PERSONAL AND PROFESSIONAL RECOLLECTIONS

by the late
Sir George Gilbert Scott

Frontispiece: Crayon portrait of Sir George Gilbert Scott
by George Richmond, dated June 27th, 1877
[reproduced by courtesy of the National Portrait Gallery, London]

PERSONAL AND PROFESSIONAL RECOLLECTIONS

by

SIR GEORGE GILBERT SCOTT

*A Facsimile of the Original Edition with New
Material and a Critical Introduction by*

GAVIN STAMP

PAUL WATKINS

STAMFORD

1 9 9 5

.

© 1995 new material Gavin Stamp
original work first published in 1879 by
Sampson Low, Marston, Searle, & Rivington

new edition published in 1995 by

PAUL WATKINS
18, Adelaide Street
Stamford
Lincolnshire
PE9 2EN

ISBN

1 871615 26 7

Printed on long-life paper and bound in real cloth

Printed and bound by Woolnoughs of Irthlingborough

CONTENTS

EDITOR'S ACKNOWLEDGMENTS

Gavin Stamp wishes to acknowledge assistance in preparing the notes in Appendix C from Kenneth Powell, Andrew Saint, Dr Andrew Sanders, Robert Thorne and Dr Clive Wainwright, in addition to help generously given him by Richard and Eline Gilbert Scott and other members of the Scott family in pursuing Sir Gilbert Scott.

GMS
28.11.94.

PUBLISHER'S ACKNOWLEDGMENTS

Thanks to John Smith of Stamford Museum for the initial inspiration; and grateful thanks to Gavin Stamp for his introduction and editorial work; and Anne Wilkins for her superb index.

The original manuscript of *Recollections* is held by the Royal Institute of British Architects (British Architectural Library), London and we are grateful for their co-operation. Formal permission to publish unprinted material from the manuscript was given by the author's great grandson, Richard Gilbert Scott, to whom our grateful thanks.

The holders of the copyright of the illustrations is acknowledged in their captions.

Several other people helped on the way with encouragement and suggestions: Marion Cutforth, Julian Lytten, Martin Smith, Ian Toplis, and proof-reader Philip Riley.

Shaun Tyas
May 1995

PREFACE

Copies of the original 1879 edition of Sir Gilbert Scott's *Recollections* have long been sought after as it is a key document illuminating the history of Victorian architecture. A facsimile edition was published in New York in 1977 by the Da Capo Press, but this provided neither the index so maddeningly lacking in the original volume nor any annotations and references to Scott's original manuscript which had been given to the Library of the Royal Institute of British Architects by Scott's great-grandson in 1974. The changes to and omissions from Scott's manuscript made by his editor were first published in 1976 by Gavin Stamp in *Architectural History*, the Journal of the Society of Architectural Historians of Great Britain, volume 19.

This edition of Scott's *Personal and Professional Recollections* is the first to combine a facsimile of the 1879 edition with material from Scott's original manuscript. This is given as an Appendix with references to enable it to be correlated with the published text, together with an annotated index to make all the information accessible and usable. We are grateful both to Richard Gilbert Scott and the British Architectural Library for making this comprehensive edition possible.

Despite Scott's prodigious architectural output, modern literature about the most famous of Victorian architects is comparatively scant. The standard biography is that by David Cole, *The Work of Sir Gilbert Scott* [Architectural Press, London, 1980] which contains a list of works and which superseded the essay by the same author in *Victorian Architecture* edited by Peter Ferriday [Jonathan Cape, 1963]. An account of Scott's career, together with those of his architect descendants, is given in the *Scott Family* volume of the *Catalogue of the Drawings Collection of the Royal Institute of British Architects* by Geoffrey Fisher, Gavin Stamp and others and edited by Joanna Heseltine [Gregg International, 1981]. There is also the catalogue to the exhibition held at the Victoria & Albert Museum in 1978, *Sir Gilbert Scott (1811-1878) Architect of the Gothic Revival*.

A comprehensive account of the 'Battle of the Styles' over the design of the Government Offices – which caused Scott such anguish and which provoked the writing of his *Recollections* – was given by in 1985 by David B. Brownlee in *Architectural History*, volume 28 (pp. 159-197), and the political and administrative complexities of the whole affair are described by M. H. Port in *Imperial London: Civil Government Building in London 1851-1915* (Yale University Press, 1995); and an even fuller history of these buildings by Ian Toplis in *The Foreign Office, An Architectural History* [Mansell, 1987], while the recent magnificent restoration of the interiors of the Foriegn Office is illustrated in *Apollo* for July 1992. The history of the Prince Consort Memorial is accounted by Stephen Bayley in *The Albert Memorial* [Scolar Press, 1981] and in *The Museums Area of Kensington and Westminster* volume of the *Survey of London* [Athlone Press, 1975]. The building of the Midland Grand Hotel is described in *St Pancras Station* by Jack Simmons [George Allen & Unwin, 1968] and in the chapters by Gordon Biddle and Oliver Carter in *Change at King's Cross*, edited by Michael Hunter and Robert Thorne [Historical Publications, 1990]. Scott's abortive involvement in the competition for the new Royal Courts of Justice is discussed in *The Law Courts: The Architecture of George Edmund Street* by David B. Brownlee [Architectural History Foundation & MIT Presss, 1984]. The Nikolaikirche in Hamburg and Scott's other designs for German buildings are dealt with by Michael J. Lewis in *The Politics of the German Gothic Revival: August Reichensperger* (Architectural History Foundation, New York, 1993). Other studies of individual buildings designed by Sir Gilbert Scott are too numerous to mention here.

The importance of Scott's writings is discussed by Sir Nikolaus Pevsner in a chapter in *Some Architectural Writers of the Nineteenth Century* [Clarendon, Oxford, 1972] and the influence of his theories together with an analysis of his architecture is given in *The High Victorian Movement in Architecture 1850-1870* by Stefan Muthesius [Routledge & Kegan Paul, 1972]. The still vexed question of Scott's cathedral restorations is discussed in *Goths and Vandals* by Martin S. Briggs [Constable, 1952], in *Restoration and Anti-Restoration* by Stephen Tschudi Madsen [Universitetsforlaget, Oslo, Bergen & Tromso, 1975], by Gavin Stamp in *A.A.Files* [vol. I, No. 1, for 1981-82], and by Wim Denslagen in *Architectural Restoration in Western Europe: Controversy and Continuity* [Amsterdam, 1994].

But Gilbert Scott has yet to join other Goths like Butterfield and Burges, Waterhouse and Norman Shaw in being the subject of a long modern biography to do his extraordinary career full justice. His own words, his Personal and Professional Recollections, still remain the most valuable key to understanding this most eminent Victorian.

Gavin Stamp
Strathbungo
May 1995

INTRODUCTION

Personal and Professional Recollections by the late Sir Gilbert Scott, R.A., Edited by his son, G. Gilbert Scott, F.S.A. was first published in London in 1879 by Sampson Low, Marston, Searle & Rivington. Its author had died the previous year, on 27th March 1878. It is a remarkable book, not least because it was the first autobiography of a British architect – probably of any architect – to be published. Memoirs had been written of earlier designers, notably Sir Christopher Wren, while Benjamin Ferrey's *Recollections of A.W.N. Pugin* and *The Life and Works of Sir Charles Barry* by his son had appeared in the previous decade – in 1861 and 1867 respectively. But not even Sir John Soane, obsessed as he was by his professional status and place in history, seems to have prepared an account of his life which he considered worthy of publication.

Along with his knighthood – granted in 1872 following the erection of the Albert Memorial – the publication of Gilbert Scott's personal and professional recollections was a clear indication of the rise in status of the architect in Britain since the 18th century. It was also a tribute to the success of Scott's own phenomenal career, for he had managed to become a household name while running what was surely the largest architectural office in Britain, if not in Europe. Scott rose to fame and fortune on the back of the Gothic Revival and the great Victorian boom in church building. At the height of his career he employed some thirty assistants and draughtsmen in the office at Spring Gardens. For better or for worse, Gilbert Scott, more than any other individual, was responsible for pioneering the modern architectural office producing work in a characteristic 'house style' which, it is clear, is not always from the hand of the nominal senior partner. And when he died, he was buried, not next to his wife in Tandridge churchyard near Godstone, but in Westminster Abbey. The funeral procession from West Brompton on 6th April 1878, took three hours and Queen Victoria sent an empty carriage. Sir Christopher Wren was not given such a send off; nor has any British architect enjoyed one since.

Scott's reputation may have fallen from its apogee in his lifetime but he has never been forgotten, while his *Recollections* has often been used both to denigrate the man and his times. In his day, however, there was no disputing Scott's eminence. He was awarded the Royal Gold Medal for Architecture and subsequently became President of the Royal Institute of British Architects. Not all may have agreed that he was 'the foremost architect of his day'; E.W. Godwin admitted in his obituary in *The British Architect* that 'I should hesitate to nominate Scott's work as those of a genius. If he had not the great gift he however possessed others which in these days are perhaps even more

c

conducive to success. He was indefatigable in business and a fervent worker. No chance was ever missed, no opportunity neglected ...' Scott's achievement could therefore not be ignored. As *The Builder* remarked in its own obituary, his was 'the most successful architectural career of modern times.' As a famous and successful man, Scott therefore became a symbol of the vices as well as the virtues of his profession and so became a focus of abuse from, in particular, John Ruskin and William Morris, when his generation's mania for church restoration came under critical scrutiny.

Scott's *Recollections* were generally well received when published in June 1879, although some reviewers were clearly surprised that a modern architect should ever have written an autobiography for publication. 'It is rather a bold thing, considering human nature for what it is, that any man should offer his own description of his life and work as the only fair and unprejudiced one...' Such was the opinion of an editorial in *The Builder* — no doubt written by its long-serving editor, George Godwin — which also complained of 'The entire want of recognition of those who were of any service to him... there is not one word of recognition of the help which he received from some journals when he most wanted it, — help which he urgently entreated in letters penned as if his professional life or death depended upon an editor's good-will.' — much the same might be said of many architects today — 'And we cannot help feeling that there is something a little undignified in the frequent imputations of malice and reviling, and other strong words, in reference to criticism which in the main was probably as honest as criticism, as the world goes, usually is.'

The (anonymous) reviewer in *The Architect* also complained of this excessive sensitivity to criticism, noting that, 'all this is nonsense, and is unworthy of Scott, who enjoyed during his life an unusual amount of respect.' The same reviewer was also dismissive of Scott's claim, in discussing the carving of detail [p. 215], that he worked by influence whereas Street achieved more personal results through drawings, concluding that, 'If instead of monopolising an amount of work which he could not perform honestly or well, he aimed to be an artist, and if for 'influence' he substituted drawings, specificatrion, and supervision, the progress of Gothic architecture would have been different, and we need not be today as far as ever from possessing a recognised national style.'

Here is the essential problem with Gilbert Scott: he did far too much. Scott was responsible for over a thousand new buildings or restoration projects which included: new government offices in Whitehall; a great national memorial; a major London railway terminus hotel; important new buildings in the ancient English universities, for the University of Glasgow and for the new University of Bombay; Preston Town Hall; hospitals, country houses, schools and vicarages; new cathedrals at home and abroad; scores, if not hundreds, of new churches as well as countless church restorations in addition to significant works at most of the great English cathedrals. Not all may have approved of his restorations; not everybody cared for his interpretation of the Gothic

d

Revival and Scott 'was, neither by taste nor temperament, an innovator.' Posterity has a higher regard for the architectural quality and apparent originality of the work of Street and Butterfield, Bodley and Burges, Godwin and Waterhouse; but there is no avoiding the best buildings designed by Gilbert Scott in any survey of the Gothic Revival.

Perhaps the fairest modern critical assessment of Scott was given in 1953 by that most subtle historian of Victorian architecture. H. S. Goodhart-Rendel, in his *English Architecture since the Regency*:

> Scott's professional position became rapidly so pre-eminent that it has been needful to point out that his success in occupying and maintaining it was due chiefly to talents other than artistic ... That the architect who, during a working career of forty years, built or interfered with nearly five hundred churches, thirty-nine cathedrals and minsters, and many other buildings besides, was a remarkable man it would be foolish to deny. That the designs he issued, the making of which must, considering their number, have been in more or less degree deputed to others, should mostly possess a strong sense of their issuer's idiosyncrasy is as remarkable as it might be unexpected .... Throughout the first forty years of Queen Victoria's reign, large buildings of Scott's constantly check the historians' progress, some of them deserving more admiration, some less. None, however, is likely to justify in our eyes the judgement of an age that has throned him on an eminence relatively loftier than that occupied by any other British architect since the day of Sir Christopher Wren.

Rendel was certainly not blind to the supreme cultural achievement of the mid-Victorian decades but his hero was G. E. Street and to some extent his judgement may well reflect the prejudices of the Late Victorians about the High Victorians. Today we take Gilbert Scott at his best more seriously, and it is clear that when he was closely involved with a project he was capable of producing architecture of great accomplishment. His major secular works seem less constrained by precedent than his too numerous ecclesiastical commissions and the Albert Memorial and the Midland Grand Hotel at St Pancras must be regarded as amongst the finest works of the Victorian Gothic Revival. Ironically, one of Scott's finest creations was in the style in which he was trained but soon abandoned in favour of Gothic. Posterity owes Scott's tormentor, Lord Palmerston, a considerable debt, for the recently restored reception rooms in the Foreign office show the reluctant Classicist to have been a master of form and materials, of colour and decoration. Well might the British Government now be proud of a complex of Victorian buildings which it tried to demolish only thirty years ago.

Gilbert Scott also founded an architectural dynasty, which is one reason why he wrote down his recollections. 'What I have written being intended primarily for my children,' Scott observed, 'I wished to give such family information as was wholly beyond their reach, but after that to give them an outline of my professional career alone, almost to the exclusion of personal and family matters.' However, he evidently thought in terms of publication soon after beginning the manuscript in 1864, for he wrote after his account of the Government Offices saga, 'I must ... privately warn my sons against publishing what may get them into ill odour with authorities.' As his editor stated in the Preface, in 1873 Scott made precise instructions about the publication of his manuscript after his death.

Scott's recollections were originally written in five leather-bound notebooks with lock clasps. He wrote in these intermittently over a period of fourteen years. The writing is in pencil and is often barely legible as 'pretty well all that I write is the product of my travelling hours' which were mostly spent in moving steam trains. Like Pugin's before him, Scott's busy career greatly depended on the advent of railway travel and much of his time was spent rushing around the country on newly completed lines to meet clients or to inspect work in progress. Indeed, Scott could not have handled such a volume of work in the more leisurely and far less comfortable pre-railway era.

Scott began writing down his recollections in 1864 when he was 53 years old. He had recently suffered a professional reverse over the Government Offices and his acquiescence in designing in a Classical style at the behest of Lord Palmerston had undermined his status as the leader of the Gothic Revival. In addition, therefore, to wishing to record family history, Scott may well have taken up his pencil to record his version of events and so to justify himself. Certainly he wrote down the first part of his memoirs up to and including the Government Offices affair in one continuous narrative which filled the first notebook and much of the second. The remainder and the first part of the third notebook (which begins with Scott's letter to *The Times*, dated 1st July 1868, about 'The Design for the Law Courts' subsequently pasted in) were filled with family matters, principally the death of Scott's third son, Albert Henry who died in 1865.

An interval of seven years followed before Scott began writing again, on 10th March 1872, in response to the devastating blow of the death of his wife Caroline. He resumed, in July, with a discussion of the Albert Memorial and then continued with accounts of his various cathedral restorations which he would later amplify. The fourth volume begins with, 'May God bless what I have to record in this book. GGS. Aug. 8. 1872.' This was the day before he was knighted by Queen Victoria. After describing that event, Scott did not resume his recollections until the 21st February 1877. In a passage excised by the editor, Scott recorded that;

> During the autumn I became painfully impressed in the costliness of my mode of living & the falling off of my practice – & as my son & daughter in law did not care for Ham, determined to remove to London, whether wisely or not God knows! We did not finally move till a year later. I am now a Londoner & have much lost in position. May God bless the change! I fear it was not quite well considered.

Scott's practice had been in decline along with his own health since he was incapacitated by a stroke in 1870 and it was also suffering from the inevitable change in architectural fashions. Nevertheless, Sir Gilbert Scott still managed to leave almost £130,000 when he died the following year.

In poor health and increasingly conscious of mortality, Scott filled the rest of this volume with more detailed accounts of his cathedral restorations, putting the record straight over his several quarrels with deans and donors, above all with the egregious Edmund Beckett Denison, later Lord Grimthorpe. This part of *Recollections* provides valuable historical evidence in an area of practice which remains controversial and is too often little understood. Indeed, Scott's work in cathedrals may be regarded as the most impressive and valuable part of his achievement; it was certainly that to which he seems to have devoted most care and attention. The fifth and last notebook was never completely filled. It contains two essays which Scott wrote in defence of his own work and principles. The first, 'The Anti-Restoration Movement', written in October 1877 was a defence of his treatment of ancient churches and cathedrals in response to the attack recently made on him by, in particular, his former assistant, J. J. Stevenson. The second was a critique of 'The 'Queen Anne' Style', the new eclectic and anti-Gothic domestic manner adopted by a younger generation of architects – not least by Scott's eldest son and his editor. The last entry in the notebook is dated January 1878.

In preparing his father's manuscript for publication, George Gilbert Scott junior usually followed the order in which the recollections were written, although he had to combine the two separate accounts of cathedral restorations to make one coherent narrative. He also had to make substantial cuts and alterations in many places. There were three main problems with the manuscript to be addressed. The first was the large amount of historical material which was purely of family interest or not of strict relevance to Scott's professional life. The editor therefore eliminated long passages describing people and customs in the area of rural Buckinghamshire where Scott had been brought up. The second was the lengthy and painful passages written in response to the deaths first of his third son, Albert, and then of his wife. The Victorians are often supposed to have been obsessed by death-bed scenes, but so personal a response, so evidently tortured by grief and by guilt, was naturally excised. Even so, what remained in the published text reveals how deeply Scott was affected by these misfortunes and how profound was his Christian faith.

However, the amount of personal and private material printed in the published *Recollections* evidently surprised and shocked some readers. The reviewer in *The Architect* complained of 'indiscretions' included by the editor as well as in the Dean of Chichester's Introduction, and made his point with an apt quotation: '"It was not his business," writes Thackeray of Macauley, "to bring his family before the theatre footlights, and call for bouquets from the gallery as he wept over them," but, as it now appears, the volume before is suggestive perpetually of posturing of this kind. Nothing is too private for publication...' But in fact it was.

It is the third broad area of editorial change which perhaps most interests the modern reader, for the younger Scott, with a conventional sense of propriety, naturally felt obliged to censor the names of people still living who had been discussed by his father in unflattering terms. One was Scott's erstwhile partner, William Bonython Moffatt (1812-87). As published, Scott's account of how his wife finally broke the partnership in 1845 [p. 130] has often been used against him, for it seems to suggest ambitious self-interest and hypocrisy. However, the original manuscript makes it clear that the association with Moffatt had become dangerous, especially at the time of the 'Railway Mania', owing to his partner's involvement in unwise financial speculation. In 1860 Moffatt was imprisoned for debt and, as Scott's obituarist in the *Building News* revealed, 'a connection of another kind between the two gentlemen has been maintained up to the time of Sir Gilbert's death, which exemplified in the strongest degree his regard for early associations.'

For not only did Scott regularly assist the wretched Moffatt with money, he contributed £20 to his legal fees when his former partner was incarcerated in the Queen's Bench Prison for debts of a thousand pounds. The memoir in the RIBA Library by Charles Hilbert Strange of his father, Charles Matthew Strange, who had been Moffatt's assistant in 1859-60, confirms Scott's version of events. Strange's diary recorded that Moffatt was 'an ugly man with hair all over his head' and such incidents as, 'Mr M. not been to bed all night, sparring with some fellows at the George and Blue Boar.' No wonder that Mrs Scott 'was most anxious upon the subject' of the partnership and boldly took the matter into her own hands.

Another area of coyness in the published *Recollections* was Scott's long account of the Government Offices saga, in which his tenacious hold on a job he did not actually win in competition did him considerable moral damage – as he well knew. Scott was not at all coy when writing in his notebooks, but there are, in fact, no great surprises in the revelation of the names of those who opposed him. Henry Garling, whom Lord Palmerston attempted to foist on Scott as a 'coadjutor' had, after all, won the original 1856 competition for the War Office, while the younger Charles Barry, who schemed so energetically to get the job from Scott, had come second in the original competition for the Foreign Office, thus beating Scott who had only made third place. Similarly, it is not surprising to find that the nefarious 'Mr B--' was Professor Donaldson who, as an ardent Classicist, had no love for the Gothic which Scott had hoped to build in the heart of Westminster.

Scott was also coy in his published references to the critics whose strictures on the Albert Memorial so clearly upset him, but here the original manuscript is not more illuminating. Scott may have been referring to critical articles written by F. T. Palgrave and Sidney Colvin, but he clearly did not know who was the anonymous author of the trenchant attacks on the 'eminent architect' and his 'ignorance of [his] own work.' This was J. T. Emmett, who published 'The State of English Architecture' in the *Quarterly Review* in April

h

1872 – shortly before Scott wrote up his account of the Albert Memorial. He was surely right to state that, 'This being my most prominent work, those who wish to traduce me will naturally select it for their attacks. I can only say that if this work is worthy of their contempt, I am myself equally deserving of it, for it is the result of my highest and most enthusiastic efforts.' These efforts resulted in one of the finest public monuments uniting architecture, sculpture and the decorative arts achieved anywhere in Europe in its time. Unfortunately, those original criticisms have had a lingering pernicious effect for, sadly, at the time of writing, the Albert Memorial is shrouded in seemingly permanent protective scaffolding because the British Government claims it is not a high priority to find the money to pay for the full restoration this national monument deserves.

However, Scott did not bother to mention, let alone refute, perhaps the most devastating criticism of his work published in his lifetime. As it came from Scotland perhaps Scott felt it could be ignored. This was the lecture given in Glasgow in 1866 by Alexander 'Greek' Thomson and published as 'An Inquiry as to the Appropriateness of the Gothic Style for the Proposed Buildings for the University of Glasgow ...' in which he observed that

> granting that Mr Scott is all that his most enthusiastic admirers would have him to be, everybody knows that his establishment being the most fashionable in the metropolis, his business is so enormous that, to expect him to bestow more than the most casual consideration upon the work which passes through his office, is altogether unreasonable. Nor could it be supposed that the magnitude of this work was sufficient to have secured more than an ordinary amount of attention at his hands, for it was nothing unusual to him.

That the University of Glasgow secured but a single brief mention in *Recollections* rather confirms the justice of Thomson's complaint.

Some of Sir Gilbert Scott's shrill protests about criticism of his work were omitted by the editor, but what remains in the published volume has a curious contemporary ring. For Scott, like so many outwardly successful architects, combined a breezy self-confidence with an acute sensitivity to criticism which easily generated pages of aggrieved self-justification. Scott's reaction to attacks on the Albert Memorial were echoed by the pained reaction of Sir Basil Spence a century later to criticism of his Home Office design for Queen Anne's Gate. In neither case does this redound much to the credit of the famous knighted architects. As A. J. Beresford-Hope (whom Scott thought an enemy) remarked after his death, 'he was often hurt in his feelings by things which he could afford to laugh at.' But he continued

> That was the general characteristic of the man, and those who had not the privilege of his personal acquaintance very little appreciated it; and with all his zeal, all his earnestness, and all his conviction, he never bore malice. He would take blows and would give blows, as every man ought to do; but I repeat – he never bore malice.

i

In most respects, Scott's *Recollections* could only have been written by a man of his generation and much of their value is an account of the private feelings of a successful professional Victorian. Scott was typical in his interest in genealogy and his somewhat obsessive concern to demonstrate respectable and ancient lineage on all sides of his well-connected clerical family – although this might seem to be contradicted by his similar concern to chart a rise from humble origins by dint of hard work and enterprise such as might be worthy of the attention of a Samuel Smiles. But that apparently smug satisfaction with worldly success which several modern commentators have held against Scott was not the whole story. An attractive aspect of his personality was a deep love of his family and a strong sense of guilt about neglecting those closest to him. Passages excised for publication suggest that Scott tended to believe he was being punished by the deaths of close members of his family. He was certainly well aware that professional success was achieved at the cost of personal sacrifice and the death of his 'dearest Carry' in 1872 produced an outpouring of guilty feelings:

> It is now too late – Oh! Lord forgive my thoughtlessness, my ignorances & my negligences! Oh my dearest wife, if thou canst hear me now forgive the faults which though knowest but too well!!... She was so much alone, owing to my best hours being at business & on journeys that I have no doubt she frequently did feel melancholy & when I returned home jaded with work & often disturbed by severe anxiety and disappointment I fear I did little to enliven her spirits ...

Certainly Mrs Scott can have seen little of her workaholic husband, especially after they moved from the Admiral's House at Hampstead out to the Manor House at Ham in 1864. In 1869 Scott moved further into the country by taking 'Parkhurst' at Leith Hill and the following year the family moved into 'Rook's Nest' at Godstone, Surrey. Even allowing for the efficiency of Victorian railway travel, it is clear that Scott's busy life meant that he was often away and even when he was working at the London office he must have usually returned home late in the evening. In view of this constant activity, it is scarcely surprising that Scott suffered a stroke while at Chester in 1870. After his wife's death, Scott moved back to Ham in 1873 and the move back to London in 1877, prompted by increasing ill-health, was to Courtfield House in Collingham Gardens in Kensington to live with his second son, John Oldrid, and his wife. Oddly, for a man so concerned with family and status, Scott never bought or built a family seat; even his country houses were rented. Perhaps there was no time to do more.

Scott tells us almost nothing about his busy office, or about his methods of working in his *Recollections*. This may seem strange, but perhaps he felt such information redundant to his architect sons. To understand how Scott operated professionally, the modern reader must turn to another published volume of architectural autobiography, that of his former assistant T. G. Jackson (1835-1924). He had been a pupil of Scott's office in 1858-61 at No. 20 (renumbered as No. 31 in 1866) Spring Gardens, an elegant late 18th century terraced house, possibly designed by Sir Robert Taylor, which was just off Trafalgar Square (on the site of the Admiralty Arch). 'Scott's office was a very large one,' he wrote in his *Recollections of Thomas Graham Jackson*, eventually published in 1950.

> Counting pupils, salaried assistants, and clerks, I think we were twenty-seven in all. I was put to work in the first floor room at the back with six others; there were about a dozen more in two rooms on the second floor; the ground floor front room, which served also as the waiting room, was the sanctum of Mr Burlison, the head man, who made the estimates and surveys. Scott's own room was the ground floor back, and farther back still were the writing-clerk and the office boys. The front room first floor was let to a Mr Moriarty, a barrister, a mysterious person whom we never saw.
>
> Of Scott we saw but little. He was up to the eyes in engagements and it was hard to get him to look at our work. I have seen three or four men with drawings awaiting correction or approval grouped around his door. The door flew open and out he came: 'No time today!'; the cab was at the door and he was whirled away to some cathedral where he would spend a couple of hours and then fly off to some other great work at the other end of the kingdom. Now and then the only chance of getting instructions was to go with him in the cab to the station. I see I wrote at the time, 'What a fine thing it is to be so busy'; but looking back from my present standpoint I find nothing in such a career to envy, and much to wonder at. It need hardly be said that it is an impossibility really to direct so large a staff as Scott's, but the work had to be done somehow. The heads of different rooms were capable men with a good knowledge of construction; Scott had a wonderful power of making rapid expressive sketches and from these his men were able to produce work which, curiously enough, did fall into something of a consistent style that passed for Gilbert Scott's and which one can always recognise wherever one meets it as coming from that office ....

This account of such breathless industry makes plausible such apocyrphal stories as Scott telegraphing Spring Gardens from a provincial railway station: "Why am I here?"

Yet Scott somehow found time not only to write long reports on the condition of medieval cathedrals but also to produce several books, many articles and to write the Royal Academy lectures on the rise and development of medieval architecture which were published posthumously. *A Plea for the Faithful Restoration of Our Ancient Churches* was written in 1848, before Scott's career really took off, while his *Remarks on Secular and Domestic Architecture, Present and Future* of 1857, although a serious statement of Gothic principles, was partly an exercise in self-advertisement and self-promotion. But *Gleanings from Westminster Abbey*, published in 1860 and expanded in 1863, rich in research and observation, was a labour of love. As he wrote, Scott's appointment to succeed Blore as Surveyor to the Abbey in 1849 was 'a great and lasting source of delight' and he treated the building with loving care and scholarly intelligence. It is fitting that he was finally laid to rest there, under a brass designed by his old pupil, George Edmund Street.

k

As Jackson recognised, the list of architects who subsequently distinguished themselves after leaving Spring Gardens is a long and impressive one which redounds to Scott's credit. His first pupil had been the church architect G. F. Bodley, whose sister Georgina married Scott's brother, Samuel King. Another early pupil was the great Street, who later succeeded where Scott failed in securing the commission for the new Law Courts in the Strand. At the memorial meeting held at the RIBA soon after Scott's death, Street recalled that, 'It is just thirty-three years ago since I first worked under him, and I can truly say that his extreme kindness and amiability to the young men in the office were such as to impress them very deeply.' Street's own annotated copy of Scott's *Recollections* is now in the RIBA Library and next to the passage where the orthodoxy of 'Middle Pointed' Gothic was discussed [p. 203] and how: 'In my own office, Mr Street and others used to view every one as a heretic who designed in any but the sacred phase,' he pencilled in the margin that:

> This is exact contrary to the facts. I used to sware by 1st Pointed & we used to call Scott's work 'ogee' because it was too late in char. My first Ch-Biscovey was of purest 1st Pointed (circa 1848) – & was designed at this time. G. E. Street.

Another pupil was George Gilbert Scott junior, Scott's brilliant eldest son who subsequently edited *Recollections* and who, as he is little known today, deserves a short note here in conclusion. He had been born in 1839 and was well qualified to deal with his father's papers, as he was not only an architect but was a distinguished historian and antiquary who had been briefly a Fellow of Jesus College, Cambridge. The younger Scott had been educated at Eton – one of the first results, perhaps, of his father's worldly success – and was an articled pupil in Spring Gardens in 1857-60. He worked with his father on restoration projects until 1863, when he entered Jesus College as an undergraduate. Although he continued to help his father in certain jobs, such as the restorations at Peterhouse, Cambridge, G. G. Scott junior was essentially in independent practice after the mid-1860s. A posthumous appreciation of his father taken from G. G. Scott junior's own notebooks is published as an Appendix to this volume.

Sir Gilbert Scott's eldest son's principal architectural achievement was St Agnes', Kennington, in South London, designed in 1874 and demolished after the Second World War. This very influential Anglo-Catholic church was conspicuous for its refined Late Gothic style with square-headed windows and containing furnishings with a strong hint of the Renaissance. St Agnes' marked Scott junior as a member of the avant-garde, along with Bodley and Sedding, who were rejecting the orthodoxies of his father's generation of Gothicists. Similarly, Scott's secular work included several vicarages designed in the 'Queen Anne' style which his father attacked at the end of his life. Scott junior was also reacting against his father's generation in his defence of Renaissance styles; he designed the New Hostel at Pembroke College, Cambridge, in an

Early Renaissance manner and whereas Sir Gilbert had spoiled Wren's St Michael's Cornhill by the introduction of 'Lombardic' tracery to change its character, his son enlarged Wren's Chapel at Pembroke with a tact that was most unusual at the time.

The younger Scott was also notable as a scholar, publishing in 1881 his *Essay on the History of English Church Architecture prior to the Separation of England from the Roman Obedience*. He shared antiquarian interests with his father, whom he helped in historical investigations, although he became increasingly uncomfortable about and implicitly critical of Sir Gilbert's church restorations. Being the professional heir to a famous architect is never easy and in several areas of life and practice he grew apart from his father. Sir Gilbert seems to have been closer to his second son, John Oldrid, with whom he went to live at the end of his life. In his will, Sir Gilbert left his practice to his two architect sons and for two years the drawings emanating from Spring Gardens were signed 'G. G. & J. O. Scott'. In fact, the two brothers did not collaborate and the practice was inherited by John Oldrid, a pedestrian architect and a dull man.

The evident estrangement between the two brothers was further exacerbated in 1880 when G. G. Scott junior shocked friends and members of his family by being received into the Roman Catholic Church. He had visited Cardinal Newman at the Birmingham Oratory shortly before and was pleased to find that His Eminence had a high regard for his great-grandfather, Thomas Scott, the 'Commentator' (whose grandson, a firm Broad Church Anglican, would have surely been dismayed by his son's conversion.) Unfortunately, Scott's subsequent career was tragic as his behaviour became increasingly unbalanced. In 1884 he was declared to be of unsound mind following a public trial under the 1862 Lunacy Act, during which J. O. Scott was implicitly criticised in a leading article in *The Times* for undue concern to prevent his brother having access to the £40,000 he had inherited from his father. After three periods of incarceration in lunatic asylums and estranged from his long-suffering wife and family, George Gilbert Scott junior died in 1897 while staying, inexplicably, in one of his father's most celebrated buildings: the Midland Grand Hotel at St Pancras.

'Middle Scott' had six children, of whom two followed in his profession: Sir Giles Gilbert Scott (1880-1960), the architect of Liverpool Cathedral – the last and one of the greatest fulfilment of the ideals of the Gothic Revival – and his younger brother Adrian Gilbert (1882-1963). The Gilbert Scott architectural dynasty has been continued in the fourth generation by Sir Giles' son Richard Gilbert Scott, who gave his great-grandfather's leather-bound notebooks containing his personal and professional recollections to the Library of the RIBA in 1974, and so enabled this special edition of the most celebrated Victorian architectural autobiography to be published.

Gavin Stamp

Sir Gilbert Scott.

PERSONAL AND PROFESSIONAL RECOLLECTIONS

BY THE LATE

SIR GEORGE GILBERT SCOTT, R.A.

EDITED BY HIS SON,

G. GILBERT SCOTT, F.S.A.
Sometime Fellow of Jesus College, Cambridge.

With an Introduction

BY THE

VERY REV. JOHN WILLIAM BURGON, B.D.
Dean of Chichester.

London:

SAMPSON LOW, MARSTON, SEARLE, & RIVINGTON,

CROWN BUILDINGS, 188, FLEET STREET.

1879.

JUSTORUM AUTEM ANIMAE
IN MANU DEI
SUNT

PREFACE.

————◆————

THE following " Personal and Professional Recollections" were commenced by my father many years
ago.   They were designed originally for the information of his family, but as the work progressed
the scope of it became enlarged.   In 1873 my
father drew up directions for its publication in the
event of his decease, and his instructions upon the
subject are precise.   " I feel it due," he writes, " to
myself that the statement of my professional life
should go before the public in a fair and unprejudiced form ; and the more so as I have been one
of the leading actors in the greatest architectural
movement which has occurred since the Classic
renaissance.   I only seek to be placed before the
public fairly and honourably, as I trust I deserve ;
and I commit this especially to those whose duty
it is to do it, begging the blessing of Almighty God
upon their exertions."   The manuscript, naturally
enough, contains much that is unsuited to publication, and which my father, had he lived to revise it
for the press, would undoubtedly have modified
or erased.   With such matter I have endeavoured,

aided by the advice of others, to deal as it may be conceived that its author would have dealt, had opportunity served. There is also much relating to purely domestic concerns in which the public could not be expected to take interest. The greater part of this has been omitted. So much only is left as appeared necessary to the completeness of the story, and valuable as an indication of character. I trust it may not be thought that too little has here been expunged, and that something may be allowed to the partiality of a son.

My thanks are due to the Very Reverend the Dean of Chichester who, with equal willingness and kindness, undertook to contribute the Introduction, and who has further given valuable aid and advice in the revision, throughout, of the proofs. I have also to thank the Very Reverend the Dean of Westminster for the permission to reprint the sermon preached by him on the occasion of my father's interment; Mr. Edward M. Barry, R.A., for a similar permission in respect of a portion of a recent lecture delivered in the chair of Architecture at the Royal Academy, in reference to my father's career; to Mr. E. A. Freeman, who was at much pains to recover a passage in one of his early pamphlets to which my father in his manuscript had referred, but of which he has given no very accurate indication; and to Mr. George Richmond, R.A., for kind assistance in regard to the engraving from his drawing, which he has allowed me to place as a frontispiece to this work.

TABLE OF CONTENTS.

———◆———

INTRODUCTION

BY

THE DEAN OF CHICHESTER.

INVITED to contribute an Introductory Chapter
to Sir Gilbert Scott's " Recollections," I willingly
undertake the task; yet have I little to offer
beyond the expression of my personal regard for
the man, my hearty admiration of the great work
which he lived long enough to accomplish.

(1.) It is impossible to survey the revival which
has taken place in the knowledge of Gothic architecture within the last forty years without astonish-
ment.   Not that our actual achievements as yet
are calculated to produce excessive self-congratu-
lation: but when it is considered out of what a
state of childish ignorance we have so lately
emerged, it is surely in a high degree encouraging
to review our present position.   And to Sir Gilbert
Scott, more than to any other individual, we are
indebted for what has been effected.   He in-
genuously acknowledges his obligations to others:
tells us at what altar he first kindled his torch:
arrogates to himself no claim to have been *facile
princeps* in his art.   On the contrary, he frankly
recalls his own failures; and recounts the steps,

slow and painful, by which he himself struggled out of the universal darkness, with a truthfulness which is even perplexing. Yet has he been unquestionably the great teacher of his generation; and by the conservative character of his genius he has proved a prime benefactor to his country also. To *his* influence and example we are chiefly indebted for the preservation of not a few of our national monuments—our cathedral and parochial churches. And (it must in faithfulness to his memory be added) a vast deal more would have been spared of what has now hopelessly perished had his counsels always prevailed—above all, had his method been more generally adopted.

(2.) In the " Recollections" which follow (would that they were less fragmentary!) Sir Gilbert has chiefly—all but exclusively, in fact—dwelt upon the great *Cathedral* restorations which were conducted under his auspices. His remarks will be read with profound interest, and will become local memorials of the most precious class, as the authentic private jottings (for they do not pretend to be more) of the great architect himself. But one desiderates besides an enumeration of the many dilapidated parochial Churches on which he was employed; and one would have been glad at the same time to be reminded by himself of the eloquent plea which was ever on his lips for dealing in a far more conservative spirit with those precious relics of antiquity. Let me be allowed in this place to say a few plain words on a subject very near to my heart—as I know it was very near to his: a subject concerning which those who have a right to be heard, and who ought to have spoken long ago, have either practised reticence or else spoken ineffectually until, I fear, it is too late for any one to speak with the possibility of much good resulting from what he says. I allude to the ruthless work of destruction which for the last thirty years has been going on in almost every parish in England under the immediate direction of our architects, and with the sanction of our parochial clergy. Verily, it is not too much to declare that with the best intentions and at an immense outlay, more havoc has been made, more irreparable mischief wrought throughout the land within those thirty years, than any invasion of a barbarous horde could have effected. We have severed ourselves, on every side, from antiquity,— have effectually broken the thousand links which used to connect us with the historic Past.

(3.) At the beginning of the period referred to, to seek out and to study the village churches of England was almost part of the education of an English gentleman. In the case of one of culti-vated taste, whatever was remarkable in their structure or in their decorations,—from the primi-tive window or singular font or rude bas-relief above the doorway, down to the fragments of stained glass, specimens of wrought iron, or vestiges of fresco on the walls,—nothing came amiss. The ancient altar-stone degraded to the pavement; the curiously-carved finials; the dila-pidated stand for the preacher's hour-glass; all found in him an appreciating patron. That the edifice itself was as a rule in a most discreditable

plight, is undeniable. The green walls, low plastered ceiling, chimney thrust through the window,
—the ponderous gallery above and the tall pews
beneath,—all were sordid and unworthy. But for
all *that*, the great fact remained that our village
churches were objects of surprising interest; full
of beauty, full of instruction. There is no telling
what a privilege it was to pass a day with one's
pencil among the many relics which they invariably
contained; and from every part of the edifice to
learn *something*. Externally, enough remained
at all events to tell the story of the structure:
within, comfortable it was to reflect that nothing
after all was so much needed as the removal of
pews, galleries, whitewash: the re-opening of
windows: the careful repair of what, through
tract of time, had vanished: the restoration of
what had been barbarously mutilated. Nothing
in short was required but what a refined taste
and strong conservative instinct might reasonably
hope to see some day effected.

(4.) And now, what has been the actual
result of thirty years of church " Restoration "?
Briefly this,—that in by far the greater number
of our lesser country churches there scarcely sur-
vives a *single point of interest*. In the case of
our more considerable structures—with a few bright
exceptions—the merest wreck remains of what
did once so much delight and interest the beholder. The door of entrance has been "restored,"
but not on the old lines: three other doors—in
order to obtain additional sittings, to exclude
draughts, and to save expense—have been so

blocked up as to make it impossible to discover what they were. The curious Norman chancel-arch has been " enlarged :" the ancient font and pulpit have been supplanted : the screen has either been painted over or else removed entirely. The windows (furnished with stained glass of the kind which it gives the beholder a sharp pain across the chest to be forced to contemplate) are wholly new, and do not assort with the edifice : a huge east window in particular (bad luck to the author of it !) has effectually obliterated the record of what stood there before it. The venerable tomb of the founder (on the ground, under a mural arch) has been built over with seats. Another mutilated recumbent figure of an ancient lord of the soil has been buried,—inscription and all. Sedilia, piscina, aumbry, niche,—ruthless hands have rendered every one of them uninteresting and unintelligible. Some exquisite tracery has been chiselled away within and without the building. A specimen of the ancient oak seats has disappeared, and a forest of rush-bottomed chairs covers the floor. There were once traces of curious fresco painting on the walls ; but they also have been obliterated. After repeated inquiry I find that the sepulchral slabs, of which there used to be several, are at the present hour either (*a*) buried, or (*b*) lying in the churchyard, or (*c*) ingeniously plastered into the wall of the tower where they cannot be seen and where they cease to be of the least interest, or else (*a*) destroyed. A prime object seems to have been to assimilate the tint of the walls to that of a cup of coffee: also to procure a surface of unbroken colour. Another leading principle has evidently been to introduce a quantity of varnished deal furniture. A third, to overlay the floor in every direction with " Minton's tiles "—except where the perforations for the "heating apparatus" have established a stronger claim. The result is that there is no longer discoverable a single inscribed stone—certainly not *in situ*—from one end of the church to the other. *When* will architects and country parsons learn that the most unmeaning, most commonplace, most *vulgar* thing with which the floor of an ancient church can be covered is an assortment of black and red tiles? Is it not perceived at a glance that they must needs be uninteresting, disappointing, and when they have procured the ejectment of ancient sepulchral stones, downright offensive? Has the parish then no history? It *had* one—a history which thirty years ago was to be seen written on the walls and on the floor of the parish church. Is it tolerable that on the plea of "restoration" these local records should all have been obliterated? How about the men who ministered to the many generations who once worshipped within these walls? Behold, they have (all but one) departed. And have they then, like a long line of shadows, left *no* material trace of their occupancy behind them? The answer is obvious. Certain of them sleep in dust, side by side, in front of the altar which they served in their lifetime; and a row of sepulchral slabs until yesterday acquainted the beholder at least with their names, dates, ages. Am I to be told that yonder assortment of parti-coloured tiles (which are to be bought by the yard by anybody, any day,

anywhere) are so much more interesting than those memorials of the past, that it is reasonable they should cause their unceremonious ejectment ?
. . . . I have said nothing about the architectural Vandalism of these last days, being without professional knowledge; but I have the best reason for knowing that the author of the ensuing " Recollections" would have endorsed every word which has gone before. O, that what has been written might avail, if it were but in *one* quarter, to arrest the work of ruin which is still steadily going forward throughout the length and breadth of the land !

(5.) I recall with interest an opportunity I once enjoyed (1869-70) of acquainting myself with Sir Gilbert's skill and conscientiousness in superintending a work of no great magnitude. The beautiful church of Houghton Conquest, in Bedfordshire, had fallen into a state of exceeding decadence; and the rector (the late Archdeacon Rose) having been encouraged to invoke the assistance of Sir Gilbert Scott, the architect paid us a visit. (I say *us*, because Houghton Rectory was the happy home of all my long vacations.) Sir Gilbert fully shared our concern at the entire destruction of the large east window, which had been half blocked up, half replaced by a wooden frame containing three vile mullions of wood. After conducting him round, the Archdeacon and I took our seats by his side on the leads of the nave, while he took a leisurely survey of the roof of the structure. " What is *that ?* " he inquired, directing his glass to the summit of the eastern gable. I volunteered the statement that it was a ruined fragment of the former cross, for such it seemed. "*That* was never part of a cross," he at last said thoughtfully; "it is part of the tracery of a window. I can see the cavity for the insertion of the glass." To be brief, it proved to be, as he at once suspected, the one necessary clue to the restoration of the east window. On the window-sill, which was honeycombed with decay, his practised eye had already distinguished traces of *four* mullions. I need not go on. A few more fragments were found built into the wall, and the entire window for the architect's purpose was recovered. He preserved everything for us, from the dilapidated screen to the old hour-glass stand. Several specimens of fresco were revealed on the walls; a curious coat-of-arms in stained glass was detected in the tower; two windows which had been closed were opened; the grave-stones were left in their places; the very reckoning of the parson with certain members of the Conquest family, scratched with the point of a knife (I suppose in the time of Queen Elizabeth) inside the arch of the vestry door, was ordered to be religiously preserved. On the other hand, a portentous Georgian pulpit, furnished with a formidable sounding-board above, and a species of pen for the accommodation of the clerk beneath, were banished. The sordid porch and plastered ceiling of the chancel were supplanted by objects exquisite in their respective ways.

(6.) I have said nothing hitherto about Sir Gilbert's personal characteristics, disposition, habits of mind. It will be found that these emerge with tolerable distinctness from the autobiography which follows. His indomitable energy and unflagging zeal, as well as the enlightened spirit in which he pursued his lofty calling: his enthusiasm for the great cause to which he devoted himself to the very close of his earthly life: these lie on the surface of his narrative. And here it is impossible not to admire the entire absence of any expression of professional jealousy from first to last; and indeed the absence of depreciatory language concerning others,—although the man who worked after Wyatt in the last century, after Blore in the present, might have been excused if he had testified both surprise and annoyance at what he was daily constrained to encounter.—A stranger, I suspect, would have been chiefly impressed by the exceeding modesty and unassumingness of his manner,—" his beautiful modesty," as one who knew him most intimately has well phrased it; adding a tribute to " his perfect breeding and courtesy,—not so much finish of manner as genuine inbred politeness." Such " graces of character," writes another friend of his, " will not soon be forgotten by those who knew him, however slightly." Obvious as it always was that he entertained a decided opinion on the point under discussion, he yet bore with the crude remarks of persons who really knew nothing at all about the matter in hand to an extent which used to astonish me. Even when conversing with those who were submissive and really only wished to learn, there was no appearance of dictation or dogmatism. His affability was extraordinary. While on this

a

head let me not fail to acknowledge his wondrous patience and kindness in matters of detail.

I must needs also again advert to the conservative character of his genius. When I became Vicar of St. Mary-the-Virgin's, Oxford (1863), I found to my distress that Laud's porch was doomed. The parishioners willingly listened to my recommendation, and it was spared. I confessed what I had done to Scott, and asked for his forgiveness if I had counselled amiss : but he commended me highly. A few feet in advance of the porch however, are two plain piers, erected in the last century,—either of them surmounted by a strange kind of dilapidated urn. Were *they* also to stand ? I presumed that the architect who had already removed the high wall which used to enclose the north side of the churchyard, and substituted for it the present elegant erection, would have been for their removal : and certainly I was not prepared to offer any resistance had I discovered that such was actually his view. But no. After a careful survey, he recommended that they should be retained, and gave me his reasons for retaining them. It was truly edifying and interesting to hear his remarks on such occasions. The thing was "historical;"—or at least it was "good of its kind;"—or it "had a certain character about it;"—or "I don't altogether dislike it." In short—for whatever reason—the end of the matter commonly was that "I think we had better let it alone."

(7.) Notwithstanding all that has gone before,

were I called upon to state my private estimate of the man, I should avow that in my account, second to no other personal characteristic was the ardour of his domestic affections : first, his love for his parents, brothers, sisters ; then his entire devotion to his wife and his children. There is many a passage in the ensuing autobiography which bears me out in this estimate. I well remember the exceeding distress which the death of his son in 1865 at Exeter College occasioned him ; an event on which he had freely dilated with his pen, but which it is thought was of too private a nature to find here so extended a record. I should also think it right to declare that in my account a deep undercurrent of Religion, as it was the secret of his strength and of his life, so was it also the secret of his heart's affections : the fountain-head too, by the way, of a certain playful joyousness of disposition which came to the surface continually, and never forsook him to the last. His general manner, however, was grave and thoughtful ; and his piety of that quiet and even reserved kind which only occasionally comes to the surface, and easily escapes observation altogether. No one about him, in fact, not even his sons, knew the strength and ardour of those religious convictions which were with him an inheritance; for (as the reader will be presently reminded) the Rev. Thomas Scott, of Aston Sandford, the commentator, was his grandfather. To his faithful valet, who had repeatedly asked him to tell him (but had been invariably put off with some evasive reply) how it happened that the lower side of his arms looked galled and sore, had in fact a *leprous* appearance, he

one day avowed as follows : " When I am praying,
especially for my sons, I feel I cannot do enough.
I feel kneeling to be but little, and I prostrate myself on the floor. I suppose that my arms from
this may have become a little galled."—He never
syllabled his wife's name in conversation with his
sons without a silent prayer for her repose ; and
when out of doors, he would always raise his hat
(the token of how he was mentally engaged) at
the mention of her cherished name.—I trust it is
not wrong to reveal such matters. One must
either practise reticence, and so conceal the character which one professes to exhibit faithfully :
or else risk offending the very persons probably
whose good opinion one would chiefly be glad to
conciliate.

JOHN W. BURGON.

The Deanery, Chichester,
 May 17th, 1879.

SIR GILBERT SCOTT.

CHAPTER I.

My motive in jotting down the following miscellaneous recollections is this :—that a man's
children have no means whatever of getting at the
particulars of his life up to the time when their
own observation and memory begin to avail them,
and that they are peculiarly apt to receive mistaken impressions. It is consequently, as it appears to me, the duty of every one who has
appeared much before the public to supply this
defect from his own memory, and thus to prevent
misapprehension.

I was born at the parsonage-house at Gawcott,
near Buckingham, on July 13th, 1811. Though my
father, like myself, was born in Bucks, I hardly feel
that I have in reality any very direct connection
with that county, clergymen being so much birds
of passage, that the place of their children's birth
seems little more than a matter of chance.

My grandfather, the Rev. Thomas Scott, so
well known by his commentary on the Bible
and other works, was a native of Lincolnshire,

B

where his father was a considerable agriculturist. I have not been able to ascertain whether the latter was a native of that county, but as his eldest son [1] took some pains to disclaim connection with families of the same name in his neighbourhood, I infer that such was not the case. He (the father of my grandfather) was born in the time of William III. (1701), and was connected by marriage with the Kelsalls of Kelsall in Cheshire, the representative of which family was about that time vicar of Boston.[2] His wife was one of the Wayets,[3] a very respectable county family. From the arms made use of by my grandfather's family, I gather that they must have sprung from the Scotts of Scott's Hall in Kent, who left Scotland in the thirteenth century.[4]

My mother's family were West Indians. Of the family of her father, Dr. Lynch of the island of Antigua, I know but little, but her maternal grandfather was the possessor, at that time, of a valuable estate known as " Gilbert's Estate."

This family settled at a very early date in Antigua, previous to which they had resided in Devonshire, one of their representatives being Sir Humphrey Gilbert, half-brother and companion-in-arms of Sir Walter Raleigh.

[1] William Scott, of Grimblethorpe Hall, near Louth. —Ed.

[2] Edward Kelsall, Vicar of Boston, 1702—1719. See Mackenzie's edition of Guillim's " Display of Heraldry," p. 68.

[3] He married Mary Wayet of Boston. One of her sisters was married to Lancelot Brown, " the omnipotent magician Brown " of Cowper's " Task," Bk. III. The family of Wayet was also settled at Tumby in Bain, in the same county.—Ed.

[4] One branch of this Kentish family was settled at Rotherham, in Yorkshire, in the reign of Edward I V.—Ed.

My great-grandfather, Nathaniel Gilbert, appears to have been a most excellent man. Living in a century of extreme deadness in religious matters, he was roused to a sense of the shortcomings of his age in this respect either by the preaching or by the writings of Wesley. He consequently joined the Wesleyans at a time when they were not considered as severed from the Church of England. At his request Wesley sent over to Antigua some ministers of his society to instruct the negroes and others, but though the whole family joined the new society, it is clear that Mr. Gilbert did not consider himself otherwise than a member of the Church of England, for he brought up his eldest son as a clergyman. Nor do I recollect even a hint of those members of the family who were living during my childhood (including my grandmother and a great-aunt, Miss Elizabeth Gilbert,) being other than Church people, although the last named treasured up most affectionately her personal recollections of John Wesley himself, and retained through life a strong sympathy with his followers. This family was indirectly connected with several good families in England, among others with that of Lord Northampton, with the Abdy's, and with the Gordons of Stocks. Sir Edward Colebrooke once told me that he was connected with the Gilberts, and Sir Denis Le Marchant also through his marriage, as also Lady Seymour, wife of canon Sir John Seymour, and Sir George Grey.

My father, the Rev. Thomas Scott, was the second son of the well-known commentator. He was born at Weston-Underwood in Bucks, during

the short period of my grandfather's residence
as curate of that village in 1780. My grandfather,
about that time, served several churches in that
district. The next year he removed to Olney,
the former curate of which, John Newton, was
his intimate friend; where he was brought a good
deal in contact with the poet Cowper, who was
his next-door neighbour. I well recollect an old
man occasionally calling on us at Gawcott, who
had known my grandfather at that early period
of his clerical life.

My Native Village.

The following notice of my native village, and
of some of its inhabitants, its customs, &c., I give
merely as a memento of times in which, though
not long gone by, there remained much more
of old manners than has survived to the present
day.

Gawcott is a hamlet of, and situated a mile and
a half from, Buckingham. It had had a chapel
in former times, as is proved by a field retaining
the name of "chapel close," and showing marks
of ancient building. How long this had ceased
to exist I do not know, probably for some centuries. The absence of a church had its natural
consequences, producing a partly heathenish and
partly dissenting population. The former of these
evils, and perhaps to some degree the latter, was
so much felt by one of its inhabitants that he
determined on refounding a church in his native
village. This excellent person, one John West,
was a man of humble origin, who had made what
to him was a considerable fortune by the trade

of a lace-buyer, that is to say, by acting as middle-man between the poor lace-maker and the trader. The difficulties he met with in carrying out his generous project were considerable. I have often heard my father say that after the church was built he had the greatest difficulty in getting it consecrated, and that he at last sent a message to the bishop (Tomline of Lincoln) in these words :—" Tell the bishop that if he won't consecrate it I'll give it to the dissenters,"—a message which had the desired effect. This church or chapel, erected during the first years of the present century, was perhaps as absurdly unecclesiastical a structure as could be conceived. Enclosed between four walls forming a short wide oblong, it had a roof sloping all ways, crowned by a belfry such as one sees over the stables of a country house. The pulpit occupied the middle of the south side, the pews facing it from the north, the east, and the west, and a gallery occupying the north side, in the centre of which were perched the singers and the band of clarionets, bass-viols, &c., by which their performances were accompanied. The font, I well recollect, was a washhand-stand with a white basin! The advowson was placed in the hands of five trustees, all being incumbents of parishes in the neighbourhood, and belonging to the then very scarce Evangelical party. My father was the first " Perpetual Curate." There was at first no parsonage, and he lived for a time in the vicarage at Buckingham (the vicar being non-resident), where my two eldest brothers (and one who died in infancy) were born. He soon,

however, raised funds for the erection of a parsonage, which, as he had a fancy for planning,
he designed himself,—and I must not find fault
with my native house. It was close to the
church.

My earliest recollections of the church bear
upon the digging of the vault for the founder and
my sitting in the gallery at his funeral, and seeing
it pass the opposite windows. This was in 1814,
so that it is a pretty youthful reminiscence, yet
though it is my earliest, it does not come to me
otherwise than any other, and does not seem by
any means like a beginning, showing that though
we forget what happened in our early childhood,
we nevertheless have no feeling of being incapable of observing and remembering it. Here, for
instance, I can recollect who dug the vault, and
who took me to church, and I have a full sense
of being conscious of who they said Mr. West
was, and of the house he had lived in, though I
was but three years old.

The inhabitants of Gawcott were a very quaint
race. I recollect my father saying that when he
first went there to reconnoitre, he found the road
to it rendered impassable by a large hole dug
across it, in which the inhabitants were engaged
in baiting a badger, a promising prelude to an
evangelical ministry among them. However he
succeeded in bringing the place in due time into
a more seemly state as to externals, though the
old leaven remained, and a certain amount of
poaching and other forms of rural blackguardism
still prevailed. There grew up amongst all this,
however, a good proportion of really excellent

people, some of whom had at one time belonged
to the previously more normal type.

The neighbourhood of Buckingham is by no
means picturesque. It is situated geologically at
the junction of the Oxford clay with the lower
oolite, and though in other districts the latter
rises into high and picturesque hills, such is not
the case with this portion of its course. It is a
plain, slightly undulated, agricultural country,
partly arable, but mainly devoted to dairy farming,
butter being the only produce for which it is
famous. It is (or rather was) here and there
well wooded with oak, is everywhere enclosed,
with a good deal of hedge-row timber, sadly dis-
figured by lopping, and there is usually some
more ornamental timber round the villages. The
latter, as a rule, retained some traces of the "Great
House" the residence of the old proprietor who
had in most instances succumbed to the all-
absorbing influence of a single family, originally
one of their own—the squire-race, but then
become the Marquises and subsequently the
Dukes of Buckingham, who from their semi-regal
seat of Stowe, some four miles from my own
humble village, lorded it over the county. An
unpicturesque country, denuded of its natural
aristocracy, is no doubt very dull and unattractive,
yet it possesses some interest in the natural and
quaint character of its inhabitants and in its reten-
tiveness of old customs. I have never met with so
many odd eccentric characters as in my native village, nor do I suppose that there were, even then,
many districts in which old customs were better
kept up. Whether they are so still, I know not.

The cottages were usually of the old thatched type, built of rough stone, or of timber and plaster. The one sitting-room known as " the house " had the old-fashioned chimney-corner, in the sides of which the master and mistress of the family sat, with the wood fire, placed upon bars and bricks, on the floor between them. In the ample chimney over their heads hung the bacon, for the benefit of the smoke, and below it all sorts of utensils for which dryness was to be desired, and high overhead as they sat there the occupants could see the sky through the vertical smoke-shaft. The room was paved with unshapen slabs of stone from the neighbouring quarry or "stone-pit" and the oaken floor timbers showed overhead, though hardly sufficiently so for a tall man to feel his head to be safe. Between one of these timbers and the floor there was placed (where babies were to be found) a vertical post, which revolved on its central axis and from which projected an arm of wood with a circular ring or hoop at its end, so contrived as to open and shut. By passing this about the baby's body the little thing could run round and round at will, while its mother was busied at her household work or at the lace-pillow. The bedroom arrangements I do not recollect, but I do not think they were so defective as those we now so often hear of, and the generality of cottages had a pretty ample garden.

The farmers did not live very differently as to general forms from the cottagers, the difference lying chiefly in the very substantial distinction between abundance and scantiness of fare. They usually lived in the "house" or kitchen, though

they (and indeed some of the cottagers) had
" parlours " which were only used when they had
company. In a corner of the " parlour" was
usually a smart cupboard called a " bofette."

I have heard my father say that Mr. West, the
founder of the church, lived in the same room
with his servants, all helping themselves at dinner
from a common dish placed in the middle of the
round table.

In the midst of this funny population we lived
almost as a stranger colony. My father was by
education a Londoner, and my mother too, though
a West-Indian by birth, had been educated in
London, as were also my grandmother and my
great-aunt, who resided with us, while our isola-
tion was rather increased, than otherwise, by my
father taking seven or eight pupils who came from
all parts of the kingdom, and by our mixing very
little indeed in local society, though we had
numerous friends at a distance, who occasionally
visited us. Our few local friends lived in the
neighbouring town of Buckingham, and now and
then a clergyman was admitted to our acquaintance : most of them, however, shunned us
as evangelicals, or as they were then called
" methodists."

My recollections of the period of my youth are
indeed very curious in this respect, I mean as to
the relations which at that time (up to 1830 and
later) subsisted between an evangelical clergyman
and his family, and the other clerical families
around them.

Now be it remembered that my father was in
his way very much of a man of the world.

Having been brought up in town, he had seen a good deal of life in one way or another. He was the farthest possible from being a sanctimonious man, and, though he made religion his primary object and guide, he did not bring it to the front or parade it in the least degree so as to give offence to others. He was, in addition to this, a peculiarly gentlemanly man, ready and well fitted for any society, and as much at home with men of rank as with his equals or inferiors. He was also a man of especially popular manners, more so than almost any man I recollect, thoroughly genial, merry, and courteous in all companies and to all comers.

My mother too was a particularly ladylike person, a hater of all vulgarity, an absolute detester of all low and unworthy motives, and ready to sacrifice any advantage rather than risk any, even the most punctilious, point of honour or high feeling. She was well-born, of a good old family called on the monument of one of them [5] (a stranger to us) in Petersham church, " generosa et perantiqua familia."

She was related to persons of good position : her grandfather and uncle were West India planters, (the former, President of the Assembly in his island), whose family had intermarried with baronets, and in one case with a marquis, so that there was no social or personal reason for our not being familiar with our neighbours, but the reverse.

[5] Thomas Gilbert. He was, says his epitaph, " Integer, probus, severe justus, fidus ad amicos, ad omnes, ad Deum ; sine promissis, sine dissimulatione, sine superstitione, firmus, benevolus, pius." He died in 1766.—ED.

Yet how many of the neighbouring incumbents ever called on us or we on them ? I may almost say not one. I have no recollection of knowing the wife, son, or daughter, of any clergyman in the neighbourhood, and none ever appeared at our table, with the exception of one or two curates who had slightly evangelical tendencies. I do not know whether this arose most from the exclusiveness of the "evangelicals," or from the repugnance felt toward them by other clergymen, perhaps from both. I recollect one highly eccentric rector hard by, a master of a college at Oxford, who had assisted the son of a farmer, who showed literary talent, to enter the church, and had signed his testimonials for deacons' orders, refusing to do the same for him when he went up for priests' orders, because he had once taken duty for my father in his absence. Of this rector I used to hear that when once led, the worse for his cups, through the quadrangle of his college, he exclaimed, " All this I do to purge my college from the stain of methodism ! " (Wesley had been of his college). This, however, was of course an extreme case, and the man both eccentric and disreputable. The ordinary incumbents contented themselves with taking no more notice of us than if we did not exist. Even common civilities were so rare, that I recollect the pleasure which my father expressed when he met with any. There were a few exceptions, and my father in one or two cases was in the habit of helping a neighbour, but as a rule no incumbents ever appeared at our table, nor any of us at theirs, nor indeed did we know more than two or three, even by sight, much less to speak to. I remember that my father used to speak with great respect of Mr. Palmer, the father of the present Lord Selborne, but no acquaintance existed between them.

Now let it not be for a moment imagined that it was because these clerical neighbours held what are now called " High Church views." Not a bit of it. No such notions existed among, or would as a rule have been understood by them. The greater part of them preached mere moral essays, which would have come almost as naturally from a respectable pagan. What most of them hated was the name of " methodist," while some of them resented the essential doctrines of the christian religion, such as the Atonement, and the influence of the Holy Spirit, which went among them by the name of " enthusiasm,"[6] and among the best of those who did not exactly define their objections, there was one sentiment in which they all concurred, that " as concerning this sect, we know that everywhere it is spoken against."

Nor was there less feeling on our own side. My father and mother would not have allowed us to associate with what they termed " worldly people," nor would they themselves be intimate with clergymen whom they considered " not to preach the gospel," so that as the result of these two influences we were absolutely isolated.

It is a curious question what the rank and file of these old " high-and-dry " men really were. I cannot see any resemblance between them and the

[6] The old toast of " Prosperity to the establishment and confusion to enthusiasm " illustrates this state of feeling.—ED.

present high churchmen; though, on the other hand, the fact remains that the high churchmen have naturally succeeded to them, and they have lapsed into the high church party. Nevertheless I do not imagine that they held any doctrine in common with their successors, unless it be baptismal regeneration, which the old men possibly held; not indeed actively, but just as a safeguard against the "methodistical" doctrine of "conversion." They held, I suppose, that the wicked suffer future punishment; but any severe pressure of that doctrine they practically repudiated. They were, I think, theoretically believers, but practically or passively disbelievers, in the principal doctrines of christianity. They did not hate evangelicals so much from differing with them on specific points, as because they pressed religion and piety as the chief aim of their teaching, whereas the high-and-dry men did not care, or take the trouble to do so, the fact being that they were not religious men.

They seem to me to have been practically Pelagians, though they knew nothing and cared nothing about what they were, being content with the consciousness that they were neither "methodists" nor "enthusiasts" and that they detested both. This, however, does not apply to the leading men of the party, many of whom were excellent, as they were undoubtedly learned, men; who held, in the main, a good and orthodox code of doctrine—so much so, that when the evangelicals came to compare notes carefully with them, they did not find very much difference, excepting that these made more of sacraments and less of conversion, of original sin, and of the influence of the Holy Spirit, and that they repudiated co-operation with dissenters in any matter whatever (e. g. in the Bible Society), while the evangelicals did not object to anything which they thought would promote earnest religion.

Many of the bishops who belonged to this better stratum of the old high-and-dry party hated the evangelicals even worse than the less moral of their opponents did. I remember one of them at a visitation, publicly rebuking a most pious and zealous evangelical for some irregular act, such as preaching in the open air, or something of that kind, and afterwards taking wine at the visitation dinner with a clergyman so noted for his immorality that he subsequently had to be *chasséed* altogether.

My father and mother were among the most admirable people I have ever met with, and the most affectionate of couples. Their marriage was purely a love-match, though strengthened by the ties of earnest piety. They had become acquainted shortly after my grandfather had taken the living of Aston Sandford, near to which is the semi-romantic village of Bledlow, on the edge of the Chilterns, of which my mother's uncle, the Rev. Nathaniel Gilbert, was rector. My mother, having lost her father at a very early age, had been brought by her mother and aunt to England, and had been educated in London, as also had my father, though they did not become acquainted till they met in Buckinghamshire, at one of the neighbouring rectories. They were married in the beautiful church of Bledlow, and such was the

simplicity of manners in that county and time that
—"tell it not in Gath"—my father took his wife
home seated on a pillion, and that from the house
of the proprietor of a considerable West Indian
estate, a man of no mean connexions, and a Buckinghamshire rector! This simplicity, however,
suited their means, which were very slender. My
parents, as I have said, were both of them what
may be called "well-bred," both by nature and
training "gentlefolk." I have often witnessed,
with admiring wonder, my father's gentlemanly
address when he met with persons of a higher
station, so superior to what we young villagers
could ever hope to attain to. He was a man of
popular and winning manner, and of a remarkably commanding aspect, so that, while he felt at
home with persons of any rank, he could at once
quell, almost with his eye, the most obstreperous
parishioner, and even insane persons, under the
most violent paroxysms, would yield to him without resistance.

My mother had been beautiful in her youth,
and, when I first remember her, was a very noble
and stately person, somewhat taller than my father,
with an aquiline nose, piercing, though soft, dark,
hazel eyes, and black hair. She was indeed a
commanding woman, though of an intensely affectionate disposition, and devoted to her husband,
her family, and the parish. Were it not for such
parents, and for our having been kept aloof from
the rough society of the place, and brought in
contact with strangers, owing to my father taking
pupils, I cannot conceive to what degree of rusticity we should have fallen! As it was, we all

came out into the world, certainly somewhat ungarnished, but rather plain than rustic. Our parents always tried to impress upon us the feelings of gentlemen, in a degree only second to their endeavours to train us up religiously.

Our village, as I have already said, was full of odd, quaint characters. I will describe a few of them.

To begin with the farmers :—Our great farmer was Mr. Law. He cultivated two large farms, one which he rented, and the other his own free-hold. We held him, and I believe rightly, to be very rich. He was nephew and executor to the founder of the church, and from him my father received the scanty endowment. He was a short, burly man, of no great talent, but a very worthy, good-natured person ; he was perpetual church-warden, and always lined the plate he held at the church doors after charity sermons with a one-pound note, with which now obsolete form of money (called, from its greasiness, " filthy lucre ") his breeches-pockets were always well filled.

Then there was old Zachery Meads, a sulky, obtuse old giant, who was never seen at church, or ever expected to do anything good.

Next there was Benjamin Warr, a splendid old yeoman, who, with his sturdy wife and a family of twenty children (most of the sons six feet high), made a fair show in one of our square pews.

Then, again, John Walker (of Lenborough, an allied hamlet), a downright, thoroughly excellent specimen of an English farmer—a man of sterling sense, honour, and excellence in every way. (By-the-bye, he is but just dead, and I saw his mourning-card but yesterday.)[7] He has, since our day, been more than once mayor of Buckingham. He was our best singer, our best yeomanry cavalier, our best dairy farmer, our most strong-headed and right-minded parishioner, and withal a really christian man.

The other farmers had nothing very marked which merits notice. They used to dress much more in the true John Bull style than is now the fashion. Their costume was a long frock coat, a very long waistcoat, divided at the bottom below the buttons, and reaching over the hips, corduroy knee-breeches, and, when not top-booted, shoes with large buckles. They usually carried a gun, and were accompanied by a sporting dog.

Among the labourers we had many very excellent men, men of real piety and worth, though I need not describe them individually. I may mention that, so far as I can recollect, these men were all decently educated, though how this came about I do not know. Indeed, oddly enough it seems to me that inability to read was less frequent forty years ago among these rustic labourers than it is now in the immediate neighbourhood of London. In our time we had sunday-schools, and there was a village schoolmaster who kept school on his own account, but we had no parish school, beyond a national school at Buckingham. The females were all employed in lace-making, which was commenced so early in life as to leave little time for schooling, yet I fancy they could very generally read, and they were by no means ignorant of Bible history and of general religious knowledge.

[7] January, 1864.

C

Among the more eccentric inhabitants of our village I may mention a man of the name of Walker, surnamed " Tom O' Gawcott," a super-annuated prize-fighter, whose great boast was that he would never " darken the doors of Jack West's church ;" but in his old age he relented, and he died a truly religious man.

One of our village characters was a Mrs. Warr, who kept a shop for " tea, coffee, tobacco, and snuff," opposite to the churchyard. As in our childish days we were not allowed to go into the village alone, " Mother Warr," as we used to call her, carried on a great trade with us in lollypops, &c., by answering our call across the road from the churchyard ; a brook ran through the village street, and she or her old husband had placed stepping-stones to aid her passage to and fro. It was quite a picture to see her in her quaint, old-fashioned dress rise at our call from her lace-pillow, and step nimbly across the brook with her sweet wares. She wore a high cap, with her hair brushed vertically from her forehead, her stay-laces showed in front, and her gown, divided at the waist and gathered up in a bundle behind, exposed to view a stiff glazed blue petticoat; she had short sleeves hanging loosely from her elbows, and large buckles to her shoes, and on sundays she added long silk gloves, a black mantilla edged with lace and a bonnet of antique cut. Personally she was tall and dignified, as became her costume, and in mind as strong as you please, and by no means disposed to be trifled with, though generally condescending and benignant. Her husband, surnamed "Old Baccy," was equally antique, though by no means her equal in other ways.

The village was as eccentric in its diseases as in its other conditions. Two of its inhabitants, both named Warr, suffered from the strangest form of madness, and poor old Molly, " Mother Warr's " sister-in-law, was one of them. I have heard that she and two others, while girls, had been seized with "St. Vitus' dance," and were kept shut up together in the same room, where at certain hours, when St. Vitus was rampant, they commenced dancing till the room was not high enough for their capers. At this particular stage in their disorder the charming influence of the fiddle, played by a boy, was prescribed, which had the effect of reducing the more active form of the attack, but in the case of poor Molly, left matters not much the better, for ever afterwards she had two fits of raving madness in the twenty-four hours—at noon and at midnight. During eleven hours she was quiet and inoffensive, though the subject to her neighbours of a strange mysterious awe, which was perhaps one of the hindrances to our venturing to the shop for our lollypops, for when we did so she occasionally served us herself, to our intensest horror, for our dread of her, even during her lucid intervals, was beyond description.

One of the two other sufferers from St. Vitus' dance was known amongst us as "Nanny White;" the success of the boy fiddler had in her case been perfect, and she had attained a good old age, not in strong health, for she was, poor old lady, tremulous through a tendency to palsy. I call her a lady advisedly, because she was what one. may term a peasant-lady. She was a person of earnest piety and of admirable conduct,—an aristocrat among the peasantry. Her income was 30*l.* a year, but she lived almost in state. We went as children once a year to drink tea with her (which was more than we were allowed to do with any of the farmers, but good John Walker), when she received us with great dignity, dressed in her best old-fashioned clothes. The good little old lady sat smiling and shaking in her arm-chair, while her waiting-maid handed about the tea and cake ; we all sat round on old high-backed chairs with twisted pillars and cane backs, which, by-the-bye, she had bought at a sale of the furniture of the latest despoiled of the neighbouring great houses (that at Hillesden, which I shall mention anon). We sat on that occasion, for the nonce, in her " parlour," while in the " house " through which it was approached was the old dresser, under which was a series of copper cauldrons of gradually diminishing sizes, presenting their highly polished interiors to the spectator. This good old woman some years after, when my father had to rebuild his church, made out of her savings a really handsome subscription as " a friend," no one but my father and mother knowing whence it came till after her death. I recollect that she had at one time for her maid and companion a young person named " Betsy Scott." I wish I knew enough of her to sketch her character. She was a " lusus naturæ," both in intellect and piety, and after her death (of consumption) my father wrote a memoir of her, embodying many letters and papers of her

writing, some I think in poetry.   I well recollect
his applying to her the quotation from Gray :—

> " Full many a gem of purest ray serene
>   The dark unfathom'd caves of ocean bear ;
> Full many a flower is born to blush unseen,
>   And waste its sweetness on the desert air."

Two of our favourite village characters were a
half-cracked man, and a semi-simpleton ; the one
known as " Cracky Meads," and the other as
" Tailor King."   The former had been a soldier,
and on his return from campaigning had found
that his elder brother had inflicted upon him a very
base injury, which drove the poor fellow out of
his mind.   After this his great desire was to
build himself a house with his own unaided hands
on a piece of waste ground by a road side.   He
made many beginnings, but what he built in the
day the young men of the village pulled down
at night.   At length, however, his perseverance
and active defence of his work prevailed, and he
succeeded in completing a very tolerable bachelor's
cottage.   He enclosed a long piece of waste as a
garden, which he successfully cultivated, and with
the help of his pension lived pretty comfortably.
He was, when unexcited, quiet, sullen, and inoffensive ; but it took only a little skilfully directed
conversation to stir him up tremendously in different ways.   His most interesting excitement
was that of warlike reminiscence, when he would
tell endless tales of his personal experiences,
sometimes enacting them with the bayonet, which
he kept under his bed, with a vigour hardly consistent with the safety of his audience.   His most
terrible movements, however, were against his

brother, upon whom his imprecations were as fearful as they were deserved. He was popular among my father's pupils, both for these displays, and for his services in getting them eggs, and boiling or frying them in his cottage, and for allowing occasionally a little indulgence in the form of a pipe of tobacco.

Poor " Tailor King " was a very different but equally amusing character. He was blessed with but a scanty store of sense, but had a double supply of instinct. His intincts were wholly devoted to sporting matters. He was always present in the hunting-field, knew of course where every meet would take place, and by long practice in the ways of the fox, could so surely prejudge his course, as by wary cuts to keep up with the hunters. The time lost to his trade by these digressions was made up for by the rewards received for occasional aid, taking home a lame dog, assisting a fallen rider or a damaged horse, and so he made his hunting pay. He could sometimes tell the very hole in the hedge through which the fox would emerge from the wood. He was an uncouth figure, his neck all on one side from catching it in a forked bough while leaping a hedge. He hunted in a light green coat, knee breeches, and low shoes. We were often sent by my mother, if she wanted a hare, to Mr. Law to ask if he would shoot one for her, and his constant reply was, " I'll go and ask the tailor," or as he pronounced it "tyahlor." We then went together to the tailor's shop, where he was sitting cross-legged at his window. " D'ye know where there's ever a hare (yahr) sittin', tyahler ?"

was the constant question, and the tailor could always tell or show where to find one. His conversation was a mixture of ludicrous simplicity with instructive cunning, and by the amusement of his talk and the general character of his instincts, he became a great favourite among us boys.

Another favourite was old "Warr of the Woodhouse," a clever skilled old woodman; but I am ashamed to say that we only cared for him when he was drunk, or "market-merry" as he called it, which took place once a week on market-day. When he died, after my leaving home, poor old "Mother Warr" and her husband retired from their shop to the said woodhouse, where they ended their days. My wife saw the old woman there in her old age, later than I did myself, and says that she never saw so picturesque a figure; tall, straight, and dignified still, in her last-century dress, sitting at her door in the wood plying her spinning-wheel.

These are a few specimens, but the whole place was full of character, even where there are no very salient points to depict. The old women seem to my recollection to belong to another age, and the sturdy worthiness of many of the men, with their funny old-fashioned way of expressing themselves, formed a most agreeable contrast to the contemporary tendency to pauperism, which was silently making way among the less estimable part of the population, who, like spotted sheep, in time infected the flock.

Our own family was a large and rapidly increasing one. My eldest brother was a youth of

remarkable talent and was viewed as a little god
by his brothers and even by his parents. This
had a bad effect on me. He was looked on as a
representative person, and all efforts were concentrated upon him. His next brother got a
little attention at second hand, and being a boy of
steady industry and good ability, he got on ; but I,
the third, was too far removed to pick up even
the crumbs, and not having a natural love of
books and nothing occurring to make me love
them, I came off but badly. I was also under
the disadvantage of having no boys of my own
age to work with ; indeed with all my faults I was
forwarder than any who were at all of my own
standing, so that at twelve or thirteen, I had to
be classed with idle fellows of eighteen or more ;
a desultory way of going on which was very injurious. I ought certainly to have gone to school,
but this was out of the question. My father was
poor, and as he took pupils himself, he was too
busy with the older ones, often men of from twenty
to twenty-five or more, to give me much of his
personal attention, so that I slipped through between wind and water. I do believe, however,
that if encouraged and helped, I should have
done well, and in mathematics I did get on fairly.

My great relief from this life of heedlessness
and rough handling was the visit of the drawing-
master. Though I never acquired any very high
powers of drawing under him, I can never be too
grateful for his help and kind encouragement.
He was a Mr. Jones, of Buckingham, who had
been in his youth patronized by some of the
Stowe family, and had been sent to London, where

he became a student at the Royal Academy, and was much noticed by Sir Joshua Reynolds, of whom he entertained an affectionate remembrance. Foolishly, however, he returned to his native town, and had consequently failed of reaching the eminence for which nature had fitted him. He supported himself as a drawing-master, and occasional portrait-painter. His visits twice a week were the very joy of my life. I remember, as if it were yesterday, and almost feel again while thinking of it, my anxiety when he was a little late in coming, my frequent glances towards the path by which he reached our garden, and my heart-felt joy when I saw his loose drab gaiters through the bushes. Mr. Jones was a mild, benignant, and humble-minded old man, and though he had not attained eminence, he was thoroughly grounded in his art. His knowledge of anatomy and of perspective was perfect, as was his acquaintance with the principles of colouring, whether in oil or water-colour, and his powers of drawing were remarkable. Yet his training had stopped short of bringing his powers to bear upon actual high-class work of his own. I often wish I had some of his drawings, I am sure they must evince the elements of genius, though unmatured, and consistently enough with this, he instilled into my mind an intense love for the subject without any ripened knowledge or skill. While, however, depreciating myself on this and other subjects, it is fair to mention that my home schooling terminated when I was only about fourteen and a half years old. The little I learned of French my mother taught me, and I might, had I worked hard, have learned it well, as she understood it perfectly, and spoke it with ease. My eldest brother had also a good French master, in whose instruction unhappily I did not participate.

How infinitely important it is for boys to feel the duty and necessity for exertion. Though I have reason to be most thankful for my success in life, the defects of my education have been like a millstone about my neck, and have made me almost dread superior society. A very little extra attention would have obviated this, for if with the same means of education my brother carried off in his freshman's year one of the highest university classical scholarships, why should not I have been a fair classic? It is one of the greatest wonders of my life to witness the way in which young men deliberately throw away their chances of eminence and seem satisfied with the bare prospect of getting a living; as if man was born, not to do the very utmost in his day and generation which the talents committed to him render attainable, but merely to exist. Old Sir Robert Peel, as I was told by his son, used to say that if any youth of ordinary ability made up his mind as to his object in life and bent all his energies to its attainment, he would be almost certain of success, and this led the son of Sir Robert to determine, when a child, that he would be prime minister, and to persevere till he became so.

Being younger than most of my father's pupils (who, in fact, were many of them matured men, who had determined late in life to read for the church), I had very little companionship, and I became a solitary wanderer in woods and fields,

and about the old churches, &c., in the neighbourhood.

I have a tolerably distinct recollection of my
grandfather, the author of the Commentary on
the holy scriptures. We used to visit him *en
masse* about once a year; it was a time of great
joy and excitement when it came round. The
post-chaise was ordered from Buckingham, and
usually was made to carry seven. My father and
mother occupied the seat, three small children
stood in front, and two sat on the "dickey," while
the fat old postboy rode as postillion. It was
some twenty-five miles to Aston Sandford, and I
think I could find my way now by my recollections
of that date. My grandfather was, as I remember
him, a thin, tottering old man, very grave and
dignified. Being perfectly bald, he wore a black
velvet cap, excepting when he went to church,
when he assumed a venerable wig. He wore
knee-breeches, with silver buckles, and black silk
stockings, and a regular shovel hat. His amusement was gardening, but he was almost constantly
at work in his study. At meals, when I chiefly
saw him, he was rather silent, owing to his deafness, which rendered it difficult to him to join in
general conversation. I well remember, when
any joke had excited laughter at the table, that he
would beg to be informed what it was, and when
brought to understand it, he would only deign to
utter a single word—"Pshaw!" One day, as we
sat at dinner, a very old apple-tree, loaded with
fruit, suddenly gave way and fell to the ground,
to the surprise of our party, and I remember my
grandfather remarking that he wished that might

be his own end, to break down in his old age under the weight of good fruit.   Family prayers at Aston Rectory were formidable, particularly to a child.   They lasted a full hour, several persons from the village usually attending.   I can picture to my mind my grandfather walking to church in his gown and cassock, his long curled wig, and shovel hat.[8]   He had a most venerable look, and I felt a sort of dread at it.   On sundays he had a constant guest at his table—the barber, to whom he was beholden for his wig.   Those who are not acquainted with the evangelical party in its earlier days can hardly understand the way in which community of religious feeling was allowed to over-ride difference of worldly position.   I recollect the same at Gawcott, where, though not allowed to associate even with our wealthiest farmer, we ever welcomed to our table a very poor brother of his, in position scarcely above a labourer, who was a man of piety, and came many miles on sunday to attend our church.   The same was the

[8] My father's recollections upon the subject of clerical dress may be of interest.   He has often told me that in the earliest period to which his memory extended, the clergy habitually wore their cassock, gown, and shovel hat, and that when this custom went out, a sort of interregnum ensued during which all distinction of dress was abandoned and clerics followed lay fashions.   This is the period which Jane Austen's novels illustrate.   Her clergymen are singularly free from any trace of the ecclesiastical character.   Later on, the clergy adopted the suit of black, and the white necktie, which had all along been the dress of professional men, lawyers, doctors, architects, and even surveyors, of men, in short, whose business it was to advise.   Of the modern developements which this lay-professional dress has received at the hands of clerical tailors, it is unnecessary to say anything. —ED.

case with the barber at Great Risborough. He was a pious man, and he walked over every sunday to hear my grandfather preach, and a place was kept for him at the dinner-table. He was, however, a superior man, and he had the good fortune to get his two sons into the church. Some time after he had settled at Risborough he found that there was an old bequest for the education (for the church) of any one of his name living at Risborough, which he at once claimed and obtained for his son. The other boy, having a good voice, was placed in the choir at Magdalen college, Oxford, when in due time he was admitted into the college, and finally into the church.

Near Aston lived my uncle, the Rev. Samuel King. He was son of an excellent man, George King, a large wine merchant in the city ; and being a pupil of my grandfather's, he formed an attachment to his only daughter Elizabeth, and married her before or during his residence at the university of Cambridge. After they left Cambridge, he took the curacy of Hartwell, near Aylesbury, where was the seat of Sir George Lee, at that time occupied by Louis XVIII. and the ex-royal family of France. Subsequently, or at the same time, he was curate of Stone, close by Hartwell, where I first recollect visiting him, after which he removed to Haddenham, nearer to my grandfather's, so that our visits were jointly to my grandfather and to him. My aunt was a gifted and lovely woman, and at that time she used to aid my grandfather in the correction of a new edition of his commentary, as did also a young man who then resided with him, Mr.

W. R. Dawes, since well known as an astronomer,
and who in his old age returned to Haddenham
and built himself a residence there. I well remember my puzzlement at hearing that certain
printed sheets, which came every morning by post,
and seemed to be viewed with great consideration,
were "proofs of the bible." I connected them in
idea with the evidences of christianity.

The whole household of my grandfather seemed
imbued with religious sentiment. Old Betty, the
cook, and Lizzy, the waiting-maid, and old Betty
Moulder, an infirm inmate, taken in on account of
her excellence and helplessness, were all patterns
of goodness, and even poor John Brangwin, the
serving-man, partook of the general effect of the
atmosphere of the rectory. Poor old fellow! I
visited him last spring, with three of my sons at
an almshouse at Cheynies, when he poured forth
his recollections of my grandfather for half an
hour together. It was sunday, and we found him
reading in the copy of the commentary which my
grandfather had left him in his will; and he told
us he had just had a cold dinner. "He never
had anything cooked o' sabbath day; Muster
Scott never had anything cooked o' sabbath
days"—a precept he had followed for more than
forty years. I regret that my recollections of my
grandfather himself are so very scanty, while my
memory of the place, and of its less important
inhabitants, and of its trifling incidents, is as
perfect as though it were of last year.

Some five miles beyond Aston Sandford runs
the range of the Chiltern Hills, the "delectable
mountains" of my youth, always forming our

horizon, though very rarely reached by us. They divided the county into two parts, as different as possible in their character; the northern, where we lived, homely and picturesque, the southern hilly and delightful. Once only in these early days I saw this beautiful part of my county, when I went to visit my aunt (the widow of the Rev. N. Gilbert), at Woburn, near Wycombe, and I well remember the pleasure I experienced. I remember our all walking up Stokenchurch hill, a coach-load of passengers forming a long procession before us.

After my grandfather's death my uncle King was presented to the living of Latimers, in this southern division of Bucks, our visits to which place were the brightest spots in my early life. My uncle was a most lively and amusing man, who, having no family of his own, devoted himself, when thrown in the way of children, very extensively to their amusement. He was a man of multifarious resources, an excellent astronomer, and perhaps the best amateur ornamental turner in the kingdom. He was a glass-painter, a brass-founder, and a devotee to natural science in many forms. My aunt was a literary person. She had received the same education with her brothers, instead of learning feminine accomplishments. She was one of those " ladies of talent " one occasionally meets with, whose company is courted on account of their superior knowledge and conversational powers. I have every reason for gratitude to them both, as I shall afterwards show.

My maternal grandmother and her sister (as

before-mentioned) lived with us at Gawcott. The former was a very excellent, quiet, unobtrusive little woman. I rarely heard anything of her husband, Dr. Lynch. He died early, leaving her with a young family, and I fancy but slenderly provided for, for the only thing I ever heard of him was, that he impoverished himself by being so easy-going, that he could not refuse any one who asked money of him. His eldest son was, during my childhood, a medical man at Dunmow in Essex, where he also died early, leaving a large family. My aunt Gilbert had accompanied my grandmother and her family to England, or possibly was here already, as her English recollections reached to a much earlier date. This must have been about 1790, as nearly as I can tell, my mother being at that time about four years old. They resided in Great Ormond street, Queen's square, which then bordered upon the fields. My aunt was a person of considerable talent, of great piety, and of an extraordinarily affectionate disposition, and withal wonderfully simple-hearted and forbearing. She devoted herself to my mother during her childhood, with an intensity of affection, exceeding probably what a child would always find agreeable.

She and my grandmother were provided for by annuities upon their father's estate, then pretty good, but ever diminishing with the decline of West India property. My mother went to a very good school (I think in London) kept by a Miss Cox, who was afterwards married to a Mr. Woodroffe, a clergyman in Gloucestershire, and my mother always kept up an affectionate correspondence with her, and they mutually visited from time to time. She was author of a religious novel entitled, "Shades of Character, or the Little Pilgrim," and of "Michael Kemp." When my mother married, my aunt came to live with her (my grandmother living for a time near her son at Dunmow). When I made my appearance on the *tapis*, my aunt pitched upon my unworthy person as her pet, and ever afterwards followed me up with an assiduity of affection which it is impossible to exaggerate. This was probably enhanced (though my conduct was not calculated to produce that effect) by her having had the charge of me, when five years old, for some months, while I made a stay on account of some casual disorder at Margate. This was in 1816, and as it was the landmark of my childhood, I will give a few reminiscences of it.

Of the coach journey to London, I have hardly a glimmer of recollection. On our arrival, however, we transferred ourselves to the house of a sort of " Gaius mine host," who dwelt hard by the coach-office where we alighted. This was a Mr. Broughton, of Swan-yard, Holborn bridge, who kept a boarding-house for travellers, with a preference for those of the evangelical party, and a still more particular preference for missionaries, and most especially for missionaries to New Zealand. This, his most powerful preference, was rendered manifest to the eye by his rooms being hung with patoo-patoos, war-rugs, and all the marvels of a New Zealand museum; and occasionally a tattooed chief or two, to his intense joy, took up their quarters under

D

his roof. All this, however, I gathered at subsequent visits.

Mr. Broughton showed his special regard for the commentator, my grandfather, by opening his house to his descendants at all times gratuitously —indeed he demanded their acceptance of his hospitality as a right. Swan-yard, which has perished in the extension of ·Farringdon street, was opposite to the then Fleet market. It was a waggon-yard, devoted to broad-wheeled waggons and straw, and the house was far from lively. At the time of our visit Mrs. Broughton, who was enormously corpulent, was laid up with the gout, and I was forthwith conducted by my aunt to the good lady's bedroom. Here I was so terrified at the sight of her vast person, enveloped in volumes of dimity, and her legs swaddled in a stupendous gouty stocking of white-and-pink lamb's wool, that I at once proclaimed a mutiny, and refused to stop in the house, in which I so resolutely persisted, that my good aunt actually yielded to me, and transferred me to the cabin of the Margate sailing-packet, which was to start in the morning.

Here we met a number of Buckingham friends, who were to join us in our lodgings at Margate. My impression of the cabin is very vivid. It was full of passengers, and I well recollect a lively and lengthened argument, in which my aunt was a warm disputant, as to whether in dealing with savages we ought to aim at civilizing before christianizing or *vice versâ*, a point on which the cabin was about equally divided. As the night drew on, the ladies and children retired to the berths which lined the sides, while the gentlemen retained their chairs. I well recollect peeping out from between my curtains, and seeing gentlemen, who had lately been warm in argument, sitting quietly asleep round tables, on which their heads and elbows were deposited.

Of the next day my leading recollection is the sweeping of the boom across the deck as we tacked, and the havoc it always threatened amongst the crowded passengers. Arrived at Margate we took lodgings on "the Fort," at the house of one, Captain Bourne; my aunt and I, and our Buckinghamshire friends all living together as one family. There was already a steamer to Margate; but it was such a new thing that the visitors and inhabitants crowded to the pier to see it come in. I well remember the excitement of seeing its approach. One of my most vivid recollections of Margate was our going with some of our friends to a Quakers' meeting at a place called Drapers, and hearing several ladies preach. I also recollect seeing a fleet of thirty-two East Indiamen pass in a row, probably under convoy, as the war was but recently over. While at Margate I lost an infant sister named Elizabeth.

After leaving Margate we visited my uncle Lynch at Dunmow, and in passing through London, my aunt stayed with an old Wesleyan friend, Mr. Jones, of Finsbury square. I remember their showing me, from his windows, gas-lamps as great curiosities. We also went to see another Miss Gilbert, a cousin of my aunt's, (we called her "Cousin Harriet.") She was a wild, eccentric person, and while we were there, went into a frightful fit of hysterics, owing to her having visited the grave of a near relation, who had been her sole companion. I have preserved two coins which this old cousin gave me that day. I will not, however, increase frivolous reminiscences. It is vexatious to think of the perversity of children's memories. I recollect the funeral of Mr. West in 1814, and this digression from my village home in 1816, as well almost as if they had happened last year. Yet of the battle of Waterloo, which occurred in the intervening year, I have not even the slightest recollection.

My aunt Gilbert was most interesting in her reminiscences. John Wesley was the great saint of her memory. I remember her telling me of his having kissed her, which she esteemed a great privilege. She had been an intimate ally of Mrs. Fletcher of Madeley, who, after her husband's death, became a sort of female evangelist " All round the Wrekin." This hill was familiar to my childish ideas from my aunt having lived so long under its shadow. The date of this I know not, but it was during the days of Mrs. Fletcher and of Lady Dorothea Whitmore. Who the latter was, I do not know, but the family I find still resides in the neighbourhood. One of my aunt's sisters had married a Mr. Yate of Madeley. Her son, the Rev. George Yate, was rector of Wrockwardine. I remember another son, a naval officer, bringing to Gawcott a flag which he had taken in the American war ; and a daughter, Anne Yate, used to visit us, (by the way it was she who took me to Mr. West's funeral). She died of consumption some few years later, " poor cousin Anne."

My aunt kept up a very extensive correspondence, and had done so all her life. One of her
great correspondents was her brother William,
who lived in America. His was a very remarkable character. He was a barrister, and a
man of acute genius, and was just rising into
fame when his mind gave way. His insanity
took a political line, and, the first rage of the
French Revolution being rampant at the time, he
went to France to ally himself with Robespierre
and the rest, but took fright, I fancy, when he
got nearer, and returned. He subsequently went
to America, as the only country with the government of which he could feel satisfied. He was a
friend of Southey and Coleridge during their early
days. Southey remarks of him in his life of
Wesley :[9] " . . . . Mr. Gilbert published, in the
year 1796, ' The Hurricane, a Theosophical and
Western Eclogue,' and shortly afterwards pla-
carded the walls in London with the largest bills
that had at that time been seen, announcing ' The
Law of Fire.' I knew him well, and look back
with a melancholy pleasure to the hours which I
have passed in his society when his mind was in
ruins. His madness was of the most incom-
prehensible kind, as may be seen in the notes
to the ' Hurricane ;' but the poem contains passages of exquisite beauty. They who remember
him (as some of my readers will) will not be
displeased at seeing him thus mentioned with the
respect and regret which are due to the wreck
of a noble mind."

Another constant correspondent was a cousin.

[9] Vol. ii. chap. 28, foot note.

Poor man, he corresponded till the last, and then came the news that he had shot himself. I remember one of my aunt's last letters to him, which was evidently intended to keep him from religious despair, for she quoted the passage: " Though your sins be as scarlet, they shall be white as snow," &c. Let us hope that he was insane. Another correspondent was a Lady Abdy, also a cousin.

My aunt's object in all these cases was a religious one, this being the main subject of her thoughts. My aunt was a poetess, she wrote a good deal, and not badly. She was in great requisition for epitaphs, &c. I wish I could get some of her longer productions. She was an admirable woman, and in my view quite an historical person. She had a large chest filled with selected letters from her correspondents, from John Wesley downwards; but this most valuable collection was indiscriminately destroyed after her death, which happened I think in 1832. A grievous error! She lies buried a little to the south of the church of Gawcott. My grandmother lived a few years longer, and was buried at Wappenham. Both were, eighty or upwards at their death.

STOWE.

We lived within about four miles of Stowe, then in its greatest glory. The Marquis (afterwards Duke) of Buckingham was the puissant potentate of the district, and Stowe was its seat of government. It was to us of great advantage, to have this centre of art and princely splendour to refer to when we pleased. It was a set-off against the otherwise almost unmitigated rusticity of the neighbourhood.

To Stowe we all made an annual pilgrimage. This was the great day of our year. It took place in early June, that we might enjoy the glories of the lilacs and laburnums. The journey was somewhat grotesque. My father rode his old horse " Jack," or subsequently "Tripod." The older boys walked, while my mother, my eldest sister, and the children performed the journey in the baker's cart, a tilted but unspringed vehicle, furnished with chairs for the occasion, and further with a large basket of provisions which were conveyed by our serving-man William to " The Temple of Concord and Victory," our traditional lunching place. I well recollect the gratification afforded by the hard-boiled eggs, &c., eaten beneath the unwonted shade of a classic temple.

Stowe was really a very fine place. It was most extensive and well wooded ; indeed the park with its woods merged gradually off into the forest of Whittlebury. It was approached from Buckingham by a perfectly straight road some three miles long, and bordered by a wide grass drive and an avenue on either side, and leading to a triumphal arch known as the " Corinthian Arch." From several other directions it was somewhat similarly approached, so that from the Buckingham lodges to those in the direction of Towcester could hardly be less than eight miles. The house had (and has) a frontage of nearly 1000 feet, though it is fair to mention that its extreme wings hardly form a part of its architecture. It is entered, properly speaking, from

behind, where it assumes the form of a convex
semicircle. To us, however, the approach was
from the garden front, which is the great architectural façade and looks south. Here the entrance is by an octastyle Corinthian portico, approached by a lofty flight of steps rising the height
of a basement storey. I well remember the kind
of awe with which this stately approach inspired
me, and how vast it appeared to my young imagination. We were welcomed under the portico
by an almost equally stately groom of the chambers, Mr. Broadway, a man of portentous aspect
and intense dignity of demeanour. He paid
special attention to us from his respect for my
father, and devoted much pains to showing and
explaining the pictures, &c. I can fancy that
I hear now the dignified and measured words in
which he introduced the pictures to our youthful
inspection : " The Burgomeister Sichs, by Rembrandt;" "The portrait of the elder, by the younger
Rembrandt," &c. His tone gave us a reverence
for the old masters beyond what our discrimina-
tion would have alone inspired. It was really a
very fine collection, and being the only one I had
seen, I feel thankful to think that I had the
opportunity through it of seeing noble art so
early. The sculpture was also fine, containing
a great number of antiques, which were mostly
ranged round a large elliptical saloon, entered
directly from the garden portico. My veneration
was greatly enhanced by the fact that one vast
room was wholly devoted to the collection of
engravings, classified in an infinite number of
portfolios, and another to similarly-arranged music,

and that the library was so extensive as to demand the services of a man of learning and position (a dignified Roman Catholic priest, Dr. O'Connor) as the librarian. One modern picture, the " Destruction of Herculaneum " (by Martin), used to fill us with wonder, as did a magnificent astronomical clock, giving the true motions and positions of the planets, and only wound up, as we were told, once in four years, i. e. on the 29th of February.

The house was in point of fact a " palace of delights," a wilderness of art, vertu, and magnificence, of which upon the whole I have not seen an equal, and it is beyond measure aggravating to think of its glorious contents having been dispersed through the folly of its possessor.

The duke of my childhood was the grandfather to the present one. He was a man of considerable ability and attainments and of portentous ambition and pride. I believe that the downfall of the family was fully as much owing to him as to his son. He literally came under the woe pronounced upon those " that lay field to field, till there be no place, that they may be placed alone in the midst of the earth," for he nearly ruined the family by purchasing estates with borrowed money, the interest on which exceeded the rental.

We made, by-the-bye, two annual peregrinations thither, for once a year we went over to the review of the yeomanry cavalry, of which the Marquis of Chandos (the late Duke) was lieutenant-colonel. It makes me feel very antique to remember that I was present at the festivities which celebrated the baptism of the present duke,

and very magnificent they were. The fireworks
were, I suppose, as fine as that time could produce.
I recollect on that day, while sitting on a bench
so placed as to overlook a very large piece of
water surrounded by beech plantations, hearing
the remarks of two old women. " Lawk, how
unkid," said one, "you can see nothin' but water!"
" Oh, bless you," replied her more knowing companion, " why, the sea's twice as big as that."

Of the architecture of Stowe I cannot say much
from memory, nor is it necessary, as it remains, I
believe, intact.

As Stowe was my introduction to classic architecture and high art, so was my liking for gothic
architecture due to the old churches in my own
neighbourhood. The district is not famed for its
ancient churches, yet it possesses several of considerable merit. Our own village was utterly
devoid of early remains, though I venerated the
old " Chapel Close," where its ancient church or
chapel had once stood. In the same way
Buckingham had lost its old church, a very fine
edifice, which fell in 1776. My drawing-master,
Mr. Jones, remembered its fall, and told me that
it had an aisle called the Gawcott Aisle. The
old churchyard remains, though the church now
stands on the Castle Hill, and a very ungainly
edifice it is.[1] There is only one really ancient
building in Buckingham, the chapel of St. Thomas
of Canterbury, now a grammar school.

The building which first directed my attention
to gothic architecture was the church of Hillesden,

[1] Its reconstruction, under my father's direction, was in
progress at the time of his death.—ED.

situated two miles to the south of Gawcott. This
is a church of late date, but of remarkable beauty.
It was our great lion, and every new comer was
taken to see it on the earliest possible opportunity,
and was appraised by me in proportion to his
appreciation of its beauties.

I always looked upon Hillesden with the most
romantic feelings. It was a beautiful spot as
compared with our neighbourhood in general ;
it was situated on a considerable elevation, surrounded by fine old plantations and avenues of
lofty trees conspicuous throughout the district.
Near the church stood the " Great House," a
deserted mansion of the time, I believe, of Charles
II. The place had, from early in the 16th century,
belonged to the family of Denton. They were
staunch Royalists, and had suffered severely during
the Great Rebellion. We used to be told that
Sir Alexander Denton, the then proprietor, after
a vigorous defence of his mansion, was taken
prisoner, and after being conducted for some
distance from his home, was made to look back to
see his residence in flames. He died in prison.
The family in the direct line had become extinct,
and its last member, having married Mr. Coke of
Holkham, became the mother of the celebrated
Mr. Thomas William Coke, afterwards Earl of
Leicester. He was the proprietor of Hillesden
in my early days, and I recollect going to the
house of a farmer whose wife boasted that they
had been playfellows when children. The house
had been much reduced in size, but what remained, though uninhabited, retained its old furniture. I particularly remember the bedrooms, the

beds being placed in odd recesses between two closets partitioned off on either side, through which you would have to pass, to get into bed, by doors in their sides. The grounds still retained their old form with terraces and a large fish-pond. There were also the stables, of earlier date, probably of Edward the Sixth's time, and a rather elegant octagonal dove-cote of brick. Mr. Coke had repeatedly refused to sell the Hillesden estate to the Duke of Buckingham, but at length it was purchased by Mr. Farquhar of Font Hill, who immediately afterwards sold it to the duke. This was a sorrowful event to me, as the duke was in my eyes the great enemy of local history. He soon destroyed the old house, and carried off the curious old sentry-box, in the form of a brick gate-pier, to Stowe, while timber began to disappear, and keepers destroyed the liberty of the woods, and the little glory which had remained departed.

The church, however, was there after all, and to it I made my frequent pilgrimages, and a little later dear old Mr. Jones used to meet me there to teach me how to sketch. These were, perhaps, the happiest occasions of my youth, and I look back upon them now with a glow of delight.

Hillesden Church is, as I have said of late date. The tower is humbler in its pretensions than the rest of the church, and is of rather early and simple "perpendicular" work. The church itself was begun in 1493, by the monks of Nutley, to whom the rectorial tithes belonged. It is a very exquisite specimen of this latest phase of Gothic architecture, and possesses all the refinement of its best examples, such as the royal chapels at

Westminster and Windsor. Indeed, I have seen no detail of that period to surpass those of this church. In plan it consists of a nave with aisles and quasi-transepts, a large chancel with north aisle, a sacristy of two stories at the north-east angle of the chancel aisle, the upper story of which is approached by a very large newel stair at the extreme north-eastern angle. This stair-turret is a very exquisite and striking feature, being finished with a sort of crown of flying buttresses and pinnacles, of which I have seen no other instance, indeed it is one of the most beautifully-designed features I know.[2] The upper sacristy has a series of radiating loop-holes looking into the church. The walls of the chancel are ornamented by stone panelling. The ceilings throughout had panels of plaster, with wood mouldings. I have since seen some which had unhappily been taken down, and found the plaster to be in thick and very hard slabs, on which were set out curious geometric figures, drawn with the compasses, as if to form the guides for painted decorations. The rood screen was perfect, and of exquisite beauty. The fittings were nearly all of the original date, and very good, though, of course, of very late character. The chief exception was the great square pew of the Dentons, a somewhat dignified work of Charles the Second's reign, furnished with great high-backed chairs.

The monuments of the Dentons were, of course, of very varied date, from Edward the Sixth's time, or thereabouts, downwards. There is, by the way,

[2] Its design was reproduced by my father in the angle turret of the new buildings at King's College, Cambridge.—ED.

a fine monument to one of the earliest of the
family (after Hillesden had come into their hands)
in Hereford Cathedral, which I have lately had
the pleasure of reinstating, after it had been lying
in pieces for twenty years.[3]   The north porch is a
very charming structure, of exquisite design and
finish.   The churchyard cross appears to be of
the fourteenth century.   I greatly hope to have a
hand in the restoration of the church to which I owe
so much as my initiator into Gothic architecture.[4]
I fear it is in a very damaged state.   I should mention the remains of painted glass which it contains.
They are beautiful fragments, in the style of
those in King's College chapel, though more delicate in finish.   The principal remains illustrate
the life of the patron, St. Nicholas.   In other
windows, where most of the glass is gone, fragments remain in the heads, containing charming
representations of mediæval cities, such as one
sees in the background of Van Eyck's pictures.

I recollect my father writing to the Duke of
Buckingham to urge his repairing this church.
The result was that his Grace whitewashed the
exterior of the tower !

Maids Morton church, the second in rank in
our district, is also of "perpendicular" date, but
earlier.   Its tower is of admirable and unique
design.   It, at that time, retained its old seats,
with fleur-de-lis poppy-heads; also a beautiful
stoup by the doorway, all which have since been
ruthlessly destroyed.

Tingewick Church was the nearest to Gawcott

[3] Cf. infra, p. 294.
[4] This wish was realized in 1874 and 1875.—ED.

of our mediæval structures.   It was a good church, containing norman arcades and a few fragments in the south wall of the same date ; the rest, I think, all " perpendicular."   The tower was attributed to William of Wykeham.   It has since undergone strange transmogrifications.   The south wall has been rebuilt, I think, twice, and much good and interesting old work destroyed.   My father, at different times, took the curacies of Hillesden and Tingewick in combination with Gawcott.

The only other church I will mention as connected with my youthful days is Chetwood.   I was never more astonished than when I first saw this church, never having before seen or heard of " early english " architecture.   It is a fragment of a small monastic church, and its east window consists of five noble lancets, with, externally, plain but bold detail.   On either side are fine triplets. Never having before seen such windows, I was greatly perplexed at them, and, failing to get the key, and being reduced to peeping through the keyhole of the west door, I was astonished and puzzled to find that the east windows had shafts with foliated capitals, a thing I had never seen and could not understand.   I remember continuing all day in a state of morbid excitement on the subject, and having no access to architectural books, it was very long ere I solved the mystery.

My taking in this way to old churches first led my father to think of my becoming an architect, and, after consulting with my uncle King on the subject, this became a fixed arrangement.   I was then about fourteen years old, and shortly afterwards my uncle very kindly offered to take me under his own charge, and to superintend me in studies having a tendency in that direction. I accordingly took up my residence at Latimer's, in 1826. I had, two years before, made a trip to London, where my eyes were opened to much which I had never thought of before. Westminster Abbey, I need not say, I was charmed with ; it was the only gothic minster I had seen ; nor did I see any other, excepting St. Albans and Ely, till after my articles had expired, in 1830! I recollect that when I saw Westminster Abbey, in 1824, they were putting up the present reredos, or rather " restoring " in " artificial stone " the old one.[5]

My uncle's instruction was mainly in mathematics ; he carried me on through trigonometry and mechanics, in which I took great pleasure. He also gave me direct instruction in architecture, of which he possessed a very fair knowledge. I was by him initiated into classic architecture, both Greek and Roman ; and a friend of his (the Rev. H. Foyster), who had been once intended for our profession, having lent me a copy of Sir William Chambers' work, and some one else a portion of Stewart's Athens, I was able to follow up architectural drawing, as then taught, pretty systematically, and by the time I was articled I had already been put through my facings to a certain reasonable extent. I think I also had access to Rickman, as I certainly got to know the ordinary facts as to the different periods of mediæval architecture. The only treatise I had before seen on this subject had

[5] This was restored anew in alabaster and marble in 1866.—ED.

been an article in the Edinburgh *Encyclopædia*, of
which I remember little but the illustrations, more
especially a west elevation of Rheims Cathedral,
in which I took, when quite a child, the greatest
delight.   I stayed, I suppose, with my uncle about
a twelvemonth, on and off.   Though a somewhat
solitary life, it was one of very great pleasure and
enjoyment.   The country there is peculiarly
charming, and so wholly different from my own
home as to be like a new world.   My love of
woodland was here transferred from oak-woods,
choked up with hazel and blackthorn, to beechwoods, through which you may wander without
obstruction.   The very wild-flowers and wild
fruits were different, while the search for chalce-
donies and fossils, among the flints with which the
woods were bestrewed, afforded amusement to my
solitary wanderings and pleasure in showing upon
my return what I had found.   My uncle was a
man of infinite resources.   Turning, carried to a
perfection probably never surpassed, mechanical
pursuits of other kinds, practical astronomy and
other branches of science, occupied his leisure
hours, while his conversation was always lively
and instructive.   My aunt, too, was a person of
great talent and attainments ; and they had occasionally at their table persons of extensive information, while they themselves visited at the aristocratic houses of the neighbourhood, and their
company was sought after, as of persons of talent
and varied information.

The twin villages of Isenhampstead Latimers
and Isenhampstead Cheynies (commonly called
Latimers and Cheynies) are situated within a mile

E

of one another, and are rivals in beauty of situation. They both overlook the charming valley of the little Chiltern trout-stream, the " Chess," which rises five miles off, at Chesham, and falls into the Colne, near Watford. This little valley is not much known to the world at large, though of exquisite beauty, and now, or formerly, containing the dwelling-places of some noble families. Cheynies was the old residence of the family of Cheyney, and later of the Russells, whose original seat there is still in existence (though now but a farmhouse), and whose mortal remains are still brought here from the more lordly abbey of Woburn, and here deposited in their final resting-place. Latimers (now, by the dictum of its proprietor, called Latimer) is one of the residences of the Cavendish family. It belonged, at the time I am speaking of, to old Lord George Cavendish, afterwards created Earl of Burlington. He was brother to a former Duke of Devonshire, uncle to the then duke, and grandfather of the present duke. He was a noted patron of " the turf," and had another seat at Holkar in Furness. His eldest son, the father of the present duke, was dead, and his next son, Mr. Charles Cavendish (the late Lord Chesham) was the expectant heir of Latimers.

The two " great houses " were both probably of the age of Henry VII. or Henry VIII. (Latimers perhaps a little later), and both were chiefly famous for their chimneys. Latimers had been spoiled in the Strawberry Hill style, with the exception of its beautiful stacks of tall octagonal chimney-shafts, in charming proportions and profile, but all alike. Cheynies had been so dismantled that its chief glory was also in these its upper regions, but unlike those at Latimers they were nearly all different in design, the shafts being decorated with varied and admirably executed pattern-work in brick.

Both still remain, though those at Cheynies have their caps reconstructed and spoiled. The house at Latimers has been rebuilt by Blore all but its chimneys. Latimers is charmingly situated, and I think my uncle's rectory was even better placed than the great house. The church was modern and vile, but the village which was in two parts, one on the hill and the other below, was very picturesque, with old timber houses, and a glorious old elm tree of towering height on the little green. The upper village is now destroyed, and the whole merged into the "grounds," perhaps to the increase of the beauty, but certainly to the diminution of the interest of the place. Latimers is a sort of hamlet of the little town of Chesham, five miles up the valley, where my brother John (now Rector of Tyd St. Giles' in Cambridgeshire,[6]) was at the time articled to a medical man, Mr. Rumsey. This was an increase to my happiness, as I could occasionally walk over and see him. My recollection of the whole district is as of a little paradise. The hills, valley, river, trees, flowers, fruits, fossils, &c., all seem encircled in a kind of imaginary halo. I fancy I never saw such wild flowers or ate such cherries or such trout as there. There I ter-

[6] Since preferred to the living of Wisbech and to an honorary canonry of Ely.

minated my childhood, and thence I emerged into
the wide world, in the prosaic turmoil of which
I have ever since been immersed.

Here, then, let me bid good-bye to my childish
years, strange, half-mythic days, full of quaint,
rough interest, full of faults and regrets, yet of
pleasure, of thankfulness, and of affection.   Oh!
that I had availed myself of the many privileges
of those my early days, of their religious opportunities, and of their means of intellectual improvement!   But regrets are unavailing.   Let me
rather thank God for my pious and excellent
parents and for the many blessings of my life,
and crave His forgiveness for my negligence and
shortcomings.

CHAPTER II.

WHILE I was under the direction and tuition of my uncle King, he and his father, Thomas King of London, were on the look-out for an architect to whom to article me. It was a *sine-quâ-non* that he should be a religious man, and it was necessary that his terms should be moderate. They happened to inquire of Mr. Charles Dudley, travelling agent to the Bible Society, who, after telling them that there was scarcely a religious architect in London, recommended Mr. Edmeston, better known as a poet than as an architect, and it was finally settled that I was to go to him on or about Lady Day, 1827.

About this time I may mention, by the way, that old John West's church had shown signs of falling to pieces, and my father, after the first perplexity was over, set vigorously to work to raise subscriptions for rebuilding it. He was wonderfully supported by religious friends in all parts of the country, and raised, I think, 1400*l.*, or 1500*l.*

Among the large subscribers I recollect Mr. Broadley Wilson, Mr. Joseph Wilson, and Mr. Deacon, all men of note in the city, also Mrs. Lawrence, of Studley Park, Yorkshire. It was unlucky that the rebuilding of the church should have been necessary at perhaps the darkest period, or nearly so, of church architecture (though not quite so bad as that of old Mr. West, to be sure).

My father was again his own architect, made his own working drawings, and contracted with his builder at Buckingham, Mr. Willmore. I cannot say much about either design or execution ; but these were days to be winked at, as no one knew anything whatever of the subject. It did, however, exceed the old church, in having a western tower and an eastern apse, and is more reasonable in arrangement, though not much more ecclesiastical.

I often wish we had it now to build. I recollect one day, when its foundations were being put in, our friend Mr. Thomas Bartlett coming to see the work, and my father telling him that he was about to place me with an architect; Mr. Bartlett congratulated me upon it, and added, " I have no doubt you will rise to the head of your profession," when my father at once replied, "Oh no, his abilities are not sufficient for that." I hardly knew which to believe. It would have been conceited to hold with the one, but I could not quite knock under to the other.

The new church was commenced, I fancy, when I was living at Latimers, but I saw a little of the work at intervals. It was my first initiation into practical building, though the lessons learned were not of the best, as Mr. Willmore was far from being a good builder. It was

built of the rough bluish limestone of our Gawcott Pits, with dressings of a freestone from Cos-
grove, near Stoney Stratford.

During my stay at home before leaving for
London, my brother Melville was born, just
twenty years after the birth of my oldest brother,
who was then at Cambridge.

My father took me to London and placed me
with Mr. Edmeston, with whom I lived at his
house at Homerton, his office being at Salvador
House, in Bishopsgate Street. The first remark
of my new master which I recollect was to the
effect, that the cost of gothic architecture was so
great as to be almost prohibitory ; that he had
tried it once at a dissenting chapel he had built at
Leytonstone, and that the very cementing of the
exterior had amounted to a sum which he named
with evident dismay.

I had no idea beforehand of the line of practice
followed by my future initiator into the mysteries
of my profession ; I went to him with a mythic
veneration for his supposed skill and for his
imaginary works, though without an idea of what
they might be. The morning after I was deposited at his house, he invited me to walk out
and see some of his works—when—oh, horrors !
the bubble burst, and the fond dream of my
youthful imagination was realized in the form
of a few second-rate brick houses, with cemented
porticoes of two ungainly columns each ! I shall
never forget the sudden letting down of my aspirations. A somewhat romantic youth, assigned
to follow the noble art of architecture for the love
he had formed for it from the ancient churches

of his neighbourhood, condemned to indulge his taste by building houses at Hackney in the debased style of 1827! I am not sure, however, that I was any very serious loser from this. Mr. Edmeston's practice was a mere blank-sheet as to matters of taste, and left me quite open to indulge in private my old preferences, or to choose in future what course I pleased.

I learned, too, in his office a great deal which I might have missed in a better one. I learned all the common routine of building, specifying, &c., so far as was practised by him, and I had a good deal of time for reading and drawing on my own account. Still, however, I confess it had a lowering and deadening effect, and it failed to inspire me with that high artistic sentiment which ought to be impressed upon the mind of every young architect.

Mr. and Mrs. Edmeston were very kindly persons, and as they had a good library, which was my evening sitting-room, I had excellent opportunities of that kind for self-improvement, and I think I took very fair advantage of them. I read much and drew much, made myself acquainted with classic architecture from books, such as Stewart's " Athens," the works of the Dilettante society, Vitruvius, &c., and with gothic, so far as the scanty means went. I thoroughly taught myself perspective in one fortnight, from Joshua Kirby, so much so that I have never had to look at a book on it again ; indeed, I used to set myself the most difficult problems, and invent new ways of solving them. I had liberal holidays at midsummer and christmas, when I went home, to my intense delight. In my summer holidays, I devoted most of my time to measuring and sketching at Hillesden, Maid's Morton, &c., and on my return I devoted my evenings for a long time to making drawings of what I had measured, most elaborately tinting them in indian ink, which was sponged nearly out twice over, according to the custom of the day. I remember indulging my rural yearnings, by designing a farm-yard and its buildings in true rustic style. I think it was on this occasion that Mr. Edmeston wrote seriously to my father, warning him that I was employing my leisure hours on matters which could never by any possibility be of any practical use to me.

I had at first only one fellow-pupil, one Enoch Hodgkinson Springbett. He was a very good sort of fellow, but without an aspiration beyond the class of practice he had been trained to ; I used to try to get him to work in his evenings without avail. His great pride was in his cards, on which he styled himself " Architect and Surveyor," and in mentioning certain gentlemen as his " clients." He was, however, well skilled in reducing the plans and elevations of Mr. Edmeston's houses to a very small scale, and drawing them with sparkling neatness in the margin of the sheet of drawing-paper on which the specification was written out in diamond text for the builder to sign as his contract. Thus I went on without a companion of my own taste, indeed for a long time without knowing a single student of architecture but Mr. Springbett. It is right, however, to mention that he used occasionally to take lessons at the drawing-school of Mr. Grayson, nor would it be right to allow it to be supposed that Mr. Edmeston's taste in the abstract was proportioned to the nature of his practice. He really took much pleasure in, and appreciated fine works, whether ancient or modern, and being a man of literary tastes, his feelings and views were by no means in unison with his practice. He was, in point of fact, a most agreeable companion, and a man of liberal and refined mind, thoroughly well-informed and well-read, in fact a most superior man in everything but his own direct professional work, viewed in its artistic aspect. He had, too, a strong appreciation of artistic drawing, and recommended me to take lessons of Mr. Maddox, an architectural drawing-master of great talent. I delayed this very long, fearing to burden my father unduly. I greatly regret this; I certainly ought to have followed up this extra tuition during the whole period of my pupilage. As it was, I did so only for a little more than the last year of the four of my articles.

Mr. Maddox was certainly a man of real ability, with a wonderful power of drawing, and a high appreciation of art. He was, however, far from being an estimable man in other ways. He was an infidel, and his conversation on such subjects was truly appalling. My lessons with him were much disturbed by my catching the smallpox, and by a very mournful occurrence of another kind, which led to a rather long absence ; but I gained great advantage from his instruction, and only wish I had had more of it. Among my fellow-pupils was Edwin Nash, who became my staunch friend. Morton Peto, who had just left Decimus Burton, and Thomas Henry Wyatt occasionally attended.

The scanty holidays I obtained, in addition to the prolonged ones already mentioned, I used to devote to walking out to see old buildings within reach of London, and in my evenings in the summer, I searched out objects of architectural interest in London itself, so that what with books and with sketching, I obtained a very fair knowledge of gothic architecture, by the time I was twenty years old, though I had hardly a thought of ever making use of it. Amongst the longer tours which helped me in my studies, I may name a pedestrian journey home, by way of St. Albans, a visit to my eldest brother at Cambridge, whence we walked over to Ely, and a journey to Northampton and Geddington, to sketch the crosses. I had twice visited Waltham cross, so that I thoroughly knew, and had sketched in detail all of the three Eleanor crosses by the time I was nineteen years old.

I well recollect the ardour with which I looked forward to seeing St. Albans. I wrote to my brother John at Chesham to ask him to go with me, or meet me there, and he came to London to accompany me. I had not, however, allowed myself time to sketch. We went on to Dunstable, and I visited Leighton Buzzard, and Stewkley, on my way home.

When I was in my articles old London Bridge was standing, though the present one was in course of erection. St. Saviour's, Southwark, was then in a certain sense complete. The choir was about that time, or just before, restored by old George Gwilt, while the nave, transepts and Lady chapel were untouched, though in a strange state externally, being faced with brick. Their interiors were, however, nearly perfect, but encumbered like other old churches with pews and galleries. The nave was a magnificent thing. There was a vast early-english double doorway, of great height and depth on the south side, and at the west was the fine early perpendicular doorway, which is given by the elder Pugin in his "Specimens," and the destruction of which is celebrated by his son in the "Contrasts." The Lady-chapel was almost a ruin, with unglazed windows boarded up : to the east of it projected a seventeenth-century chapel, containing the tomb of Bishop Andrewes. To the north of the church was a large vacant space, where the cloisters, &c., had stood, on the eastern side of which there still remained some remnants of the monastic buildings. There was also a late archway, to the north of the west front, leading into the open vacant ground. There was a fine late norman doorway on the north of the nave formerly leading into the cloisters.

The fate of this noble church is melancholy but instructive. Old George Gwilt had restored the choir, and, with his son, had devoted to the work the most anxious and praiseworthy study. The style being by no means then understood, he had taken the utmost pains in studying it wherever he had the opportunity, and to whatever criticisms his work may be open, the result was on the whole highly to his credit.

This anxious painstaking did not, however, suit

the parishoners, and when the transept was to be proceeded with, they placed it in the hands of another architect, Mr. Wallace, who knew little or nothing of gothic architecture, and made but a poor affair of it. About this time, a parish squabble arose on the subject of the Lady chapel, and happily Gwilt offered, if funds could be raised, to give his services gratuitously, and we see the happy result. A few years later Mr. Wallace was deputed to report on the state of the roof of the nave, and with that perverse thoughtlessness which even in our own day characterizes such reports, he condemned it at once as unsafe, the ends of the beams being decayed.

Now about the same period a well-known architect had done the same at St. Albans, and had his report been followed out to its natural consequences we might have to deplore that glorious nave as a thing of the past; but another architect, Mr. Cottingham (let us give him all praise for the act), offered to guarantee the safety of the roof, and to give his services gratuitously to save it, which he effected by inserting cast-iron shoes to the decayed beam ends. At St. Saviour's no such happy interposition took place, the condemned roof was taken down in haste before arrangements were made for a new one. Parish squabbles, spreading over several years, caused the nave to remain a ruin, exposed to the ravages of the elements, till at length another surveyor was found to condemn it *in toto*, and to erect in its stead the contemptible structure now existing. Thus did London lose for ever one of the most valued of her ancient edifices.

Hard by St. Saviour's were, and I fancy are now, the ruins of the Hall of the Bishop of Winchester's palace, with its beautiful round window. The latter still exists, though immured in a warehouse wall.

Crosby Hall, which was close by our office, was then a packer's warehouse, and was divided into three stories, an arrangement not so conducive to the appreciation of its beauty, as to the close inspection of its roof.

Austin Friars Church was much as it is at present (or rather was until the late fire), barring the external cementing, which was not yet done.

Winchester House, close to Austin Friars, was also then standing, an Elizabethan mansion erected by the Lord Winchester, to whom most of the property of this religious house had been granted.

St. Bartholomew's, in Smithfield, possessed somewhat more of its accompaniments than it now retains ; one side of the cloister existing, and a good deal of the south transept, though in ruins. A great fire occurred there in 1830, by which some parts were lost; but I recollect that it brought to light the lower part of the walls of the Chapter-house, with fine early arcaded stalls.

The ancient bridge over the Lea at Bow, may also be mentioned amongst the remnants of antiquity I then knew, but which have since perished. Waltham Cross was then unrestored, or rather unspoiled.

The monotony of my life was from time to time

relieved by short visits from my eldest brother, on his journeys to and from Cambridge. He was a most amusing companion, and his little visits filled me with delight. My father, too, occasionally came to town, as did others of my family. I had at first no friend that I cared for but Robert Rumsey, the son of the medical man at Chesham, with whom my brother John was placed; he had been a pupil of my father's, and was articled to Messrs. Longman, the publishers. We were very great friends. He subsequently gave up the business for which he had been intended, and became a stipendiary magistrate in the West Indies, where, I fancy, he still continues.

Later, however, a great change came to me as to companionship, through my brother John coming to London to attend the hospitals. This was a very great relief and pleasure, and we almost lived together, always meeting to dine together at an eating-house in Bucklersbury.

Mr. Edmeston was a dissenter at that time, though I think he subsequently joined the church; and I alternately attended service at the episcopal chapel at Homerton, known as "Ram's chapel," and at the "Jews' chapel," Bethnal Green, of which my old friend and kind patron, Mr. King (my uncle's father), was perpetual warden. On those alternate Sundays I dined and spent the day at Mr. King's house in London Fields, Hackney, and I shall never be sufficiently grateful for the kindness both of Mr. and Mrs. King, which was continued by the latter after her husband's death.

The incumbent of the "Jews' chapel," was Mr.

Hawtrey, a very gentlemanly person, and the curate was a noble old gentleman of the name of Fancourt.   There was a tendency amongst the congregation to those views known at the time as " New Lights," and which subsequently culminated in Irvingism.   I was one day startled at hearing thanksgivings offered up in the name of Miss Fancourt, the curate's daughter, for a miraculous recovery from a long illness.   The miracle had been performed through the agency of the Rev. Pierrepoint Grieves, an Oxfordshire clergyman.   It created much excitement at the time, and was unquestionably a very marvellous circumstance, though doubtless capable of being explained by natural causes.   Mr. (afterwards Bishop) Alexander was a frequent preacher there, and Dr. Wolf was worshipped as a sort of demi-god, though not without a full appreciation of his eccentricity.

My last year was ushered in by a great pleasure, followed up by the greatest affliction I had ever experienced.   My next brother, Nathaniel Gilbert, three years my junior, had, since I left home, grown up into a very charming and noble-minded youth, of excellent ability, most amiable and genial disposition, and with a fine vein of semi-humourous, semi-romantic sentiment, which gave interest and expression to all he said. Early in 1830 he was articled to Messrs. Bridges and Mason, of Red Lion Square, who most generously offered to forego their premium, out of consideration to my father.   He took well to his new occupation, and promised great success.   My delight at having him in London was more than I can express, for I loved him as my own soul.

My very office-work was gilded by the prospect of meeting him in the evening, which was managed by mutual arrangement. One evening after he had been in town a month, he told me he had a bad headache. I did not think much of that, as he had been rather subject to them; but the next evening he failed to meet me, and on calling where he lived (the house of my excellent friend, Mrs. Boyes, then of Charterhouse Square), I found that he was ill.

The illness increased day by day, and my poor mother was hurried up to attend him. It was soon evident that it was a case of brain-fever. And one evening, when I had hurried from the office to see how he was, I was bluntly told by the servant boy, that he was dead! I shall never forget the stunning effect of the announcement; my legs gave way beneath me, while incoherent sounds were involuntarily uttered, and I was with difficulty helped upstairs by my two brothers, Tom and John, who had hastened down to break the mournful news to me. It was my first introduction to sorrow, and deep, deep it was. My health suffered much from it for some time.

My poor brother Nat was but sixteen years old, but a fine well-developed fellow, of a noble countenance, and a fine bold disposition. I recollect some time earlier that he, and a pupil of my father's of the same standing, apprehended and secured a man who had been committing a robbery. And about the same time, when the inhabitants of Otmoor in Oxfordshire rose against the carrying

F

out of an enclosure act, and the Bucks yeomanry were called out, he jumped on to one of the cannons as they passed through our village, and rode fourteen miles on it to see the fight.

He lies buried in the churchyard of St. Botolph's, Aldersgate, where in 1841 I erected a monument to his memory, with an inscription which my father had given me some years earlier.

I will, however, turn to more cheerful topics.

My father's first cousin, the daughter of his eldest uncle, William, had married Mr. Oldrid of Boston, and when I was, as I suppose, about eleven, had brought her son, John Henry,[1] to Gawcott as a pupil. She had three daughters, the eldest of whom, Fanny, had once in these early days accompanied her to Gawcott, when it was supposed that my eldest brother was attracted by her. Some years later she and her two sisters went to school at Chesham, and on two occasions they spent their Christmas holidays at Gawcott, and an infinitely merry time it was. It was during these visits that my feelings towards my present dear wife,[2] the youngest of these cousins, grew up. My brother Nat was then at home, and the merriness of our party was perfect. I was not, however, aware that I was wounded, till the pain of parting began to be felt. But more of this anon.

I must of necessity wind up the account of my pupilage with the narration of two circumstances. One was that during the latter period of it,

---

[1] Sometime lecturer at St. Botolph's, Boston, and since then Vicar of Alford.—ED.

[2] She departed this life February 24th, 1872.—ED.

Mr. Edmeston very kindly appointed me and Springbett, joint clerks of the works to a small building, a proprietary school. We attended on alternate days, and to my no small advantage, though perhaps not to that of the building. The other circumstance was one which had a very strong influence on my subsequent life, though whether more for good or ill it is not easy to say. Certain, however, it is, that it was attended with many advantages, but also with much vexation of spirit.

The circumstance was this.

A builder named Moffatt, having taken a contract under Mr. Edmeston, induced him to receive his son, then about sixteen, as a pupil. Young Moffatt was a remarkably intelligent, though uneducated boy, a native of Cornwall. I remember before I saw him, Mr. Edmeston describing him to me with great satisfaction on the score of his bright intelligent appearance. It devolved upon me to help him through our office text-book, " Peter Nicholson's," and I found him ready in the extreme. He had been brought up at the bench, which was then always the case with a young builder, and was in theory held to be a good thing for an architect. He could do anything and everything which wood and tools could produce, from a four-panel door to the finest piece of cabinet work, and knew all the practical lore of the timber merchant, the builder, and the mechanic, a class of knowledge which I perhaps almost unduly appreciated, and which with the brightness of his uncultivated parts won for him in my mind a sort of regretful respect.

He was subject to lameness, the result of a fever, and soon becoming unable to go to town, and Mr. Edmeston having established a branch office at Hackney, near where Moffatt lived, it was arranged that he should be placed there, and I used to go in the mornings to instruct him in architectural drawing, Euclid, practical Geometry, and I think perspective, in all of which he got on remarkably well, so long as I continued at Mr. Edmeston's. I also persuaded him subsequently to take lessons of Mr. Maddox.

After I left, he continued at Mr. Edmeston's city office for some time, till getting sick of having next to nothing to do, he rebelled, and refused further attendance ; but I shall have plenty to say of his subsequent progress before I have done.

On leaving Mr. Edmeston's about Lady Day 1831, I went for a month to visit my uncle and aunt King at Latimers, where I again saw my merry cousin, Carry Oldrid. My uncle met with a serious accident while I was there, by the breaking of a ladder, by which we were getting to the roof of the house, the ladder breaking between his feet and my hands, so that he fell to the ground while I escaped. Happily he was not very seriously hurt, though he long felt the effects of it. This threw me all the more into the society of my favourite cousin, and fanned the spark already kindled.

I may note here as an archæological memorandum, that during this visit I walked over to King's Langley, where I found a farmer, on whose ground was the site of the ancient monastic establishment, digging up the foundations of the church ;

many of the bases were exposed to view, exhibiting the plan of a cross church of the first order.   I
compared it at the time to Westminster Abbey.
I recollect that the bases were of purbeck marble,
and belonged to columns surrounded by eight
detached shafts, with larger piers at the crossings.

The farmer was taking a plan of it before the
removal of the bases.   I mention this because it
is not generally known.   I fear the plan can
hardly now be extant.

This visit to Latimers was one of peculiar
delight.   The April of 1831 was as bright and
genial as the May was severe, and both in one
respect symbolized my own feelings.   The
Latimers country was charming that April.   The
tender green of the beechwoods, luxuriant before
its wonted time, and relieved at all points by the
blossom of the wild cherry ; the snowy splendour
of the cherry orchards ; the hedgerows and woods
gemmed with wild flowers, and all nature rejoicing
in the all too early spring, offered enjoyments almost
intoxicating to one who had not seen the country
at this season for four years, and now saw it in an
unusually exquisite spot, and at an antedated
season ; but this was accompanied by something
much more fascinating, the society of my cousin,
who was the constant companion of my walks.

On my proceeding at the end of this enchanted
sojourn, to Gawcott, oh how plain and homely
everything looked!   My dear sister, Euphemia, was
quite hurt at my admiring nothing.   The very
primroses were pale and colourless compared with
those at Latimers.   The plain homely Oxford
clay district, with its lopped hedgerow timber and

its oakwoods, looked sadly prosaic after the beauties
of the Chiltern land.　My sister suspected a deeper
cause, and privately suggested it to my mother,
who, with the decision and commanding force which
were her characteristics, at once brought me to
book, and absolutely prohibited any further indulgence of such sentiments, partly on account of my,
for long years to come, dependent position.

I really had not indulged specific and acknowledged intentions, though certainly harbouring
warm sentiments, but this lecture determined me
to resist them for the present at least, and my
state of mind was aptly symbolized by the deep
snow and sharp frost, by which May was ushered
in, which killed and blackened the precocious
growths of the too early spring to a degree which
I have never witnessed since, and which was said
by the knowing ones, but mistakenly, to be beyond
the powers of summer to restore.

I spent a couple of months at home sketching,
making sundry drawings, &c., and then paid a visit
to my eldest brother, who was settled at Goring
on the Thames, a charming spot, where I also
sketched a little among the old churches, &c., and
indulged a few thoughts of my cousin Carry, who
had recently been there.　Shortly afterwards I set
out on the longest journey I had yet taken, a visit
to my uncle at Hull.

On this journey I sketched a good deal, and
saw much which delighted me.　I went to Peterborough, Stamford, Grantham, Newark, Lincoln,
Howden, Selby, York, Bridlington, Beverly,
Boston, Tattershall, &c.　I also had a pleasant
coasting trip to Scarborough and Flamborough

Head. My visit to Hull, too, was a very merry one, and I formed a more intimate friendship with my cousin John,[3] which has lasted ever since. On my return I saw my cousin Carry again, but followed the prudential counsels of my mother, as closely as I could.

This journey was a very great advantage to me; it opened out and extended greatly my knowledge of gothic architecture, and tended to reduce my shy, taciturn, and somewhat gauche manner, a point in which I was by nature at a great disadvantage.

I now entered upon the second stage of my professional life. Returning to London, I obtained many introductions to architects and others, several of whom gave me good advice, varying with their particular practice or antecedents. I think it was Mr. Waller, a well-known surveyor, who advised me to put myself with a builder; and, obtaining an introduction to Mr. (now Sir Samuel Morton) Peto, I placed myself with him and Mr. Grissell, his partner, giving such services as I could offer, in return for having the run of their workshops, and of their London works.

It is impossible for me to exaggerate the advantages of this arrangement in giving me an insight into every description of practical work; and that on a scale and of kinds greatly differing from what I had been accustomed to. I was specially stationed at the Hungerford Market, then in progress of erection under Mr. Fowler, to

[3] Afterwards Vicar of St. Mary's, Hull. He died in 1865. —ED.

whose very talented and excellent Clerk of the Works (the late Mr. Colling) I was under very great obligations for kind and continued aid in my pursuit of practical information. The work was constructed on principles then new. Iron girders, Yorkshire landings, roofs and platforms of tiles in cement, and columns of granite being its leading elements.

I got much information, too, in the joiner's shop, from the foreman, from the clerks in the office, and especially from assisting in measuring up work, usually with the foreman. I had at one time to assist two surveyors of eminence, Mr. Roper and Mr. Higgins, in measuring up all the work in a row of houses in which Mr. Peto and Mr. Grissell lived, in furtherance of some arrangement under the will of the late Mr. Peto, and a most valuable lesson it was.

I ought, too, to mention the advantage of constant reference to Mr. Fowler's working drawings, some of the best and most perspicuous I have ever seen, and of selecting from Messrs. G. and P.'s office copies of specifications by different architects, which I was kindly allowed to take to my lodgings, and make copious extracts from.

I may mention that my brother John and I lodged together during a part of this time in Warwick Court, Holborn, where I continued to live long after he had left town, and where my stay was from time to time enlivened by visits from my cousin John from Hull, and sometimes from my father and my uncle John, and now and then by my eldest brother taking for some weeks together the duty of his rector, who held a plurality, being incumbent of one of Barry's Islington churches.

My stay with Grissell and Peto, though I seem to have made much of it, was not of long continuance. It became necessary that I should be doing something for my living ; and Mr. Peto did not quite relish my prying so closely as I was wont, into the foundations of the prices of work and materials, though both he and Mr. Grissell were most kind towards me. I accordingly some time in 1832 entered the office of my very excellent friend, Mr. Henry Roberts, who had recently obtained by competition the appointment of architect to the new Fishmongers' Hall, at the foot of new London Bridge.

Mr. Roberts had, subsequently to his original period of pupilage, been for a considerable time in the office of Sir Robert Smirke, whose tastes, habits, modes of construction, and method of making working drawings, he had thoroughly imbibed. He had subsequently made the lengthened continental tour customary in those days, and had not, I think, very long been in practice since his return. He was in independent circumstances, and was a gentlemanly, religious, precise, and quiet man. I was the only clerk in the office at the time, though he subsequently took a pupil, so that I had the advantage of making all the working drawings of this considerable public building, from the foundation to the finish ; and of helping in measuring up the extras and omissions, as well as of constantly seeing the work during its progress.

This engagement lasted two years, and though

most beneficial to me, it seems almost a blank in my memory, from its even and uneventful character. I recollect that during that time I once ventured into a public competition for the grammar school at Birmingham. I also got a picture one year (I don't recollect trying again) into the exhibition, and attended a course of Sir John Soane's lectures, at the Royal Academy. I often contemplated becoming a student there, and chalked out Gothic designs, but I never followed it up. I do not think I did much in sketching at this time, Smirkism and practical work having for a time chilled my own tastes ; nor had I any advantages of artistic study. It was a dull, blank period, and I think I was to blame for it.

I have little recollection of my visits home during this time, though in the course of it I lost my aunt Gilbert. I remember, however, one visit. My father being presented by the Bishop of Lincoln (Kaye) to the living of Wappenham, Northamptonshire, eleven miles north of Gawcott, I went with him to reconnoitre, and, having to build a new house there, I supplied him with a very ugly design, founded on one of Mr. Roberts' plans, which his old builder, Mr. Willmore, took care to spoil and slight, as much as he thought necessary for his own purposes. About this time, also, I was requested by my friend, Henry Rumsey, who had succeeded to his father's practice at Chesham, to plan him a house there. My taste seemed under a cold spell, and the design, though convenient enough, was wholly devoid of any attempt at architectural character. He wanted to employ several local tradesmen and I named my old fellow-pupil Moffatt as clerk of the works, who was also to get a good deal of the joiner's work done in London under his father. Thus was recommenced an acquaintance productive of such marked influence on my future career. Moffatt performed his duties most efficiently and cleverly, but with so little tact as to make an enemy of his employer for the very acts by which he was best promoting his interests, while I lost in my friend's esteem by defending my representative.

In the spring of 1834, Mr. Roberts kindly gave me the appointment of clerk of the works to a small work at Camberwell, which I superintended throughout its erection, which was very rapid, and was completed in the autumn of the same year. My conscience tells me that this arrangement was much more beneficial to myself than to the building.

I now made up my mind to attempt to get into practice, but previous to doing so, I took three months' holiday, which, foreign travel being out of the question, I spent partly at Wappenham, and on visits to my uncle King and my eldest brother, and partly in a sketching tour, on which I was accompanied by my friend Edwin Nash. I sketched a good deal during this interval, and did something towards recovering my old but dormant tastes. My stay at my father's new home was very delightful to me, but how much more precious had I known that it was my last visit to him. His health had evidently much failed him of late, and I heard whispers of deadly maladies, but they seemed as idle tales to my sanguine mind.

Alas! how soon they proved far otherwise.

While we were on this tour we heard the news of the destruction of the Houses of Parliament.

I remember with great interest the many evenings spent in hearing the debates within the walls of old St. Stephen's, where I was familiar with the eloquence of Peel, Stanley (afterwards Lord Derby), O'Connell, Lord John Russell, and others, with the early efforts of the then youthful and blooming Gladstone, and the quaint absurdities of old Cobbett.

The old St. Stephen's resembled a rather sumptuous methodist chapel, all its real architecture being concealed by wainscotting and round-topped windows, denying every hint of the real ones. When I saw it on my return to London, how changed was its aspect! It seemed as if the subject of an enchanter's spell, and converted suddenly from a mean conventicle into a Gothic ruin of unrivalled beauty, glowing with the scorched but quite intelligible remnants of its gorgeous decorative colouring. The destruction of this precious architectural relic is the single blot upon the fair shield of Sir Charles Barry.

About this time the new Poor-law Act had come into operation, and my friend Kempthorne, just returned home from his continental tour, had, through the interest of the Chief Commissioner, who was a friend of his father's, been employed to prepare normal designs for the proposed Union workhouses.

Being inexperienced, he, in an unhappy moment, called in the aid of his old master, Mr. Voysey, who, though a clever and ingenious practical man, had not one spark of taste, and took a very exaggerated view of the necessity for economy. The assistant commissioners were instructed to press upon the newly-formed boards of guardians the desirableness of employing Mr. Kempthorne, the commissioners' architect; and thus poor Kempthorne was placed under the real disadvantage (though seeming advantage) of having a vast practice thrust upon him before his experience had fitted him to conduct it, while he embarked with a set of ready-made designs of the meanest possible character, and very defective in other particulars.

While visiting my brother at Goring about Christmas, 1834, I received a letter from Kempthorne, telling me that a set of chambers next to his own, in Carlton Chambers, Regent Street, was vacant, and that if I liked to take them, he could find employment for my leisure time, in assisting him with his Union Workhouses. I closed with this and was soon ensconced in my new chambers and busied on work even more mean than that of my pupilage. This had not, however, continued more than a few weeks, when one morning Kempthorne entered my room with an expression on his countenance which soon showed me that he was the bearer of heavy tidings. He soon broke to me, kindly and gently, for he was a good, kind fellow, the sad intelligence of the sudden death of my father.

Here was a stunning blow, of which I had experienced no parallel! I will not go into our family grief, my poor widowed mother's prostration, nor the sudden break-up of our happy home. After the first flood of grief was passed, and my father's honoured remains were deposited alongside of those of old John West, in the church at Gawcott, action and decision became the necessities of our position.   My two eldest brothers were fairly on their own hands, and my eldest sister was married to my cousin, the Rev. J. H. Oldrid, who had succeeded my father at Gawcott.   I was the eldest of six still unsettled in life, and I must adopt my course with promptitude, or my chances in life were gone.

The two steps I took were, first to write a kind of circular to every influential friend of my father's I could think of, informing them that I had commenced practice, and begging their patronage, and secondly, to quit Kempthorne, and to use my interest to obtain the appointment of architect to the Union Workhouses in the district where my father had been known.   Both steps were happily attended with success.   Several friends placed small works in my hands, and I succeeded by a strenuous canvass of every guardian in obtaining appointments to four unions in our immediate district.

This was a success for which I have to thank a gracious Providence, and without which I really do not know what course I could have taken.   Now, however, I found myself in a few months in what was to me good practice, though for a time unproductive, and involving considerable outlay, in which I was helped by my mother out of her scanty means, and—it would be contemptible if I allowed pride to lead me to ignore it—by my share in a fund, which was, wholly unasked, subscribed as a testimonial to, and a help to the descendants of, the Commentator, my grandfather.

If the three previous years come back to my memory as a mere blank, those which succeeded seem an era of turmoil, of violent activity and exertion. For weeks I almost lived on horseback, canvassing newly formed unions. Then alternated periods of close, hard work in my little office at Carlton Chambers, with coach journeys, chiefly by night, followed by meetings of guardians, searching out of materials, and hurrying from union to union, often riding across unknown bits of country after dark, sudden sweet peeps in at my poor mother's new home, (a nice old house at Wappenham, where my brother had, by Bishop Kaye's kindness, succeeded my father at the rectory,) with flying visits to Gawcott and elsewhere, as occasion served.

I employed one clerk, and had invited Moffatt to come to help me in preparing my early working drawings, which he did with the utmost diligence and efficiency, and on the works of one union commencing, and those of others within reach being about to commence, I recommended him as resident superintendent of a little circuit of buildings within a few miles of one another. He accordingly took up his residence at one of those places whence he was to ride the round of the others.

By some strange coincidence of circumstances an influential magistrate in Wiltshire had become acquainted with, and taken a fancy to Moffatt, and had invited him down there, promising to use his influence in getting him appointed architect to the Amesbury Union House. He went accordingly and succeeded, and we made the plans and working drawings at my office.

An anomalous state of things was thus set up. I was architect to four union workhouses in one district, to which Moffatt was clerk of the works, while he was architect to one in a distant part of the country, the drawings for which were made at my office. This led him to come and make a formal proposal to me. I agreed to this proposal, and it became the foundation of our future partnership. I will here stop these hard, dull incidents, and speak of a circumstance of a very different and more interesting character.

Early in the period which I have been describing, during one of my visits to Wappenham, my mother had told me that my cousin Carry Oldrid had just come on a visit to Gawcott, and that if my old feelings continued towards her, she did not desire me to be influenced by what, three or four years previously, she had said. I met my cousin at Buckingham, and, thus set free, my old sentiments came back upon me like a flood. I spent a day or two at Gawcott in her society, and I soon found myself over head and ears in love. In a few months we were engaged, though without any near prospect of marriage. This afforded a softening and beneficial relief to the too hard, unsentimental pursuits which at this time almost overwhelmed me, and to which I must now return.

The effect of Moffatt's new arrangement was magical. He followed up union-hunting into

Devonshire and Cornwall with almost uniform success, and my poor little quartette of works round my old home soon became as nothing, when compared with the engagements which flowed in upon us as partners. Moffatt's own exertions were almost superhuman, and when I recollect that no railways came to his help, I feel perfectly amazed to think of what he effected.

When I first set about this poor-law work, I considered the look of the buildings as wholly out of the question, and felt myself bound in a great degree to the arrangements laid down by the published plans of the commissioners, though I attempted better construction than they prescribed. I recollect a competitor, Mr. Plowman of Oxford, who was both a builder and an architect, saying of one of my earliest specifications, that it was one of the best he had ever seen, but impossible to be carried out in a workhouse on account of the cost. This I found to be true, for Kempthorne's plans and specifications, in which everything had been cut down to the very quick, had given the scale of estimate which the commissioners led the guardians to expect, so that for a long time it was unsafe to venture beyond it. Architecture and good finish, or even any great improvements in arrangement, were at the time hopeless, and one was driven to the wretched necessity of viewing one's profession, as represented by one's chief works, merely as a means of getting a living, excepting that when competitions became frequent, there was an excitement and speculation about them, which added a certain kind of interest to otherwise most uninteresting work. Competition

G

soon, however, produced other effects. Variety
became necessary, or where was the ground-work
for competition ?   Thus improved arrangements
began to be aimed at.   Perspective views were
naturally regarded as attractive elements in a
competition, and to give them any interest there
must be something to show, so that external
appearance began timidly to be thought of, and
estimates stealthily to creep upwards, and many
a row and uproar did this produce, to the joy
of the disappointed competitors.

The competitions for union workhouses were
conducted on principles quite peculiar to themselves. They were open in every sense, and
each of the competitors was at liberty to take any
step he thought good. They used first to go
down and call on the clerk, the chairman, and any
of the guardians who were supposed to have any
ideas of their own, and after the designs were sent
in, no harm was thought of repeating those calls
as often as the competitor pleased, and advocating
the merits, each man of his own arrangement. On
the day on which the designs were to be examined
the competitors were usually waiting in the ante-
room, and were called in one by one to give personal explanations, and the decision was often
announced then and there to the assembled candidates. Moffatt was most successful in this kind
of fighting, having an instinctive perception of
which men to aim at pleasing, and of how to meet
their views and to address himself successfully to
their particular temperaments. The pains he took
in improving the arrangements were enormous,
communicating constantly with the most experi-

enced governors of workhouses, and gathering ideas wherever he went. He was always on the move. We went every week to Peele's coffee-house to see the country papers, and to find advertisements of pending competitions. Moffatt then ran down to the place to get up information. On his return, we set to work, with violence, to make the design, and to prepare the competition drawings, often working all night as well as all day. He would then start off by the mail, travel all night, meet the board of guardians, and perhaps win the competition, and return during the next night to set to work on another design. I have known him travel four nights running, and to work hard throughout the intervening days, a habit facilitated by his power of sleeping whenever he chose. He used to say that he snored so loud on the box of the mail as to keep the inside passengers awake. He was the best arranger of a plan, the hardest worker, and the best hand at advocating the merits of what he had to propose, I ever met with; and I think that he thoroughly deserved his success, though it naturally won him a host of enemies and traducers.

I meanwhile carried on my own private poor-law practice through Northamptonshire and Lincolnshire, which was viewed by us as my privileged ground. I built, I think, at that time two union-houses in Bucks, five in Northamptonshire, and four in Lincolnshire, in which I stood alone. I also had a certain amount of practice of other kinds. I lived, like Moffatt, in a constant turmoil, though less so than he. The way in which we used to rush to the Post Office, or to the Angel at

Islington, at the last moment, to send off designs and working drawings, or to set off for our nocturnal journeys, was most exciting, and one wonders, in these self-indulgent days, how we could stand the travelling all night outside coaches in the depth of winter, and in all weathers. The life we led was certainly as arduous and exciting as anything one can fancy in work, which in its own nature was so dull as our business in the abstract was, but one's mind seems to shape itself to its day, and I believe I really enjoyed the labour and turmoil in which I spent my time.

These were the last days of the integrity of the old coaching system, and splendid was its dying perfection! It was a merry thing to leave the Post Office yard on the box-seat of a mail, and drive out amidst the mob of porters, passengers, and gazers. As far as Barnet on the north road seven mails ran together with their choicest trotting teams passing and repassing one another, the horns blowing merrily, every one in a good humour, and proud of what they were doing. Then the hasty cup of coffee at midnight, and the hurried breakfast had joys about them which I seem even now to feel again. One coach I travelled by—" the Manchester Telegraph "—cleared eleven miles an hour all the way down, stoppings included. It was a splendid perfection of machinery, but its fate was sealed, the great lines of railway being in rapid progress. Our shorter journeyings we did by gig and on horseback, though they often extended through the length and breadth of a county.

I had in the midst of all this confusion made

myself decently acquainted with geology, which, with my old church-hunting tendencies, added greatly to the interest of my journeys. I was in fact an enthusiast on this subject; and though I had not time to follow it scientifically, I obtained a very good practical knowledge of the stratification and geological productions of the greater part of the country. My sketching of gothic architecture was at the time but scanty; having to fight for bare existence, I directed my efforts mainly to the matter before me.

In 1838 (June 4th) I was married to my dear cousin Caroline. We took apartments until we could find a house, and about the end of the year we settled down at No. 20 (now 31), Spring Gardens, where my two eldest sons were born in 1839 and 1841. From this date my practice began to take a more legitimate and less abnormal line; and though I soon afterwards became actual partner with Mr. Moffatt, this partnership was not of permanent duration.

In 1838, shortly after my marriage, I competed for a church with success. This was at Lincoln, and I cannot say anything in its favour, excepting that it was better than many then erected. Church architecture was then perhaps at its lowest level. The era of the " million " churches of the commissioners had long past, and Barry's four churches at Islington, which were really respectable and well intentioned, and liberal in their cost, had been succeeded by an abject fry, the products of the " Cheap Church " mania, in which all decency of architectural finish and construction was ground down to the very dust, to meet an idolized tariff of so many shillings a sitting.[4]   My first church (except one poor barn designed for my uncle King) dates from the same year with the foundation of the Cambridge Camden Society, to whom the honour of our recovery from the odious bathos is mainly due.   I only wish I had known its founders at the time.   As it was, no idea of ecclesiastical arrangement, or ritual propriety, had then even crossed my mind.

Unfortunately everything I did at that time fell into the wholesale form ; and before I had time to discover the defects of my first design, its general form and its radical errors were repeated in no less than six other churches,[5] and which followed in such rapid succession as to leave no time for improvement, all being planned, I fancy, in 1839, or early in the succeeding year.

The designs for these churches were by no means similar, but they all agreed in two points— the use of a transept of the minor kind,[6] which happened to be suggested to me by those at Pinner and Harrow, and the · absence of any regular and proper chancel, my grave idea being that this feature was obsolete.   They all agreed

---

[4] This tariff system is not yet closed.   A district of so many thousand souls is still held to require a church of so many hundred " sittings " at the cost of so much a-piece.   The proportion—grotesque as it sounds—of " sittings " to souls has to be adjusted, and the area of each laid down in square feet and inches.—Ed.

[5] At Birmingham, Lincoln, Shaftesbury, Hanwell, Turnham Bridlington Quay, and Norbiton.

[6] Curiously enough, an old English tradition, derived from Saxon times, and prevalent in England and Ireland all through the middle ages.—Ed.

too in the meagreness of their construction, in the contemptible character of their fittings, in most of them being begalleried to the very eyes, and in the use of plaster for internal mouldings, even for the pillars.

This latter meanness had been forced upon me, for at first I aimed at avoiding it, but the cheap-church rage overcame me, and as I had not then awaked to the viciousness of shams, I was uncon-cious of the abyss into which I had fallen. These days of abject degradation only lasted for about two years or little more, but, alas! what a mass of horrors was perpetrated during that short interval! Often, and that within a few months of this period, have I been wicked enough to wish my works burnt down again. Yet they were but part of the base art-history of their day. In 1841 I was em-ployed by Mr. Minton to design him a church, the first to which I put a regular chancel, but in some other respects, hardly an advance on the others, though before its completion I had awakened to a truer sense of the dignity of the subject.

This awakening arose, I think, from two causes operating almost simultaneously: my first ac-quaintance with the Cambridge Camden Society, and my reading Pugin's articles in the "Dublin Review." I may be in error as to their coincidence of date. The first took place in this manner. I saw somewhere an article by Mr. Webb, the secre-tary to the Camden Society, which greatly excited my sympathy. Just at the same time I had become exceedingly irate at the projected destruction by Mr. Barry of St. Stephen's Chapel, and I wrote to Mr. Webb and subsequently saw him on the

subject. I was introduced, I believe, by Edward
Boyce. Mr. Webb took advantage of the occasion
to lecture me on church architecture in general,
on the necessity of chancels, &c., &c. I at once
saw that he was right, and became a reader of the
" Ecclesiologist." Pugin's articles excited me almost to fury, and I suddenly found myself like a
person awakened from a long feverish dream, which
had rendered him unconscious of what was going
on about him.

Being thus morally awakened, my physical
dreams followed the subject of my waking thoughts.
I used fondly to dream of making Pugin's acquaintance and to awake, perhaps, while on a night
journey in high excitement, at the imagined interview. I had heard of Pugin as a boy, ten or eleven
years before, at Maddox's. I had again heard of
him and his " Contrasts " from my ardent and excellent friend Charles Bailey, who had often helped
me with my drawings, and I had more recently got
to know more of him in this way. I had undertaken in 1838 (or thereabouts) a large workhouse
at Loughborough. The contractor for a part of
the work was a strange rough mason from Hull,
named Myers. While engaged under me at
Loughborough, he competed with success for the
erection of a Roman Catholic Church at Derby,
nearly the first which Pugin built.[7]

Myers was a native of Beverly, and had been ap-
prenticed to the mason to the minster, from which
he had acquired an ardent love of Gothic architecture, and this now dormant tendency was roused
into energy by his being brought into contact with

[7] St. Mary's, a really beautiful work.—ED.

Pugin. Eternal friendship was sworn between them, and Myers was the builder of nearly every subsequent work of Pugin's.

I made my crusade in favour of St. Stephen's an excuse for writing to Pugin, and to my almost tremulous delight, I was invited to call. He was tremendously jolly, and showed almost too much *bonhomie* to accord with my romantic expectations. I very rarely saw him again, though I became a devoted reader of his written, and visitor of his erected works, and a greedy recipient of every tale about him, and report of what he said or did. A new phase had come over me, thoroughly *en rapport* with my early taste, but in utter discord with the "fitful fever" of my poor-law activity. I was in fact a new man, though that man was, according to the trite saying, the true son of my boyhood.

It was, I suppose, while the awakening was commencing, that I was invited to compete with a small number of architects for the erection of the Martyrs' Memorial at Oxford. This was in 1840, and it seems strange that one so unknown in matters of taste, should have been named on a select list for a work like this. I owed it, I fancy, to the kind influence of my friends, Mr. Stowe and Major Macdonald, with two members of the committee, and to a third member, Dr. Macbride, having been a friend of my father and of my grandfather: when I received the invitation I threw myself into the design with all the ardour I possessed. My early study, full ten years before, of the Eleanor crosses was a good preparation. I obtained every drawing of old crosses I could lay hand on, and devoted my best endeavours to producing a design suited to the object. I succeeded. That this was before my awakening to a true feeling for church architecture, is proved by the defects of the accompanying addition to St. Mary Magdalene's church ; but I fancy the cross itself was better than any one but Pugin would then have produced.

An amusing incident occurred at, I believe, my first interview with the committee. I found them in disagreement as to the best stone for the monument. The commissioners for selecting stone for the Houses of Parliament, had not long before made their report in favour of the purely mythic stone of Bolsover Moor. One party favoured this imaginary stone, for its warm colour ; another, the white variety of magnesian limestone from Roche Abbey, on account of its fine grain. I ventured on the suggestion, that by visiting the district, it might be possible to find a stone uniting these qualities, when Dr. Buckland snubbed me with great scorn, saying that such a suggestion might have been made in years gone by, when little was known of the geological productions of the country, but that now, when every variety of stone was so well known, it was hopeless to look out for new ones. I happened, however, though without scientific knowledge, to have nearly as practical an acquaintance with stone quarries as Dr. Buckland, and I did not see the force of the argument. I therefore started off with Moffatt for the magnesio-calcareous district. The first quarry we went to was that at Mansfield Woodhouse, which, on the discovery of the Bolsover delusion, had been re-opened for the Houses of Parliament ; this stone did not meet my wishes, being too coarse in grain, and not pure enough in colour. On describing, however, to the foreman of the quarry what I was seeking for, he at once told me he could show me what I wanted ; and, taking a hammer and walking with us across a few fields, he brought us to an ancient and long-disused quarry, grown over with brushwood, and on striking off a fragment from the rock, presented to me the very stone which my imagination had pourtrayed ! My delight was excessive. The committee at once, though at a great increase of cost, adopted it, and in their next report attributed the happy discovery to the pre-eminent geological skill of Dr. Buckland.

The stone is perhaps the finest in the kingdom, though it is not to be obtained in large blocks, and is very costly in the quarrying. The rock is still known by the name of "The Memorial Quarry."

About this time, or shortly afterwards, two important works came into our hands by public competition : the Infant Orphan Asylum at Wanstead, and the Church of St. Giles, Camberwell.

The former of these works is a magnificent institution : one of the many which own the well-known Dr. Andrew Reed as the founder.

Nothing could exceed the energy with which Moffatt threw himself into this competition, the most important by far into which we had then entered, nor the pains he took in thoroughly mastering its practical requirements. The planning was

chiefly his, the external design, which was Elizabethan, mine. We succeeded. The first stone
was laid in great state by Prince Albert, and the
building opened by Leopold, the King of the
Belgians.

The old Church of St. Giles, Camberwell, was
burnt down in 1840, and there was a public competition for designs for its re-erection. We competed, sending in a very ambitious design, groined
throughout with terra-cotta. No one had an idea
whose our plans were. The competition being
close, we adhered scrupulously to its regulations.
Mr. Blore acted as assessor, and reported in our
favour. Tenders were received for our design,
and came in, I think, pretty favourably, but a
parish opposition being excited, and a poll called
for, a compromise was at length made, and we
were commissioned to prepare a less costly design,
which resulted in the present structure.

My conversion to the exclusive use of real
material came to its climax during the progress of
this work, and much which was at first shown as
of plaster was afterwards converted into stone,
the builder promising to accept some other change
as a compensation. He died before the completion of the work, and his executors ignoring
this promise, a good deal of dissatisfaction ensued,
though, I must say, they had a very cheap building, and the best church by far which had then
been erected. The pains which I took over this
church were only equalled by the terror with
which I attended the meetings of the committee,
though, I think, they nearly all continued my very
good friends, and were very proud indeed of their

building. The then incumbent was the Rev.
J. G. Storie, a remarkable person. He was a
man of great talent, and personal and moral
prowess, the most masterly hand at coping with a
turbulent parish vestry I ever saw. His only
great fault was that he was a clergyman, instead
of, as nature intended, a soldier or a barrister;
but this was the fault of his parents or guardians,
not his own. He was a thorough man of the
world, and immersed in the society of men of his
own taste. I greatly admired, and, to a certain
extent, respected, while I feared him, for he was a
man whose very look would almost make one
tremble, when his wrath was stirred. He was
determined to have a good church, and so far as
his day permitted, he got it, and after all the little
rubs we had, I view his memory with respect and
friendship. His expensive habits led him to sell
the advowson, which was his own, with a covenant
for immediate resignation. The sale was effected,
and the covenant performed before the purchase-
money was paid, and those who wish to know the
rest may inquire for themselves. However this
may be, poor Mr. Storie was reduced to poverty,
from which he never recovered.

By a strange coincidence, a triple announcement was one Sunday made in the new church.
The choir had struck, the bellows of the organ
had burst, and the vicar had resigned.

Our great mistake in the church was the use of
the Caen stone, an error fallen into by many at
that time and later. It reminds me of a funny
incident relating to the Oxford Memorial. The
Chapter of Canterbury had presented three fine

blocks of Caen stone for the statues of the three bishops. I much desired to sketch carefully, for the benefit of the monument, the details of the noble tomb of Archbishop Peckham, and took occasion to stop at Canterbury for the purpose. The verger, however, soon told me that no sketching could be permitted without an order. The Dean (Bishop Bagot), was away at his See. Canon Peel had gone out, Archdeacon Croft, whom I knew, was not to be found, and my last resource was Dr. Spry. I called at his house and sent in my name, with full particulars of my mission and its objects. The Reverend Doctor was at his luncheon, I heard the " knives and forks rattling," no " sweet music to me," and after more than one attempt, was sent off with a peremptory refusal.

One of our great works at this time was Reading gaol, and few brought me greater annoyance, I think unjustly. Our design was chosen by the Inspector of Prisons, Mr. Russell, though he made great alteration in its arrangement.

Like the Poor-Law Commissioners, he was interested in not frightening the magistrates by a high estimate, and he almost pledged himself to us, that from his experience, he knew we might safely name a particular sum.

Had the usual course of a builder's estimate been followed, the error would have been discovered in time, but the Inspector further prescribed a course which prevented this. He advised the magistrates to contract only for a schedule of prices, and to have the work measured up when completed. Thus the work went on, and we did everything as well as possible, making a capital work of it, but when measured up the result may be imagined ! The Inspector of course made us the scape-goats, which perhaps served us right for being so easily gulled. I doubt, however, whether it was more costly than other prisons, and it is unquestionably a first-rate building.

I must in fairness confess that cost was our weak point. This was not intentional, but resulted from a combination of circumstances. The turmoil of competitions, crowding one upon another, left little time for more than the roughest estimates, though we did employ a regular surveyor upon them. Then the degradation of feeling as to cost, from which the public was just emerging, and our own ardent and sanguine ambition for improvement, all tended in the same direction ; yet I must confess to a certain carelessness on this point, which was decidedly reprehensible. Where there is no competition, an architect can gradually raise the ideas of his clients, from the undue lowness which so generally characterizes them, but in the case of a competition there is no chance of this, and this is one reason why, as soon as I was able, I was rejoiced to kick down the ladder which had raised, but at the same time endangered, me.

From about the time of my marriage, I had resumed my Gothic sketching to as great an extent as my hurried life permitted, and the subject of restoration soon forced itself upon my attention. I think the first work I had to do with of this kind was the refitting of Chesterfield church, and here I cannot say much for my success.   Galleries were forced upon me, contrary to the wish of the Incumbent, Mr. (afterwards Arch-deacon) Hill.   I found the rood screen to have been pulled down and sold, but we protested, and it was recovered.[8]   I recollect that there existed in the church, as I found it, a curious and beautiful family pew or chapel, enclosed by screen-work, to the west of one of the piers of the central tower. There are two such chapels now in St. Mary's church, Beverly.[9]   This was called the Fol-jambe Chapel, and was a beautiful work of Henry VIII.'s time.   What to do with it I did not know, it was right in the way of the arrangements, and could not but have been removed.[1]   I at last deter-mined to use its screen work to form a reredos, and if I remember rightly, it did very well.   I mention these unimportant matters merely for the sake of adding that the " Ecclesiologist," in alluding to this work some years afterwards, when they had begun somewhat to run me down, for purposes of their own, coolly stated that I had had the rood screen sold, and that it had only been recovered by the exertions of the parishioners ; and that I had converted the material of a jacobean screen into a reredos, a fair specimen of their criticisms, when they had an object in view.   My real initiation, however, into the various considerations affecting the sub-ject of restoration was the work undertaken at

[8] There is no such screen now in Chesterfield Church.—Ed.

[9] They have also disappeared.—Ed.

[1] This is a good typical example of what is misnamed " re-storation."   The removal of ancient remains to make way for "necessary" modern arrangements, would be more naturally termed " innovation."—Ed.

St. Mary's, Stafford. The circumstances attending the commencement of this work were so remarkable that I will briefly detail them.

I had, about 1838, made the acquaintance of
Mr. Thomas Stevens, then assistant poor-law
commissioner for the counties of Stafford and
Derby. Mr. Stevens was the only son of the
rector and squire of Bradfield, near Reading, and
as chairman to the union there, had so successfully
taken up poor-law work, that he was persuaded to
join the commission. He was a thorough man of
business, a sound churchman, and a lover of Gothic
architecture. His head-quarters were at Lichfield,
where he attended daily service at the cathedral,
so far as his journeys permitted, a *lusus naturæ*
surely amongst poor-law commissioners.

I first met him at Sir Thomas Cotton Shepherd
Shepherd's, near Uttoxeter, when we formed a
lasting friendship ; and he shortly afterwards got
me to meet him at Bradfield, to consult together
as to the restoration of the church, a work which
was happily postponed till ten years later. The
next year he married, was ordained, and took the
curacy of Keele, in the county of Stafford.

In 1840 or 1841 he wrote to me, telling me that
Mr. Coldwell, rector of Stafford, was most anxious
to restore his church, if only he could get funds,
and suggested my writing to him, offering to make
a survey and report, with a view to facilitating
that object. I did so, and made my report, but
Mr. Coldwell's appeal was but faintly responded
to. Mr. Stevens, being about to return finally to
Bradfield, I visited him on his last day at Keele,
and we went together to Stafford, where we found

H

Mr. Coldwell in despair of ever effecting his wishes. On my return to town I found a letter from Mr. Stevens, telling me that, on reaching Bradfield, he had found a letter awaiting him from a friend, whom he did not yet name, asking his advice as to the appropriation of a sum of 5000*l.* devoted to church building or restoration, and expressing a preference for Staffordshire.

Mr. Stevens had already recommended St. Mary's, subject to the condition that another like sum should be raised by public subscription. The challenge was accepted, and the sum quickly raised, so that the despair of the rector was suddenly changed to joy and thankfulness.

The principal parishioner was, and is, my truly excellent friend, Mr. Thomas Salt, the banker,[2] whose brother-in-law is the Rev. Louis Petit, since so well-known by his architectural writings, and his truly marvellous sketches.

Mr. Petit raised some considerable objections to certain parts of my proposed restorations, on the ground of their not being sufficiently conservative, and wrote a very important and talented letter on the subject.

I differed from him, not in principle, but on the application of the principles to the matter in question. I wrote stoutly, and I think well, in defence of my own views, and the correspondence was, by mutual agreement, referred to the Oxford and Cambridge Societies, who gave their verdict in my favour.

The whole case is given in the account by me of the restoration in Masfen's " History of St. Mary's Church," to which I would specially refer.

[2] He died a few years since.—ED.

Whether I was right or wrong in my views I am doubtful, but the result was a happy one, for embedded in the later walling we found abundant fragments of the earlier work, which enabled me to reproduce the early English south transept with certainty, and a noble design it is.

I employed, during the earlier part of this work, the services of my now deceased friend, Edwin Gwilt, son of old George Gwilt, the restorer of the choir and Lady chapel of St. Saviour's, Southwark. He was conservative to the backbone, and where stonework had to be renewed, he went on the principle of making every stone, and even every joint of the ashlar, correspond to a nicety with the old.

The pains we took in recovering old forms and details were unbounded, and though too little actual old work was preserved, I believe that no restoration could, barring this, be more scrupulously conscientious.

The most serious practical work was the repair of the central tower, whose four piers had become so crushed that they had to be nearly rebuilt, a dangerous work, which it has since been my too frequent lot to repeat, and a most unenviable lot it is.

Let me impress two or three great principles on the mind of those who have to undertake such works. I. Be assured that no amount of shoreing can be too much for safety, no foundations to your shoreing too strong, and no principles of constructing it too well considered. II. Use the hardest stone for your new work which you can procure, and spare no pains in bonding it, and tying it together with copper. III. Be very slow in your operations, excepting at critical junctures, where the very contrary is necessary; be careful in your principle of moveable supports, as you cut away old work; set every stone in the very best cement, and run in the core with grout of the same material. IV. Key up well at the top, and leave your shoreing a long time after the work is done, and then remove it with the greatest care. V. (Though more properly first.) Tie your tower well together with iron before you begin, and take especial care of your foundations. Above all, have a thoroughly practical clerk of the works, neither too young, nor too old.

The shoreing must be all of undivided timbers, and often of four or more such balks, bound and bolted together into one by irons.

The fittings of St. Mary's were not very successful; but, as a whole, it was beyond question the best restoration then carried out, nor have many since been in the main much better. My valued friend, Mr. Jesse Watts Russell, of Ilam Hall, was a munificent patron of this work; and this led to a friendship which has lasted unshaken ever since.[3]

I may here mention that during the years I have been chronicling, our poor-law work still continued; but that we were erecting a very different class of building, usually in the Elizabethan style, and in many cases of really good design. I may mention especially those at Dunmow and Billericay in Essex, Belper, Windsor, Amersham, and Macclesfield. Some of these, indeed, went almost as much too far in this direction, as the earlier ones in meanness.

---

[3] He died some few years after this was written.—ED.

We competed frequently, too, at this time, for county lunatic asylums, though with less success. The vigour with which my partner entered upon these, and his assiduous energy in obtaining the opinions of practical authorities on questions of arrangement, were beyond all praise. These competition drawings were usually prepared at his private house at Kennington, where he gave up all his sitting-rooms, and peopled the house with clerks, who had all their meals together, and had half an hour for a good game in his grounds, every other minute of the day being devoted to the closest work, in which he, and often I, joined as zealously as any of them.

Meanwhile, my church practice rapidly increased in quantity and in merit. I recollect with regret one work of restoration to which I devoted my very best energies, but which was rendered abortive by one false step.

Designs were advertised for, for the restoration of the beautiful chapel of St. Mary on Wakefield Bridge; and I devoted myself with the greatest earnestness to the investigation of the relics of its destroyed detail. I was seconded by Mr. Burlison, then clerk of the works to the church at Chesterfield, and by examining the heaps of *débris* in the river wall, &c., we discovered very nearly everything; and I made, I believe, a very perfect design, illustrated by beautiful drawings, the perspective views being made by my friend Mr. Johnson. My report I viewed as a masterpiece. I succeeded, and the work was carried out, and would have been a very great success, but that the contractor, Mr. Cox, who had been my carver and superintendent to the Martyrs' Memorial, had a handsome offer made him for the semi-decayed front, to set up in a park hard by. He then made an offer to execute a new front in Caen stone, in place of the weather-beaten old one; and pressed his suit so determinedly, that, in an evil hour, his offer was accepted. I recollect being much opposed to it; but I am filled with wonder to think how I ever was induced to consent to it at all, as it was contrary to the very principles of my own report, in which I had quoted from Petit's book the lines beginning,—

" Beware, lest one lost feature ye efface," &c.

I never repented but once, and that is ever since.

The new front was a perfect masterpiece of beautiful workmanship, but it was new, and, in just retribution, the Caen stone is now more rotten than the old work, which is set up as an ornament to some gentleman's grounds. I think of this with the utmost shame and chagrin.

During all this distracting period we lived in the same house in which my office was placed. I fear it was wrong towards my wife to subject her to such disturbances, particularly as her health, after the birth of my second son, was very indifferent. In 1844, however, we happily moved to St. John's Wood, where my other three boys were born.

I have little recollection of the visits from or to my relations at this time. It seems, to look back upon, like a tumultuous sea of business and agitation, leaving no time for the claims of natural affection, or of friendship, though I hope it was not so bad as my memory seems, by its blankness, to suggest. We used, however, in most years, to go to the sea-side, and on one of these occasions I made my first continental trip of one single day. It was simply to Calais, where my sketch-book tells me I must have worked violently, for I made many sketches.

At this time we were regular attendants at the church of St. Martin-in-the-Fields, where Sir Henry Dukinfield was incumbent, and after leaving Spring Gardens, we continued to go there in all seasons and weathers, till Sir Henry resigned the living. We had the greatest respect and affection for this excellent man, which continued up to his death, and he was godfather to our youngest child, who is called after him.

My wife made, in most years, long sojourns with her parents at Boston, and my hasty runs down there were a great relief and pleasure. Mr. and Mrs. Oldrid were admirable people, most sterling characters. A triple union had made our families in every way one, and our mutual visits were periods of great pleasure and happiness, as well as of great advantage to my wife.

I may here mention that during this period the Cambridge Camden Society, with many of whose views I strongly sympathized, and who had been at one time most friendly, had suddenly, and with no reason that I could ever discover, become my most determined opponents. My subsequent success was, for many years, in spite of every effort on their part to put me down by criticisms of the most galling character. No matter how strenuous

my endeavours at improvement, everything was
met by them with scorn and contumely. I believe, though I did not know it at the time, that
this partly originated in a mistake. They had
recommended me to the restoration of a church in
Berks, and a parish opposition having been got
up against restoring the ancient and very fine
open seats, Archdeacon Thorpe, the President of
the Society (in whose archdeaconry it was situated),
went with me to a parish-meeting, to endeavour to
quell the opposition. His eloquence and archidia-
conal authority were alike unavailing, and the
farmers carried their point against him, to his no
small chagrin.[4] I fancy that the members of the
Society vented their vexation upon me, though I
was as earnest in the cause as they, and that they
believed the adverse vote was to have been actually carried into execution, whereas I had
watched my opportunity, and had effected by
default, what the archdeacon had failed to carry by
assault, and I had in fact gained my point to the
full, without saying a word about it, so that I had,
in reality, a double claim upon their approval.

I suppose that I was not thought a sufficiently
high churchman, and as they fell in at the time
with my very excellent friends Carpenter and
Butterfield, they naturally enough took them
under their wing. This no one could complain
of : but the attempt to elevate them, by the systematic depreciation of another equally zealous
labourer in the same vineyard, was anything but
fair. I never would, however, publicly com-

---

[4] The chancel of this church I did not do. It was done
some years later by a local clerk of the works.

plain, and my constant answer when urged to do so, was, "that those who are rowing in the same boat must avoid fighting." I therefore bore with their injustice patiently, chiefly grieving that the leading advocates of so great and good a cause should not act on principles better calculated to recommend it to the moral perception of the public. I think it right to mention these facts, though it is many years since I have had any cause to complain, and though I now number many of the leaders of the Society among my most esteemed friends. I remember one amusing little key to their line of conduct. They had criticized one of the very best churches I had ever built (and one in which all their principles were carried out to the letter) in a way which led to a remonstrance from the incumbent, who pointed out glaring errors in matters of fact. The line of defence they took was this, that as they had had nothing on which to ground their critique but a small lithographic view, the onus of any errors they might have fallen into, did not lie with themselves, but with the architect, who had abstained from submitting his working plans for their examination.

With all its faults, however, the good which the Society has done cannot possibly be over-rated. They have, it is true, like all enthusiastic reformers, often pressed views, in themselves good, too far, and their tendencies have at times been too great towards an imitation of obsolete ritualisms ; but in the main their work has been sound and good. Their reprobation of bad work has never been blameable, indeed at the present time,[5]

[5] About 1860.—ED.

it is too mild by far.   It is, I think, the duty of
such a Society to rebuke the atrocities of false
architects with unflinching courage.   What I complain of is, their attempt just at this period, to
crush those who were labouring strenuously in
the same cause, and the same direction with themselves ; and that, with the sole object, so far as I
could ever ascertain, of the more easily elevating
others whom they viewed as more distinctly their
own representatives.   To expose the misdoings
of ignorance and vandalism was their duty ; to
point out the shortcomings of their fellow-labourers
would have been a kindness ; but to treat friends
and allies with studied scorn and contumely,
through a series of years, because they had not
sworn implicit allegiance to their absolute *régime*,
was discreditable to the sacred cause which they
professed to make the object of their endeavours,
and ended in undermining their influence, through
the obvious self-seeking it evinced ; thus damaging
the movement they otherwise had so ably advocated.

Even Pugin himself could not escape their lash,
his single sin being his independent existence.
It is vexatious to reflect that the vigour of the
Society, and its tendency to unfair dealing, seem to
have varied directly   But it must be remembered
that it was then young and vigorous, was naturally somewhat intoxicated by success, and was
especially open to the constant temptation of such
bodies to rate the success of the Society itself
above that of the cause, and consequently to
estimate persons rather by their loyalty than by
their merits.

CHAPTER III.

HAVING arrived at a point closely approaching to what I view as the most important era in my professional life, I will offer a few observations upon the position of the great revival of Gothic architecture at this period (viz. about 1844), and also as to my own humble share in it, up to that date.

It is almost vexatious when we consider how great an event that revival really has been, to recollect, at the same time, how unconscious one felt of this fact during its earlier years.

I call these its earlier years, because I hardly view those which preceded 1830 (or even a later date), as belonging to the period of the revival at all. Writers on this subject are wont to talk about Strawberry Hill, and a number of such base efforts, as the early works of the revival. They may be so in a certain sense, but one can scarcely trace much connexion between them and the work of its really vigorous period, and, as I personally know little, and knew nothing, about them, I will leave them wholly out of the question.

When I first commenced sketching from Gothic buildings (which was about 1825, though I had taken delight in them a few years earlier), I did

not in the smallest degree connect my feelings
towards them with any thought of the revival of
the style.   I think that a very base church at
Windsor, (putting aside the ludicrous " Gothic
Temple " at Stowe, which belongs I suppose to
the Strawberry Hill type), was the first modern
Gothic building I ever saw.   This was, I fancy,
about 1823,[1] and bad as it is, I recollect its giving
me some pleasure.   On a visit to London the
next year I remember seeing the yet baser church
at Somers town, since celebrated by Pugin in his
" Contrasts."   I do not think that this was very
gratifying to me, though, during the same visit, I
recollect seeing with extreme delight the restoration of the reredos in Westminster Abbey, then
in hand :   that of Henry VII.'s chapel had, I
think, been already completed.   The great majority
of new churches were still classic, and I remember
that in 1826, when my father had to rebuild his
church, the idea of making it " Gothic " was considered quite visionary, nor am I conscious of any
practical object occurring to me while studying
Gothic architecture till many years after this time.
I did so, purely from the love of it.

A great deal is said, too, as to the influence on
the public taste of different publications, in leading
to the appreciation and the revival of mediæval
architecture, and it would be unfair to ignore such
influence.   I believe, however, that the effect was
really of a reciprocal kind.   The natural current
of human thought had taken a turn towards our
own ancient architecture, and this led to its investigation and illustration, while such investigation

[1] The church was, I find, erected in 1822.—ED.

and illustration in their turn reacted upon the mental feelings which had originated them ; so that, by a kind of alternate action, spread over a series of years, the mind of the public was, both awakened to a feeling for the beauties of the style, and instructed in its principles. So far as I was personally concerned, my love of Gothic architecture was wholly independent of books relating to it; none of which, I may say, I had seen at the time when I took to visiting and sketching Gothic churches. The first prints I had met with bearing upon the subject (for I do not think that I read the article) were in the " Encyclopedia Edinensis," where, under the head of " Architecture," were two or three engravings illustrative of our style; the west front of Rheims Cathedral, an internal view of Rosslyn Chapel, and a view of an Episcopal church at Edinburgh. The latter, by-the-bye, must have been a very early work (as it was about 1823 that I saw this print), and it was, I fancy, rather in advance of its day. After this I saw nothing tending in the same direction, beyond one volume of Lysons' " Magna Britannia," till after I had left home to read with my uncle in 1826, and then what I saw was very slight, Storer's " Cathedrals " being the choicest and dearest to my memory. It must have been very long afterwards that I first became acquainted with any of Britton's works.

So far, then, as my own consciousness goes, books had little to do with the earnest stirring up to a love of the subject which I experienced. I was unconsciously subjected to the same potent influence which was acting upon the public mind, and which was rather the cause than the effect of the publications which subsequently so much aided it.

Among the books which did most to aid the revival in these early days was Pugin's (sen.) "Specimens of Gothic Architecture." This, though it first appeared in 1821, came out in its present more perfect form in 1825. Its great utility was that it set people measuring details, instead of merely sketching, and its practical effect was to lead architects, who attempted to build Gothic churches, to give some little attention to detail. The specimens given were mostly of late date, but the spirit of the work, rather than its actual contents, was its great value, and the several volumes of "Examples" which followed carried on the same feeling.

There can be no doubt that it was the share taken by the younger Pugin in these works, and what he saw of their preparation, which stirred up within him that burning sentiment which has produced such extraordinary results. I should be disposed also to attribute to the first of these publications a share in the merits of Mr. Barry's Islington churches, which, with all their faults and their strange commissioners' ritualisms, were for this period wonderfully advanced works. They were going on while I was in my articles (1827-30), and I doubt whether anything so good was done (excepting by Pugin) for ten years later; indeed, in their own parish nothing so good has been done since. For myself, I can hardly say too much as to the benefit derived from Pugin's "Specimens." I found them at Mr. Edmeston's when I was first articled to him, and they at once had the effect of leading me to the most careful measuring, and laying down with scrupulous accuracy, of the details of the works I sketched. Indeed, the greater part of my holidays was spent in making such detailed measurements. All thanks and honour then to the older Pugin, however much our *illuminati* may sneer.

So far as I was personally concerned, nearly another decade had to pass before my studies became practically productive. I followed up sketching with more or less assiduity according to circumstances, but still with little thought of its becoming practically useful; I still pursued it solely from the love of it. Once during this period I, for practice sake, entered into a competition, and chose my favourite style. I have by me also two designs for gothic churches, which I made with an idea of submitting them, as probationer's drawings, to the Royal Academy. They have some merit, though showing most extraordinary notions of ritual. I have already said that church architecture during this period had gone back. Barry's Islington churches were princely compared with those of this dark decade; and my own awakening attempts, from 1838 to 1841, were as bad or nearly so, as the rest, pressed down as I was on the one hand by the intensity of the "cheap church" mania, and on the other by an utter want of appreciation of what a church should be.

From this darkness the subject was suddenly opened out by Augustus Welby Pugin, and the Cambridge Camden Society. From that time on to 1844 was the great period of practical awakening, and by the end of it the revival was going on

with determined and rapid success.   By this time
"shams" had been pretty generally discarded by
all architects not hopelessly in the mire.   The old
system of solid and genuine construction had
generally been revived, and truth, reality, and
"true principles" were accepted as the guiding
stars of architecture; while a more correct ritualism
had been, so far as the opposition of party feeling permitted, to a considerable extent adopted.
Pugin's own works were, of course, limited (or
nearly so) to the Roman Catholic Church.   Their
clergy had sunk fully as low as our own in their
notions of ecclesiastical arrangement and design,
and he had much the same difficulties to contend
with as we had.   His success was wonderful, for,
though his actual architecture was scarcely worthy
of his genius, the result of his efforts in the revival
of "true principles," as well as in the recovery
of all sorts of subsidiary arts, glass painting,
carving, sculpture, works in iron, brass, the precious metals and jewellery, painted decoration,
needlework, bookbinding, woven fabrics, encaustic
tiles, and every variety of ornamental work, was
truly amazing.   Amongst Anglican architects, Carpenter and Butterfield were the apostles of the
high church school—I, of the multitude.

I had begun earlier than they, indeed, Camberwell church dates before their commencement;
but as they became the mouth-pieces—or hand-
pieces—of the Cambridge Camden Society, while
I took an independent course, it followed that they
were chiefly employed by men of advanced views,
who placed no difficulties in their way, but the
reverse; while I, doomed to deal with the pro-

miscuous herd, had to battle over and over again
the first prejudices, and had to be content with
such success as I could get. The one, cast
seed only into good ground: the other, as luck
would have it, over the wayside, upon stony
ground, or among the thorns; and only now and
then, quite exceptionally, and by some happy
chance, upon a bit of good soil. Each was a
necessary work. Mine was unquestionably the
more arduous, and was not, perhaps, the least
useful, though far from being the most agreeable,
while it led to thankless abuse from both sides.
I look back, however, upon my labours at that
time (1841-44) with some satisfaction, and believe
that they have in the main effected much good.

The circumstance which brought about a new
era in my professional life was this.

Late in the summer of 1844 my attention was
called by a city friend to the advertisement for
designs for the rebuilding of St. Nicholas' church,
at Hamburg, which had been destroyed by the
great fire. My friend had been requested (though
quite informally) to induce one of the English
church architects to enter the lists of this European competition, and he fixed upon me.

Strange to say, I had not then seen anything of
continental architecture, excepting during part of
two days which I had spent at Calais. I at once,
however, made up my mind that the style of the
design must be German gothic, and that I must
without delay make this my study. I accordingly
set out on my first continental tour, and unbounded was the enthusiasm with which I undertook it. I was accompanied by my brother John,

I

and at first by a young lawyer, my friend Mr. Smith, and a young barrister, Mr. Cameron (both long since departed).

Oddly enough, it never occurred to me that France should be my first field of study ; I knew what had been written by Whewell, Petit, and Moller, but I had not gathered this fact from what they had said. I began with one of the worst countries for pointed architecture, Belgium, though to me it was then an enchanted land. I visited with great delight Bruges, Ghent, Tournay, Mons, Hal, Brussels, Mechlin, Antwerp, Louvain, and Liege.

My companions were very agreeable, but I experienced what every architect must feel who travels with lay companions, the inconvenience arising from the incompatibility of their objects with his own. They had always " done " a place before my work was well commenced, and had I listened to their wishes, I should have obtained scarcely any advantage from my tour. As it was, I worked very hard and got through a great deal, but it was by fighting hard against adverse circumstances.

I would strongly advise architects to travel only with architects, or even alone rather than with lay fellow-travellers.

I got a fair day's work at Tournay owing to a great festival then going on, which amused my con-voyageurs, and at Hal I had a luxurious day while they were visiting Waterloo. The pictures we did enjoy in common, and certainly they are a great source of delight in Belgian travel. In some places one of my companions was set as a watch over me to see that I did not cause them to miss the trains, and I was consoled by the assurance that once arrived at Cologne, they would give me as much time as I liked.

Leaving Belgium, we took the customary line by Aix-la-Chapelle to Cologne. There my legal companions had done everything by the end of the first day, and I, now out of all patience with lay intervention, got up the next morning at four or five and started off on my own hook to Altenberg, leaving them to take their own course while I took mine, and arranging to rejoin my brother a few days later.

I sketched pretty well everything at Altenberg, to the very patterns of the glass, and I got a good day at Cologne, on which I half worked myself to death. I here found that I was in a great strait, I could not make up my mind whether in studying for my Hamburg design, I ought to follow the semi-Romanesque, of which Cologne supplied such a field of study, or the "complete Gothic" of the cathedral and of Altenberg. I was not then aware of the French origin of the latter style, or my decision might perhaps have been different.

Leaving Cologne, I rejoined my brother at Bonn, and proceeded up the Rhine, visiting Swartz,—Rheindorf, Andernach, Laach, Coblentz, Oberwesel, Bacharach, Mayence, and Frankfort, and, my brother's patience exceeding that of my lawyer friends, I was able to work fairly. Passing Remagen, I saw the little chapel then recently erected at Apollinarisberg. Its architecture is bad, but I was much interested by seeing the frescoes in

I 2

course of operation, never having seen art of this class before.

Near Zinzig, we passed a long procession of priests and peasants whom, after a long puzzle with our driver, we ascertained to be pilgrims on their way to Treves, to pay their devotions to the Holy Coat, then being exhibited. They sang hymns as they went on their way, and were accompanied from the village by the clergy and people of the place, who, after going a mile or so to see them on their way, took an affectionate leave of them and returned. We saw another party of pilgrims afterwards at Coblentz; and an English gentleman who had been to Treves, told us that such was the vastness of the crowd that it took him a whole day to get from his hotel to the cathedral and back.

At Frankfort we were greatly interested by the conversation of Dr. Schopenhauer, an old German philosopher, who usually took his meals at the hotel at which we stayed. I think I never met a man with such grand powers of conversation; but, alas, he was a determined infidel. I have since met him twice at the same hotel: the last time was as late as 1860, when I with some difficulty drew him out into conversation, which deafness rendered less easy than formerly, and I was quite astonished at his brilliancy, and, but for his infidelity, at the noble philosophical tone of his thoughts and conversation. I meant to have sent him some books on the evidences, &c., of Christianity, but I forgot it; and when I went to Frankfort last year, and looked out for him, I found his portrait hanging over where he used to sit, betokening that he had departed. May it be that his philosophy had previously become christianized.

My brother John was at this time in a transitional state between medicine and divinity. He had given up his first profession, and was keeping his terms at Cambridge previously to entering the Church ; and the long vacation being now nearly over, he was obliged to hasten our journey. We accordingly set off on a long diligence drive from Frankfort to Hanover, which took us two days and two nights, to the best of my recollection, beside one night on which we rested at Cassel. I had a peep only at the exterior of St. Elizabeth's church at Marburg, while breakfast was going on. I certainly ought to have stopped, as it was the most important church in some respects that I had seen in Germany.

We spent a Sunday at Hanover, and the next day went by rail to Brunswick, with which I was very much pleased ; and then to Magdeburg, whence we took a night journey by steamer to Hamburg.

Here my brother left me, and I stayed on to get local information, and took a diligence journey to old Lübeck, to my great delight, and thus completed my tour.

On leaving Hamburg by steamer for London, I struck out on the first morning of the voyage my design for the church—I have the sketch now—but a stormy sea soon put a stop to work. The voyage took, I think, three days and four nights, during most of which I was in bed ; and, on reaching home, I was so ill as to be laid up for

several days, during which time, however, I was
enabled to complete my general design, on the
drawing out of which all force was put, as I had
only a month left on returning to my office. The
style I chose was somewhat later than I should
now adopt, being founded rather on fourteenth
than on thirteenth century work. I thought at
the time that it was earlier. My journey had
enabled me to catch the general spirit of German
work at that period, though I afterwards found
that I had not done so perfectly. My design was,
however, in the main a good one, and the drawings were admirably finished, all hands being put
upon them, though the best elevations were made
by Mr. Coe and Mr. Street, the last-named
coming out now for the first time, to my observation, in the prominent way which has since
characterised him. The drawings, which were
very large and numerous, were sent off by a
steamer, which would, under ordinary circumstances, have delivered them by the time prescribed ; but an early frost had stopped the
navigation of the Elbe, and they arrived three
weeks after the time ! My agent, however, Mr.
Emilius Müller, was indefatigable in his nego-
tiations, and the delay was condoned.

When my drawings arrived and were exhibited
with the rest, the effect upon the public mind in
Hamburg was perfectly electrical. They had
never seen Gothic architecture carried out in a
new design with anything like the old spirit, and
as they were labouring under the old error that
Gothic was the German ("Alt Deutsch") style,
their feelings of patriotism were stirred up in a

wonderful manner. My design was to their apprehension far more German than those of any of the German architects. Professor Semper, my most talented competitor, had grounded his design on that of the cathedral at Florence, and Heideloff, Lange, and others had made more or less of failures, while an English architect of the name of Atkinson (the future Siberian explorer), then living at Hamburg, who had made a powerful effort, had failed of making his design German. Mr. Müller kept me constantly supplied with extracts from the newspapers, &c., which for the most part advocated my design with enthusiasm. One writer indulged in a poetical effusion, while by another I was compared to Erwin von Steinbach.

I subjoin extracts from two out of a multitude of such papers in my possession. These must have appeared within a few days of the arrival of my drawings ; the second, I fancy, may have been by the Rev. Pastor Freudenthiel, one of the clergymen of St. Nicholas, who is well-known in Germany as a poet.

From the " Hamburger Neue Zeitung," 23rd Dec., 1844.

Baupläne für die neue St. Nicolai Kirche.

Von allgemeinstem Interesse ist gewiss die Ausstellung der 39 eingelieferten Baupläne für die neue St. Nicolai Kirche, von besonderem Interesse für den Kunstverständigen aber, zu sehen wie verschiedenartig und wirklich bunt die Combinationen hier ausfallen, die historisch-architectonischen Elemente in den Ideen oft nur restaurirt sind, so dass man den Mangel natürlicher Schöpfungskraft, welche das Angelernte und Ueberlieferte beherrschen und vergessen machen soll, unmittelbar gewahrt— wie die Manifestationen der Ideen oft selbst geschmacklos und antichristlich sind, indem hier eine halbe Pagode, dort ein halber griechischer Tempel zum Vorschein kommt. Natürlich aber fehlt es auch nicht an tüchtigen kernigen Anschauungen, die würdevoll und edel aufgefasst sind, wie die unter No. 32, "Das Werk und nicht der Meister"—No. 25, "Erhaben ist der Baukunst Streben," etc., doch—"die Letzten werden die Ersten sein!" No. 39, "Labor ipse voluptas" — wurde durch den Frost zu Cuxhaven zurückgehalten, und es ist die Krone von Allen. Das Characteristische dürfte hier vornehmlich sein: die reine Entwickelung des historisch-technischen Begriffes christlicher Baukunst in originaler Klarheit und Majestät. Die Phantasie des Künstlers ringt hier gleichsam mit den Monumenten der Geschichte und der Steg wird verherrlicht durch seine saubere architectonische Zeichnung. Solchen Münster und man wird ihn ewig bewundern in seiner Herrlichkeit!—Auch darin lebt der Geist Erwin's von Steinbach.

From the "Nachrichten," January 2nd, 1845.

Ein Mauerstein zum Bauplane der St. Nicolai-Kirche mit dem Motto: "Labor ipse voluptas."

Wie hast Du aufgebaut, Du wack'rer Meister,
So kühn den Bau in Deinen Künstlerplan,
Vernichtend jenen eitlen, leeren Wahn,
Dass deutsche Kunst mit uns'rer Ahnen Geister
Zu Grabe ging für alle künft'ge Zeit!
Hat Albion Dich vormals uns geboren,
Dich hat die deutsche Gothik auserkoren,
Als Herold ihrer Pracht und Herrlichkeit!
Das ist der Münster, der mit heil'gen Schauern
In Strassburg füllet jede Menschenbrust;
Das ist der Dom zu Cöln, der heil'ge Lust
Erschuf, zu bauen jene mächt'gen Mauern,
Die fromm der Ahn in alter Zeit begann,
Ein Engel musste lichtvoll Dich umschweben,
Als, Meister, Dein Gebild erstand aus schönem Streben
Das stolz und kühn nun strebet himmelan!
Mein Hamburg, auf, zum allerschönsten Bunde
Erbaue solch ein Werk nach schwerer Zeit,
Dass staunen alle Völker! Weit und breit
Durchdringe jedes Land die hehre Kunde,
Dass nun Sanct Nicolaus in lichter Pracht
Verherrlicht wieder unsers Hamburgs Mauern,
Dann wird der spät'ste Enkel nimmer trauern
So lang der Thurm die Vaterstadt bewacht,

Dass frommer Glaube bei den Ahnen schwand,
Dass nicht aus Nacht ein Gottestag erstand.
Ja, ihm verkünden noch geweihte Sagen
In Liedern gross und hehr die fromme Kraft,
Mit der ein Gott begeistert Volk geschafft,
Als Armuth mit der Armuth sich verband,
Um Gaben mild aus ihren armen Händen
Durch langer Jahre Zeiten fortzuspenden ;
Bis schön vollendet jenes Werk erstand.
Es wird der Glaube einst zum sel'gen Schauen,
Die Hoffnung wandelt sich in Gottvertrauen,
Nur Liebe bleibt—Drum lasst uns ewig bauen
In jeder Freudenzeit, in schwerer Stunde
Ein jedes Werk auf ihrem reinen Grunde.

It must not, however, be supposed that all the notices were as favourable as these, many were so, and went very much into detail, and several pamphlets appeared on the same side. Some, however, were written by persons favourable to other styles, and to other architects, and were in some cases violent in their opposition.

As it may perhaps not be uninteresting to know the line which at this time I took in my advocacy of Gothic architecture, I will subjoin some extracts from the paper by which my design was accompanied.

" A strong feeling has for some years existed in most parts of Europe in favour of the study and careful investigation of the principles of that beautiful but long-neglected style of architecture of which such glorious examples are to be found in the ecclesiastical edifices of Germany, France, England, and other northern countries. This feeling, and the investigation consequent upon it, has almost universally removed the absurd prejudices of the last three centuries, which, by making the architecture of Greece and Rome the standard for all other countries, however differing in climate, manners, or religion, condemned as barbarous all the indigenous productions of the countries inhabited by the Teutonic nations. A careful examination, however, of these works which have been so ruthlessly condemned has convinced every inquirer that, so far from being barbarous, they are the greatest productions of human art, the most perfectly suited to the climate, manners, and natural materials of the countries where they exist, and, above all, that as sacred edifices they excel all other buildings in the appropriateness to the spirit of the religion from which they have emanated. The style of these exquisite buildings has a strong and natural claim to be used for ecclesiastical purposes by the architects of all nations of northern Europe, as being that style which spontaneously rose and developed itself among all the nations of German origin under the peculiar influence of the Christian religion. That this style did not owe its origin or developement in any degree to the particular influence of the Church of Rome is fully shown by the fact that it never arrived at any great perfection south of the Alps, that it was there considered as a foreign style, and that its extinction in the sixteenth century was commenced by the efforts of the ecclesiastics at Rome, and was carried out through the influence of Italian artists.

" It was natural that when, after three centuries of neglect, the beauties of our native architecture began again to be appreciated, disputes should arise between the different branches of the great

Teutonic family for the honour of its first invention. Warm and elaborate arguments have accordingly taken place : Germany, France, and England
have zealously pressed their claims, with more or
less success, according to the ingenuity of their
respective champions. The subject of dispute, it
must be confessed, has been unimportant, but, like
the study of alchemy, though fruitless in its immediate object, it has tended much to promote the
successful investigation of more practical and
important questions. These frivolous inquiries
have now merged into the practical and detailed
study of the principles of this noble style of architecture, and questions as to its origin and its
inventors have given place to the more important
inquiry of how it can most successfully be revived
and re-established. England has taken her place
among other nations in the study and revival of
ecclesiastical architecture, and among others the
architect who has prepared the accompanying
design has made this the leading object of his
labours, and it is the opportunity afforded by your
liberal advertisement of preparing a design in
some degree worthy of the ancient models, to the
study of which he has devoted himself, that has
induced him to enter upon the present competition,
which he does rather for the delight he feels in the
subject than from any great hopes of success," &c.

Again, on the choice of the variety of pointed
architecture to be made use of,—

" In tracing the history of an art which was
subject to continual and uniformly progressive
change it is a matter of considerable difficulty to
determine at what precise period it had arrived

at the greatest degree of perfection. The taste of individuals may vary much on the merits of such a question, and where every phase of that art possesses peculiar merits and beauties of its own, the feelings of the same person may be subject to much change, according to the impressions produced upon the mind by the contemplations of specimens of different periods. As, however, the gradual progression of ecclesiastical architecture in northern Europe commenced with a style which was evidently barbarous, but rose by degrees to the highest degree of beauty and excellence, and as unquestionably it afterwards became lowered and corrupted and finally extinguished, it is clear that it must have had a culminating point, and that there must be one period at which it had obtained its greatest perfection. To ascertain this point with accuracy is an important object to those engaged in designing a church, which ought not to be less perfect in its character than corresponding works of the best ages of art.

"From a very careful consideration of the ancient churches of Germany, France, and England, the author of the present design has been led to fix the end of the thirteenth century, viz. from 1270 to 1300 A.D., as the period at which the most perfect ecclesiastical architecture is to be found; very fine specimens are certainly to be met with both earlier and later than these dates, but still within these limits appears to be comprised the period of the fullest developement of the style. That this was a marked era in the history of church architecture is proved by several circumstances in which it differs from other times. The architects of the different nations of Europe, in the first instance, imitated the later works of the Romans, but in the course of time they re-modelled these into a style peculiarly their own, which style is known by the name Romanesque, Lombardic, or (though erroneously) Byzantine. In the working out of this change each nation took its own course, and the architectural styles resulting from this change widely differed in different countries. During the twelfth century, however, each began to introduce the pointed arch, accompanied by other features novel to the established manner. During the transition each nation still took its own course. We accordingly find the buildings of this period in Germany, France, and England, widely differing from one another. Towards the end, however, of the thirteenth century they appear, by a remarkable coincidence, to have all arrived at the same point, though reaching it by different routes. It is true that each country still retained its peculiar taste and characteristics, but the essential principles and elements, at this period, more nearly coincided than at any other, and from this point they seem to have again diverged, till they at length differed from one another as widely as before. Each, though in different ways, departed from the simple principles of taste, and introduced into their archi-tecture those fantastic and corrupted details, which at length led to the extinction of the style, and a return to the architecture of ancient Rome.

"Another peculiar feature which marks the era which has been named, is, that at that epoch, the ornamental foliage was in every instance imitated from nature. The enrichment of earlier buildings had been derived from classic antiquity, but in the course of years had grown into a new style, neither classic nor natural. At this period, however, the artists fell back upon nature, and we find all the foliage and ornaments of that time to be copies of real leaves and flowers ; while at a later date nature was again departed from, and merely conventional forms again made use of. The same distinctive features may be traced in the sculpture, stained glass, decorative painting, jewellery, and other ecclesiastical arts of that period, which will be found to evince a purity of taste and feeling never before reached in the same countries, and not generally retained in later times.

"A careful examination of the architecture of this date will show that it possesses in its most perfect form all the peculiar characteristics of pointed architecture, that it retains no trace whatever of the objectionable features of former styles, and that it is at the same time free from the defects which were subsequently engrafted upon it. Every form is perfect and elegant in its design, from the grandest features to the most minute ornaments. Individual buildings may have their own particular defects, but there is no imperfection inherent in the style. It is equally suited to the most simple and to the most magnificent structures, being susceptible of the greatest simplicity without becoming mean, and of the utmost extent of decoration without the risk of exuberance."

I then go on to show that it would be inconsistent to imitate the local characteristics of the
old buildings in the immediate district, because
these arose from difficulties as to materials, &c.,
which then existed, but have since ceased, recom-
mending rather " To take advantage of the varied
beauties exhibited by German churches of corresponding style in *general,* than by those of a
particular district; and to endeavour so to treat the
subject as we may imagine that the ancient artists
would have done, if they had possessed all the
practical advantages which can now be obtained."

I give these lengthy extracts, not from any
value they possess in themselves, but in order to
show the progress of thought upon such subjects
then attained.

The decision on the design was for some time
delayed ; and, during the interval, the mask of
concealed names was so completely dropped, that
my design was constantly spoken of as the
" Scottisch " design, and I was enabled to defend
myself personally against some attacks made upon
it. At length it was determined to call in Sulpice
Boiserée, and Zwirner, the architect to Cologne
Cathedral. The former could not personally
attend ; but he wrote a sort of essay on the subject, which was considered to coincide with my
own views. Zwirner, however, went to Hamburg, and I was advised by my agent, Emilius
Müller, to be there in case of being wanted. I
accordingly crossed from Hull, and arriving early
on a Sunday morning, was roused from my slumbers by the indefatigable Müller, who had discovered that he was wrong in advising my

presence. I had accordingly to remain *incognito*
for the day, and the next morning to retire to
Lübeck, where I remained for some days. As ill-
luck would have it, it was found out by my competitors that I had arrived; and as Zwirner had
gone, with one of the committee, to spend the
Sunday at Lübeck, I had actually met him
(though unseen) on the road, which afforded a
fine card for the invention of a conspiracy. Of
this, however, I was ignorant, and I remained in
my retirement until I heard that the decision was
in my favour, and then returned to Hamburg. I
stayed there for a considerable time, to make
arrangements for commencing the execution of
the work. I went there again in September and
October of the same year, when a contract was
entered into for the foundations, and we formally
broke ground on October 8th, 1845 (L.D.)

During this visit I made the acquaintance of
that admirable man, the Syndic Sieviking, the
founder of the celebrated Raumen Haus. I have
never met a more accomplished gentleman, or a
more charming and excellent man, or one of a
more elegant mind, or more refined feelings.

A difference of opinion had arisen as to
whether transepts should be added to my design,
omitting the second aisles. This alteration was
eventually carried. I may mention that I had
been studying German, though in a very moderate
degree, from the time that there seemed a
prospect of my success; and that my assistant,
Mr. Burlison, had done so more successfully, and
had spent some time this year at Hamburg, in
order to get up practical information. My clerk

of the works was Mr. Mortimer, a very talented man, who had been engaged for me in that capacity at several buildings, among which was St. Mary's, Stafford. Of this valued coadjutor, and his untimely end, I shall have to speak hereafter.

I returned home by way of Holland, for the purpose of making myself acquainted with the use of trass or tarras in water cements. I visited on my way Bremen, Osnabrück, Münster, and Xanten. The latter contains an admirable church, which had some influence on the maturing of the Hamburg design. In Holland I visited Arnhem, Utrecht, Amsterdam, Haarlem, and Rotterdam. The journey from Hamburg to Xanten was by diligence, as were most of my inland journeys in Germany for some years later.

The information I obtained in Holland was most serviceable, and was conclusive in favour of tarras. I brought some of it home with me, and followed up experiments which were equally conclusive in their result. The pains taken in Holland on government works in the preparation of mortar is truly amazing. I went into a shed where eighty people were employed; they were in four divisions, twenty facing twenty, all armed with a kind of hoe. The materials for the mortar (consisting of trass and dry slacked hydraulic lime) were placed in two lengthened heaps between two twenties of men, who, at the word of command from a kind of sergeant, commenced mixing the ingredients in the most careful and systematic manner. This done, the two ranks shouldered arms, and a man ran through the shed

K

with a watering-pot, sprinkling a small quantity of water on the powder, after which the mixing was repeated as before. Again the aquarius ran through, and again the mixing was repeated; and this went on till the mortar was reduced to a state of paste, and no apothecary's salve was ever better manipulated. The mortar is tried from time to time by means of wedge-shaped bricks stuck together, and the cohesive power tested by weights in a scale hung to one of them, the result being formally booked by the clerk of the works. The work upon which they were engaged was a fortification on the banks of the old Rhine. There was a mighty cistern, elevated high above the works, from which proceeded india-rubber hose with brass nozzles; every bricklayer having the command of one of these, and directing the jet of water against every side of every brick before laying it, lest one particle of dust should weaken the adhesion of the mortar.

About this time a constantly increasing desire had grown up in my mind to terminate my partnership with Mr. Moffatt. My wife was most anxious upon the subject, and was constantly pressing it upon my attention, but my courage failed me, and I could not muster pluck enough to broach it. At length Mrs. Scott "took the bull by the horns." She drove to the office while I was out of town, asked to see Mr. Moffatt privately, and told him that I had made up my mind to dissolve our partnership. He was tremendously astounded, but behaved well, and the ice thus broken, I followed up the matter vigorously. This was during the latter part of

1845, and at the close of the year an agreement was entered into, dissolving our partnership then and there " de facto," but taking one year as a year of transition, and delaying the actual gazetting of the dissolution until the close of that year.

Though Mr. Moffatt occasionally kicked hard at this, I must do him the justice to say that he behaved fairly and straightforwardly throughout. We came to an agreement of this kind : we valued the probable receipts of our several works and of outstanding bills, and divided the works into three portions, one for myself, another for Mr. Moffatt, (each taking our allotment " for better or worse"), and a third to pay a debt owing to our banker. This arrangement turned out better for me than for him, as his works having a certain amount of speculation about them, he lost a good deal of the estimated value of some of them. As, however, they were in their nature and origin his own works, it did not seem unfair that he should stand the brunt of this. The year 1846 was to me a time at once of thankfulness and of anxiety. I was most thankful to be freed from a partnership which, with many advantages, had become the source of much annoyance ; at the same time it was " hard lines," after having been ten years in practice of the most unprecedented activity, to have put by next to nothing, and to have to set aside the proceeds of many works to cover a debt, which was the result of easy-going and bad management on my own part, and of some extravagance on that of my partner.

My connexion with Mr. Moffatt, as will have

been gathered from the statements made earlier
in this sketch, was by no means a premeditated
one.   It had grown up spontaneously and almost
independently of my will.   People wonder, I have
no doubt, how two persons, so contrary in their
tastes and dispositions, could have joined in partnership, and blame my judgment in permitting it.
I have only to say, in reply, that I never thought
of partnership until it came about wholly without,
and almost against my own will.   Nor had I
any reason to think otherwise than favourably of
my partner.   He was very talented, very practical,
and very industrious.   Nor am I sure, with all its
drawbacks, that I have not gained more than I
have lost by the connexion.   My natural disposition was so quiet and retiring, that I doubt if I
should have alone pushed my way.   My father
used to be seriously uneasy on this head, and he
never believed that I could get on in the rough
world.   Mr. Moffatt supplied just the stuff I was
wanting in.   He was thoroughly fitted to cope
with the world; he saw through character in a
moment, and could shape himself precisely to the
necessities of the case and the character of the
people he had to do with.   This enabled me,
through a sort of apprenticeship of ten years, to
learn to rough it on my own account.   Strange
to say as time went on, he seemed gradually to
lose his power of acting wisely.   I had by that
time chalked out a practice for myself, wholly
different from that for which he was fitted, and
at length I was enabled to separate from him, and
to keep my own practice, making over his own to
him.

I was now a free man, but I had almost to begin life over again. I wrote a circular, which I sent far and wide, publishing my separation to the world. I almost wonder to think how readily practice came to me in my single name; but "Scott and Moffatt" had become so well known as a *nom-de-guerre*, that it took very many years to get rid of it altogether, and now at the end of eighteen years I occasionally get a letter so addressed.

The fact is that we had made ourselves a name such as few architects have ever made at our age, and had done more perhaps than had ever been done in the first ten years of architectural practice.

I fear we were disliked by our fellow-professionals for our almost unheard-of activity and success. This, however, was only the natural jealousy of competitors, and I do not think that it was founded on any just reason. Happily, I had come to the determination to avoid competitions for the most part, though without making any resolution which would debar me from them when they seemed from special circumstances desirable. I have the greatest reason to be thankful that my subsequent practice has, for the most part, come to me without competition and unasked-for, and that this has freed me from much of that professional jealousy which follows a frequently competing architect. I do not, however, think that I could have got into such practice without a long previous course of competition, and I would not recommend young architects, as a general rule, to try the experiment.

I was thirty-five years old in the midst of this year of transition, and I recollect congratulating myself on the old saying,—

"He who ever means to thrive
Must begin by thirty-five."

From this time my life seems to have usually run in so smooth a course that I hardly know what to say about it that is worth saying.

In that year (1846) I appear to have made two journeys to Hamburg. The first was in April: I went *viâ* Calais, visiting Dunkirk, Bergues, Pope-ringhe, and Ypres, to which place I had been directed by my dear friend Syndicus Sieviking to study for the future Rath-Haus of Hamburg, for which he considered the Halles there as a most suggestive model; and highly delighted I was with it. I then went by Aix-la-Chapelle, Dusseldorf, Neuss, and by diligence across Westphalia to Min-den, whence I visited some of the quarries, situated in a splendid country, which supply Hamburg; thence to Halberstadt, and by Magdeburg, to Hamburg, and returned by sea. The next journey was in September. I went by sea, and on this occasion, on September 24th, 1846, the first stone of the church was laid in great state (L. D.). I returned by way of Brunswick, Hildesheim, and Cologne, visiting stone quarries and sketching.

I ought to have mentioned that I had been violently attacked in the "Ecclesiologist" for un-dertaking a Lutheran church. I wrote a formal defence, to which they refused admission.

The following is the text of my defence thus suppressed :—

" *To the Editor of the 'Ecclesiologist.'*

" SIR,—In your last number I find that you have made some rather severe remarks upon me with reference to the new church of St. Nicholas, Hamburg. Had these remarks been founded upon correct premises, I should not for a moment deny their justice; but as this is far from being the case, and as the natural inference from what you say would be, that I was about to erect a church for a community which disbelieved the most essential doctrines of Christianity, and to dishonour the symbols of our faith by using them as mere decorations of a building which is to be used by those who deny that faith, I think it necessary to trouble you with a few lines to show how unjust an impression your remarks are calculated to make.

" Now, nothing can be more manifest than the injustice of attributing to any community opinions, which, though possibly held by individuals professing to be its members, are directly opposed to the authorized doctrinal standards of the community itself, and to do so, certainly but ill-becomes any member of a church like our own, which retains within its pale, and even within its priesthood, persons professing almost every variety of doctrine from the Romanist to the Socinian. If your principle was to be fully carried out, surely no one could conscientiously build an Anglican church, as such a building would in all probability be used at one period or another by persons, who, though belonging to the same communion, might hold doctrines which he must consider to be little, if at all, short of heresy.

"Now the position of the Lutheran body is in this respect very similar to that of our own. Its authorized tenets have generally, I believe, been considered to differ but little from those of the church of England; indeed, where they chiefly differ, the Lutheran doctrines have generally been thought to approach nearer to those of the Roman-ists than do those of our own communion. On the other hand, however, there are many professed Lutherans, whose opinions are at direct variance with those of the body to which they belong: but are we to select the views of these persons, and lay them down as the doctrines of their church? The fact is, that the class of religionists of whom you speak, so far from being the genuine type of their church, are, I have every reason to believe, a small and constantly decreasing minority.

"Their doctrines (if such they may be called) are not indeed the genuine offspring of Germany at all, but had their origin in the philosophical and infidel spirit which gave rise to the French revo-lution; and I am happy to find that they are now, for the most part, confined to a section of the older ministers, and are almost universally repudiated by the younger members of the community.

"Of the actual doctrines of the Lutheran church it would be very much out of my place, were I indeed able to do so, to speak in detail. As re-gards those, however, to which you particularly refer, I may say, first, that wherever the confession of Augsburg has been adopted, instead of explain-ing away the doctrine of the Holy Trinity, that mystery has been held in exactly the same manner as it is by the church of Rome, and by our own church, and the three creeds have been retained in the form in which they are received by the Western Church in general.

"On the subject of the Sacraments, it is well known that they hold much stronger views than many of the English clergy. Their views on the Real Presence are too well known to need remark: and on the subject of Baptism they agree with our own church, according to the strongest interpretation of its articles and offices. Luther, for instance, makes such observations on the subject as the following:—'The laver of regeneration is one that not superficially washes the skin and changes man bodily, but converts his whole nature, changing it into another, so that the first birth from the flesh is destroyed, with all the inheritance of sin and damnation.' Again he says, 'This (that is, the old man) must be put off with all its deeds; so that, being the children of Adam, we may be made the children of God. This is not done by a change of clothing, or by any laws or works, but by a *renascence* and a renovation which takes place in baptism.' Again, 'Those who extenuate the majesty of baptism speak wickedly and impiously. St. Paul, on the contrary, adorns baptism with magnificent titles, calling it the washing of *regeneration*.' Again he speaks of the fanaticism of those who speak of baptism as a mere mark, and adds that as many as have been baptized have taken, beyond the law, a *new nativity*, which was effected in baptism. Surely no one, whatever his opinion may be on this subject, can call this ' scoffing at regeneration:' and even Dr. Pusey, who is certainly not preju-

diced in favour of the German reformers, speaks
with satisfaction of their retaining the ancient
doctrine of baptism, and of the clearness of their
perceptions on the subject. If we view the
Lutheran community in the spirit of ecclesiologists,
we shall not, I think, deny them a large share of
praise as having preserved more of the ancient
fittings of their churches than any other, not
excepting the Romanists, and certainly not ourselves.

"Mr. Pugin remarks upon this in one of his
works, stating that he could, when first entering
an ancient Lutheran church, hardly perceive that
it was in the hands of Protestants; and again, in
his 'Glossary,' under the head of 'Tabernacle,'
he speaks of the fine preservation of one, and the
existence of several others in churches which are
in the hands of Lutherans, but of the demolition
of that in Cologne Cathedral, and the probable
destruction of that at Louvain by the Romanists.
Indeed, it is to churches which are 'occupied by
the Lutherans' that we must look for examples of
the movable fittings of mediæval churches. While,
for instance, one party in our own church is searching, with but little success, for ancient stone altars;
and another is much more successfully seeking for
judgments against new ones, the Lutherans quietly
and universally retain and use their ancient stone
high altars, and even the minor altars which are
not used are still preserved, so that most of their
large churches contain more specimens of ancient
altars than our reformers have allowed to remain
in our whole island. I know, for instance, a single
Lutheran church which contains upwards of thirty

of them. But it is not alone the altars which they have retained, but almost every accompaniment of the altar : such, for instance, as the magnificent triptychs, gorgeously decorated with paintings and imagery, which retain their places not only over the high altars, but in many instances even over the small and disused altars in other parts of the churches. Many of these are of the most magnificent description and in perfect preservation, and several of them are frequently to be found in a single church.

"Again, every high altar retains its ancient candlesticks, not for ornament only, but for almost daily use. The magnificent tabernacle, a feature almost unknown in England, still stands by the side of the altar, or forms a recess with richly-decorated doors in the wall near to it. Figures of the Blessed Virgin, of exquisite loveliness, still occupy the niches. The rood-lofts often remain decorated with splendid sculpture, or with panels filled by most beautiful paintings of saints, or other Catholic subjects. Above, very frequently, hangs the rood itself, never having been removed, as in England, from its place. Pendant lights, both for lamps and candles, often containing beautiful niches and figures, still hang from the vaultings, and ancient brass candlesticks are still attached to the walls ; paintings, needlework, and, indeed, every kind of decoration are frequently to be met with, such as we retain hardly a remnant of. They have, indeed, not only preserved what is ancient ; but, at periods subsequent to the Reformation, have added multitudes of new decorations, particularly paintings of Scriptural subjects, often in vast numbers, though of course partaking of the general decay of art common to the period; but still showing that the fanatical dread of such decorations was unknown among them, and a feeling that the 'teaching of the Church' should be displayed upon its walls. In the present instance there has been, as you state, a dispute as to the proper style to be adopted for a church: one party favouring, not as you say, a pagan temple; but the style of the Romanesque period in Italy, and the other the German style of the thirteenth century. The latter having prevailed, it is only common justice, after the manner in which you have thought proper to speak of them, to inquire a little into the grounds which have led them to this determination; and, for this purpose, I cannot do better than refer to one of the pamphlets which has been published on the subject, and you will find that the author treats the matter precisely on the same principle as you would do yourselves, and carries out the details of christian symbolism in a spirit which you could not but approve, though you might not go with him in all his details.

"After treating at great length on the unsuitableness of all other styles for a christian church, he proceeds to lay down this general axiom, that 'The outward building of stone should present an image of the spiritual Church of Christ,' and after some interesting remarks upon the spiritual edifice—particularly on the threefold grace of Light and Life and Love, imparted by Christ to his Church—and also on the promise of Christ to be present with it in the Sacraments, and in the preaching of the Word, and in prayer, he proceeds, 'The place now for the assembling of Christians for the public worship of God is the material church, this as a work of the christian congregation which is itself imbued with the Life of Love in the Light of the Gospel ; and must, in conformity therewith, bear witness to the same threefold grace.   The outward fabric must itself present an image of the Light and Life and Love which are the essential characteristics of the Christian Church.   Does not the Apostle say of the christian congregation, "Ye are the temple of the living God, as God hath said, I will dwell in them and walk in them."   Thus will we also demand of the house of the congregation, that as a christian edifice it may present itself as a temple of the living God, in which the Spirit of God may dwell and walk.'

   " He then states that such a work have our fathers achieved, ' or much rather,' he adds, ' may we say, has the Spirit of God itself erected ;' and that 'in the same spirit in which the Apostle says, " Ye also, as living stones, are built up a spiritual house," have also our fathers breathed into the inanimate stones a new life, and built them up into a spiritual house of God ; so, therefore, may we justly say of such a building, as the Apostle Paul did of the Christian Church itself : " Ye are God's building, and are built upon the foundation of the Apostles and Prophets, Jesus Christ Himself being the chief corner-stone, in whom all the building, fitly framed together, groweth into an holy temple in the Lord." '

"He next proceeds to give a general outline of the manner in which the symbolism of church architecture is expressed, commencing with the prevalence of the cross from the very foundation of the church, to the heaven-aspiring points of its steeples. The frequent use of the cross as the form of the massive foundation of the church, he considers to be an emblem of the Rock upon which the Church is built ; and, from thence, he carries out the principle, not only where it is palpably intended, but even through the details of the architecture, where, though the intention is not evident, the principle of the cross is constantly recurring.

"He then adverts to the prevailing upward tendency of every feature in a Gothic building, following it out from the lower features to the 'steeple, which, with the glance of the eye, draws also the heart unchecked to the cross above, and seems as the leader of the choir to exclaim, ' sursum corda ;' and to hear from the whole congregation of pinnacles around the echo, ' habemus ad Dominum.'

"He speaks of the clustered pillars as emblems of brotherly love, each helping to bear the other's burden, and each assisting the other in its upward striving, till all meet in the heaven's vault above. ' As the aim of all is the vault of heaven, so the soul of all is the free spirit of love—nothing servile is to be seen, no architrave checks with its oppressive burden the upward striving, everything, it is true, bears and serves, but it is the service of free love.'

"It is needless to go through the details, but

they all show the same general spirit and intention. I will, however, quote a few passages to
illustrate the spirit of the writer more fully. After
remarking that the symbolical allusions of Gothic
architecture may be traced through a thousand
features, but all in unison with the whole, and all
bearing witness to the same spirit: 'But the
festive garment and ornament is first put upon
such a building by the hand of sculpture and
painting. As the christian spirit strives to em-
brace and to penetrate all spheres of life, so the
Gothic building draws all arts into its service.
The christian church has become what it is in the
course of the historical developement of the kingdom of God upon earth. This historical developement then, together with all the branches of the
earthly creation, are presented in a Gothic church,
and more particularly in statues, reliefs, paintings
&c. There we see the whole creation, from the
beginning to the last day, Moses and the Prophets
and the Kings of the Old Testament. The
holiest place is occupied by the Lord of Lords,
the King of Kings, and around Him are the
Apostles and Evangelists; more distant are the
martyrs and fathers of the church to the latest
period, with the representatives of the worldly,
but protecting power, emperors, kings, and princes.'
He then shows how every kingdom of nature is
made to bear its part in symbolizing the kingdom
of grace, and he adds—'The richest fulness of
sculpture abounds in the wide portals, as if in-
vitingly pointing towards rich and blissful treasures of the Spirit which are contained in the interior of the building. The revelation of God is

most evidently set forth in a Gothic minster, &c., &c.'

" He closes this branch of his subject by remarking that the same system may be carried out in many other ways ; 'for as the spirit of christianity is a living one, the symbolization of christian art must be infinitely various.'

' I will only notice one other point, which is the earnest manner in which this writer urges the position of the font near the entrance of the church. 'Here placed,' says he, 'it reminds and admonishes each person, on his entrance, of his baptismal vow, which he has once solemnly confirmed, as bound in covenant with his Lord and God. There in the sight of the pulpit, and in the direction towards the altar, ought the font to stand, that here it may hold our sight directed, both to the word of the gospel and to the sacrament of the altar, that by means of these, we may obtain that forgiveness which, through the journey of life from our baptism to the partaking of the altar of the Lord, we so continually stand in need of.

" ' The whole course of the christian's life lies between the sacrament of baptism and that of the altar. As he receives baptism at the entrance of life, so would he desire at his exit from the same to receive the Lord's Supper as the latest Viaticum. The font, therefore, should take its place at the beginning, as the altar at the termination, of the whole building.'

" I will add but one more quotation. 'Without pious faith, without warm love, and a heartfelt devotedness, never, and nowhere, was anything truly great or holy accomplished. Such a living faith is, however, not an exclusive privilege of (Roman)[2] catholicism. Do we protestants, therefore, at the present day wish to erect houses of God as great and noble as those of our fathers? then must we build up ourselves onwards and onwards, as living stones into a spiritual house, a temple of the living God. Unless endued with life and light from above, we cannot perceive the sacred glory which beams around Gothic architecture. Without these our heart remains dead, a cold rock against the floods of faith and of love; but by means of these the stone having received life, bears a mightily convincing witness that of these stones God has raised up children to Himself.'

"Such have been the arguments, and such the tone of feeling, which have led the citizens of Hamburg to select, as you say, the style of a 'Gothic cathedral,' rather than that of a pagan temple.

"Now, let me ask, are persons capable of such sentiments, to be treated as heathen men or as infidels, and to be denied the very externals even of christianity? Much rather, should we not rejoice to find among them such warmth of feeling, and such depth of sentiment, backed as it is by a noble liberality, which it would be well for us, if we had more of amongst ourselves, and which, considering the awful calamity from which they are but just recovering, reflects the greatest credit upon their christian feeling. Lastly, may we not fairly hope that the practical carrying out of such

[2] The word "Roman" is not in the original; it was inserted by my father.—ED.

L

sentiments may be made a means of stirring them up to still more elevated zeal, and leading them to restore that ancient discipline, which has been of late years but too much neglected, and to remedy all those evils which we, as members of the church of England, cannot but deplore ?

"I am, sir,

"Your obedient servant,

"GEORGE GILBERT SCOTT.

"July 30th, 1845."

The next year, I visited the Saxon Switzerland in search of stone quarries, and went on to Prague. Indeed from that time, I was in Germany nearly every year, though as yet, I remained ignorant of France.

In the autumn of 1847, while at the lakes with .Mrs. Scott, I received intelligence of my appointment as architect to the refitting, &c., of Ely Cathedral, which opened out before me a new field. It was from the excitement produced in my mind by Dean Peacock's description of Amiens Cathedral, which he had visited that autumn, that I was led, as late as the end of November, to make a short run over to France, chiefly to Amiens and Paris.

My eyes were at once opened. What I had always conceived to be German architecture I now found to be French. I thoroughly studied the details of Amiens, and those of the Sainte Chapelle, which bore most closely on my previous German studies, and I returned home with a wholly new set of ideas, and with many of my old ones dispelled. It seems curious that I should have been twelve years in practice, before I became acquainted with French architecture, yet I was the first among English architects, as I believe, to study it in detail in any practical way, and with a practical intention. In 1848, the *annus mirabilis,* my tour was from Hamburg to Bamberg, Nuremberg, Strasburg, Freyburg, and Oppenheim. So deserted was the continent by Englishmen that year, that I travelled ten days without seeing one, or hearing our language spoken. I was at Frankfort at the time of the German Parliament, when I spent a Sunday afternoon in writing a letter to my friend Reichensperger, who was a member of it, on the necessity of founding the revived German Empire on a basis of religion. I remember saying that the old empire had been so based, and had stood a thousand years, and that if the new one were not so, it would inevitably fail.

The next morning I went (by appointment with him) to see the sitting of the parliament. I found them in a state of perfect uproar and confusion, and with difficulty learned, that it was owing to having just received intelligence that Prussia had signed an armistice with the Danes without asking their leave. A fortnight later this turmoil culminated in the murder of several of the members, and the overthrow of the attempted revival of the Holy Roman Empire. Among the friends of this period, I may mention Herr Reichensperger, M. Gerente sen., Herr Zwirner, Dean Buckland, and Lord John Thynne.

The most important works to be noted since 1845,[3] are the following :—Bradfield Church ;

[3] Up to the year 1862, or thereabouts.—ED.

Worsley Church, which was begun when I was in partnership with Mr. Moffatt ; St. Mary's, Nottingham, which was finished by him ; Watermore, near Cirencester ; Weeton, near Harewood ; Bilton, near Harrowgate ; Aithington House, Yorkshire ; the restoration of the churches of Aylesbury, Newark, and Nantwich, and the designs for the Cathedral of St. John, Newfoundland. Also new churches at West Derby, Liverpool ; Holbeck, near Leeds (a special work); Sewerby, near Bridlington, where difficulties arose from the fads of my employer ; the restoration of Ellesmere church, and the rebuilding of St. George's, Doncaster ; additions to Exeter College, Oxford, and the new chapel there ; the new churches at Haley Hill, Halifax, and on Ranmore Common, near Dorking. Then followed the competition for the Rathhaus at Hamburg, and that for the Government offices in Whitehall ; the restoration of Hereford, Lichfield, Salisbury, and Ripon Cathedrals. Of civil and domestic buildings, I will here mention the houses in Broad Sanctuary, Westminster ; Mr. Forman's house at Dorking ; Mr. Manners Sutton's, near Newark ; Sir Charles Mordaunt's, Walton Hall, Warwick ; and Mr. Sandbach's, near Llanwrst ; the Town Hall at Halifax, which came to nothing ; the Town Hall at Preston, and Brighton College. And I also carried out several semi-classic works, among which I will name the chapel at Hawkstone ; the remodelling of St. Michael's, Cornhill ; Partis College, and the chapel of King's College, London.

In 1848 I read the first paper I had written for

a public meeting, excepting, by-the-bye, one on the origin of the stone of which Stonehenge is composed, written about 1836, for the then existing Architectural Society, but which I could not muster courage to bring forward.

My paper was on the truthful restoration of ancient churches, and it was read before the architectural and archæological society of the county of Bucks, at Aylesbury. It was a somewhat impassioned protest against the destructiveness of the prevailing restorations, and was preceded by an address from the Bishop of Oxford (Dr. Wilberforce), in which (probably to propitiate some low-church dons), he took almost the contrary line, inveighing against popish arrangements, &c., &c. I was so irate at his paper that my natural timidity vanished, and I gave double emphasis to all I had written.

The bishop, however, had the better of me, for a rood-loft in the neighbouring church of Wing, which I had been for some time defending against threatened destruction, was forthwith pulled down, asking no more questions, and the bishop's address was appealed to as the authoritiy. I cannot resist a wicked joke apropos to this case, which had been made shortly before in the same town. I had been called in to report on the central tower of the church, and had found it to be very dangerous. At a dinner to which I was invited on this occasion, an obtuse old cleric wisely remarked, " What a mercy it was that the tower did not fall during the bishop's visitation." " Not at all," replied a witty barrister, " not at all, I'd match Sam to dodge a falling church with any man," and reverence for the episcopal bench did not prevent a general burst of laughter, excepting perhaps from the excellent cleric. While upon Aylesbury, I must tell a good joke of another kind. It happened that the vicar had been long annoyed by the church clock striking twelve while he was reading the communion service, and that very week the sexton had completed an ingenious contrivance to prevent the disturbance. His scheme was to fasten the clapper up, by pulling a wire which reached down into the church, and which, when in action, he fixed to a hook which he had driven into a pew beneath the tower. When the hour of trial came, the clock made violent spasmodic efforts to strike twelve, and at every abortive stroke, it lifted up the corner of the crazy old pew, and let it down again. The congregation, fresh from the alarm caused by my report, came to the instinctive conclusion that the tower was coming down, and, emulous of the character given to their diocesan, rushed from the supposed falling church *en masse*.

My paper was repeated at Higham Ferrers, before the Northamptonshire and Bedfordshire societies, and I published it in 1850, accompanied by a number of fragmentary scribblings—a person who appears in print for the first time, having usually a number of miscellaneous arrears to provide for. It was dedicated to good Dean Peacock, whose friendship had become one of my greatest sources of pleasure.

As I have since become a confirmed scribbler, and, as I believe, I have more reason to be satisfied with the papers I have written in the way of

business than with those written later for public
reading, I will refer to a few reports which may
be of interest, although some are already named.[4]

My first report on St. Mary, Stafford, and the
correspondence with Mr. Petit on the same
church; my report on the chapel upon the bridge
at Wakefield; on Ely Cathedral; on St. Peter's
and St. Sepulchre's churches, Northampton, in the
papers read before the society there; a report on
Westminster Abbey made for Mr. Gladstone
about 1855 or '56; reports on several cathedrals,
Hereford, Salisbury, Worcester, Ripon, &c.; and
one, on the royal tombs (though I do not now
agree to its recommendations); on Gloucester,
Lichfield, and St. David's cathedrals, several reports; on the priory churches at Brecon, and
many others. See also four lectures read at the
Architectural Museum, five at the Academy, one at
Leeds, and one at Doncaster (a paper on Old Doncaster church); two papers read at the Institute of
British architects, and one before the Architectural
association. See also an early letter to the Ecclesiologist about St. Stephen's Chapel, a subject on
which I had got up a great agitation.

In 1849 I was, wholly unexpectedly, appointed
architect to Westminster Abbey; the appointment
having just been resigned by Mr. Blore. This
was a great and lasting source of delight. I at
once commenced a careful investigation of its
antiquities, which I have followed up ever since,
and the results of which I have frequently communicated *vivâ voce* to meetings of societies, &c.,

---

[4] It is hoped to publish in a collected form the most important
papers, reports, &c., of the character here referred to. — ED.

on the spot, and, more recently, in a written form. I also devoted much time to the similar investigation of the Chapter-house, the results of which I have frequently exhibited.

My communications in the early period of my appointment were chiefly with the Dean, Dr. Buckland, though also with Lord John Thynne, the Sub-Dean. Dr. Buckland was excessively jovial and amusing, though it was clear that he was wearing himself out by his desultory, though indefatigable, way of attending to business. No one was denied him, on whatever subject he called. I have known him, after seeing people at the Deanery for hours together, on every imaginable subject—practical, scientific, and visionary—run up to the roof of the Abbey with me; and, after scampering over every part, suddenly recollect that he had had no breakfast, although he had come from Islip, and it was two o'clock. Could it be wondered that his mind should give way under such a regimen?

His last sermon was on the occasion of the thanksgiving for the cessation of the cholera, and his text was, " If the prophet had bid thee do some great thing, wouldest thou not have done it? How much rather then, when he saith unto thee, Wash, and be clean." In the course of the sermon he quoted the seventeenth article, as against our poor, that they had given themselves up to " wretchlessness of most unclean living."

Under Dr. Buckland I restored to its place the beautiful iron grille to Queen Eleanor's monument, which had been removed in 1823; I also restored the grille of the tomb of King Henry

Vth, which had been broken up into a thousand pieces, and lay scattered in "the Old Revestry." We also newly capped a great number of the flying buttresses, and completed the eastern pinnacles.

During the long period of the poor Dean's illness, Lord John Thynne most ably filled his place, and considerable works were carried on. Among others, I may mention the new choir-pulpit; the enclosure of the choir from the transepts, which had been left open when the choir had been refitted under Blore; the iron sanctuary screen and altar-rail; some ameliorations in the lantern above; the stained glass in the south clerestory of the choir, and in the north transept; also the re-opening of the ancient entrance to the dormitory (now the library); and the completion of the vaulting of the vestibule to the Chapter-house, which had lost two bays, and one half of which was walled off. I also introduced the use of a solution of shell-lac, with which we have gone on gradually indurating all the internal surfaces. This was first applied to the royal tombs, and promises to stereotype the work in its present condition for an indefinite time.[5] Other extensive practical repairs have also been effected.

During this time the new houses and gatehouse in Broad Sanctuary were erected, under an act

---

[5] This process, which has proved perfectly successful in the interior of the Abbey Church, was tried as an experiment in the bay of the cloister which aligns with the entrance of the Chapter-house. As to its success in this case, under conditions intermediate between those of external and internal architecture, I am myself very doubtful.

of parliament for the improvement of this part of Westminster.

My communications with Lord John Thynne have always been of the most agreeable kind, and I believe I may number him among my best friends. Through him I have had works placed in my hands by the Duke of Buccleuch, and the Earls of Cawdor and Harewood, besides others.

The Abbey to me has been a never-failing source of interest, though sometimes of annoyance, owing to the little appreciation which exists of the value of the remains of the ancient monastic buildings, and the necessity in some instances of destroying objects of antiquity in order to comply with pressing practical wants. On the whole, however, I have done much to preserve and bring to view such objects. I refer to my published paper, called "Gleanings from Westminster Abbey," as containing notices of the majority of these discoveries. About 1854 I was requested to make a formal report to the Sub-Dean (with a view to its being forwarded to Mr. Gladstone) on the general state of the Abbey. I do not think I have a copy of this, but it ought to be preserved as a public document of some interest and value. The nave pulpit is a recent work for which the funds were mainly provided by Sir Walter James.

The name of James reminds me of my most talented and excellent friend, the Rev. Thomas James, whose death we have had very recently to deplore. I made his acquaintance about 1846 in Northamptonshire, when he was one of the secre-

taries to the Architectural Society. His knowledge and judgment in all matters relating to
church antiquities were of a high order, and he
was for some twenty years the life and soul of
that, the best of the local societies. This society
has counted among its active members, besides
Mr. James, the Rev. Ayliff Poole, Rev. E. Hartshorne, E. A. Freeman, Esq., the Rev. Lord
Alwyne Compton, and other excellent ecclesiologists and antiquaries. Mr. James was a most
amiable and zealous man, and an excellent writer.
He wrote many articles for the *Quarterly Review*,
amongst others one on Northamptonshire. He
has been one of my best friends for some eighteen
years. He died of a cancer in the liver this last
autumn, 1863, at about fifty-two or three years
of age.

In 1848 my friend, the Rev. Thomas Stevens,
commenced the restoration, or rather the partial
rebuilding and enlargement, of his church at
Bradfield, which had been in contemplation
some ten years previously. Though executed
so long since, I still view it as one of my best
works. Mr. Stevens is a man of very strong
views and will, a detester of everything weak,
mean, or unmanly. As a natural consequence
of this disposition, he took a very determined
liking to the transitional, or what we usually called
the "square abacus" style. In this preference,
as a matter of taste, I strongly concurred, though,
as a matter of theory, I held with the use of the
early decorated as the point of highest perfection
in the style generally. I elaborately discussed
the question, shortly after this date, in a paper

attached to my " Plea for the faithful restoration
of ancient churches," from which it will be seen
how I hung back upon the "square abacus"
variety.   Many were the friendly and jocose dis-
putations we had on the point.   I was always
willing to be beaten, as this gave me an excuse
for using a favourite, though, as I thought, not
theoretically correct style.   Mr. Stevens got to
employ the term "square abacus" as a moral
adjective, used in the sense of manly, straight-
forward, real, honest, and all cognate epithets,
and "round abacus" for what was milder, "ogee"
being used in the sense of mean, weak, dis-
honest, &c.   This drilling probably made me
ready at a later time to fall in with the French
system of using the square abacus irrespective
of date or of other details.   At an intermediate
period I made use of the transitional style, using
it in conjunction with tracery, and with a certain
amount of natural foliage (without reference to
French types) as a fair developement on eclectic
principles.   The period over which the work at
Bradfield church extended was a time of great
pleasure, owing to my constant and most friendly
communication with Mr. Stevens.   He is perhaps
the most valued friend I have had, a thoroughly
staunch, firm character, a thorough man of
business, of undaunted courage and determination, and a strenuous follower out of whatever
he undertook.   Some years later he founded, in
connexion with the church of Bradfield, St. Andrew's College, a school which has had a wonderful run of success, owing to Mr. Stevens' admirable
and courageous management of it.   Of the build-

ings of the college I do not claim to be the architect; it was not built out of hand, but grew of itself, bit by bit, as it was wanted, each part being planned by Mr. Stevens, helped a little by myself or by my clerk, Mr. Richard Coad. The hall is the part I may chiefly claim as my own.[6]

A direct result of my connexion with the college was my appointment as architect to the new church in the Isle of Alderney, its founder, the Rev. J. Le Mesurier, having resided at Bradfield. This church is also in the "square abacus" manner. I must say that this is still the style I, on the whole, most delight in, though it is no doubt in some respects imperfect, and I am inclined to think that, even relinquishing the Gallic mania, which has for so long had possession of our minds, a legitimate style may be generated by its union with later developements.

In 1851 I joined my friend, Mr. Benjamin Ferrey, in a short tour in Italy. We met at Berlin and proceeded by the Saxon Switzerland and Prague to Vienna. Here we gave a day to St. Stephen's, with which I was most agreeably surprised. We went, partly by rail, partly by diligence, to Trieste, and thence by steamer to Venice.

My special recollections of this early part of my journey are first, the affected delight of the hotel-keeper at Berlin at seeing me; my vanity accepted it (inwardly) as a tribute to the architect of St. Nicholas at Hamburg, but, unluckily for

---

[6] The stained glass in its western windows is one of the earliest works in this material designed by Mr. E. Burne Jones.—ED.

my self-love, he proceeded to tell me that I was
the greatest of English poets; and I found that
he took me, or pretended to do so, for Sir Walter
Scott.   The next is Ferrey's depression of spirits
at the dulness of the country in north Germany,
and his sudden delight at reaching the Saxon
Switzerland.   He seemed as if he would jump
out of the carriage window.   We were amused,
in passing through the suburbs of Dresden, to see
a well-known incumbent of Westminster, in plaid
trousers, black tie, and a wide-a-wake, sitting
swinging his legs on a balk of timber by the road-
side, smoking a cigar.   Oh, tell it not in Westminster!   The fourth incident related to Ferrey's
own wide-awake, which persisted in blowing off his
head, while crossing the Simmering pass outside a
droschky, which at length threw the Styrian driver
into such convulsions of laughter that he fell off
the carriage, but cat-like came down on his legs.

In crossing the Adriatic, I was delighted at the
first evidence of a southern climate, in the vast
tunny fish, which followed our course, ever and
anon leaping far out of the water, and pursuing us
again as swiftly as before.

At Venice, all was enchantment!   No three
days of my life afford me such rich archæological
and art recollections.   We both worked hard,
and did much.   I here met Ruskin, whom I
knew before, and we spent a most delightful
evening with him.   On this occasion I made
the acquaintance of my valued and now lamented
friend, Sir Francis Scott, whose friendship I kept
up until his premature demise last autumn, 1863.
At Venice I also made three other valuable

acquaintances, Mr. Gambier Parry, of Highnam
Court, David Roberts, and Mr. E. W. Cooke.
We urged Roberts to take Vienna on his way
home, which gave rise to two noble pictures
of the interior of St. Stephen's. My impressions of St. Mark's were stronger than I can
describe. I considered it, and still continue to do
so, the most impressive interior I have ever seen.
The Venetian Gothic, excepting the ducal palace,
disappointed me at first, but by degrees it grew
upon me greatly. Ferrey was enraged at it, and
I could continually hear him muttering the words,
"Batty Langley," when he heard it spoken favourably of. We both, however, joined heart and soul
in our devotion to the ducal palace, and spent
much time in sketching its details. The Byzantine
palaces also attracted my attention a good deal,
especially the Fondaco dei Turchi. Unhappily
want of time led us to leave Torcello and Murano
unvisited.

From Venice we went to Padua. Early in the
morning I looked out into the twilight to see if
anything in our line was visible, when what was
my delight to see a splendid Gothic domestic ruin
close behind our hotel, and what my disgust at its
soon turning out to be a sham, painted upon the
back wall of the yard. I called Ferrey and played
off the trick successfully on him, and was next day
paid off by him in kind at Vicenza.

We worked tremendously hard at St. Antonio,
and at the Arena chapel, and great was our delight
in both. The next day we went to Vicenza and
Verona. The latter place charmed us beyond
measure, and we worked very hard for a day and

a half, and thence proceeded to Mantua, where
among other things I made precisely the same
sketch of the tower of the cathedral which Street
made the next year. I had done the very same
by the tower of St. Zeno at Verona. From
Mantua we went by Modena to Bologna. I
ought to have mentioned that we met with Anthony Salvin the younger, who accompanied us
and interpreted for us. Ferrey and I tried a little
speculative Italian on our own account at Bologna,
asking an elderly gentleman of benignant aspect
where we should find the church of San Stefano.
He, seeing that we had exhausted our knowledge
in the question, made no reply, but, taking one of us
by the button, he led us silently through two or
three streets, and, conducting us into the very
middle of the church, shook hands with us both in
dumb show, and departed. San Petronio struck
us much by its vast proportions and wonderful use
of brick, though this is internally concealed by
whitewash. From Bologna we proceeded to Florence. Again we had three days of the purest
delight. I worked violently to the last day,
timing myself strictly to the work I was to do
every hour of the day ; and at last, to my intense
disgust and dismay, forgot San Miniato. Next to
my three Venice days, these at Florence occupy
the choicest corner of my art recollection.

Thence we went to Sienna, and had the hardest
three hours' work in my life, and the pleasantest.
It was really too bad to hurry in such a manner,
but Ferrey was in fits at the idea of crossing the
Alps in the snow, and we had reached the end of
October. We spent one working day and a Sun-

day at Pisa, again with unalloyed delight, and
again worked hard and got through much. Here
we met with a young English architect, who had
the happy knack of giving offence to the police
authorities, and great was our dread of the effects
of his conversation, as overheard by the Austrian
officers, who crowded every café. We escaped,
though we afterwards found that our friend had
been arrested at Verona for sketching the fortifications. I had encountered Austrian soldiers
throughout nearly the whole of my journey; even
Hamburg that year was garrisoned by Austrians,
and from Saxony to Tuscany they were continuous. We were greatly struck by their fine
persons and equipments; but when Ferrey, as we
were crossing from Trieste to Venice, was describing them ecstatically to an old English officer just
returned from India, the reply he received was,—
"Aye, but if they ever go to war with the French,
you'll see how the French will walk into them,"
—and so we have seen, eight years later.

I am hurrying over the architectural part of our
tour, but to go into particulars would be endless,
and the buildings are too well known to need it.
We were, suffice it to say, delighted, and worked
as hard as men could do from morning to night.
We usually breakfasted by twilight, to get every
hour of the day for hard work. I only regret that
we were so chary of our time, and did not stay
longer.

We went from Pisa to Genoa, and the snow
had already come, and had covered the Carrara
mountains most gloriously. I shall never forget
looking back upon them as we walked up the hill

M

at Spezzia in the morning, and seeing them again radiant in fiery glory in the last rays of the setting sun. I never saw, nor since have seen, anything more magnificently splendid. In a few minutes it had vanished into cold grey.

Of Genoa my recollections are of chilling cold, warmed only by my enthusiastic delight in the western portion of the cathedral, both within and without. I have written my impressions of this in a paper given in the appendix to my work on "Domestic Architecture." It is the best Gothic architecture I saw in Italy, and I am convinced it is the work of a French architect, or of an Italian fresh from France, though it is carried out in more than all the exuberance of coloured material peculiar to Italian art.[7]

The fear of snow led us to pass through Pavia without stopping, and to spend but a day at Milan. Haste, alas! without good speed, for the snow overtook us at Como, and we had to cross the Alps after all, through six feet of snow, and in sledges (i. e. deal boxes nailed on ash poles) with some twenty men to dig a way for us, and nothing to be seen but snow and fog.

In going by diligence from Como to the pass, one of our horses jumped over a precipice. I was asleep at the time, but Ferrey, who saw it, woke me up in dismay. Happily the traces had broken

[7] This work should be compared with the north and south portals of the west front of the cathedral of Rouen. A comparison of the two works leads to the conclusion that both were executed by the same artist, or guild of artists, and that the originators of both were not Italians, but northern Frenchmen. — Ed.

and let him go, but a tree caught him, and we drew him up again by ropes.

On our return (which was all in the fog) we looked in at Freiburg, in Breisgau (which I had seen three years before), and were much charmed. We were shown over by an old acquaintance of mine, the commissionaire whose quaint English books and letters had before amused me, and whose worthiness had interested me in him.

On our journey home we made the acquaintance of, I believe, a nobleman from the neighbourhood of Leghorn. He was going to London, and thence to Paris. He was a most conversational man, and not afraid to proclaim himself to be one of the most timid of his race. His greatest dread was lest there should be an *émeute* during his stay at Paris. He called on Ferrey and myself in London "*pour prendre congé,*" and set off for Paris, where, on the very morning after his arrival, occurred the celebrated "*coup d'état.*" We heard of him no more.

In spite of all the violence now indulged in, against every lesson learned south of the Alps, I must say that I gained very much by this journey, and much desire to repeat it. I was convinced, however, that Italian Gothic, as such, must not be used in England, but I was equally convinced, and am so still, that the study of it is necessary to the perfecting of our revival, and I have detailed my impressions on this head in the paper already referred to. What, however, with the folly, on the one hand, of men who adopt Italian Gothic, with all its purely local peculiarities, and, on the other, of those who, from a mere rabid

and unintelligent prejudice, condemn unheard any
one who thinks that any practical hint can be imported from Italy, one is compelled to abstain from
making much use of any lessons one has learned
there. I trust this double folly will in time be
outgrown.

This year the Great Exhibition had taken up
much of my attention. I had had a model prepared of the church at Hamburg, which occupied
a very conspicuous place in the nave ; perhaps the
finest of Mr. Salter's models.

I had also a restoration prepared of one end of
the monument of Queen Philippa. This had taken
a very long time to work out by the most careful
study of the original. I had during the previous
summer been constantly giving snatches of time to
it, and as the niche work was all gone, excepting
some detached fragments preserved in the Abbey,
and the parts immured in the adjacent monument
of Henry V., I had obtained leave to make inci-
sions into the base of that tomb, by which means I
brought to light the whole design, including two
niche-figures and one exquisite little angel, one
of the many which adorned the tabernacle-work.
I had to work at this by the help of candles and
looking-glasses. When engaged one day with
Mr. Cundy, the Abbey mason, on this work, the
thought suddenly occurred to me that some of the
lost portions might have found their way into the
Cottingham Museum. I suggested this to Mr.
Cundy, and as that collection was at the time for
sale, he went and searched, and at length found
one of the large canopies and other fragments on
the chimney-piece of Mr. Cottingham's office.

After some months they were recovered, and all (with the fragments before mentioned) refixed in their places. It was said that Mr. Cottingham had bought them, thirty-five years earlier, from the Abbey mason. The restoration of the end was executed by Mr. Cundy, mainly at his own cost. The figures were by Mr. Philip, and the coloured decorations by Mr. Willement. It is now in the South Kensington collection, and is the property of the architectural museum.[8]

I had some other things in this exhibition, but my great interest was in Pugin's court. The last time I saw him was there, on the occasion of the opening. How little did I think how soon that burning light was to be extinguished! Had I known this, how anxiously should I have striven for more intimate acquaintance!

During this year, Mr. Cottingham's museum being for sale, I wrote a letter in the *Builder*, urging its purchase by the Government, as the nucleus of a collection of mediæval specimens for the use of carvers and others. This was without avail, but it originated the architectural museum. I had a call, in consequence of my letter, from a strange person, Mr. Bruce Allen, who told me that he had long had a plan of the same kind in connexion with a school of art for art workmen. After my return from Italy he pressed the matter, and invited to a meeting a number of architects, to whom he proposed his scheme, chiefly for the school of art. After several meetings, it was determined to establish an architectural museum, and to allow

[8] It is now in the architectural museum in Westminster.—ED.

Mr. Allen to carry on his school of art as a private speculation of his own within the museum, to which he was to be curator. The matter went on but sleepily for some months, when I determined to take it into my own hands, and nail my flag to the mast. I accordingly wrote private letters, and sent circulars to every one I could possibly think of, begging both annual subscriptions and donations to a special fund for starting the collection. The labour I gave to it was immense; I called on all such people as seemed to need it, and frequently over and over again. The number of times I wrote and called on Mr. Blore, without getting in reply one word or one penny, was amazing. Street discouraged it, as tending to copyism. Butterfield gave very cold support. Poor Pugin was just laid by. I nevertheless obtained liberal support, got up a good list of annual subscribers, and some 500*l.* in donations. Specimens poured in from all quarters (not always good ones); I lent nearly the whole of my large collection, and employed agents and workmen all over the country to get new casts. M. Gerente acted as my agent in France, and he got us an excellent lot of casts. Later on Ruskin gave, or lent us, his whole collection of Venetian casts, and some very fine French ones. Much of Cottingham's museum came to us, and before long we had formed a very wonderful collection.

We had taken a very extensive and most quaint loft, in a wharf at Cannon Row, Westminster, which we soon completely filled. There we used to have lectures in the midst of our specimens. There Ruskin has poured forth his most telling eloquence. There we held annual conversaziones, when 500 or 600 persons were presided over in the cock-loft by the prince-like Earl de Grey, and were addressed often by some of the first men in the country ; but, above all, here were our carvers taught their art from the best ancient models, and our students acquired a degree of skill and taste in the drawing of architectural ornament which had never before been reached, nor has (since the removal of the museum) been retained. These were the days of our pride, and I confess I even now feel a pardonable exultation when I call to remembrance the share I took in bringing about such noble results. No movement ever made in our day, had equalled this in its effects both upon workmen and students. Our cock-loft was the centre of their artistic study and improvement, and to myself and others engaged in the work it was a source of constant and almost daily delight and interest. During my journeys I was ever looking out for objects of art, whose representation might enrich our collection ; and even in the gardens, in the fields, or by the seaside, the very leaves and flowers seemed to connect themselves with our art-scheme, and to suggest plans for illustrating all such productions as would lend suggestions to art.

The vision was, however, soon clouded. Funds failed; I had allowed my enthusiasm to outrun our finances, and a heavy debt stared us in the face. We made an appeal for aid to the Prince Consort, and a deputation, consisting of Earl de Grey, Mr. Clutton (the Hon. Sec.), and myself, waited on his Royal Highness to

state our case.   He received us graciously, and
promised   and   gave   aid,   becoming   also   our
" patron."   He took occasion, however, to read
us a not very complimentary lecture on the state
of architectural education in this country, which
he described as contemptible in the extreme.   It
was clearly a *ricotto* of one of Mr. Cole's, being
the key to his own course in always employing
builders instead of architects.   There was much
truth in what he said, though the true result
should have been a strenuous movement to improve the artistic education of our profession,
rather than to employ in our stead, and cry up
as our superiors, builders and military engineers,
who make no pretence whatever to æsthetical
training.   I might, had dates coincided (of which
I am uncertain), have replied that, defective as
was the training of English architects, there
stood before his Royal Highness two of them,
who, having in three several instances accepted
invitations to compete in foreign countries with
architects from all Europe, and for buildings
of first-rate importance, had in each instance
carried off the first prizes, and that two of these
European competitions had been in his own
country, and the third in France, while in two
at least of them (one in each country), the highest
authorities had been consulted, or had taken part
in the decision.

   We were referred by the Prince to Mr. Cole
and Mr. Redgrave, who took up the case with
some favour, and met our committee to arrange
joint action.   The result was an annual subscription of 100*l.* (which they were not pledged to con-

tinue), on condition of the free admission of the
students of their school of art.   This lasted, however, but a single year, 1855.   South Kensington
was then but in embryo, and nothing could be
permitted elsewhere.   Accordingly, when we
applied in person for the continuance of the subscription, Mr. Cole told us that, their schools being
now about to be removed, our collection would
cease to be available to them, and the payment
must consequently cease.   He then delicately
suggested that if we were to change our *venue*,
and petition for a grant of space in their new
building, rent free, it might be favourably entertained, and we were shown on a plan of the
building a noble gallery which might be at our
service, with attendance, lighting, warming, &c.,
gratis,—"All these things will I give thee, if thou
wilt fall down and worship me."   The gallery
was to be fitted up for us, and the collection removed and re-arranged at the public cost.   Never,
in fact, was hook better baited for hungry fish.
The suggestion was laid before the committee.
There were those who, like Laocoon, suggested
fears of the Greeks, even when in so generous a
mood.   In fact, we all secretly felt that our fate
was sealed.   The Syren voice was understood,
but could not be resisted; stern poverty constrained
us to the shore.   Meanwhile, when they saw that
we nibbled, the bait was gradually and studiously
reduced.   Our wrath was great, but our poverty
was greater, and at last the compact was signed,
with the fullest consciousness that we were
doomed to be engulphed; I had written the word
before I recollected one of the epithets of Mr.

Cole, " the modern Ingulphus." It is now about
eight years since we removed to South Kensington,
and I can truly say that I have never felt any
satisfaction in the museum since. There followed
continual and systematic encroachment, the resistance of which was deemed a personal affront,
to be avenged by further encroachments, and, as
a climax at last, our refusal of some absurd proposal was made an excuse for our receiving notice
to quit, the joint consequence of our having *done*
the work we were invited for, and of their knowledge that, as we could never get other premises,
our collection was at their mercy. Our capitula-
tion and our making over the collection on loan
was followed by its removal and re-arrangement
without our leave or knowledge. All this, however, would be as nothing were it not that our
students were frightened away by distance and
red tape, and the beneficial effects of the collection
thus seriously reduced.

These annoying circumstances have been, I
confess, much mitigated by the noble collection
brought together under the same roof by the
department, and the first-rate art-library since
added to it, so that I am ready to condone all
past offences, and now recommend all art students
to lodge near South Kensington, and to avail
themselves of its unprecedented advantages for
the pursuit of their studies.

In 1853, the great parish church of St. George
at Doncaster was burned down. Ferrey had refitted the old church, and I thought that we should
be appointed joint architects, as he proposed, and
I was willing to accept, but, owing to some local

differences, this arrangement was negatived, and I was appointed singly.

I did all I could to bring them to what had been suggested by Ferrey, but in vain.

My first anxiety on undertaking this great work was to ascertain whether any part of the ruins could be worked up into the new church. I found this impossible. I then devoted my attention to the restoration, on paper, of the old church from its ruins and fragments, and in this I met with great success. Mr. Burlison stayed there several weeks and thoroughly overhauled everything. We traced out the whole history of the church, which we found to be a skeleton of transitional early english, gradually overlaid with different ages of perpendicular work.

I read a paper on the result of these investigations before the Oxford architectural society, which is published in Jackson's history of St. George's church.

The next question related to style. The tower was a noble work in early and bold perpendicular, and as its entire design had been recovered, I was anxious to reproduce it. The question then arose whether I ought to make the rest of the church coincide with it in style. Yorkshire contains much of the best early perpendicular, e. g. at York in the Minster, at Beverly Minster (in the east window and the west end), at Bridlington (in the west front), and at Howden (in the Chapter-house). I was well acquainted with all these of old, but I determined on a systematic revisiting of them with a view to forming a deliberate opinion. My conclusion was that, noble as these specimens are, and excellent as are their details, their great merits arise from their similarity to the preceding style, and that we had better adopt that earlier style at once, and, adopting it, take it at about its best stage, and, further, that there was no harm in accompanying this by a reproduction of the perpendicular tower.

The old church was insufficient in size for the wants of the parish, yet had acquired a part of its size by a disproportionate widening of its aisles. I could not of course reproduce this.[9]   I therefore increased the radical scale of the church, repro-portioning it with reference to its earlier form.   I found, however, that much greater length was necessary, and I wanted to add a bay to the length of the nave, but the Archbishop had spoken, and still spoke, so strongly against enlargement, that I unfortunately had to give this up.   Still, however, the church is some twenty feet longer than the old one.   I will not go further into a description of the church.   I certainly took great pains with it, and believe it to stand very high amongst the works of the revival.   It has been brought almost *ad nauseam* before the public by my friend, and at the time my tormentor, Mr. E. B. Denison.[1]   He was, however, a strenuous supporter of doing the work well, and was a very liberal contributor to the funds ; and were it not that he has an unpleasant way of doing things

---

[9] Aisles are valuable in the point of view of accommodation in proportion to their width, the least useful part of an aisle being that nearest to the pillars. In Newark church, to my mind one of the best proportioned churches in England, the aisles are wider than the nave.—ED.

[1] Now Sir Edmund Beckett, Q.C.—ED.

which makes one hate one's best works, I should have far more reason to thank than to complain of him. My comfort was, however, much more seriously interfered with by a despicable and untrustworthy man, whom I had the misfortune to fall in with as a clerk of the works, and who had contrived to ingratiate himself (for the time) with Mr. Denison, so much so as to cause much that was annoying; but I will not dwell upon disagreeables. The work was well carried out, and every improvement proposed was ably advocated by Mr. Denison. He, like my friend Mr. Stevens, was a determined advocate of anything strong, bold, and forcible, and the lessons he read me on this have been most useful. It is true he carries this to excess, and, barrister-like, advocates it by faulty arguments, which, woe be to the luckless wight who ventures to expose; but his views are in the main strong, sound, and true, so that there is no good done by sifting them for a few fallacies, which any one who knows anything of the subject is as well aware of as he is himself. My project of reproducing the original design of the tower was subsequently modified into the reproduction of its general forms in an earlier style. I am not proud of this tower. I missed the old outline, and I never see it without disappointment, though I do not think that this feeling is generally participated in.

I built another church there on a general scheme of Mr. Denison's. I wonder whether I have the original sketch. It would be amusing.[2]

[2] This church, close to the Great Northern Railway Station, has since been altered by Sir Edmund Beckett, or rather by a very competent local architect under Sir Edmund's direction.—ED.

Late in 1854 I competed for the new Rathhaus, or Hôtel de Ville, at Hamburg, a second European competition. I founded my design according to the wish of my departed friend, the Syndic Sieviking, upon the Halles at Ypres, but changed the detail entirely. I confess that I think it would have been a very noble structure.

Early in 1855 this competition was decided in my favour, but the execution was postponed *sine die*, owing to the funds set apart for it being required for the improvement of the navigation of the Elbe. I sent a small view of it that year to the Exhibition at Paris. The following remark terminates the notice of it in a pamphlet by M. Adolphe Lance:—"L'hôtel de ville de Hambourg sera une des plus belles et des plus raisonnables constructions de ce temps-ci. Heureux l'artiste qui y aura attaché son nom, heureuse la ville qui pourra le compter au nombre de ses monuments."

I was named one of three architects who had the examining and passing of English works in architecture for the Paris Exhibition, my coadjutors being Professors Cockerell and Donaldson. I contributed very largely myself, sending two views of the church at Hamburg, one of the Rathhaus design, one of the interior of Ely Cathedral, a drawing of my restoration of the Westminster Chapter-house, and a number of others. I received a gold medal.

I spent a little time in Paris on this occasion, and saw very much in the Exhibition to give me pleasure. As usual, however, I devoted most of my time to sketching from old buildings.

In 1855 I had received a hint from Mr. Hard-wick, R.A., that I had better put down my name on the list of candidates for the Royal Academy, and in December I was elected an associate. The only notable circumstance connected with my associate-ship was that, during an interregnum, in which Pro-fessor Cockerell had ceased to lecture, I was, in con-junction with Mr. Smirke (also an associate), called upon to deliver lectures there. I gave five such lec-tures, and I must say that, if they were not good ones, it was not for want of pains, for I did all in my power to render them so, and am vain enough to believe that they contain much that is original and meritorious. They were most elaborately illustrated by bold chalk sketches and drawings; on these I, my sons, pupils, and assistants worked most assiduously. On one occasion I actually went into France on a special sketching tour in December, to get materials for my lecture. A nobler set of illustrations was probably never seen to any lectures. They numbered on one occasion upwards of seventy, and far more than covered an entire side of the great room at the Academy. They were many of them from sketches made expressly for the occasion; some were from sketches obtained from others, very many were enlarged from my older sketch-books, and some were taken from published works; indeed, every source was laid under contribution to make my lectures thoroughly explanatory in every way. I often think of publishing them, but the trouble and the cost interfere.[3]

---

[3] They are now published with illustrations as a posthumous work.—ED.

It is a pity that we have not two professorships at the Academy—the one for classic, the other for gothic architecture. It is sad that the latter should be either utterly neglected, or else taken up by one who has not made it his special study, nor cares about its revival, except to head deputations to discourage it.

About this time I erected the church at Haley Hill, Halifax, the munificent work of Mr. E. Akroyd, the great manufacturer. It is, on the whole, my best church; but it labours under this disadvantage, that it was never meant to be so fine a work as it is, and consequently was not commenced on a sufficiently bold and comprehensive plan. Nothing could exceed the liberality and munificence of its founder, and I think he was well satisfied. I confess I hardly am so, as I know how much finer it would have been, had it been more developed as to size.

CHAPTER IV.

I NOW arrive at the period of the competition for
the Government offices in the autumn of 1856.

I will first mention that it found me hard at work,
writing a treatise on " Domestic Architecture." I
had long felt that some book was needed, putting
forth in a popular way, free from exaggeration, the
applicability of our revived style to general uses ;
and, at the same time, the inconsistency of giving
it a queer, antiquated garb, and the necessity of
making it conform loyally and willingly to the
habits and requirements of our own age. This
book, as pretty well all that I write, is the product
of my travelling hours. People often express a
wonder how I write lectures, books, &c., in the
midst of my engagements. I simply do so by
employing my time on such work while travelling. I carry a blank book in my pocket, and
write in pencil as I go. I find that it rather
amuses than fatigues me, and that my thoughts
are freer at such times than at any other ; while
in a night journey I often warm up to more
enthusiastic sentiments than at other times I have
leisure for. This book took me a very considerable time to write, and its publication was delayed
because it was finished at the wrong time of the

year—for books, like other things, may be in or out of season.

This great competition, then, found me in rather a prepared state of mind. I was not, however, content with this; but, long before the programme came out, I set to work to put myself systematically through my facings. My family being, as was usual in the latter part of summer, in the Isle of Wight, I retired to a great extent from active engagements, and set myself to design the elements which I thought best suited to a public building. I designed windows suited to all positions, and of all varieties of size, form, and grouping; doorways, cornices, parapets, and imaginary combinations of all these, carefully studying to make them all thoroughly practical, and suited to this class of building. I did not aim at making my style " Italian Gothic ;" my ideas ran much more upon the French, to which for some years I had devoted my chief study. I did, however, aim at gathering a few hints from Italy, such as the pillar-mullion, the use of differently-coloured materials, and of inlaying. I also aimed at another thing which people consider Italian—I mean a certain squareness and horizontality of outline. This I consider pre-eminently suited to the street front of a public building. I combined this, however, with gables, high-pitched roofs, and dormers.

My opinion is, that putting aside the question now rife as to whether we should, or should not, introduce foreign varieties of Gothic, my details were excellent, and precisely suited to the purpose. I do not think the entire design so good as its elementary parts. It was rather set and formal. With all its faults, however, it would have been a noble structure ; and the set of drawings was, perhaps, the best ever sent in to a competition, or nearly so.

A little before the competition, but subsequent to my designing the speculative elements of it, I had a good opportunity of trying these elements beforehand. Mr. Akroyd had asked me to design a town-hall for Halifax, to suit a site which he favoured. I made a design, which I flatter myself was as good a thing of its kind, and of its small size, as had been made at the time ; nor do I think I could now do better. It was the first-fruits of my studies for the Government offices ; and, in my opinion, was better than any subsequent design for these buildings.

When my designs for the public offices were exhibited,[1] they excited much attention ; indeed, they were, by those who favoured Gothic, considered generally the best, though opinions were divided to some extent between them and the designs by Mr. Street and Mr. Woodward. Indeed, few comparatively, as were the Gothic designs, they were by far the best in the exhibition, putting aside, perhaps, those of Sir Charles Barry, which were visionary, and founded on the diminutive elements of the present Board of Trade buildings.

The judges, who knew amazingly little about their subject, were not well-disposed towards our

---

[1] They bore the following motto :—" Nec minimum meruere decus vestigia Græca ausi deserere et celebrare domestica facta."—ED.

N 2

style, and though they awarded premiums to all the best Gothic designs, they took care not to put any of them high enough to have much chance. The first premium for the Foreign Office was awarded to a design by my old pupil Coe ; the first for the War Office to one (not bad by any means) by Garling. Barry and Banks came second for the Foreign Office, and I third.

I did not fret myself at the disappointment, but when it was found, a few months later, that Lord Palmerston had coolly set aside the entire results of the competition, and was about to appoint Pennethorne, a non-competitor, I thought myself at liberty to stir. A meeting took place at Mr. Beresford Hope's, at which Charles Barry, myself, and Digby Wyatt were present; and, if I remember rightly, it was agreed to stir up the Institute of Architects. To the best of my memory, the Government had just changed, and Lord John Manners had taken the Office of Works, when a deputation from the Institute laid the matter before him. The result was the appointment of a select committee to inquire into the subject. This committee had Mr. Beresford Hope for its chairman, and included Lord Elcho, Sir Benjamin Hall, Mr. Tite, Mr. Akroyd, Mr. Stirling, Sir John Shelley, Mr. Lock, Mr. Lygon,[2] and others.

It appeared, on the evidence of Mr. Burn, who had acted as one of the architectural assessors to the judges, that while the assessors were of one mind as to the order of merit among the designs, they did not coincide with the decision of the judges; and, further, that they had agreed in

---

[2] Now the Earl Beauchamp.—ED.

placing me second for *both* buildings, while no one was on any showing first for both ; moreover, that they considered second for both (the two being essentially parts of the same group) to be a higher position than that of first for only one.[3] I was thus in a certain sense lifted up from my third place and placed upon the balance between second and first. The committee reported that the two styles were equal in convenience and in cost, and, stating what I have just detailed, they recommended the Commissioner of Works virtually, though not in terms, to make his own choice between my design and that of Messrs. Banks and Barry.

They reported in July, 1858, but no decision was come to till late in November, when I learned that I had been appointed (L. D.).

I at once received instructions to revise my design with reference to sundry considerations named. Meanwhile, the notion of erecting a War Office had been given up, and the Indian Government were in treaty for that part of the ground which faces King Street; and as the Secretary of State for India (Lord Stanley) had actually drawn up a minute for my appointment to that building also, Mr. Digby Wyatt, at that

---

[3] It may be well to give here the order in which the premiated competitors were placed by the judges :—

War Office.	*Foreign Office.*
H. B. Garling	Coe and Hofland
M. B. D'Hazeville (of Paris)	Banks and Barry
T. E. Rochead	*G. G. Scott
*Pritchard and Seddon	*Deane and Woodward
C. Brodrick	T. Bellamy

The Gothic designs are marked in this list by an asterisk.—ED.

time official architect to the India Office, called upon me, and made a proposition that we should undertake the work in conjunction, to which I willingly agreed. The designs were made and approved, and the working drawings ordered and proceeded with for both buildings, when Mr. Tite[4] commenced a violent opposition in Parliament, in which he was, unhappily for me, supported by Lord Palmerston. It is of no use fighting this battle over again now, but I refer to the papers on the subject. Suffice it to say that the statements made both by Mr. Tite and by Lord Palmerston were as absurd and unfounded as anything could be.

I wrote in the *Times* the next day, showing their utter fallacy. On a former occasion, while the subject was before the select committee, I went, or sent round, to all the public buildings I could think of, and measured the area of their windows, and on comparing them with those of my design I was able to show to the committee that my design provided half as much light again as the average of buildings of the same class. Tite was a member of that committee, yet he had the face to state that my designs were deficient in window-light, and encouraged Lord Palmerston to do the same. In my letter in the *Times* I showed this up pretty vigorously ; but a second attack followed, in which all this unfair misstatement was again brought forward, with a quantity of poor buffoonery which only Lord Palmerston's age permitted.

[4] The architect of the new Royal Exchange, and M.P. for Bath.—ED.

I was well defended, but the Government, being weak, promised to exhibit the drawings in the House of Commons before they were to be executed. One leading member of our profession was so irate at my letter in the *Times*, which he considered to reflect upon English architects in general, that he proposed moving the Institute to reverse the recommendation of their council to award to me the annual Royal Medal of the Institute, and was only dissuaded from attempting to inflict that gratuitous dishonour upon me by strong remonstrances. I had not, I think, then become aware that he was Lord Palmerston's private tutor in matters of architectural lore. As this gentleman had for many years acted in a very friendly way towards me, I have never allowed his conduct in this matter to provoke me to any unkindly act. I shall have to say a little more about this presently. I confess that though I knew, till then, nothing of my recommendation for the medal, I did feel deeply this attempt to kick me, while prostrate and in deep perplexity and trouble : and I cannot reconcile it with the character and generosity which this gentleman has usually evinced. I fancy, however, that his somewhat morbidly correct ideas as to competition rendered the fact of the work being given to a man, who obtained only a third premium, very galling to him, and had much to do with his conduct. Still, as he agreed in throwing overboard Messrs. Coe and Hofland, while Barry and I were reported, virtually, by the select committee, to be on an equality, I fear that personal feeling, together with an hostility to my style, had an even stronger influence.

However all this may be, it cannot be denied that I was cast down from the eminence I had attained. The "very abjects" now loaded me with their miserable abuse, and, though I went on with my working drawings, I felt that my position was sadly altered, and the chance of carrying out my design forlorn. It was comforting, under these dejecting circumstances, to observe how generously a certain select number of persons of influence rallied round me, and cheered me in the conflict. Not only was I warmly and vigorously aided by the *Saturday Review*, the *Ecclesiologist*, and by the Gothic party pretty generally, but a number of members of parliament stuck nobly by me. I wish I knew all their names, but I will enumerate a few : Lord Elcho, Mr. Dudley Fortescue, Mr. Charles Buxton, Mr. Stirling (who had been one of the judges in the competition), Sir Edward Colebrook, Sir Stafford Northcote, Mr. Danby Seymour, Mr. Pease, Col. Tinney, Sir Morton Peto, Sir Joseph Paxton, and Mr. Akroyd.

Digby Wyatt, though no Goth, held loyally to our compact, and we went on in a forlorn hope. Even Mr. Disraeli told me that there was no chance of carrying it, but Lord John Manners held firmly to his own decision, and met the attack in parliament manfully, and with great success. Indeed, the opponents trusted to numbers, and cared little about argument, while Lord Palmerston didn't care a straw what buffoonery he gave vent to, for the greater the twaddle he talked, the louder of course was the laughter, and that was his deadly weapon.

So things went on, and had the Government

stood, I should perhaps have carried it in the
small days of August. But, alas! the ministers
were left in a minority on their " Reform Bill,"
and dissolved parliament. Then followed the
sudden invasion of Italy, and the *canard* that
Government had been playing into the hands of
the Emperor of the French, which was believed
just long enough to serve, with the pseudo-
Reform cry, to lose the elections. I am no politician, though tending to conservatism, but at that
time I certainly did take an interest in the elections. At length, however, the fatal day arrived,
the Government resigned, and my arch-opponent
became once more autocrat of England.

It was a considerable time before a Commissioner of Public Works was nominated, and I lived
upon the slender hope that he might be favourably
inclined.

At length Mr. Fitzroy took the office, and
personally he actually was on my side, but was
nevertheless bound to uphold Lord Palmerston's
views. I forget the precise order of events, but
the builders' estimates were by that time in a
forward state, and were allowed to come in, and
they turned out very satisfactorily. Lord Palmerston, however, sent for me, and told me in a jaunty
way that he could have nothing to do with this
Gothic style, and that though he did not want to
disturb my appointment, he must insist on my
making a design in the Italian style, which he felt
sure I could do quite as well as the other. That
he heard I was so tremendously successful in the
Gothic style, that if he let me alone I should
Gothicize the whole country, &c., &c., &c. About

the same time my drawings and a model were exhibited in the tea-room of the House of Commons, and when the vote for the building came on, there took place another memorable debate on architecture, in which Lord Palmerston gave way to another flood of his secret mentor's second-hand learning, Mr. Tite talked nonsense, and some fair speeches were made, especially by Lord John Manners and Lord Elcho, on my side.   The matter was left an open question to be decided the next session, when I was to exhibit designs in both styles.

It was, as I suppose, about this time that a deputation of M.P.'s waited on Lord Palmerston to advocate the cause of Gothic architecture.

Since Satan accompanied the angels on the mission narrated in the Book of Job, there has seldom been wanting a " devil's advocate " when anything delicate has had to be transacted, and so it was now.

They unluckily invited that worthy, vain old busy-body, Mr. A——, who had been trying to make himself look clever in the tea-room by finding mare's-nests in the shape of non-existent errors in the arrangement of my plans, and he must needs come and tell his foolish tale at the deputation.   The faults he found were wholly imaginary, and the arrangements had been the result of long thought and patient consultation with the heads of departments, but no one there knew anything about this, and so a wound was given me by a pretended friend, who had been admitted by mistake, and—thanks to him—Lord Palmerston found no difficulty in letting off all friendly arguments like water out of a tap.   I think it was on this occasion that, having discovered the error of his argument about " shutting out the very light of day," he said, " This Gothic architecture admits the sun from its very rising till its setting, so that my friend the Speaker, who necessarily goes to bed late, and has no shutters to his windows, can get no sleep for it."

It was about the same time that, on going to the lobby of the House, I, by the merest chance, discovered that one of my opponents in the original competition had just brought a paper, arguing his own claims, for distribution among the members. I obtained one, went home and wrote a reply, got 600 copies struck off in no time, and, it having been on a Friday that these papers were sent round, I got mine distributed to the members from house to house before the next sitting.   I had, by the request of the editor of some periodical, written (anonymously) a conspectus of the arguments contained in my book on " Domestic Architecture " and elsewhere, in favour of our style, under the name of " The Gothic Renaissance."   This I had printed in a separate form and similarly distributed. Indeed, I did everything that man could do, nearly my entire time being devoted to the fight.

About the middle of August I heard that a deputation of architects was going up to Lord Palmerston to pat him on the back and encourage him in his determination to overthrow the work of his predecessors.   I was foolish enough, on hearing it, to call on a leading member of the profession, a Mr. B——, to protest against this.   He professed innocence of all privity to the scheme, but told me that, if asked, he should not decline to join it.

My necessary exertions being for the time over, Mrs. Scott persuaded me to go, with our elder sons, to spend a day or two at the Oatlands Park Hotel near Chertsey, for relaxation after my anxious toils and sorrows. The next day was a Saturday, and on that day there appeared in the *Saturday Review* a most cutting article, showing up the ignorance and folly of Lord Palmerston's architectural essays in and out of parliament. On returning from fishing with my sons, I received a message from Mr. Burn, who, to my surprise, I found to be laid up with a severe illness in the same hotel, saying that he had just seen my name in the visitors' book, and wished I would call upon him. I did so, and, though he was very ill, found him very jovial, and he talked a little about the Government Offices, but said he wanted to go into the subject more at leisure with me, and arranged that I should call again on Monday. When I did so, he opened conversation by saying, "Whoever do you think came down to see me yesterday (Sunday) but B——? I don't know what he came about, but he said he was so anxious to know how I was that he thought he would run down on Sunday afternoon and see me." He then proceeded to say, " I asked him if he had seen the article on the Government Offices in yesterday's *Saturday Review*, and I said to him, ' By the lord Harry, it is the best thing I ever read in my life.' " B—— was *mum*, while Mr. Burn proceeded : " I don't know who it is that backs Palmerston up, but I am convinced, by what he says, that there's some idle fellow in our profes-

sion who keeps prompting from behind the scenes."
B—— had had enough of it and departed! I
was able to tell Mr. Burn, what he had by his
spirited reception prevented B—— from telling
him himself, that Mr. B—— had come down to
canvas him for the deputation, with a view to
being able to quote him as agreeing with its
objects, but the broadside he had received had
silenced him, and he went back from his Sunday
trip "with a flea in his ear." I now found to my
satisfaction that Mr. Burn, the senior assessor of
the competition, approved distinctly of my appointment, though till then (barring our cursory introduction years before) he was a perfect stranger to me.

The deputation took place during the same
week. Mr. B—— again was master of the cere-
monies. Sidney Smirke, the first speaker, assert-
ing (with his hair perhaps on end) that, if they
began in King Street with Gothic, it would never
stop till it had reached Charing Cross. Tite
repeated his heavy common-places, and spoke of
Charles Barry and H. B. Garling as the successful
competitors : poor Coe had no friends.

I have not, after an interval of many years,
ceased to feel that the conduct of those architects
who attended on this deputation was in a high
degree unprofessional. I am happy, however, to
say that I have never permitted any such feeling
to show itself in my intercourse with them, or to
cause any personal breach.

There can be little doubt that the deputation
had been arranged with the cognizance of Lord
Palmerston, and that it greatly strengthened his
hands. I tried to get up a counter address, but

the Gothic architects did not come forward in sufficient force to make it worth while. This cold-heartedness was the greatest damper I had met with. I must, however, name some who exerted themselves in the most generous way, and who willingly signed the address :—Mr. Joseph Clarke, Mr. Benjamin Ferrey, Mr. John Norton, Mr. Ewan Christian, Mr. George Goldie, Mr. Raphael Brandon, Mr. T. W. Goodman, Messrs. Pritchard and Seddon, Mr. T. P. St. Aubyn, Mr. Arthur W. Blomfield, Mr. William Slater, Mr. William White, Mr. T. H. Hakewill, Mr. John L. Pearson, Mr. E. Welby Pugin, Mr. William Burges, and Mr. S. S. Teulon.

Shortly afterwards Lord Palmerston sent for me, and, seating himself down before me in the most easy, fatherly way, said, " I want to talk to you quietly, Mr. Scott, about this business. I have been thinking a great deal about it, and I really think there was much force in what your friends said." I was delighted at his supposed conversion. " I really do think that there is a degree of inconsistency in compelling a Gothic architect to erect a classic building, and so I have been thinking of appointing you a coadjutor, who would in fact make the design!" I was thrown to the earth again. I began at once to bring arguments against the proposal, but the blow was too sudden to allow me to do justice to my case *vivâ voce;* so on my return I immediately wrote a strongly and firmly worded letter, stating that I had been regularly appointed to the work, that Mr. Gladstone had assured me that my appointment would be respected, that he (Lord Palmerston) had done the same both personally and in parliament. I dwelt upon my position as an architect, my having won two European competitions, my being an A.R.A., a gold medallist of the Institute, a lecturer on architecture at the Royal Academy, &c.; and I ended by firmly declining any such arrangement. I forget whether he replied. I also wrote, if I remember rightly, to Mr. Gladstone.

Thus closed this stage of the business, and, being thoroughly knocked up (or down, as you may please to call it), I retired with Mrs. Scott and my family to Scarborough to recruit.

I was thoroughly out of health, through the badgering, anxiety, and bitter disappointment which I had gone through, and for the first time since commencing practice, twenty-four years before, I gave myself a quasi-holiday of two months, with sea air and a course of quinine. During this time, however, besides the work sent down to me from time to time, I was busying myself in preparing for the next campaign. I saw that, with Lord Palmerston, Gothic would have no chance, and I had agreed to prepare an Italian design. I felt that I could not, while a stone was left unturned, make a design in the ordinary classic form; I had, however, such faith in Gothic, that I always believed that "something would turn up" in its favour.

To resign would be to give up a sort of property which Providence had placed in the hands of my family, and would be simply rewarding my professional opponents for their unprecedented attempt to wrest a work from the hands of a brother architect, after he had not only been regularly appointed, but had commenced the business, had even made his working drawings, and had received builders' tenders.

The way in which the matter was left in parliament was that I was to prepare an Italian design, which, with the Gothic one, was to be laid before parliament the next year. The course I determined on was to prepare a design in a variety of Italian, as little inconsistent with my antecedents as possible. I had, in dealing with Lord Hill's chapel at Hawkstone, and with St. Michael's church, Cornhill, attempted, by the use of a sort of early Basilican style, to give a tone to the existing classic architecture; and it struck me that not wholly alien to this was the Byzantine of the early Venetian palaces, and that the earliest renaissance of Venice contained a cognate element. I therefore conceived the idea of generating what would be strictly an Italian style out of these two sets of examples; Byzantine, in fact, toned into a more modern and usable form, by reference to those examples of the renaissance which had been influenced by the presence of Byzantine works. To the study of this I devoted myself while at Scarborough, and I produced elementary sketches which contained much that was, in my opinion, really valuable, as giving a new tone to semi-classic ideas. After my return to town, I worked out these ideas into new designs for both buildings, and not, as I think, without considerable success. The designs were both original and pleasing in effect; indeed, Lord Elcho, to whom I showed them before laying them before the authorities, thought them better than the Gothic design, and rejoiced that good was likely to come out of evil.

I at length showed them to Mr. Cowper, who, I should have stated, had, on the unexpected death of Mr. Fitzroy during the recess, come into the Office of Works. Mr. Cowper was, of course, under the control of Lord Palmerston. Left to himself, he would, I believe, like Mr. Fitzroy, have preferred the Gothic design; and now, as I equally believe, liked the Byzantinesque one. He was, however, so far as this question went, in the hands of a strong master, and, after a few civil remarks, merely said that he would make an appointment with Lord Palmerston.

About this time a friend called, and told me he was sure that something secret was being trans-acted with one of the original competitors, for when, in casual conversation with this gentleman, he had referred to the Foreign Office, so extra-ordinary an expression had come over his coun-tenance that he was convinced that some mischief was brewing. Some time later another friend told me that he had discovered that a design for the Foreign Office was being prepared by this architect! He also asked me if Lord Palmerston had not once proposed to make him my coadjutor in the matter, and if it was not the case that I had refused. I now saw how matters stood. Lord Palmerston had hoped at first to be able to thrust this gentleman upon me as a colleague; but, failing that, had secretly encouraged him to make a design, that he might have " two strings to his bow." I do not remember the order in

O

which these revelations came to me, relatively to other circumstances ; but they probably explain the fact that Lord Palmerston allowed several weeks to elapse, after I had shown Mr. Cowper the designs, before he made any appointment with me to see them. When he did so, he kept me wait-ing two hours and a half in his back room (during a part of which I heard him very deliberately going through his luncheon in the next room), and then sent me away unseen. At length, however, I showed him the design. He was very civil, and I thought he liked it. Indeed, I believe that he did, but thought it hardly consistent with his previous professions to admit it.

After this I saw Mr. Cowper, and told him that I thought Lord Palmerston was favourably impressed. Having occasion to go at once to Hamburg, I left the matter, as I thought, in a tolerably satisfactory position. While abroad, however, I received a letter from Mr. Cowper, saying that I was mistaken in my impression as to Lord Palmerston's feelings, and that I must modify the design, and make it much more like modern architecture.

This led, on my return, to a number of futile attempts, and in the midst of them I heard by a side wind that the competitor to whom I have referred had not only made a design, but that it was actually at the Office of Works, and under consideration !

Now indeed a crisis had arrived, and some strong step must be taken. I accordingly drew up a formal account of all which had transpired, stating what I had heard as to these proceedings, and entering a decided protest against the course thus secretly taken.

This protest I sent to Mr. Cowper, and informed my supporters in the House of Commons of what had been done.

This seems to have quashed the project, and shortly afterwards I was directed to make some modifications in my semi-Byzantine design to meet the opposing views half way. The design was then referred to the joint opinion of Messrs. Cockerell, Burn, and Ferguson.

I had frequent interviews with these three gentlemen, and I have every reason to be grateful for the kind consideration with which I was treated by them. Professor Cockerell, being a pure classicist, had the greatest difficulty in swallowing my new style. He lectured me for hours together on the beauties of the true classic, going over book after book with me, and pouring forth ecstatic eulogies on his beloved style of art. I did not argue against his views, which I respected, but rather took the line of advocating variety and individuality, and of each man being allowed to follow out his individual idiosyncrasies ; but it was a bitter pill for him. He kindly desired to aid me, but his tastes went all the other way. Ferguson, on the contrary, was strongly in favour of my views. They embodied in great measure what he had been for years advocating, and he would have gone to the full extent of my newly generated variety of "Italian." Mr. Burn did not go strongly into the question of style, but took the thing up in a determined and sturdy manner in the light of upsetting an unjustifiable combination against a

brother architect. He stood by me most manfully and sternly. He and Ferguson together
brought over Cockerell to their views, and they
made a joint report in favour of my design, subject to a few modifications, of which Ferguson
disapproved, but which he conceded to please
Cockerell.

I cannot say much in favour of the design as
now approved. My first idea had been toned
down, step by step, till no real stuff was left in
it. It was a mere *caput mortuum*, as is invariably
the case where a design is trimmed and trimmed
again to meet the views of different critics. Like
the man with his two wives in the fable, one had
pulled out all the black hairs, and the other all
the grey ones. I hoped, however, to throw more
life into it in the execution, and I even encouraged
to myself the most forlorn hope that the House
of Commons might still decide in favour of the
Gothic design. The drawings went again before
parliament; the House of Commons had no
liking at all for the new design, but let it pass
after another architectural debate, and so it stood
at the end of the session of 1860, and thus my
second great campaign was over.

As in the previous year, Lord Palmerston,
when parliament was once safely prorogued, lost
no time in changing his tone. I found that
something was "up," through my friend Mr.
Hunt [5] (the professional adviser to the Office
of Works), who sent for me and offered some
very serious though mystic advice to me to
comply with any directions I might receive, or

[5] Now Sir Henry Arthur Hunt, C.B.—ED.

I should be in danger of losing my appointment. I may here mention that during all these wearisome delays, the India Government, growing naturally sick of such childish trifling, had fought shy of their verbal agreement to share the site with the Foreign Office, and had quite justifiably commissioned Mr. Digby Wyatt to look out for another. I was thus in danger in that quarter also. They were the further moved to this, because Sir Charles Wood did not like the arrangement made by Lord Stanley, that they should have the King Street front, while the Foreign Office should have that towards the park.

I was sent for to Lord Palmerston on September 8th, 1860, when he told me that he did not wish to disturb my position, but that he would have nothing to do with Gothic; and as to the style of my recent design, it was "neither one thing nor t'other—a regular mongrel affair—and he would have nothing to do with it either:" that he must insist on my making a design in the ordinary Italian, and that, though he had no wish to displace me, he nevertheless, if I refused, must cancel my appointment. He did not stop for a reply, but went on to tell me that he had made an agreement with Sir Charles Wood which necessitated an entire alteration of plan. The India Office was to share the park front with the Foreign Office. The State Paper Office was to be removed, and the building was to project irregularly into the park, leaving the King Street front as a future work.

I came away thunderstruck and in sore per-

plexity, thinking whether I must resign or swallow
the bitter pill, when whom should I meet in Pall
Mall but my friend Mr. Hunt. I at once told him
what had transpired, and he in return told me what
had given rise to the advice which, a few days
earlier, he had kindly volunteered. He had been
consulted by Mr. Cowper[6] as to whether they could
not fairly get rid of me (as, I suppose, a troublesome,
contumacious fellow). He (Mr. Hunt) had put the
case in this way : that I was regularly appointed
by his (Mr. Cowper's) predecessor, and had performed, without any shortcomings, the duties committed to me : that it was no fault of mine that a
change of masters had taken place whose tastes
were different, and that it would be a very serious
injury to me to displace me, and one for which no
pecuniary compensation would make amends. On
the other hand, that employers had an undoubted
right to prescribe the style of the building they
desired to erect, and that, in the case of an heir
succeeding to an estate after a new mansion had
been designed, though good feeling suggested the
continuance of the same architect, it was a fair
condition that he, on his part, should be willing to
conform to the views of his new client. By these
arguments alone he had quieted the impatience of
my employers, now stirred up to a climax, and he
conjured me to act in conformity with the views
which he had suggested. He urged the claims of
my family, whom I had no right to deprive of
what had become their property as much as my
own, for a mere individual preference on a question
of taste, &c., &c. I saw Mr. Digby Wyatt shortly

[6] Now Mr. Cowper Temple.—ED.

afterwards, who, very disinterestedly, urged strongly the same view—I say disinterestedly, for had I resigned he would beyond a doubt have had the whole design of the India Office, instead of a half of it, committed to his hands.   I was in a terrible state of mental perturbation, but I made up my mind, went straight in for Digby Wyatt's view, bought some costly books on Italian architecture, and set vigorously to work to rub up what, though I had once understood pretty intimately, I had allowed to grow rusty by twenty years' neglect.

I devoted the autumn to the new designs, and, as I think, met with great success.   I went to Paris and studied the Louvre and most of the important buildings, and really recovered some of my lost feelings for the style, though I fell, ever and anon, into fits of desperate lamentation and annoyance, and almost thought again of giving up the work.

That winter my youngest boy but one[7] had a severe fever at St. Leonard's, and I was detained for six weeks from business, but I went on with my design.   While I was from home under this affliction, I was elected a Royal Academician, the pleasure of which was sadly alloyed by the circumstances of the time.   I succeeded my dear friend Sir Charles Barry, who had died suddenly during the autumn.

My new designs were beautifully got up in outline; the figures I put in myself, and even composed the groups, for, though I have no skill in that way, I was so determined to show myself not behindhand with the classicists, that I seemed to have more power than usual.

[7] We were five, all boys.—ED.

The India Office, externally, was wholly my design, though I had adopted an idea as to its grouping and outline, suggested by a sketch of Mr. Digby Wyatt's. This I thought very excellent, although in his own drawing he had done but little justice to the conception. Lord Palmerston highly approved of the design, and it passed the House of Commons in the session of 1861, after a very stout fight by the Gothic party, who naturally and consistently opposed it strenuously. I aided this opposition a little myself, for feeling the new design (as to its plan and outline) to be even more suited to the Gothic style than the old one, I had a splendid view made of a mediæval design adapted to the altered plan. It was by very far superior to any which I had hitherto made, and I placed it with my other Gothic designs in the exhibition at the Royal Academy, as a silent protest against what was going on. I further had a copy made of this view, and had nearly succeeded in getting it exhibited to the House of Commons with my classic design on the same plan, but Mr. Cowper was too canny for me, and thus, after more than two years' hard fighting, I was compelled to "eat my leek."

The struggle through which I had fought the matter, step by step, was such as I should never have faced out, had I known what was before me. Indeed, at the commencement, nothing would have induced me to volunteer a classic design; but the battle, though long one of style, came at last to be almost for existence. I felt that I should be irreparably injured if I were to lose a work thus publicly placed in my hands, and I was step by step driven into the most annoying position of carrying out my largest work in a style contrary to the direction of my life's labours. My shame and sorrow were for a time extreme, but, to my surprise, the public seemed to understand my position and to feel for it, and I never received any annoying or painful rebuke, and even Mr. Ruskin told me that I had done quite right.

Such was the length of time over which this business spread, that, though my designs were commenced before my son Gilbert's term of architectural pupilage began, his five years had expired before the foundations were begun to be excavated. It is now seven years and a half [8] since I set about my first sketches, and the work is only in certain parts first-floor high. Great, however, as has been the annoyance of which I had been the victim, I am determined by God's help to do my very best, just as much so as if the style was of my own choosing.

I am ashamed to have occupied so much space in detailing these heartless and almost heart-breaking vexations, and will now leave the subject.

[8] Written in 1864.—ED.

CHAPTER V.

I will now make a few observations upon the progress and position of the revival during the period which I have been passing over, viz. from 1845 to the present time, 1864.

Up to that time (1845) the revival in this country had been essentially English. I am not aware that, with the exception of a few works by Mr. Wylde,[1] any foreign idea had crept into it. I believe my own journeys into Germany, and subsequently into France, gave the first impetus in the direction of foreign architecture, and that was but a slight one. I think it was in 1849 that I drew a series of designs for capitals of the foreign type, and my pupil, Mr. Alfred Bell, followed them out further for St. Nicholas at Hamburg, my types being those which I had sketched at the Sainte Chapelle.

In my essays on various subjects at the end of my book on Restoration (published in 1850) I do not recollect any tendency to foreignism. Those essays are not a bad modulus of the mind of the revival at that time; that on the selection

[1] As a fine example of Mr. Wylde's design, St. Martin's Northern schools in Castle Street, Endell Street, may be mentioned.—Ed.

of a style, was intended to be corrective of the tendency of the "Ecclesiologist" towards late decorated. Their dictum had been in favour of the earlier stage of the flowing decorated, or, as my friend, Mr. E. A. Freeman, used to say, they would call it in their own nomenclature, "the early late middle pointed." The three western bays of the choir at Ely were at that time their beau-ideal, forgetting that the outline and proportion of these were derived directly from the Norman bays with which they came in conjunction. So imperious was their law, that any one who had dared to deviate from or to build in other than the sacred "Middle Pointed," well knew what he must suffer. In my own office, Mr. Street and others used to view every one as a heretic who designed in any but the sacred phase ; and I well recollect, when I was, at Holbeck, obliged to build in early English or "first pointed," the sort of holy and only half-repressed indignation and pity to which it gave rise. The revived style was one, and its unity was "Middle Pointed." I held this as a theory myself. They held it as a religious duty, though they now seem to have forgotten this phase in the history of their faith, and are very irate when it is referred to. So tyrannical did this law continue to be, that when I first busied myself in forming the Architectural Museum, it was with fear and trembling that I introduced some early English specimens. I held out against the revival of this style of foliage myself, but I feared that its admission would, among the stricter sort, condemn the whole institution.

How curiously reversed have these Medo-

Persic laws since become. Tyranny has been equally rampant, but it has persecuted what it once enjoined, and now its supporters have got back once more into the old groove, and are equally tyrannous in the old line. The introduction of the foreign element in a systematic way, may, perhaps, have been due to Mr. Ruskin, certainly it came on shortly after the publication of his " Seven Lamps." This, undoubtedly, set people upon Italian Gothic. For my own part, I never fell into this latter mania ; I held that there was much to be learned from Italian Gothic, but that it should not be really adopted at all. Others took a contrary view, as Mr. Bodley, in his design for the memorial church at Constantinople.

The French casts in the Architectural Museum had, no doubt, a strong influence in bringing about the revival of that class of detail ; and, as regards myself, my frequent sketching tours in France and Germany, and my having constantly to make use of these details in my working drawings for Hamburg, had a great tendency in the same direction. As yet I held and thought, in my innocence, that every one, or nearly every one, held to nature as the source of foliated ornamentation. I had, during my earlier practice, made use in early English work of the conventional foliage ; but subsequently I had come to the conclusion that, though it was lawful to revive bygone forms of a merely mechanical character, it was inconsistent to revive bygone conventionalism in matters originally derived from nature ; and that while we might imitate the architecture of another period, we must always go to nature direct (though perhaps aided by suggestions from art) for objects of which nature was the professed origin, and that if we saw fit to conventionalize, the conventionalism should be our own.

It was, I suppose, about 1853 or 1854 that I wrote a lecture on such subjects for the Architectural Museum. I entered into it with intense enthusiasm, and actually got up, as well as I was able, the subject of botany, so far as concerns the English wild plants. I followed this up, not scientifically, it is true, but with a delight and an avidity which I can hardly describe, and my lecture was of a very impassioned character.

I remember longing most earnestly to discover a leaf, from which one might suppose our early English foliage to have been derived. The nearest I could find was an almost microscopic wall-fern, and certain varieties of the common parsley. One night I dreamed that I had found the veritable plant. I can see it even now. It was a sear and yellow leaf, but with all the beauty of form which graces the capitals at Lincoln and at Lichfield. I was maddened with excitement and pleasure ; but while I was exulting, and ready to exclaim, "Eureka! Eureka !" I awoke, and behold it was a dream.

I remember after this, or another lecture on the subject, in which I had stated my theory against revived conventionalism, Mr. Clutton (our secretary) came behind me, and whispered in my ear, "You've been preaching heresy." I thought my theory so certain, that I never discovered his meaning till 1856, when he and Mr. Burges made

their competition design for the cathedral at Lille.
This was really the first occasion on which the
Ecclesiological Society's law, as regards the
" Middle Pointed," was set at nought. The
Ecclesiologists had actually at one time doubted
whether it would not be right to pull down Peterborough Cathedral, if only we could rebuild it
equally well in the " Middle Pointed " style ; and
now they were forced to swallow a veritable
" First Pointed " design, and to sing its unwilling
praises. Clutton and Burges certainly had the
credit of overthrowing the old tyranny, and even
some of its most rigorous abettors soon found it
necessary to outvie each other in setting at
nought their former faith, and in trying who could
be the *earliest* in the style of their buildings.
One thing, however, never changed, the intole-
rance shown by them for all freedom of thought
on the part of other men. Every one must per-
force follow in their wake, no matter how often
they changed, or how entirely they reversed their
own previous views. Nor was anything more
certain than this, that however erroneous their
former opinion might have been, their views for
the time being were right, and that every one
who differed from them was a heretic, or an old-
fashioned simpleton. It had many years before
been a saying of mine, that there was no class of
men whom the Cambridge Camden Society held
in such scorn, as those who adhered to their own
last opinion but one ; and this sentiment has
been the great inheritance and heirloom of their
imitators.

Let it not, however, be supposed that I object

to changes of taste or opinion ; on the contrary, I conceive them to be the necessary accompaniment of a state of active and tentative progress. Nor even do I object to an earnest belief in the particular phase in vogue ; this is the natural consequence of earnestness and zeal in the work in hand. What I do protest against, is the custom of taking the cue from some self-elevated leader of their own, and, whatever the circumstances may be, treating with pitying scorn every one who does not chance to fall in with the new rule or opinion ; even those who have no power of art in them setting themselves up as lights, because of their adhesion to the latest promulgated dictum of the clique, and those of a superior class neglecting often their own special training, in the intensity of their self-satisfaction at belonging to the privileged party, whose great moral rule is to trust in themselves, and to despise others.

Still, in spite of these foibles, the revival was progressing vigorously ; probably these very weaknesses were the mere outbreakings of over-excited pulsation, and the eccentricities, which were growing upon the revived style, were perhaps like the diseases which human beings are expected to pass through once and then to have done with.

I feel uncertain sometimes whether the breaking down of the "Middle Pointed" régime was a move for good or ill. There was, to say the least, a theory in that rigorous code. It was argued, and with some force, that in the nature of things it is anomalous to revive an old style ; that the history

of art, while its stream was pure, was one of continuous and natural progress, the stream never
returning upon its own course, and every developement being the offspring of its immediate predecessor; that this natural course had been broken
by the classic renaissance, since which event all
had been confusion, until at length we were left
without a distinctive style of our own; that at
this juncture, by a coincidence of feelings and
circumstances, our old architecture came to be,
without premeditation, revived, and that it was
the duty of those who guided that revival to see
that its course should not be wildly eclectic, but
that we should select once and for all, the very
best and most complete phase in the old style,
and taking that as our agreed *point de départ*,
should make it so thoroughly our own, that we
should develope upon it as a natural and legitimate
nucleus, shaping it freely from time to time to
suit our altered and ever altering wants, requirements, and facilities, just as if no rude change had
ever taken place. Assuming this theory to be
sound, it was further argued that the " Middle
Pointed" is the true point of perfection which we
should take as our nucleus of development; that
however admirable may be the vigour of the
earlier phases, and whatever beauties we may
find in the later, this middle style has the undoubted merit of completeness. It may be less
vigorous than its predecessor, but it has purged
itself of the leaven of early rudeness, and has so
completed all its parts as to meet every practical
necessity, while it has not commenced the down-
hill road of enervation and decay. One thing

was also in its favour, that the theory had become so generally accepted, that this phase might really, and without affectation, be said to be already thoroughly revived and adopted as our own, and that we really were in a position to take it as our starting point, and were actually doing so with considerable success. I had added to this theory, in my own version of it, that we should endeavour to import into this revived style all which was valuable in other varieties, the vigour of the earlier work, and all useful developements of the later. I refer on this point to my remarks on future developement in my little volume of 1850,[2] and I was certainly trying, with some success now and then, to carry the theory into effect.

There is then some ground for doubt how far the break-down of this theory, which followed immediately upon the Lille competition, was of advantage to the cause. Its most ludicrous feature was, the pious devotion to "First Pointed" in its most ultra-Gallic form, which at once began to inspire the minds of those who, before this, had given an equally religious tone to their adhesion to "Middle Pointed," now in its turn become semi-impious. I confess I was disposed for one reason to welcome the change. I had long felt the slavery of being morally debarred from making use of the earlier style, in which I secretly delighted, and was glad to have a little more freedom, without being subject to the jibes of self-constituted critics. This was, however, a vain imagination, as exclusiveness is never at a

---

[2] "A Plea for the faithful Restoration of our Ancient Churches" (T. H. Parker), chapter iii.

loss in forging new fetters to take the place of those worn out. Not that this is of any great consequence, as some bond of union is unquestionably needed, and no one should be weak enough to allow his own judgment to be biassed by the fads of others, unless he sees that their judgment is to be relied upon as sound.

There can be no question that a kind of chaotic state of things has ensued upon the dissolution of the " Middle Pointed" confederation. This, while it has perhaps done good by encouraging a tentative striving after new developements, and the introduction of many elements of value into the revived style, has nevertheless weakened the movement by destroying its unity, and by bringing it back very much to what it had been at first, a system of eclecticism, the very thing which we were striving to avoid.

There has, in fact, been no end to the oddities introduced. Ruskinism, such as would make Ruskin's very hair stand on end ; Butterfieldism, gone mad with its endless stripings of red and black bricks ; architecture so French that a Frenchman would not know it, out-Heroding Herod himself ; Byzantine in all forms but those used by the Byzantians ; mixtures of all or some of these ; "original" varieties founded upon knowledge of old styles, or upon ignorance of them, as the case may be ; violent strainings after a something very strange, and great successes in producing something very weak ; attempts at beauty resulting in ugliness, and attempts at ugliness attended with unhoped-for success. All these have given a wild absurdity to much of the architecture of the last seven or eight years, which one cannot but deplore : but at the same time it must be allowed that much of the best, the most nervous, and the most original results of the revival, have been arrived at within the same period. The worst things have in fact been produced by men, not drilled by the study of ancient work, but " climbing in some other way." It is their works which disfigure our streets with preposterous attempts at originality in domestic architecture. The really trained men, who have thoroughly studied ancient work, though they have not been exempt from great eccentricities, have nevertheless produced very fine works of art, full in many cases of original developement. I believe now, that the " wild oats " of this period may be considered as sown, that we are getting back into a very reasonable groove, and may trust that the days of mere eccentricity are passed, and I cannot but hope that we shall get into a condition of liberal unity, in which our efforts will be brought to act in one direction, not by a scornful bearing towards one another, but by a general conviction of the reasonableness of the course which we are taking.

Just now, indeed, the contemptuous line is chiefly adopted by a somewhat old-fashioned clique, of which the head is my valued friend, Mr. J. H. Parker of Oxford. These early pioneers in the revival, horrified at the wildness of these later days, have taken upon them to abuse, not the ignorant pretenders who have brought disgrace upon our cause, but the most talented of our band. No insult indeed is sufficiently bitter against every one who learns a single lesson abroad, or attempts the smallest originality of his own. Our tendency to wildness has given some excuse for this, and I do trust that a little common-sense exercised on both sides will soon put an end to a state of things which is bringing much scandal upon the revival, and is greatly rejoicing its opponents.

As regards myself I gradually fell into the use of French detail, not exclusively, but in combination with English. In domestic architecture I do think that I struck out a variety eminently practical, and thoroughly suited to the wants and habits of the day. Had I carried out my designs for the Government offices, this developement would have been realized; as it is, it is hardly known. I have carried it out to a certain degree at Kelham Hall,[3] but that is, in its ideal, rather more Italianized than my own more deliberate developement would have been; still, however, that house shows it fairly. Mr. Forman's house at Dorking[4] was built earlier and on a less pretentious scale, but it contains a great deal of what I was then working out. Sir Charles Mordaunt's, at Walton near Warwick, contains it in a minor form, and worked out with less sufficient funds, as does Hafodunos House, near Llanwrst.[5] The Town Hall at Preston also exemplies it, and the Rector's house at Exeter College, though in a less degree. One feature in all these buildings is the ample size of the windows.

[3] Near Newark, the seat of J. H. Manners-Sutton, Esq.—ED.
[4] Pipbrook House.—ED.
[5] The seat of H. R. Sandbach, Esq.—ED.

My friend Parker is very irate at the whole of these developements. He says they are Italian, French, or anything else, and wants me to make everything purely English, indeed he would make it Tudor. Now I distinctly aver, that if we were to build houses really like the old Tudor mansions, people would not in these days live in them. We must have large windows, plate glass in large sheets, sash windows if we like, and every convenience of our day. These clearly demand a new expansion of the style, and I boldly say that none has been proposed so good as this. The tide is rather setting against it now, because of its non-English form, and I am myself desirous, as soon as the vortex of business gives me a little leisure, to go again over its details carefully, and to Anglicize them, without sacrifice of essentials. Thus far I go with the present turn of feeling, but I see no sense, after for years labouring to bring domestic architecture into a practical form, in at once giving up all the results to a mere change of fashion. The general tendency at the present moment is to return to English detail. I hold with this to a certain extent. We were certainly going too far the other way, but if by doing this we have introduced any features bolder, more manly, more reasonable, more useful in any way, or have added to our store elements which tend to enrich it, and to increase our legitimate resources, let us not, in the name of common sense, throw them away again. Anglicize if you please, and I go all the way with you, for we were running wild on foreign detail ; but retain all the good you have picked up in your wanderings, and use it up in your reformed architecture.

I will offer a few remarks on our progress in the subsidiary arts, beginning with that of carving.

It has been a drawback to my own artistic success that, being one of the first of the revivers, I had, as it were, to grow with my own work, instead of being previously trained for it. Had I, for instance, known my future lot, how assiduously should I have practised myself in my youth in the drawing and designing of foliage, and in all the branches of decorative art as connected with Gothic architecture. I had no kind of idea of ever wanting them, and wonder that I practised them even as much as I did. The consequence of this want of knowledge of the future has been that I was unprepared, in my personal artistic training, to do justice to the developement in which I have had to take a prominent part, and have had to work up the subject, as I was able, in the midst of the vortex and turmoil of distracting business. I had it in me, but I had no leisure to stop to cultivate it. In spite of these great disadvantages I do believe that I have done as much as most men to forward the art of carving; but had it not been for them, I am sure that I should have done very great things in this direction. I have had a vast deal of bad carving done for me, it is true, some of it detestable. This has been mainly owing to the extent of my business, which has been always too much for my capacity of attending to it, added to the disadvantages before mentioned. Nevertheless where my real influence has been brought to bear, the results have been very different, and would have been very far more so, had it not been for these disadvantages, which I could not by any means get over.

I remember that, as early as 1840, my anxiety about the carving for the Oxford memorial was most intense, and though the result is not very high, I do think that, considering the time, it was remarkable. The carving at Camberwell church, which is conventional, is another fair specimen (barring the human heads, which I then thought as detestable as I do now). My carver then was a Mr. Cox, who continued to do my work for some years. When we founded the Architectural Museum, I turned my attention very much to French carving, of the type of that in the Sainte Chapelle, and later I urged the adoption of a bolder style, using natural foliage in a great degree, but attempting to get something of the boldness of the best conventional types. I think that this has been admirably attained by Mr. Brindley [6] in some of my later works, as at Kelham Hall, Wellington College Chapel, and the Town Hall at Preston. These are examples of carving of a very high order. My friend Mr. Street, during this period, has been working up the pure conventional foliage, Mr. Earp [7] being his handpiece, and he has done very great things. I think that his work and mine together, for the last few years or so, have been a noble developement. He can lay claim to his, more personally than I can to mine,

---

[6] Of the firm of Farmer and Brindley, whose studios are in the Westminster Bridge Road.—ED.

[7] His studios are now in the Finchley Road.—ED.

as he gives drawings, while I do my work by influence ; but the results in both cases are of a high order.   Let us push on to perfection in this noble race.

Metal-work has, during the period in question, made considerable progress, though it has suffered from its share of the eccentric mania of the day. Mr. Skidmore[8] can claim an eminent place both in skill, progress, and eccentricity.   My own individual share has not been great, excepting that I have had one or two great works carried out, such as the choir-screens at Lichfield and Hereford cathedrals.   Both of these were designed in full by myself, and are carried out according to my designs, in general ; in both, however, as in all his works, Mr. Skidmore has "kicked over the traces" wherever he has had a chance.   In some cases the work has gained, and in some suffered from this. Original ideas have been imported, but a certain air of eccentricity has come in with them.   On the whole the works are both very fine, and especially the latter.   I believe that Mr. Street has made great progress in metal work, acting through a smith at Maidenhead.   I have only seen a little of his work, but that was first rate.

With gold and silver work and jewellery I have had nothing to do.   This is foolish of me, as I delight in nothing more, but my avocations will not permit me.   I hope that the Memorial to the Prince Consort will be a success in the way of metal-working, if not invaded by interference on the one side or by wildness on the other.

How far stained glass has progressed, I am

[8] Of Coventry.—ED.

unable to form an opinion.   The universal mania
for earliness and eccentricity has here been rampant with a vengeance, and *cliqueishness* has had
its full swing.   I recollect about 1855, just before
Mr. Clayton[9] established himself in practice, he
designed for me several windows for the clerestory
of the choir of Westminster Abbey ; and though
the windows themselves were late thirteenth century, he was so strong in the old " Middle Pointed "
theory, that he insisted upon treating his draperies,
&c., in the style of the middle of the fourteenth.
In 1860 when he was employed to fill some windows in the north transept, so great had been the
change in his views, that he could, with the utmost
difficulty, be kept from making his glass earlier in
style than the stonework itself, and his figures
absolute scarecrows.   Yet I believe that he has
never been considered early enough, or grotesque
enough, in his views for the more learned.   Personally I have always been under the disadvantage
of having had no time to obtain such a mastery
over this subject, as would enable me to exercise
that strong influence which I should have desired.
My theory is, that if there is real merit in early
christian art—of which I am perfectly convinced—
its merit must of necessity be independent of, and
separable from, its defects and its quaintness ; and
that if we believe in our own great revival, we are
bound to show our faith by discriminating the
faults from the merits of our originals, and by
endeavouring to produce an art which avoids the
one while it retains the other, and adds to this
whatever of better instruction and skill our own

[9] Now of the firm of Clayton and Bell.—ED.

age can afford. This theory I, from year to year, endeavour to dun into the heads of those with whom I have to do. Alas! as an Hibernian once said, "The more I tell them to do it, the more they won't do it at all." Either they are such simple zealots as to believe in the faults of their masters as implicitly as in their merits, or else they do not really believe in the revival, and treat the old examples merely as viewed through a Wardour Street shop-window, or, as Simonides views an early codex, as things made only to be forged. I believe the former to be their real view, but I beg them to apply their common-sense to the subject for a little time, and then to act freely for themselves. As it is, one constantly sees in painted glass, things which in *Punch* would pass for very good jokes, and caricatures in *Punch*, which, in glass, would be viewed as true christian art.

Hardman, or rather his artist Powell, has had the advantage or disadvantage of a long drilling under Pugin. It made him a first-rate glass-painter, but on the death of his great master, instead of turning to old examples, he has been content to work on upon the material bequeathed to him, which has become from year to year more diluted, and its loss by dilution being unsupplied by any infusion of new strength, he has sunk for the most part into little more than an agreeable prettiness, though he occasionally when he brings his mind to bear strongly upon a particular work, produces really fine things, and his sense of pleasant colouring is certainly stronger than that of a great majority of our glass-painters. The works he did for Pugin have been as yet barely surpassed, e. g. those in the Houses of Parliament.

The art of glass-painting has suffered a great loss from the crochets and ill-nature of a man who of all others was the best qualified to help it forward. I refer to Mr. Whinston. He had devoted years to the study of old examples, and no man more thoroughly understood them. From his profession and education one would have expected him to prove a wise and judicious moderator between the excesses of over-excited partisans of conflicting views. He might have done infinite good had he taken up that position. As it is, he has absolutely thrown away his vantage-ground by imitating the worst excesses which he ought to have corrected, and by appearing as the almost exclusive advocate of a single type of glass-painting, and the unmeasured abuser of every one who in the smallest degree differs from him. This unhappy course has left him literally without influence, which I the more deeply regret as I am one who admires with him the particular phase to which he has attached himself, and go almost the whole way with him in my reprobation of some of the follies which excite his wrath, and I feel that his influence and censorship, had they been judiciously used, would have been of the most essential service to the cause. As it is, his bitter invectives render it impossible for any one to converse with him on the subject, excepting a few persons who have submitted to act in subserviency to his dictation, and who being, naturally, persons of no great mark, are very far from representing in their works any great advantage received from his instruction. In one respect, however, he has been eminently useful. He has, in conjunction with Messrs. Powell of Whitefriars, effected very important improvements in the manufacture of glass for the purposes of glass-painting.

Another great loss which this art has sustained arose from the premature death of the elder M. Gerente, of Paris. This gentleman, educated to another profession, had so earnest a feeling for art, and directed that feeling so strongly upon glass-painting, as to devote several years exclusively to the study of it, and to tracing and drawing from ancient examples throughout France. He told me that, after he had made up his mind to become a professional glass-painter, he would not allow himself to execute a single work, till he had devoted four years, exclusively to the study of ancient glass-paintings. He was a man of most vigorous talent, of great originality of conception, and at the same time a very learned antiquary. From such a man, though at first too antiquarian in the treatment of his works, the greatest results might have been hoped for, but Providence willed it otherwise. After escaping, almost miraculously, the dangers of the Revolution of 1848, in which he was taken prisoner by the mob, and actually set up for execution and the muskets levelled at him, when he was saved by the accidental interference of one of his own workmen, and afterwards was engaged in actual fighting for twenty-four hours together; he was cut off in the very next year, after only eight hours' illness, by the cholera. He called on me one day in great agitation; he had just lost his father by that disease, and, after watching him through his illness, had been seized with such a panic that he fled precipitately to England, convinced that if he stayed in Paris he should die of it. A fortnight afterwards Le père Martin called upon me, and told me that Gerente had returned, had been immediately seized with cholera, and had died !

He was succeeded by his brother, educated as a sculptor, who has followed up with considerable success his elder brother's methods.

Among the most promising artists in this department are Clayton and Bell, both of them men who took to art directly and solely from a natural genius for it. Mr. Alfred Bell was a pupil of my own. He was recommended to me by the clergyman of his native village, himself an amateur artist, who had aided his early genius. His productions at that early age (fourteen) were most remarkable, and, during the whole time that he was with me, nothing he had to do seemed to present any difficulty whatever to him. Since then he has reverted to his original bent for painting, rather than architecture. I only regret that he, owing to circumstances, and perhaps to an over-confidence in his own unaided powers, too much neglected a regular drilling in the elements of art. This has prevented his natural talents exhibiting themselves to full advantage. Mr. Clayton has been better drilled, and has a stronger turn of mind, and were it not for the two great banes of glass-painting, a morbid love of queer antiquated drawing on the one hand, and the destructive effect of over-pressure of work on the other, very great results indeed might be anticipated from them. They were the first in this country who became glass-painters, because they were artists; but it is a destructive profession, and if the greatest artist who ever lived had become in early life a glass-painter, and had had a great run of business, I do not hesitate to say that his future fame would have been ruined. No real art can stand against a constant high-pressure and working against time. Some of Clayton and Bell's productions are of a high character, but a large proportion are damaged or ruined by one or both of the influences above-mentioned. Their works are by no means whatever proportioned to their ability.

Ill-luck seems inseparably attached to this most unhappy art. Three distinct misfortunes dog its course at every step. First, the multitude of mere pretenders, or, at best, men of very slender artistic feeling and less skill, who disgrace and drag down the art which they profess. Secondly, the absurd rage for antiquated drawing, which exercises a ruinous influence upon it. This may be divided into two classes : one, that of the pseudo-artists, who imitate or pretend to imitate old drawings, merely to mask their inability to do anything better. Their grotesqueness is that of incapacity. The other is that of artists of a better class, who, as a simple matter of choice, follow the oddness of old work. This is the grotesqueness of error. The third misfortune is the natural consequence of the second. A number of persons, whether glass-painters or others, disgusted at the folly of this deliberate grotesqueness, run at once into the opposite mistake, and seek to remedy the evil by means of copies in glass of

actual picture-painting. This again divides itself
into two classes : the pretenders, who, though
incapable of producing works of art at all, calculate
(and successfully) upon the prevalent ignorance,
and produce wretched, mawkish attempts at
picture-painting, which a large proportion of the
public believe in and cry up as something very
fine, but which is really the most sickening of all
things. The culminating specimen of this is,
perhaps, the east window of All Saints Church,
Hastings. The second class consists of really
good or tolerable artists, who, falling into this
mistake, do all the mischief in the world by, as it
were, gilding an error by art which would otherwise be pretty good. The leaders of this are the
Munich painters and their patrons in this country,
and the culmination of the error is to be seen in
Glasgow Cathedral.[1] It is perhaps fortunate that
these painters make use of such contemptible
architectural decoration in their windows that no
one who has any real knowledge is, in this country,
deceived by them. A few classic architects, a
Dean or two, and a mixed multitude of the semi-
ignorant public form the list of their patrons.

The annoying thing is, that those who know
better give them the best possible excuse for their
error, for it becomes a fairly open question whether
a person will choose reasonably good art united
with erroneous principles, or sound principles
wedded to a grotesque art. It was vexatious
enough that Clayton and Bell, from whom better
things might have been hoped, and who have produced fine work (as in St. Michael's, Cornhill)

[1] And in the Chapel of Peterhouse, Cambridge.—ED.

should, for the most part, deliberately follow in the wake of the incapables: but it is yet more so, when a society of painters of the highest class, having been formed with the express intention of uniting high art with true principles, are found producing works yet still more strange than those of any of their predecessors.[2]

Let us hope against hope.

In decorative colouring I fear that we are not much more in advance. Our architects must become artists, and then, and not till then, shall we have a chance of success. Pugin did great things, but I cannot say much for subsequent progress. In mosaic work and inlays I think we have done better; indeed I cannot but think that this is one of the most promising branches of decorative art, and one of the most important, inasmuch as our climate demands decoration which cannot be injured by damp.

In encaustic tiling we have made little progress since Pugin's time. No one has equalled him in the designing of patterns, though I think that Lord Alwyne Compton greatly excels him in arrangements; while Godwin, of Hereford, comes far nearer to the texture of old tiles than Minton does.

Incised stone in some degree trenches now upon tile-work, and offers a wide field for progress. I hope that the introduction of it by Baron Triqueti into Wolsey's chapel at Windsor will prove a cause of advancement in that art, as

[2] From the date of this critique it is evidently only to the very earliest works of Messrs. Morris and Co. that reference is here made.—ED.

the employment of enamel mosaic in the same chapel will also, as I trust, in its own particular direction. The use of high art (as painting and sculpture) in connexion with the revived style, has not yet made great progress, though I think it will do so. I will not dwell upon this question; for my individual views on the subject, I would refer to my lecture delivered at Leeds in 1863, and entitled, " The Gothic Renaissance," and to my book on " Domestic Architecture."

My latest engagement of importance has been the Memorial to the late Prince Consort. I was invited to enter a competition for this, with some half-a-dozen other architects. I sent a single design for the memorial proper, and several for the Hall, which was proposed at the same time. My design for the monument was accepted. My idea in designing it was, to erect a kind of ciborium to protect a statue of the Prince; and its special characteristic was that the ciborium was designed in some degree on the principles of the ancient shrines. These shrines were models of imaginary buildings, such as had never in reality been erected; and my idea was to realize one of these imaginary structures with its precious materials, its inlaying, its enamels, etc., etc. This was an idea so new, as to provoke much opposition. Cost and all kinds of circumstances aid this opposition, and I as yet have no idea how it may end; I trust to be directed aright. [March 10, 1864.]

April, 1865.

I confess that few things perplex me more than the question of our position as the Gothic Revivalists.

Q

We commenced, as I have often said, without premeditation, acting spontaneously from mere love of it, without combination, without even comparing notes, with no thought of overthrowing or supplanting the vernacular classicism, but merely from an ardent and newly-generated affection for our old architecture; which led, first, to the mere study of it, and then, as a natural consequence, to its reproduction. Reproduction gradually ripened into revival, first for ecclesiastical purposes, and then for general use : our zeal increasing as we went on, we now began to flatter ourselves that we should eventually supplant the classicism of the day. Our love of the Gothic led us to a condemnation of the Classic, of which at first we had never thought : till at length we came to entertain a sort of religious horror of all styles of pagan origin. The formal and specific character which the revival now assumed, naturally led to a more systematic action. At first, free choice was allowed in the variety of Gothic which each man should adopt for any of his works. Gradually this was seen to be inconsistent with an organized revival, and it became necessary to unite in the adoption of our one style. The "middle-pointed" was soon fixed upon, though some (including myself) held, that whatever was valuable in other styles should be translated into it, so as to make it more comprehensive of all which was good. Some among us hated other varieties as much as they did classic, or perhaps even more, and seemed to think the use of perpendicular, or Norman, or even early pointed as nothing short of heresy. This absurdity was, however, a mere exaggeration of consistency, for if the revival was to be a great reality, it must have a consistent nucleus; so that it became necessary for a man, whose taste for the style was of an eclectic and general character, to put restraint upon himself for the sake of maintaining the unity and consistency of the movement.

I must confess that I regret the rude breaking-up of this consistent theory. It was begun by the transference of the claim of sovereignty from middle to early pointed : this was followed up by the attempering of the early style with foreign features; and eventually by the exclusion of English Gothic, in favour of French with a mixture of Italian, and often by a violent exaggeration of foreign character. This, in its turn, produced a reaction toward our own architecture, and at the same time in favour of a later style. Had this brought us back to where we once were, with all the advantage of what we had gathered during our wanderings, it might have been advantageous; but all our movements are in excess, and we seem for the time at least, to be at sea again, without chart or compass. All must now be very English and very late; while by some, liberty is again proclaimed, and men are left to adopt any style they may fancy, from the twelfth century to the eighteenth, while a few still adhere to the exaggerated early French or half Italian in vogue a few years back.

There is one great advantage attendant upon these changes, in that they have produced a liberal spirit as to the varieties of our own architecture, which renders our restorations more conservative, and our knowledge more general; while a study of foreign architecture cannot fail to supply us with much valuable matter, even though we do not actually adopt foreign styles. Still, however, our position is anomalous. I confess to thinking that while the foreign rage was upon us, we were generating a secular style peculiarly suited to our own wants: but unhappily this was caught up by an ignorant and untutored rabble, and so caricatured and exaggerated, that its very originators came to hate it, and can now hardly make use of their own developements without exposing themselves to ridicule, as adhering to exploded notions, and as abetting their own vulgar imitators. This reaction may well lead to an anglicizing of the variety thus developed, which would be in itself desirable: though I confess to an opinion that a little touch of Italian character has the advantages of facilitating the use of brick, with the square sectional forms which the nature of that material suggests; of severing purely secular from religious architecture in the minds of the public; and of avoiding a too severe clashing between our gothic and our classic street architecture. If all this can be obtained without departing too far from English types, so much the better. A slight infusion of Italian feeling may also have the advantage of admitting the free use of round and segmental arches, which I feel to be essential to secular architecture.

In our church architecture we have, as I consider, little reason to depart far from our own types; though I confess, even here, to a tendency to eclecticism of a chastened kind, and to a desire for liberty to unite in some degree the merits of the different styles.   We ought, I think, to have periodical conferences between the leaders of the revival, with a view to keeping as much as may be together; though unfortunately in these days the publicity of these conferences is sadly against their efficiency.   I believe that a sort of free-masonry is almost essential here, the differences of opinions among architects, and the contemptuous feelings entertained by one clique towards another, militating sadly against agreement.

CHAPTER VI.

In the above reminiscences since 1845, I have
confined myself almost wholly to professional
topics, indeed my intention has been to limit
myself, after the first part of the work, to such
subjects.

What I have written being intended primarily
for my children, I wished to give such family
information as was wholly beyond their reach, but
after that to give them an outline of my professional career alone, almost to the exclusion of
personal and family matters. I will however
mention that my mother died at Wappenham in
1854. She had for a long time been in very bad
health, having suffered from an oppression of the
brain (whether of an epileptic or paralytic kind
I do not know), which had the effect of undermining her memory to a very painful degree. I
believe that it was brought about in some degree
by the intensity of her sorrow at my father's death,
and it was furthered by a sort of excess in her
religious devotions. She would shut herself up
every day for, I think, two hours (or it might not
have been quite so much) for religious reading and
devotion in a cold room in all seasons, and gave
way no doubt to emotions calculated to overstrain

the mental system. Her piety was of the most
ardent kind, only equalled by her affection for her
family. She lived, from the time of my father's
death, in a good old house opposite the Rectory at
Wappenham, a house which my father had occupied while the Rectory was being built, and which
(as he really only occupied the latter for a year or
so) I got to view as "my home." During my
early "workhouse" days I was always dropping
in there on all occasions. Later on I went there,
I fear, less and less frequently till the time of my
poor mother's decease, though always feeling it to
be my old home. I grieve to say that from that
time I felt that I had lost my boyish home, and
although my brother and his family were there,
and though my sister Mary Jane lived in a cottage
built for her in the village, I have never been at
Wappenham again. This has, during the last two
months since my dear sister's decease, caused me
the most poignant grief. I have felt like one
awakening from a feverish dream, and have almost
madly wondered where I have been and what
I have been doing. I earnestly advise young
persons diligently to keep up communication with
their relatives. You do not seem to need it at the
moment, and you feel as if you could do it at any
time, but when death makes a breach in the family
circle, then it is that one's neglect comes back upon
the conscience in a way which is almost overwhelming. It seemed at one time as if it would
affect my reason.

In 1848 we lost my father-in-law, Mr. Oldrid,
under circumstances peculiarly painful and distressing. He was an excellent man, of sterling

and exemplary worth. Both he and my mother died, I believe, in their seventieth year. My mother-in-law, Mrs. Oldrid, died some years later, and reached, I think, her eightieth year. She was a person of great excellence, and of a very powerful mind, which retained all its vigour and freshness till the very last. For many years I saw much more of her than of my own mother, the one being in full vigour and energy, while the other was almost laid aside from the malady I have mentioned. She frequently came to stay with us in town, and we often visited her at Boston, which became a third home to me. Her conversation was always lively, amusing, and instructive. She was a sort of female mentor in our family, while at the same time she was the life of our party, when she was with us. She departed this life after a painful illness in 1857. Mr. and Mrs. Oldrid lie buried in the family vault in the church-yard at Leverton, near Boston, where Mr. Oldrid had a small estate.

My uncle King died in Jersey in 1856. My aunt King followed him two months later, to the very day, and thus nearly the entire generation had passed away, which had been the guides and guardians of my youth, and here I would say, " Make me to be numbered with thy saints in glory everlasting."

On my mother's side of the family, Mr. Nathaniel Gilbert of Antigua, her first cousin, the head and the last of the Gilbert family[1] came

[1] Southey, in his life of Wesley, says of him, " Mr. Gilbert was a man of ardent piety . . . Being enthusiastic by constitution, as well as devout by principle, he prayed and preached in

over to England for some years (I suppose about 1845), and lived here in very good style for a long time, occupying Stocks, near Tring, the seat of his cousin Mr. Gordon. When, however, the duties on free-grown and slave-grown sugar were equalized, he returned precipitately to Antigua, where he found his circumstances almost ruined by the change. He shortly afterwards died, leaving the estate to his widow (and cousin) with a remainder to her sister, and after her to the Bible Society. I daresay the reversion could be purchased of them for an old song. The estate has been so much reduced in value, that my sister Mary Jane, whose income depended on it, in some degree, was put to some inconvenience for several years by the failure of supplies fron the old family source.

As regards my own personal history, I will only say that, since we ceased to reside in Spring Gardens, we have lived in all happiness, first at St. John's Wood, and then at Hampstead, watching the growing up of our five boys, and have every reason to bless God for the happiness and prosperity He has granted us, nearly the only drawback to which has been my wife's delicate health.

his own house to such persons as would assemble to hear him on Sundays, and encouraged by the facility of which he found himself possessed, and the success with which these beginnings were attended, he went forth and preached to the negroes. This conduct drew upon him contempt, or compassion, according as it was imputed to folly or to insanity. But he had his reward ; the poor negroes listened willingly to the consolations of Christianity, and he lived to form some two hundred persons into a Methodist Society, according to Mr. Wesley's rules."— Ch. xxviii. p. 332.

In the earlier part of these remarks I have
alluded to my sister Mary Jane's death. This
was the first breach in our immediate family circle
of brothers and sisters since the death of my
brother Nathaniel in 1830, a space of nearly
thirty-four years. How much do we owe to
Almighty God for so long sparing us from so
bitter a grief. Mary Jane had been for some
time in very weak health, though I had hoped that
she was getting over it, but this last year (1863)
she was attacked more violently than before, and
in the autumn it was seen that her sickness would
be unto death. My brother Samuel and his excellent wife most kindly asked her to stay with them
at Brighton, knowing well that it was to die
there. I will not attempt to describe her character, nor the circumstances of her illness and
departure. They will, I trust, be sketched by a
more able hand, but it is delightful to think how
cheerfully and happily she passed away from this life
to a better, knowing well that her end was coming,
and preparing for it with all cheerfulness and
deliberation, both in temporal and spiritual things.
Her character was one of exquisite beauty ; I have
never known anything to surpass it. I saw her
several times during her illness, and no word or
expression but of happiness passed her lips. I
saw her within a few hours of her death, and
when I bid her good night she said, "We shall
meet in heaven." Before I could get back in the
morning her sweet soul had taken its flight. This
was on the 22nd of January last (1864), her age
being within a few days of forty-three years. She
was a burning and a shining light, and had been

made instrumental, as one may fairly hope, to the salvation of many souls. Our family, with the exception of my two sisters Euphemia and Elizabeth, met at her funeral. She lies in the churchyard of Hove, near Brighton. It was a peaceful and pleasant family party, for, though the occasion was mournful, a halo of sacred cheerfulness seemed to hover around every memory of our departed sister.

I confess, however, that when alone my feelings were very different, and for some time I suffered from severe depression, which disappeared when I was in company. I believe I shed more tears for my sweet sister than I had ever shed in an equal time before. I was, in fact, haunted with my own neglectful conduct, and was only consoled by the assurance of my two surviving sisters that she attributed it wholly to the necessities of my peculiar practice. I am now threatened with a second grief. My dear sister Euphemia is suffering from a disease which they say must be fatal, and which is of a most painful nature. Nothing could be more touchingly beautiful than the correspondence between her and our sister Mary Jane during the last few months; each being conscious of the seeds of dissolution working within them, and each more anxious, and grieving more, for the other than for herself. How earnestly do I wish that I could experience the sentiments which have so wonderfully supported them in these grievous trials.

March 23rd, 1865.

I re-open my book after closing it for twelve

months, and I must recommence on subjects similar to those with which I closed it. Two most heavy afflictions have come upon me during the interval ; the one expected, the other absolutely unlooked for. My dear sister Euphemia departed this life in perfect peace on February 8th last (1865). I will return to this subject by-and-by, but during our long anticipation of this sad event who would have thought that one of the strongest of our dear boys would be snatched away from us before her ? My son Albert Henry was born in August, 1844, a few days after our removal from Spring Gardens to St. John's Wood. During his infancy and early childhood he showed some tendency to water on the brain, accompanied by a very early intellectual developement. Happily his health, in the course of a few years, was re-established ; though we did not for a long time venture to send him to school, but committed his education to private tutors, all of whom in succession gave us the most flattering accounts of his promise and talents. We had, indeed, abundant evidence of the high order of his mind, both as to power and tone, especially evinced by his facility of composition, which from a very early age was remarkable. He went for a short time to St. Andrew's College, Bradfield, where his progress was very satisfactory, but he was obliged to leave, owing to a slight indisposition, which led us to think that he needed home care, and he accordingly completed his preparation for the University under private tuition.

He went to Exeter College, Oxford, at the beginning of 1864, and we are told by the rector

and the tutor that his progress during the one year
of his continuance there was really remarkable,
and his conduct in every way exemplary; indeed,
he won the respect and affection of all who knew
him there.

During his long vacation we were in search of a
new place of abode, Hampstead being too cold for
our younger boys, and, after many disappointments and difficulties, we found a suitable residence
at Ham, in choosing which, and in moving into it,
our son Albert was of great assistance, though he
was obliged to return to Oxford before we were
quite settled. Who would have imagined that, while
removing for the health of our younger children,
we were so soon to lose their elder and far stronger
brother. He had been exceedingly charmed with
the place when he first visited it with me in
September, and when he returned in the winter
he at once availed himself of its facilities for
boating, and nearly every day went with his
brother Alwyne on the river for a row in a
boat, which he had hired for the vacation. How
little did we think that this harmless recreation
would be the cause of so much grief! Often
did I feel exultation at the thought that Alwyne,
who could not stand even the commencement of
our Hampstead winters, should be able now to
row every winter day on the Thames without any
inconvenience; little thinking that, though the
frail boy stood against it unhurt, the strong man
was destined to quail under its effects.

Albert felt no evil from this exposure till within
a week of the end of the vacation. On Saturday,
January 21st, he rowed as usual in the morning,

and, after an early dinner, went with Alwyne to town. The day was sharp and frosty, but with us at Ham pretty bright, though in London there was a most dense fog. They were late in return- ing, having found no little difficulty in groping their way about town. The next day (Sunday) Albert complained (as I have since heard) of a little stiffness in the limbs, but nevertheless went twice to church. On Monday I still knew nothing of his being unwell, but I afterwards heard that he complained of stiffness, and said that he would try to row it off. After rowing he had a long run after a dog. The next day he was very stiff, and we afterwards heard that, while reading logic with Alwyne, which he usually (and very kindly) did in the afternoon, he lay down on the floor of his room, and said he felt as if he was going to have rheumatic fever. We heard nothing of this; but a medical man, Dr. Julius, who was attending my son Gilbert, saw him and gave him some trifling medicine, saying that it was only stiffness from rowing. I was out all that day. The next morn- ing (Wednesday) he was still very stiff, with pains in all his joints, even to the fingers and toes; but the medical attendant, when I told him that I feared it was rheumatism, said he thought it was not. In the evening I found him much worse, and hardly able to walk, and the doctor at once said that it was rheumatism. We put him into a hot bath and got him to bed, but in the night he suffered acutely, and the next day was utterly helpless, unable to move hand or foot. I had to be away that day at Salisbury, to attend the first meeting of the restoration committee. On my return at night I found him very ill, and the next day he continued the same. We then, with great difficulty, carried him down into a larger room. On Saturday he seemed better, the rheumatism having left his limbs to a considerable degree, but the doctor announced that his heart was (as he said, slightly) affected. He had been somewhat delirious at times, but during Sunday night became more so, and on Monday, January 30th, 1865, he departed without pain, and apparently without consciousness, at about half-past three in the afternoon. He was interred in Petersham Churchyard on the following Saturday. I earnestly pray God never to let his image be dimmed in my memory, but to keep it ever fresh in my thoughts. I doubt not that our Gracious God will make his dear soul an object precious in His sight, and will train it to ever higher and more exalted happiness.

April 21st, 1865.

I will mention that among a very large number of letters of condolence of the kindest character, addressed to us on this sad event, I received one written by the direction of the Queen, expressing her warm sympathy with me in my loss.

My sister Euphemia, whose illness and death I have already alluded to, departed this life in perfect peace. Her last days were happily much more free from suffering than had been feared, and her mind was in a state of the most heavenly and childlike quiescence, happiness and love. Her life had been one of constant labour for the good of others, and of constant, unremitting, and

untiring work.   Her great characteristic was energetic, strong-willed devotion to doing good. While
in health, she was a person of almost herculean
power of work, and was always at it; and she
continued this far into her illness, and, in lessen-
ing degrees, even towards the close of it.   The
love and veneration felt for her in the three places
where she had thus ministered (Gawcott, Boston,
and Alford), were unbounded.

She added to this robust side of her mental
constitution, a great tenderness of spirit, and an
earnestness of affection, such as one would hardly
have expected from one of so strenuous a turn of
mind.   Her letters breathe a strong, yet tender
love, which is quite beautiful; and when her illness
came upon her, this became yet more marked.
She was a very beautiful letter-writer, and I very
much wish a collection of her letters could be
made.   My still heavier loss, which preceded her
death by but eight or nine days, has, in some
degree preoccupied my mind against the sorrow
which her loss would otherwise have caused me;
but I feel that one of the very dearest companions
of my early life has been taken from me, and
one of the most loving of relatives and best of
religious counsellors, though, alas, too little consulted.

June 17*th,* 1865.

I open this book again to record bereavements.

At the beginning of May, 1865, I lost my
cousin John Scott of Hull,[2] the eldest male cousin

[2] Vicar of St. Mary's. He preached his last sermon on
Easter-day.—ED.

on my father's side, and one of the loved companions of my youth.

I cannot now stop to commemorate him, as death has since come far nearer to me, and has removed one of the dearest of my circle of brothers, and perhaps the very one who seemed the least likely to be cut off.

My brother Samuel King Scott was seven or eight years younger than I, having been born in November, 1818. He was consequently but a child of eight or nine years old when I left my early home: I well remember him, at that time, as the blithest, most lively and humorous of our family, and every one's favourite. " Sammy King is just the thing," was a favourite rhyme in our nursery, and expressed rudely the general feeling towards him. His little strokes of wit, even in those days, were vernacular amongst us, and I have often told them to my own children. Years afterwards (I do not recollect whether before or after my father's death) he was articled to Mr. Stowe, a surgeon at Buckingham, a little before my brother John went into partnership with him.

These were my early days of workhouse building, and as Buckingham was the centre of my first batch of unions, I was often there; and I have a lively recollection of the delight I then felt in my young brother's company. I used to arrive by mail-cart at seven in the morning, just as he was getting up, and sometimes on a cold morning I turned into his bed to supplement my night's rest; which had been divided between the top of the mail to Aylesbury, a short bout of bed at a public-house there, and what one could get balanced on

R

the mail-cart between there and Buckingham. These little visits were peculiarly delightful to me, Sam was so jolly and cheery, and his master, Mr. Stowe, was so kind, and took such an interest in my special pursuits, as well as in my favourite study at the time, geology.   Later on, my brother John and his wife added to the pleasure of these little flying visits, so that they are among quite the bright spots in my memory.   Sam was treated in Mr. Stowe's house not as an apprentice, but rather as an adopted son.

Years rolled on again, and we had him in London " walking the hospitals."   I was then married, and we lived in Spring Gardens, where he used to come whenever his work allowed ; and very happy we were when he came, though he was working so hard, and I was so busy, and travelling so much about the country, that our communications were after all but scanty, though very, very pleasant. One of his hospital friends, now an eminent physician, told me the other day that he was the general favourite amongst them.   "They all had their quarrels," he says, " among themselves, but none of them ever quarrelled with him, though all went and told him of their quarrels."   I ought to say, that at this time, and I think a good deal earlier, he had become a sincerely religious character, and I never heard of a single act or word of his inconsistent with a strictly conscientious christian life, though this did not for a moment clash with the natural cheeriness of his lively and humorous disposition.

As soon as ever he had passed his examinations, he became a candidate for the office of house-surgeon to the Sussex County Hospital at Brighton, but seeing that another candidate had a better chance than he, he desisted, and accepted the post, which chanced to be also vacant, of surgeon to the public dispensary there. The duties of this office seem to have been that of doctor-general to the poor of Brighton, and he worked at this for more than a year desperately hard, so much so, as to injure his health; but by doing so he won golden opinions among the most estimable inhabitants of the town, as also among the medical practitioners. This led to his being selected by one of the first surgeons there, Mr. Philpot, brother to the present bishop of Worcester, as his partner, and subsequently his successor.

About 1846 he married a daughter of Dr. Bodley, a highly respected physician, who had formerly practised at Hull, where he had been an intimate and valued friend of my uncle and his family; but who had retired, and then was living at Brighton.

He was peculiarly happy in his marriage, its only drawback being that his family increased at an unusually rapid rate: so that before he had freed himself from the burdens incident to commencing practice, he found himself surrounded by a large party of children. No man, however, has led a happier life in every possible way, nor was any one in his position more loved, valued, and respected. He was the kindest and most hospitable of men; always ready to do good, devoted to his work, and withal a strict, consistent, and unswerving christian man. I hear of him wherever I go, and always in the same strain, and the feelings enter-

tained towards him at Brighton were warm beyond
expression.

He was of a wonderfully hearty constitution,
and of intense powers of enjoyment; and for many
years he relieved the monotony of active practice
by a month of pedestrianism in the summer. He
had "done" every part of Switzerland, while the
Highlands, North Wales, and the Lake district
had their turns, and sometimes the less romantic
parts of the country: for such was his zest for
nature and scenery that no one beauty suffered
with him by contrast with another, so that the
South Downs or the Surrey hills were as charming
to him as if he had never visited Snowdon, Ben
Nevis, or Mont Blanc; and he enjoyed a little
country residence he was in the habit of taking
for his family on the borders of Ashdown forest,
with as great a zest as the valleys of Switzerland,
or the borders of the Westmoreland lakes; with
which latter district he was as familiar as a mountain guide. His knowledge of geology, botany,
and other branches of natural science, rendered
these trips the more delightful.

Last summer, 1864, he went again to the Lakes
with his two eldest boys, my nephew the Rev. T.
Scott, my son Albert, and another friend, and a
most delightful tour they made, thoroughly ex-
ploring all the western half of the district; and,
stout as he was, they say that he was the most
indefatigable of the party, often continuing his
mountain walks after some of the younger ones
had been obliged to desist.

This proved to be his last expedition. It is
now seen that his mountaineering was a mistake.

A stout man of forty-five, working hard, early and late, day and night, for eleven months in the year, is unfit, however strong and vigorous he may feel, for exercises belonging either to youth or to the trained pedestrian. He was conscious of no effects but what were good, but something was going on within, of which he felt nothing. The strong man was failing at the heart, but the danger was unknown and unfelt. So exuberant were his sensations of health, that he delighted in playing with his constitution. He habitually rose at six, exercised himself for half an hour with heavy dumb-bells, and then plunged into a cold bath. The powerful machine was overstrained at its one weak point.

Early last April he went with one of his sons, and my own son Alwyne, to a place on the South Downs, and there for the first time felt an oppression in going up hill. The next week he felt it again, and more sharply, in walking over the downs to see the review of the Volunteers. It came on yet more heavily when he was called out soon afterwards to see a patient in the night, and shortly after this it came upon him with such overwhelming violence as to prostrate his strength and compel him to retire from work.

I ran down to see him at his little retiring place near Ashdown forest, and found him changed, from vigour to feebleness, a broken, prostrated man; still in his languor rejoicing in the beauties of nature, and supported by the consolation of religion, cheerful and happy, though evidently conscious of his position.

He was delighted to see me, but I left him with

a strong feeling on my mind that I had looked upon him for the last time, and I wept bitter tears after straining myself to get the last peep of him standing at the farmhouse door to see me off. For a few days we had better accounts, but ten days after I had left him, he was suddenly called to a better world, June 9th, 1865.

Last Tuesday we committed his body to the tomb, to rest not far from that of our dearly loved sister, Mary Jane, in Hove churchyard. Nineteen years before I had been present at his wedding in the same church.

Thus within less than a year and a half I had followed to the grave, from the same door and to the same churchyard, a dear sister and brother, next to each other in age, and nearer yet in goodness and love, both far younger than myself, and one far stronger: both far better. They were both pleasant and lovely in their lives, and in death were not far divided.

My dear brother's heart was found to have lost a large portion of its muscular fibre, which his physician attributed to a slow chronic inflammation brought on by too violent exercise; a practical warning to the strong man not to glory in his strength.

He was followed to the grave by, I believe, all the medical men in Brighton. His friend and pastor, Mr. Smith, declared, after the funeral, that he had never met with a more thorough-going, consistent christian, or a man more estimable in every relation of life, and that he never expected to find his equal. "The memory of the just is blessed."

All his brothers were present at the funeral, and many others, both friends and relations.

March 10*th*, 1872.

I have neglected this little chronicle now for nearly seven years—years of mercy and prosperity in most respects.

In 1870 I was threatened with a fatal disease, being suddenly attacked, while at Chester, in the heart and lungs.

I was detained at the deanery for five weeks before I could return home : [3] my dear wife went down there to be with me, and she brought me home, and by God's mercy, I was, in the course of the following spring, sufficiently restored to resume my usual engagements.

Now after yet another year, a terrible blow has fallen upon me. My wife had repeatedly been threatened with heart disease, but had been hitherto mercifully relieved. Last spring she had a very alarming attack, but again recovered. In December last, while staying in London, she was attacked by very acute rheumatism in the right shoulder, which was followed by a return of the symptoms of disease of the heart. Again, however, this gave way to remedies, but again returned. She suffered from frequent faintness, drowsiness, and swimming in the head, with pain and stiffness about the region of the heart. Dr. Bence Jones, who was consulted, made rather light of it, though his remedies did not much relieve her. She seemed

[3] Nothing could have exceeded the kindness of the Dean and Mrs. Howson under circumstances which cannot but have occasioned to them great inconvenience.

to get weaker, and sometimes kept her room. At length some other trouble complicated the attack. She kept her bed, and although I usually went three times in the night to see her, while a servant constantly sat up with her, I was blind, or nearly so, to the danger; though I confess to suffering from an indescribable internal alarm. Oh! what dismay and grief came at length upon me, when, on February the 24th, she was snatched away from us during sleep!

Her loss is to me that of one of the wisest and best of earthly companions, helpers, and advisers. She was a person of very strong and clear intellect; of quiet and decided perception of the right thing to do, under any emergency; and she was gifted with that decision and courage in which I was myself naturally deficient.

She has, over and over again, given me advice of the greatest importance in my profession; she was the means of terminating (a quarter of a century back) my partnership with Mr. Moffatt, for while I hesitated and delayed, she took the matter into her own hands, drove to town while I was away, called on my partner, and unflinchingly communicated to him my decision.

In training up her children, and managing her household, she was exemplary, and her intercourse with her friends and neighbours were such as to secure a lasting friendship and a sincere regard, which did not cease when we removed from the neighbourhood in which we had been living. One of her most striking characteristics was her wide-spread and open-handed charity. None came to her and went away empty.

My wife was my second cousin, her mother being the daughter of Mr. William Scott of Grimblethorpe Hall in Lincolnshire, the eldest brother of my grandfather, the commentator. My mother-in-law had known my father in their youth, but they had been for many years separated, until, in 1821, she brought her only son to Gawcott as a pupil. From that time, the families became intimate, and on one occasion Mrs. Oldrid brought her eldest daughter Fanny to Gawcott, when the foundation was laid of the regard felt for her by my eldest brother, which subsequently culminated in their marriage.

I did not form the acquaintance of my cousin Caroline Oldrid till the winter of 1828, when she, and her sister Helen, being then at school at Chesham, came over to spend their Christmas vacation with us. I have often heard my wife tell with great zest of this. They were to have stopped through the holidays at Chesham, but getting thoroughly sick of it, they asked leave to go to Gawcott, nearly thirty miles off. They walked over to Amersham to meet the Buckingham coach, sending on their luggage, and arrived just too late, or else the coach was full, I forget which. They were not, however, to be stopped, and at once ordered out a chaise and posted through the snow to Gawcott. I arrived from London for my Christmas holiday a few days later, and there I met for the first time my future wife.

She was then a most merry girl of seventeen, and a most happy Christmas we spent together. Nothing could exceed our merriment, and our constant fun and jokes. My sister Euphemia and my brother Nathaniel were there, and we were all in joyous happiness together.

I well remember when our happy meeting came to an end, what a vacancy and a sort of pang I felt, which whispered to me that some feeling hitherto unknown was stealing into my heart.

Not long after this, my eldest brother followed up his early love, and was married in the beginning of 1830 to Fanny Oldrid. I saw her sister again for a short time, on her way from Boston to Goring, where my brother was then living. My next meeting with her was at Latimers in April 1831, when we were thrown much together, and my early feelings were greatly fostered. I saw her again, for a day or two, that year at Boston on my return from Hull. I well remember drinking wine with her at a picnic at Tattershall Castle out of the same silver cup with an indescribable feeling of pleasure. Again I saw her in London about 1833, and two years later, in the course of the summer of 1835, we were engaged. She was now a matured woman of twenty-four, merry and full of life and fun as before, but she had seen much in the interval to subdue and chasten her spirits, and had become deeply religious.

I was not even now in any fit position for marriage, and our engagement extended over nearly three years, during which I regularly visited Boston. In this I was facilitated by my employment in the erection of several Union houses in the county. We were married on June 5th, 1838, being each a little under twenty-seven years of age. Our wedding tour was by Southwell and Matlock

to Malvern, thence to Bristol, and home by way
of Oxford.

At first, we had no house of our own, and lived
in lodgings, my office continuing to be at Carlton
Chambers, but soon we found a house to our mind,
in which we could unite the two—No. 20,⁴ Spring
Gardens, where my practice has ever since been
conducted, during a period of thirty-three years.

As our family, however, and my practice both
began to increase we removed (1844) to St. John's
Wood, where we lived for many years.

My wife was ever an admirable helper to me in
my business, always ready with wise advice and
encouragement. At one time, after my separation
from Mr. Moffatt, we were for some years in
straitened circumstances, but she always encouraged me to face them out boldly, and by
God's blessing they gradually mended till at
length we became very prosperous.

My practice took me much from home, and she
led a comparatively solitary life. Her great relaxation was when we went to the sea-side, which
we did every year, unless some other tour to
Wales or to the Lakes engaged us. She occasionally went with me on my professional
journeys, but after the birth of our second son,
her health was much undermined, and she became
an indifferent traveller. Once, I remember, we
took a little voyage in an open sailing boat, round
the Isle of Wight, with much enjoyment. Later
on, we took to driving excursions in an open one-
horse chaise, which we repeated very often for
many years, going down in this manner to the

⁴ Now Number 31.—ED.

sea-side, usually to the Isle of Wight. This delightful custom we kept up to the very last year of her life. On one occasion we went from London, in our own carriage, to the further side of Devonshire.

One of our earliest excursions (not made in this way, though) was to Skegness in Lincolnshire, the retreat of her youthful days. I shall never forget our enjoyment of this plain, unfrequented coast. I used to take my work with me, and often, there and elsewhere, have I marked out my designs on the sand in a large scale, repeating them, perhaps, on paper in the evenings.

Our favourite watering-place, however, was Shanklin, where we very often went, occupying usually the residence of the absentee squire, a rather large though cottage-like house, with charming gardens and thick plantations. My wife delighted in the seclusion of this quiet spot.

On one occasion we took another house there, the grounds of which extended to the very edge of the " Chine," and which proved to be haunted.[5]

---

[5] I well remember the circumstances. Every evening after dark, footsteps, as of a man pacing slowly up and down the verandah, upon the garden front of the house, were distinctly to be heard. We at first took it to be the gardener. Finding that this was not the case, we boys used to lie in wait, and when the footsteps were heard, leap out into the verandah. I can well recollect doing thus upon a bright moonlight night, and our amazement at finding no one. This failing, we stretched strings across the track, so as to render it impossible for any one to walk there in the dark without stumbling, but these interfered in no way with the even regularity of the strange footfalls. Another time we strewed the flagging with sand, and when the footsteps were again heard, we went out with a lantern and carefully examined the sanded pavement: not

Our last visit to the Isle of Wight was some twelve or thirteen years back. After staying a time at Shanklin, but not in our favourite home, we took a house at Niton, called La Rosière, which we greatly liked. We found, however, by repeated experience, that, much as we loved this charming island, it did not really suit my dear wife's health, being too relaxing. We, one year, tried Sea View, near Ryde, but at last we gave it up, and in future

a trace of any kind was to be found. I do not remember that we ever thought of there being anything supernatural in the matter, only the noises were unaccountable, and so, strongly piqued our curiosity. Our groom, who slept in the house, came one morning about this time to my mother, and asked for leave to go to his home. When pressed for his reason for this sudden wish, he stated that he had in the early dawn seen by his bedside a ghostly female figure, from which he inferred that his mother, his only female relative, was in danger. He was with some difficulty persuaded to wait the result of a letter to his mother, who of course was found to be well enough. We thought no more of this, judging it, in spite of the extraordinary impression which it had evidently made upon him, to be nothing but a dream of indigestion. More than a year after this, we happened to meet some friends of ours, who, as we then found, had occupied the same house during part of the following season. They asked us whether we had not been disturbed by ghostly noises and so forth, and told us that they had themselves been so annoyed, that they had had to leave the house, and that after giving it up, they had ascertained that every one in the village knew the house to be "haunted," but that the fact was carefully kept secret lest the letting value of the villa should suffer. The village story goes, I know nothing of the truth of this, that in that house in about 1820, a wicked uncle murdered his niece and ward in a cellar, which is accessible only by a trap-door in the floor of the room in which our groom slept. The old gentleman is said to have been accustomed to pace up and down that verandah after dark, for many years, during which the crime remained undetected. I attach no particular value to these facts myself, but as my father has referred to them; and the evidence is first-hand, it went to St. Leonards, where we had bitter experience of fevers during two succeeding winters, due not to the place itself, but to the bad construction of the houses we happened to take. We persevered, and in subsequent visits found it perfectly healthy. We at that time were living at Hampstead, which we found too cold for some of our boys in the winter; which led to the painful break-up of our party every year, my wife and the younger ones spending the winter at St. Leonards. She thus became almost an inhabitant of that place, and formed many friendships, becoming known there, as was the case wherever she resided, as a ready helper of the poor.

The causes above referred to led us, in the autumn of 1864 to leave Hampstead, after a long search and many projects, for Ham, near Richmond. I have already related the most heavy trial which overtook us very shortly after making this change. It was a life-long sorrow to my dear wife.

On one occasion only my dear wife went with me abroad. Her health had rendered her so poor a traveller that she always shrank from it; but at length, in 1863, she made up her mind to venture, and was in the highest degree delighted. Our tour was not long as to distance, though it spread

it may be worth while to give it. The footfalls, the attempts made to discover their cause, the fact that the groom made that statement to my mother, and that he was beyond a doubt sincerely alarmed, I can vouch for. I also heard myself the statement of the lady who rented the house the next season. Of the rest I can only say—

> " I know not how the truth may be,
> I tell the tale as t'was told to me."—Ed.

over some time. We went by Boulogne and
Amiens to Paris, where we stopped a fortnight in
a pleasant private hotel overlooking the gardens of
the Tuilleries. We then went on to Rheims, and
thence, by the exquisite valley of the Meuse, to
Namur and Brussels, where she stayed, with our
second son and a friend, while I made a rush to
attend the consecration of my church at Hamburg.
We returned by steamer from Antwerp to London.
Curiously enough, I have never myself been abroad
since then,[6] not liking to leave her for so long a
time as it would have required.

One of our subsequent trips was into Devonshire. We went in our own carriage, with post-
horses hired at Petersham, travelling by stages of
twenty or thirty miles, by Reading, Marlborough,
Chippenham, Clifton, Bridgewater, and Minehead
to Lynton, where we stayed a fortnight. We had
great fun in going from Minehead to Lynton.
Our Petersham post-horses not being trustworthy,
we drove four-in-hand from Minehead over the
noble piece of table-land, 1100 feet high, which
intervenes. At Lynton we were lodged in the
best situated house in the place, belonging to Sir
—— Smith. The situation was simply enchant-
ing, but to my wife it was like an exquisite prison,
as she could never get down to the sea nor visit
the finest scenery. We accordingly transferred
ourselves, again with four horses, to Westward-
ho, and subsequently drove straight across the
country to Sidmouth. Finally we drove back
through Dorset and Wilts, along the old, but
now unfrequented roads—a beautiful mode of

[6] This was written in 1872.—ED.

seeing the country, though subject to the inconvenience arising from the deterioration of the inns.

After 1869, we never returned to Ham, but, after a visit to Worthing and Brighton, we took for three years a charming residence—Rook's-nest, near Godstone.

This place was an elysium to my dear wife, though trouble followed us up. On the day of our arrival there her eldest sister[7] died. The next summer she had to go into Lincolnshire to nurse her second sister, whose life she was the means of saving.

Towards the end of 1870 my own health failed, and she had then to go to Chester to nurse me. Shortly afterwards she was herself attacked in the heart. Our eldest son, and subsequently our second son John, were also taken ill, and then came my greatest trouble—her own illness and departure, brought about mainly, as I think, by her solicitude for others.[8]

My dearest wife, as I have said before, was a deeply religious person. Although she read extensively on all subjects, those bearing upon religion were her favourite topics. Her early training, like my own, had been strictly " evangelical." Her parents had at one time, owing to the wretched state of the church at Boston, become Baptists, and she was not baptized until she was adult. This took place at Latimers church in

[7] Wife of the Rev. Thomas Scott, Rector of Wappenham, Northants, my father's eldest brother.—ED.

[8] My father, after her death, made it a practice, so often as the thought of her recurred to his mind to pray silently for her, and whenever, being out of doors he had occasion to mention her name, he was accustomed to raise his hat while he offered this tribute of natural piety.—ED.

1831. I was there at the time, but did not witness the service. Old Mr. King, my uncle's father, was one of the witnesses, and we have a Bible which he gave her on the occasion.

She was ever after, and had been in heart before, a devoted member of the Church of England; though broad and liberal in her views, and delighting in piety wherever met with.

When we first married, and for many years afterwards, we attended St. Martin's Church, where Sir Henry Dukinfield was vicar. She greatly delighted in his ministrations, and even when we moved to St. John's Wood, we continued to drive twice on the Sunday to St. Martin's, till he resigned the incumbency. He was godfather to our youngest son, Dukinfield Henry; his other sponsors being Mr. and Mrs. Austen, who chanced to be connexions of Sir Henry, though my dear wife's acquaintance with them was independent of this, having been formed much earlier, during her visits to my brother at Goring, where the Tilsons, of whom Mrs. Austen was one, resided; my wife and Mrs. Austen were devoted friends.

Her most intimate friend when at Ham was a Roman Catholic, an excellent and deeply-injured lady, who used on one day in every week to spend an afternoon with her, confiding to her in private her deep sorrows.

The following letters were written to me by this lady, on hearing of my dear wife's decease:—

" My dear Mr. Scott,—I cannot indeed find words adequate to express my sorrow and sym-

pathy at the sad intelligence contained in your
most kind letter just received. I heard the report
on Sunday evening, but would not believe it, until
I went on Monday morning to see Mrs. Ham-.
mond, from whom I found, alas, that it was but
too true. If I feel overcome with sorrow at the
loss of so dear a friend, what must be the grief
of her bereaved husband and children! and truly
does my heart bleed for you. Under so severe a
blow nature must have its vent ; but I know that
you will not grieve as those without hope, for your
dear wife has literally ' gone to sleep in the Lord,'
and she whom you so deeply mourn is only gone
before, to await that happy day when you will
both meet again in the bosom of your God. I feel
that I cannot thank you sufficiently for having, in
the midst of your own heartrending sorrow, so
thoroughly appreciated my friendship towards our
dear departed one. That our good God may be
with you all in your trouble, is the sincere prayer,
my dear Mr. Scott, of yours most sincerely, and
with the deepest sympathy,

" K. H."

In a postscript, she speaks of her as one of
the most Christian women she has known. Again
she writes : " If the prayers of an habitually
sorrowful heart can avail aught, rest assured that
in my communion to-morrow I will pray for you
and yours with all the fervour of my soul, that our
good God in His own good time may heal the wound
He has Himself inflicted, by taking from you the
best of wives, and from your sons the tenderest of
mothers. In this neighbourhood there is but one

wail of woe from all, both gentle and simple, who have had the privilege of her acquaintance."

From the Rev. G. W. Weldon,[9] a man of great piety and talent, with whom she was on very friendly terms when living at St. John's Wood, I received the following :—" I have just read with sorrow the tidings of your recent sad bereavement. Though years have passed since we met, the deep feeling of personal attachment for her who is gone has never changed. Allow me to add my sympathy to that of your other friends. By bitter —very bitter experience—I know what the heart feels at such a crisis, and how little even the kindest words avail to touch the sore spot. I shall only add one word, and that shall be in the form of a prayer. May the Lord soon accomplish the number of His elect, and hasten His kingdom."

I ought to have mentioned, among our summer outings, that of 1868, when, instead of going to the seaside, we took a furnished house for a couple of months at Wrotham, in Kent.

Wrotham Place is a pleasant old Elizabethan house, in part perhaps earlier, of red brick and stone, very picturesque, and with a fine old hall, now used as a sitting-room ; my wife loved it much, and greatly enjoyed her stay there, and the more so, as the country around is very beautiful, and as she there made several very agreeable friendships.

She possessed a noble mind, and was devoted to reading and deep thought, sometimes indulging in speculative views especially as to the unseen

[9] Now of St. Saviour's, Chelsea.—ED.

S 2

world. Every book which she could get on such subjects she read with avidity. She was also much addicted to mental study.

She took much interest in my profession, and often aided, encouraged, and corrected me in its pursuit. Her criticisms on my designs were always true, and, as I usually followed them, were very serviceable.

My profession, and its overbearing and per-plexing demands on my time and on my thoughts, although it provided her with the means of living in great comfort, was also a cause of much loss of happiness. I was always working under high pressure, ever in a hurry, too often therefore out of humour, and in the evenings jaded, tired and oppressed. My days were usually spent away from her, and my time was greatly taken up by long journeys, so that her life was on the whole a very solitary one. Our having no daughters greatly added to this disadvantage. I wish I could look back upon having done my utmost to introduce amusements and recreations to compen-sate for this, but alas! I did not. My life past is made up of subjects for regret. All I can say is, that I worked hard, and endeavoured to provide for her and for my children what they needed for their material well-being.

In appearance, my wife was, in her latter years, very remarkable, for though she lived to be sixty years of age, she had scarcely any appearance of the effects of age upon her, and few supposed her to be even fifty. There was not a wrinkle on her face, and her hair was very little touched with grey. She was peculiarly dignified and stately in her deportment. She only once ventured in any formal way into print. I wish I had encouraged her to do so more. This was a little pamphlet on the state of the lower orders, in London more especially, and is, in many respects exceedingly good.

CHAPTER VII.

July 11*th*, 1872.

I RESUME, after an interval of some seven years, the statement of my personal and professional reminiscences.

I think I had stated before this interval the preliminary circumstances of the Memorial to the Prince Consort. As, for example, that I had, for my own personal satisfaction and pleasure, at the time when a monolithic obelisk, 150 feet high, was thought of, endeavoured to render that idea consistent with that of a christian monument. This I effected by adding to its apex, as is believed to have been done by the Egyptians, a capping of metal, that capping assuming the form of a large and magnificent cross. The (so-called) "Iona" cross is, in fact, the christian version of the obelisk, and though the idea of a cross of metal on a colossal obelisk is different from this in type, it is not so in idea. The faces of the obelisk I proposed to cover with incised subjects illustrative of the life, pursuits, &c., of the Prince Consort. The obelisk was to have had a bold and massive base, at the angles of which were to be placed four granite lions, couchant, after the noble Egyptian model. The whole was to be raised on an elevated platform, approached by steps from all sides. I showed the drawing to the Queen, though not till after the idea of the obelisk had been finally abandoned.

I made my design for the actual memorial also *con amore*, and before I was invited to compete for it. Though I say *con amore*, in one sense it was the reverse, for I well remember how long and painful was the effort before I struck out an idea which satisfied my mind. Why this was so I know not, but such was the effort that it made me positively ill. My revilers will say that this ought to have been the result of my success, rather than of my previous failures; be this as it may, I remember vividly the contrary fact, and the sudden relief when, after a long series of failures, I hit upon what I thought the right idea.

I do not recollect that this was derived consciously from the ciboria which canopy the altars of the Roman Basilicas, although the form is the same, but it came to me rather in the abstract as the type best suited to the object, and proved then to be an old acquaintance appearing, for the first few moments, incognito.

Having struck out the idea, which, when once conceived, I carried out rapidly, the two next thoughts which occurred to me were, first, the sculptured podium illustrating the fine arts; and secondly, the realization in an actual edifice, of the architectural designs furnished by the metal-work shrines of the middle ages. Those exquisite productions of the goldsmith and the jeweller profess in nearly every instance to be models of architectural structures, yet no such structures exist, nor,

so far as we know, ever did exist. Like the
charming architectural visions of the older poets,
they are only in their primary idea founded upon
actual architecture, and owe all their more gorgeous clothing to the inspiration of another art.
They are architecture as elaborated by the mind
and the hand of the jeweller; an exquisite phan-
tasy realized only to the small scale of a model.

My notion, whether good or bad, was for once
to realize this jeweller's architecture in a structure
of full size, and this has furnished the key-note of
my design and of its execution.

The parts in which I had it in my power most
literally to carry out this thought were naturally,
the roof with its gables, and the flèche. These
are almost an absolute translation to the full-size
of the jeweller's small-scale model. It is true
that the structure of the gables with their flanking
pinnacles is of stone, but the filling in of the
former is of enamel mosaic, the real-size counterpart of the cloissonné enamels of the shrines,
while all the carved work of both is gilded, and is
thus the counterpart of the chased silver-gilt
foliage of shrine-work. All above this level being
of metal, is literally identical, in all but scale, with
its miniature prototypes. It is simply the same
thing translated from the model into reality, having
the same beaten metal-work, the same filagree,
the same plaques of enamel, the same jewelling,
the same figure-work in metal; and each with the
very same mode of artistic treatment which we
find in the shrines of the Three Kings at Cologne,
of our Lady at Aix-la-Chapelle, of St. Elizabeth
at Marburg, of St. Taurin at Evreux, and in so

many other well-known specimens of the ancient jeweller's craft. For the perfect carrying out of this idea I am indebted to the skill of Mr. Skidmore, the only man living, as I believe, who was capable of effecting it, and who has worked out every species of ornament in the true spirit of the ancient models.

The carving has been equally well executed by Mr. Brindley.

The shrine-like character I proposed to carry out in the more massive parts of the structure by means of the preciousness of the materials. In one respect I failed. The use of marble for the arches, cornices, &c., proved to be too costly, which led me to content myself with Portland stone. The rest, however, is all of polished granite or marble from the platform upwards, while below that level unpolished granite is used.

The sculptors, with three exceptions, were not nominated by me, but by the Queen, the exceptions being Mr. Armstead and Mr. Philip, who have executed the sculpture of the podium and the bronze figures at the angles; and Mr. Redfern, who modelled the greater part of the figures in the flèche. I must say of the latter that the models were much superior to the execution in metal. Of the sculptors of the podium, Mr. Philip had long been known to me, and Mr. Armstead had come under my notice during the great Exhibition of 1862 through his beautiful figure-groups on the Outram shield, and his designs for historical subjects for Eatrington Hall, Warwickshire. Being men of less established fame than the older sculptors, they undertook the work at a far lower price than these would have done, and, as it proved, to their own cost.

In my own opinion the result places them on quite as good an artistic footing as most of their more academic companions; indeed, I am mistaken if to Mr. Armstead will not be eventually awarded the palm among them all, or at least an equal position with the best.

I think I ought to have exercised a stronger influence upon the sculptors than I have done. My courage rather failed me in claiming this, and I was content to express to them my general views both in writing and *vivâ voce*. I should mention, however, that before the work was commenced a large model of the entire monument had been prepared under my own direction. This was made by Mr. Brindley, but the sculpture was by Mr. Armstead.

The sculpture had been drawn out in a general way on the first elevations, partly by Mr. Clayton and partly by my eldest son. From these general ideas Mr. Armstead made small-size models for the architectural model, and imparted to the groups a highly artistic feeling.

Without derogating from the merits of the sculpture as eventually carried out, it is but just to say that I doubt whether either the central figure or a single group, as executed, is superior to the miniature models furnished by Mr. Armstead. They remain to speak for themselves; while the two sides of the podium and the four bronze figures on the eastern front, which he designed, give a fair idea of what his models would have proved, if carried out to the real size.

I mention this in justice both to him and to myself, as his small models were the carrying out of my original intention, and have in idea been the foundation of the actual result.

The sculpture was placed under the special direction of Sir Charles Eastlake; after his death under that of Mr. Layard; and finally under that of Mr. Newton, so well known as the discoverer or recoverer of the Mausoleum at Halicarnassus.

The enamel subjects were not only designed, but drawn out in full-size coloured cartoons by Mr. Clayton, and from these executed by Mr. Salviati, at Venice.

The structural work has been admirably carried out by Mr. Kelk, and his representative, Mr. Cross.

I have been the more particular in my outline of this work at the present moment, because the memorial has just now (last week) been opened by the Queen, complete (in the main), with the exception of the central figure, which has been delayed, first, by the lamented decease of Baron Marochetti; and, since then, by the long illness of Mr. Foley, contracted while correcting his model in situ.

The Queen has been graciously pleased to award me on the occasion the honour of knighthood. Oh that she were with me who I confess to have so long and so earnestly wished might live to be the beloved sharer of this honour; now in her absence but a name!

I shall have, I believe, to bear the brunt of criticisms upon this work of a character peculiar, as I fancy, to this country. I mean criticism premeditated and predetermined wholly irrespective of the merits of the case. I need not enumerate in full the various strictures which have already been made. Most of them are groundless, some wholly untrue, some merely stupid, and most of them simply malicious. I will name, however, a few.

1. That the supports of the flèche are invisible, being concealed within the haunches of the vaults : a fault, however, if such it be, which it shares with all the great flèches of the middle ages.

2. That the angle piers do not appear strong enough for their work. This is, of course, a matter of feeling : to my eye they do look strong enough, and in some points, where they have been accidentally increased, they look too bulky. I will, however, say that they did look too slight in the original drawing, a defect which I was probably the first to perceive, and which I corrected with great care.

3. That much of the height of the flèche is lost. So is it in the case of every spire that ever was erected, as they are all of necessity much higher than they appear. I will only add upon this point that the greatest fault in the design, in my own own opinion, is that the flèche is too high. I was rather driven to this by a particular influence, and I now regret it.

4. That the outline of the flèche is broken. This is due to the figure-sculpture, but it was never intended to have a purely pyramidal outline like that of a shrine.

5. That the podium being of white marble weakens the structural effect.

This is in theory true, but the difficulty was deliberately faced, inasmuch as the sculptured podium is the very soul of the design, and is well worth a minor sacrifice. The high relief of the figures will, when the first glare has gone off, relieve this whiteness, while the vast counterforts of sculpture at the angles compensate for any loss of apparent strength, and the plain massiveness of the whole of the substructure tends to the same result.

6. That the great mass of steps takes off from the height of the superstructure.

This I wholly deny; its effect is the reverse.

This being my most prominent work, those who wish to traduce me will naturally select it for their attacks. I can only say that if this work is worthy of their contempt, I am myself equally deserving of it, for it is the result of my highest and most enthusiastic efforts. I will also congratulate our art, so industriously vilified by the same party, on this, that if the Prince Consort Memorial is worthy of contempt among the works of our age, it argues favourably of the present state of the art among whose productions this is selected for vituperation.

The following is a letter written to me spontaneously by Mr.[1] Layard, whom I had not seen for some years.

July 14*th*, 1872.

My dear Mr. Scott,—I have been in England since the beginning of last week, and I have visited the memorial almost every day that I have been in London. I must offer you my warmest congratulations upon the great success which has been achieved. It is a magnificent

---

[1] Now Sir Austen H. Layard, English Ambassador to the Porte. — Ed.

monument, which will be an honour to the country and to you. I had always been of opinion—an opinion which on more than one occasion I have expressed to the Queen—that when the memorial was completed and fully exposed to view, men of knowledge and of fair and impartial judgment would be astonished at its beauty and originality. Judging from what I hear said around me, this is the case. Of course there will be adverse criticisms: the most perfect work in the world would not escape them, but they are not worthy of notice, and will in a very short time be forgotten. Those who have had anything to do with the Press know from whence these criticisms generally come, and can trace the motives for them.

In this case they appear to represent the opinions of one prejudiced and unfriendly man, opposed to the judgment and taste of the million. I am convinced that if so grand and splendid a monument had been erected in Italy or in Germany, our countrymen would have gone many hundreds of miles to see it, and would have pronounced it an example of the vast superiority of foreign over English taste. But I am equally convinced, that such a monument could not have been erected out of England. I trust that the statue of the Prince may soon be in its place, and that it may worthily complete this glorious shrine.

Yours very truly,
A. H. LAYARD.

July 11*th*, 1872.
When I left off, in 1865, the account of my

professional career I had not mentioned the terminus of the Midland Railway which had not indeed then come into my hands. I was persuaded (after more than once declining) by my excellent friend Mr. Joseph Lewis, a leading director of that Company, to enter into a limited competition for their new terminus. I made my design while detained for several weeks with Mrs. Scott by the severe illness of our son Alwyne, at a small seaside hotel at Hayling in September and October, 1865. I completely worked out the whole design then, and made elevations to a large scale with details. It was in the same style which I had almost originated several years earlier, for the government offices, but divested of the Italian element.

The great shed-like roof had been already designed by Mr. Barlow, the engineer, and as if by anticipation its section was a pointed arch.

I was successful in the competition, and the building has ever since been in progress, having been undertaken in sections, of which the last is now ordered.

This work has been spoken of by one of the revilers of my profession with abject contempt. I have to set off against this, the too excessive praise of it which I receive from other quarters. It is often spoken of to me as the finest building in London; my own belief is that it is possibly *too good* for its purpose, but having been disappointed, through Lord Palmerston, of my ardent hope of carrying out my style in the Government offices, and the subject having been in the meanwhile taken out of my hands by other architects, I was glad to be able to erect one building in that style in London. I had carried it out already in a few instances, in the provinces; of which the most remarkable are the Town Hall at Preston, Kelham Hall in Nottinghamshire, and the Old Bank at Leeds.

About the same time I was commissioned to erect the new University buildings at Glasgow, a very large work, for which I adopted a style which I may call my own invention, having already initiated it in the Albert Institute at Dundee. It is simply a thirteenth or fourteenth century secular style with the addition of certain Scottish features, peculiar in that country to the sixteenth century, though in reality derived from the French style of the thirteenth and fourteenth centuries. I think the building, though as yet incomplete, has been a success.

I ought to have named in conjunction with the Prince Consort Memorial, the decoration of Wolsey's Chapel at Windsor as a memorial of the same kind.

The vaulting of this chapel, formerly of timber and plaster, has been carried out in stone with panels of mosaic; and the walled-up window of the west end is filled with figure-work in the same material. It was my intention that the walls below the windows should be covered with frescoes by Mr. Herbert, but for these were substituted, at the suggestion of her Royal Highness the Princess of Prussia, subjects in marble-inlay by Baron Triqueti.

This has been a source of deep disappointment to me, as it will, I fear, be to all lovers of art. The Baron's work is not, in my opinion, worthy of his fame or of its object, and I have had myself to suffer through it a good deal of vexation, more perhaps through the injudicious ardour of his friends than from any intention of his own. I have no doubt that my traducers will, when the time comes, be delighted with this opportunity of blaming me for matters wholly beyond my control.

Within the last year or two I have gone on with the government buildings, completing the group by the erection of the Home and Colonial Offices. I have had to make several attempts at the design for these latter offices, owing to new directions from successive administrations; and finally my scheme has been greatly impoverished for economy's sake. The principal damage has been done by striking off the two corner towers, which are much needed to relieve the monotony of so vast a group. I live in hopes of their restitution.

THE NEW LAW COURTS.

I have now to chronicle a great failure. I was invited, early in 1866, to compete, with a limited number of architects, for the New Law Courts. At first I declined, owing to some absurd conditions then exacted, but on the withdrawal of these, I consented, and at once threw myself vigorously into the work. The instructions were unprecedented in voluminousness, and the arrangements were beyond all conception complicated and difficult, which was further enhanced by the insufficiency of the site. The business of every conceivable department of the law had to be

T

studied, and its officers consulted over and over
again. It took me, I think, from April to September to get up my information and throw it into
anything like shape, and at length I succeeded in
packing together, in what I had reason to think
a good form, every room required, to the number,
I should think, of some thousands. We were told
that arrangement alone was to settle the competition, so I neglected the purely architectural
work until a late period. Then, however, I took
it vigorously in hand, working at it at odd times,
while my more practical study was going on, and
then taking a month at the sea-side for this
department exclusively, besides much subsequent
work, upon my return home. No previous competition had involved me in such an amount of
labour.

I do not know that my general architectural
design was of much merit, though I think that it
was fully as good as any recent work I know of
by any other architect. Of its parts, I am bold
to say, that many exceeded in merit anything that
I know of among modern designs. I say this
especially of the portico towards the Strand, of
the internal cloister, and of the domed central
hall; nor were other parts devoid of merit, but I
refer to the drawings (some of which, by the way,
were spoiled and vulgarized by bad colouring,
through which much exquisite outline drawing was
unhappily ruined). The two surveyor-assessors
awarded the greatest number of marks to Mr.
Edward Barry, and the second greatest number
to myself, while the heads of law offices awarded
the greatest number to me, and the second to

Mr. Waterhouse. The competition judges wishing to follow the advice of the assessors (now added to their own number), desired to give their verdict in favour of Mr. Barry, but as his architecture was approved of by no one, they conceived the idea of linking on to him some other architect, in whose architectural powers they had more confidence, and they pitched upon Mr. Street, whose arrangements no one had ever spoken in favour of.

I at once protested against this as a palpable departure from the conditions, which were, not to take the sum of two men's merits and balance this aggregate against the single merits of others, but to weigh each man's merits one against another. Mr. Street complained of my protest, and I then wrote to the government, stating that if the judges reaffirmed their decision, I should abide by it.

They did very unjustly reaffirm it, but the law officers of the crown cancelled their decision as unfair. As, however, I had engaged to stand by the reconsidered verdict of the judges, I felt bound to adhere to my promise, and I withdrew from the competition; though I was vain enough to feel convinced that my merits (architecture and plan together) were greater than those of any other competitor, an opinion to which I still adhere. Mr. Waterhouse was perhaps the closest rival, but Mr. Street had but a poor plan, while his architecture was unworthy of his talent, and had evidently been very much hurried; while Mr. Burges, though his architecture exceeded in merit that of any other competitor, was nevertheless eccentric and wild in his treatment of it, and his plan was nothing.

Laughably enough the competition ended in Barry, who had been buoyed up by Street's architecture, being cut adrift, and Street, who had only come in under Barry's wing, being declared the winner; as illogical and unfair a decision as could well have been come to; yet practically a good one, as it ensured a noble work: for an able and artistic architect can surely make a good plan, while no amount of skill in mere planning can by itself enable a man to produce a noble building. I am myself content. I was not beaten, for the first decision, which went against me, was declared null and void, while before the final decision, I had withdrawn from the competition. So ended the effort of three quarters of a year.

At first several of the designs were highly extolled. Mr. Layard told me that he thought mine one of the finest things he had ever seen. But in time some of the great unknown of the public press came in with their wretched revilings, and young Pugin, galled at not being a competitor, added his vindictive abuse, until at last it was set down as proved that the whole set of designs was a parcel of useless rubbish.

I am a partial witness, but I can only say I do not believe a word of it.

If it would have been my lot (had I succeeded) to have suffered the bullying and abuse which has been heaped upon Mr. Street, I cannot say that I regret my want of success. That which I had suffered eight years before in respect of the government offices, was quite as much as I could then bear. It is well that this second load of persecution has fallen upon a man of spirit and

nerve calculated to bear it. I heartily wish him
the highest success.

I consider that this great competition did me
harm, simply as a conspicuous non-success, and
as exposing me to the gibes of enemies, whom I
had innocently supposed not to exist, but whom it
brought out of their lurking-places. I have now
no doubt that beside the opposition provoked by
envy and jealousy, I had become unpopular with
my own party, through having given way at the
last in respect of the style of the government
offices. I had made a desperate fight, but I suppose that many were unaware how desperate and
earnest a struggle I had made, or, if aware of this,
would think that when finally overcome I ought
to have resigned, rather than give way. I have
already given my reasons for not doing so. The
claim of party had grown up artificially. I had
been educated to classic architecture, and had
practised it early in life. My tastes, by degrees,
had led me to abandon it, and my zeal, to aim at
supplanting it by the revived style, but whether
this feeling of earnest partisanship should over-
ride the claims of one's family in a case in which
I had fought to the last gasp, and where the property of the work had long been mine, I leave
others to judge. After a severe mental struggle I
decided otherwise, and I think I was right, but I
do not blame those who take the contrary view;
though the course I took has unquestionably rendered me less popular with the men of my own
party, and perhaps also with my opponents, as the
opposition which I encountered was almost as
much in favour of others, as it was against the

style itself ; and its main object was to force me to resign in favour of one or another of my opponents, one at least of whom took an active personal part in the agitation.

It should be always remembered that not only had I been formally appointed architect to the Foreign Office, and had subsequently been appointed (in conjunction with Mr. Digby Wyatt) architect to the India Office, but that the designs and working drawings had been made, and builders' tenders received for the work, and that nothing but this agitation about style stood in the way of the immediate commencement of both works.

I believe that the style of domestic Gothic which I then struck out has been the nucleus on which much which has since been carried out has been founded. As Mr. Ruskin says of his own suggestions, it has often been barbarized into something very execrable, but it has also been the foundation of much which is fairly good ; so that I have not reaped the fruit of my own labours, and as, during the never-ceasing changes of fashion, this style has gone rather out of vogue before I have had much opportunity of carrying it into execution, it follows that when I myself make use of it, I have often the credit of being the imitator of my own copyists.

A race of detractors of me and of my work has since arisen, the mildest of whom say that I have fallen off since my defeat by Lord Palmerston. I do not think that they have any ground for this statement, as some of my best works are of subse-

quent date, or were commenced about that time;
e. g. Kelham Hall, Preston Town Hall, the Leeds
Bank, the Glasgow College, the Prince Consort
Memorial, the Midland Terminus, the Albert
Institute at Dundee, and St. John's College
Chapel at Cambridge.

My design for the Albert Hall was, I think,
worthy of more consideration than it has received.
I wish that I had adopted a pointed-arch style
instead of the round-arch byzantine, but I was
warm on that style at the moment, and wished, too
much perhaps, to propitiate the non-gothic party.
I designed it during a tour in Perigord, among the
half byzantine churches of south-western France,
making it a completion of the idea of St. Sophia: a
central pendentive dome, surrounded by four semi-
domes. I made two other designs for this hall,
the one Gothic, the other byzantine, besides a
sketched variety of the main design worked out
with pointed arches. I should mention that these
designs were not, like that eventually carried out,
intended for a vast music hall, but as what was
called a "hall of science," a place for great scientific gatherings.

During all this period a constant agitation was
going on at the Institute of British Architects,
upon the periodical election of their president.
The Gothic men went in for Mr. Beresford Hope,
but were twice defeated, once by Professor Donaldson and once by Mr. Tite. At length, however,
the hopes of Hope were realized. After Mr. Hope,
Mr. Tite had a second innings, and then the
Council in 1870 selected me as their nominee. I
however declined to stand feeling that my ex-

tensive engagements, my distance from London,[2] and the claims of my family upon my spare time forbade it.   I felt also that I was not by nature fitted for such a post.

I have during this period held the office of Professor of Architecture at the Royal Academy.

Circumstances have been much against the due performance of my duties here.   I have, however, given a good many lectures, but they have been interrupted; first by the interval of rebuilding, secondly, by my own serious illness in 1870-71, and in this year by the terrible bereavement which I have suffered.

The best of my recent lectures have been those on vaulting, and I was preparing for this year a course of lectures on domes.

I hope, if spared, to publish my professional and ante-professorial lectures with ample illustrations in the style of those in Viollet le Duc's dictionary.[3] The illustrations of all my lectures have been almost profuse, and many of them are very excellent drawings by my pupils and assistants, my sons and myself.

ELY CATHEDRAL.

I was appointed to this, my first Cathedral restoration, in 1847, my special work being the re-arrangement of the choir.

The original choir had occupied the space

---

[2] My father was then living at Rook's-nest near Godstone. — Ed.

[3] These have been published since my father's death by Mr. John Murray.—Ed.

beneath the tower, and extended (I think) two
bays into the nave.[4]   When the central tower fell
in 1320, and Alan of Walsingham built the existing octagon, he left the choir in the position in
which he had found it, extending across the area
of his new octagon.   Thus it remained until the
time of Essex in the last century, who wholly did
away with this arrangement, pushing the altar on
to the east end of the presbytery, and making the
choir two full bays short of reaching to the octagon.
(See Bentham's two plans.)   My work was not to
carry the choir westward to its old place under
the crossing, inasmuch as this would have injured
the effect of the octagon ; at the same time that
the unoccupied space eastward (formerly devoted
to shrines) would, as things now are, have been
useless.

I contented myself with leaving the choir and
sanctuary to occupy the eastern arm of the cross,
with the exception of two bays to the east, left as
an ambulatory.   I wished this to have occupied
three bays, but to this the Chapter would not
consent.

I re-used Walsingham's stalls, as far as they
would go, designing new desk-fronts, &c.

This was the first case in which an open screen
had been adopted in our cathedrals, and I devoted
infinite pains to its design.   There was no ancient

---

[4] This position of the choir, which we are apt to regard as
exceptional, is in reality the old and normal one, the tradition
of the Basilica, and of the earliest Christian Churches.   Thus
St. Alban's, Gloucester, and Westminster represent the primitive
tradition, while Lincoln, York, and Salisbury exhibit the more
modern and abnormal arrangement, the great ecclesiological
innovation of the middle ages.—ED.

choir screen remaining. I returned only one stall on either side, as is (now) the arrangement in Henry VII.'s chapel. The stall usually occupied by the Dean is here the Bishop's throne. He thus represents the Abbot, and has done so since A.D. 1109, while the Dean, since the dissolution of the monastery, has represented the Prior.

The Bishop wanted much to have a throne in the usual position, but I would not consent to the obliteration of an early tradition.

I suggested the filling in of the wide niches over the stalls, with reliefs, which has been gradually carried out and is now complete.

I placed the organ, partly in the triforium and partly overhanging the choir, founding its design upon those of mediæval organs (e. g. Strasburg), and I placed the organist in a gallery in the aisle, passing the trackers upwards.

Subsequently I refitted St. Mary's chapel as a parish church.

Under my suggestion, and with my co-operation, the ceiling of the nave was painted by Mr. Le Strange and Mr. Gambier Parry. I suggested to Mr. Le Strange the ceiling of St. Michael's at Hildesheim as a model. The pulpit, the restoration of the western doorway, the pavement of the nave, the strengthening of the west tower, the restoration of the lantern tower, and the strengthening of the south side of choir and east side of south transept, have since been carried out under my direction.

The design of the central lantern I most carefully investigated from ancient evidences, and can speak of most of it with much certainty.

The great evidences were the mortices and the carpenters' marks. It was clearly proved by Dean Goodwin to have been a belfry, as I had supposed, contrary to the opinion of Mr. Le Strange.

The interior of the timber lantern has been decorated by Mr. Gambier Parry, but with this I have had nothing to do. I am now completing the great turrets and pinnacles of the octagon. I have made a strong move towards rebuilding the lacking north wing of the west front, but it has not hitherto been vigorously taken up. I wrote a paper on Ely Cathedral while abroad in 1873. This was read at the bisex-centenary festival of St. Etheldreda's foundation, in my absence, by my eldest son. It is published in a book upon the festival.

These works were mainly carried out under my dear friend, Dean Peacock, one of the noblest of men: the lantern work was a memorial to him. The actual restoration of the fabric of the choir had been commenced before my appointment, and was managed up to that time by the Dean and Professor Willis. The internal work of the western tower had already been completed by them, and the reconstruction of the apse of the south-western transept went on only partially under my direction. Indeed, coming in, as I did, in the midst of these works, my connexion with them generally was but partial, though it increased as they went on. I had nothing to do with the works at Prior Crawden's chapel, which were carried out by a minor canon, a disciple of Willis, and were nearly finished when I was appointed. I was assured, by the clerk of the works, that the seat behind the altar was deliberately carried out wrongly as a little bit of annoyance to the Ecclesiological Society. It looks now as if there had been no altar.

I gave very much study to this cathedral apart from actual works executed, and many matters of interest turned up from time to time. The screen, stall-work, pulpit, &c., were executed by Messrs. Rattee and Kett.

WESTMINSTER ABBEY.

I was appointed to this charge, I think, in 1849. This is an appointment which has afforded me more pleasure than any other which I have held. My work here has been very much a matter of investigation, and up to a certain date is fairly chronicled in " The Gleanings." Since that time, however, many other things have come to light. I may mention the bases of the piers of the Confessor's church, in the sanctuary ; a compartment and numerous capitals from the Norman cloister ; and some fragments belonging to the shrine of St. Edward, e. g. a piece of the return of the cornice of its western end over the reredos. The fact has also been ascertained that the whole of the shrine had been taken down, and had been rebuilt in Queen Mary's reign, and that even the steps had been reset and misplaced, the marks worn by pilgrims' knees (still very distinguishable) being quite out of their proper places.

We have found too, among other things, a compartment of ancient grisaille glazing, the hatch of the kitchen, the kitchen itself, the lower parts of St. Catherine's chapel, extensive fragments of terra

cotta figures walled up in the westernmost part of
the triforium, a beautiful fragment of Torregiano's
Ciborium,[5] and other objects of interest.

I had, almost immediately after my appointment
as architect of the Abbey, devoted a great amount
of time to investigating, and making measured
sketches of, the Chapter-house, then occupied as a
record office, and I was, therefore, well prepared
when, many years later, the work was actually
placed in my hands. I may truly say that this
was a labour of love, and that not a point was
missed which would enable me to ascertain the
actual design of any part, nor was any old feature
renewed of which a trace of the old form remained.
I know of no parts which are conjecturally restored
but the following :—the external parapet, the pinnacles, the gables of the buttresses and the roof.

In my drawing, made long before, I had shown
the shortened window over the internal doorway
as of five lights. I did so because some of the
bases of the mullions remained which showed the
window to have been of five lights. Why then, it
may well be asked, in the restoration, has it been
made of only four lights like the other windows?
I will explain why.

All the other windows have ancient iron ties at
or near their springings. These are of round iron,
but hammered flat where they pass the mullions.
Now the west, or shortened window, had lost all

---

[5] This baldachino, which is figured by Sandford, in his
"Genealogical History of the Kings of England," p. 470, and
is described by him as the tomb of Edward VIth (whose body
was laid beneath the altar of the Blessed Virgin which it
adorned), was destroyed during the Great Rebellion.—ED.

its tracery, and was walled up with voussoirs of the vaulting ribs. On removing these, however, we found the iron tie still in its place, and it was flattened, like the others for three (not four) mullions. It was clear, therefore, that the west window had been like the others. How comes it, then, that the bases of mullions tell another tale? Why, it was clear, from fragments of tracery found, that the window had been renewed by Abbot Byrcheston, when he rebuilt the bays of the cloisters opposite to the chapter-house entrance, and in the same style with them. He therefore had altered it from a four to a five-light window, and had moved the mullion bases, although he left the old tie in its place, flattened out for three mullions, as he had found it.

The cloister has been partially restored with much care. The mosaic pavement of the sanctuary has been restored, where it had been shortened eastward, the old matrices having been found and refilled. A concrete, containing chips of glass mosaic, was found under the altar pavement.

The reredos, which I found in plaster, has been restored in alabaster and marble, with great care and precision.[6] The five central canopies were found to be modern, and to occupy the space of a recess, intended no doubt for a rich retabulum. This has been restored. Some curious papering was found behind the masonry of the reredos, where it abutted against the pillars, on which were painted coats of arms.

During this time Abbot Ware's *Customary*[7] has come to light, and has been examined, together

[6] In 1866.—ED.   [7] Liber consuetudinarius.—ED.

with many other documents bearing upon the
history of the church and buildings.

The mason of the Abbey, when I was first appointed, was Mr. Cundy: subsequently Messrs.
Poole have occupied this post, who have also
carried out the restoration of the Chapter-house.

My own works at the Abbey have not been
extensive. They consist of two pulpits, three
grilles, an altar-rail, the gable and pinnacles of
the south transept, sundry tops of pinnacles, a
new altar-table in the sanctuary of the church,
and another in Henry VII.'s Chapel; but the
most satisfactory has been the hardening of the
decayed internal surfaces with shellac dissolved
in spirits of wine. The Abbey has also been
warmed, which will tend, I hope, to its durability.
The bronze effigies of kings and others have been
cleaned, and the ancient gilding exposed.

I have planned a great sepulchral cloister on
the south side of the Abbey buildings, extending
along College Gardens; but I see no prospect of
its being carried into execution.

We are now engaged in restoring the eastern-
most of the portals (in this case a quasi-portal) of
the north transept. We have found them to be
gabled, as shown in Loggan's view, and we find
very much of the evidences of the old design.
May I be spared to see them all perfected.[8]

I commenced these works under Dean Buckland, whose place was soon taken by Lord John
Thynne, who has retained, as sub-dean, a general

[8] The work is still in progress, and the western portal of this,
so-called, Solomon's porch is now approaching completion, but
the great central one has not yet been commenced.—ED.

directing power. Dean Stanley, however, has now assumed the lead, and takes infinite interest in the works.

HEREFORD CATHEDRAL.

The western towers having fallen about 1796, the nave had been wretchedly dealt with by Wyatt.

When I was first appointed to continue this restoration, the former work, carried on under Mr. Cottingham, had been suspended for many years.

He had repaired the nave, the internal crossing with its piers, the interior of the sanctuary (from the crossing to the altar-space enclosure), the east end of the Lady Chapel externally, and also most of the interior of the same. The parts through which I had to carry on the work were the transepts, the choir-aisles, the eastern transepts, and the north porch; together with the rearrangement of the choir, and the replacement of the monuments removed during Mr. Cottingham's work.

The reparations were carried on with the most scrupulous regard for evidence, and with the least possible displacement of old stone: the last being rendered most difficult by the extreme decay of the external work, the stonework being often hollowed out by internal decay, even where it appeared upon the surface comparatively sound. The present state of the central tower will illustrate this.

Among lost features recovered, I will mention the circular windows which light the eastern triforium of the north transept. These had been converted into perpendicular windows, though

retaining their early circular arches : no suggestion remained of what they had originally been.
It one day occurred to me that they might have
been circles, and being in the green to the eastward of the transept, I held up a half-a-crown
piece, fitting it, in perspective, to the window arch,
when I found that its lower edge just touched the
sill.   This led me to cut into the inserted work,
when I discovered the circles, with even the
grooves for their cusps, and some of the curious
pear-shaped cusps themselves.   The restoration
of these is absolutely exact.   The eastern pinnacles of the Lady Chapel had been rebuilt by
Cottingham, but the side ones were wanting.
Some of these I found stowed away in the crypt,
and I rebuilt those on the north side, partly out of
old materials.   The monuments removed by Mr.
Cottingham were scattered about in all directions,
and I could not have recovered their positions had
it not been for the aid of the Rev. F. T. Havergal,
one of the Priest Vicars, whose knowledge and
research were of the greatest possible importance :
all that we could identify were replaced in their old
positions.

I was interested in discovering among these a
monument to one of my old friends, the Dentons
of Hillesden,[9] which I replaced as near its old
position as I could; but I subsequently found,
to my regret, that parts of its altar-tomb and
heraldic remains had escaped my notice.   I
applied to Lord Leicester, the representative of
the family, for aid to its more perfect restoration,
but in vain.

[9] Cf. ch. i. pp. 45, 46.

U

The beautiful stall-work of this cathedral had been removed by Cottingham, and had been, for some twenty years, stowed away in the crypt, all in fragmentary pieces. It was a part of my task to fit these together and rearrange them.

I do not know whether I was justified in the course which I took with regard to this. There was at that time a violent agitation, first, for opening out the choirs of our cathedrals; and, secondly, for making, where practicable, the choirs more proportioned to present uses, so as to give no excuse for using them for congregational purposes. I was so far influenced by this fancy as regards screens, (be it right or wrong), as to have laid down a rule for myself to open out choirs in cases where no ancient screens existed, but not otherwise. I also yielded so far to the argument for choirs, proportioned to practical needs, as to think that, as in this case the old dimensions and landmarks had been lost for twenty years, I was at liberty to adopt what seemed to be a more convenient arrangement. The old choir had extended through the crossing into the nave, the eastern arm forming only the sanctuary.[1]

My rearrangement made the eastern arm the choir, giving up the transepts as well as the nave to the congregation. Practically, for ordinary purposes, this was a gain; for great diocesan uses it was a loss. From an antiquarian point of view it was an error. I leave it to others to judge

---

[1] Cf. note on Ely Cathedral, ch. vii. p. 281.—ED.

of it.   I confess I do not think .I should now do the same.

I do not believe that Cottingham had found an old screen: at any rate, he left no relics of it.   The metal screen in its present form came about in this way: Mr. Skidmore was anxious to have some great work in the exhibition of 1862, and offered to make the screen at a very low price. I designed it on a somewhat massive scale, thinking that it would thus harmonize better.with the heavy architecture of the choir.   Skidmore followed my design, but somewhat aberrantly.   It is a fine work, but too loud and self-asserting for an English church.   The reredos had already been erected by Mr. Cottingham, jun.   The decoration of the north transept was carried out by Mr. Octavius Hudson.

I had the pleasure of carrying out this work under the kind and friendly assistance of my dear friend, Dean Dawes, for whom I conceived a sincere regard.

The tower is in a very bad state, and I hope its restoration will soon be undertaken.   The old roof marks had been obliterated by Mr. Cottingham.

The builders employed were Messrs. Ruddle and Thompson, of Peterborough.   The clerk of the works was Mr. Chick.

LICHFIELD CATHEDRAL.

My work here was mainly the opening out and rearrangement of the choir.

I succeeded, rather against my will, Mr. Sidney

Smirke, who had restored the south aisle of the nave, and had really commenced upon the choir.

This choir had been dealt with by Wyatt in the most extraordinary manner possible. It had originally been of very early pointed work, almost or quite transitional in character, but had, in the fourteenth century, been rebuilt from the arcade upwards in rather late decorated; the outer order of the arches being also reconstructed in that style. The older columns had been octagons with a triple shaft on every side. The fourteenth-century architect had removed the shafts facing the choir, in order to gain width, and had corbelled his vaulting shafts above the stalls. Wyatt had disregarded both of the old dates, and, by the help of cement, spikes, and tar-cord, had converted the columns and arches (towards the choir) into copies of those of the nave. When I was first called in, this cement work had been partly removed, and the mutilated work behind it presented the most difficult enigma. I believe that I recovered the design absolutely, but some parts of it were discovered through remains so slight that, though conclusive, their interpretation was of intense difficulty.

I was greatly aided in this investigation by the qualities of the stone employed, for the fourteenth-century architect had used a different stone from that of the older work.

Wyatt here, as at Salisbury, had removed the old altar-screen, and had extended the choir through the Lady Chapel to the extreme east end. He had enclosed the area thus formed, by blocking up its arches with wood-work and glazing, so that the choir could not be seen at all from the nave. He had left the old choir-screen of the fifteenth century, but this had unhappily been taken down before I was called in, and I do not recollect that the idea of replacing it was ever suggested. I erected an altar-screen on the site of the ancient one, and put up a metal screen between the choir and the nave. No old stalls remaining, new ones were introduced, over which it was always intended to place grilles, but this has never been carried out; so that this, from being the closest of quires, is now the most open.

Colouring was found about the bosses of the groining, which I desired to have restored by Mr. Octavius Hudson, but this was not approved by the chapter.

The work has, at a later period, been extended to the Chapter-house and the Lady Chapel, and it is now contemplated to extend it to the exterior of the west front. Wyatt had, by the help of Bernasconi, translated this fine work into Roman cement: we hope to retranslate it into stone.[2]

I have had the privilege of working at Lichfield under several very marked men. The greater work was carried out in the time of Dean Howard, but, from his great infirmity, he was not able to take so active a part as he would otherwise have done. Nothing, however, was decided upon but in the fullest consultation with him, and he threw himself into it with all possible zeal and with the greatest mental energy. He was a most charming man, and kept up a cheerful, lively, and even jocose and buoyant spirit, under circumstances of

[2] This work is now in progress.—ED.

very great bodily suffering, which he bore with the most christian and heroic submission. I may indeed say that he rose above his sufferings in a manner of which the mere recollection is quite edifying.

His second in command was Mr. Precentor Hutchinson, a really wonderful man. I had known him for years as a great promoter of church extension in the diocese, and when he joined the chapter he rose at once to the circumstances, and did his work right nobly. I do not know how to describe him, as he united in a marvellous manner the finest disposition and temper, the richest humour, and the most energetic activity and zeal. I delighted in him, and, I need not say, deeply deplored his unexpected loss.

He was succeeded as precentor by another right wonderful man, Archdeacon Moore. Again I am unable to describe him. Dean Stanley has done so to the life. A grander man I never knew. He seemed, in conversation, to unite in himself the characteristics of Lichfield's two great men, Johnson and Garrick; and at the same time to blend with them the great charm of the generous open-hearted man of the world. Two such precentors have rarely succeeded one another.

He also is gone, but he enjoyed at the age of eighty-three all the vigour and life of middle age; indeed, very far more than often falls to the lot of a man at any age.

Dean Champneys I saw but seldom. I always found him a very kind and agreeable man. Lately the Deanery has fallen to the lot of my valued friend and patron Dr. Bickersteth, formerly Archdeacon of Bucks, under whom, I hope, the west front, the great gem of the cathedral, now set in paste, will be reset in genuine stone.

An intensely vexatious circumstance occurred during the earlier period of my connexion with Lichfield.

The ordinary work of the cathedral was carried on by a staff of masons, permanently engaged, under a foreman. At that time Professor Willis went to Lichfield to prepare himself for a lecture on the cathedral. He did not communicate with me, but carried on his examinations with the assistance of the foreman of masons. I subsequently learned that, while in company with this man, he had discovered, upon the upper surface of the string course of the triforium of the transepts, the marks of the setting-out of the groining shafts of the early-English work, which from that level upwards was removed, or altered, in the fifteenth century. No communication whatever was made to me upon the subject, and the first I heard of it was from a complaint, made I think by Professor Willis himself, that the stones, on which these invaluable evidences had existed, had been removed by this very foreman, who, with the exception of the professor himself, was the only man who was aware of their existence. The man's excuse was, that as Professor Willis had taken notes of them he did not think there was any need to preserve them, and, as his men had nothing else to do in the winter, and the stones were somewhat out of repair, he had set them at work to renew them. I must say I think the professor was exceedingly blameable in entrusting such evidence, thus discovered, to the sole guardianship of an ignorant mason, and in making no communication whatever to me, as the architect to the cathedral; but the occurrence is more important as showing the danger of keeping on these staffs of masons, who, if they have nothing else to do, employ themselves in doing irreparable mischief. What has now become of the professor's notes I know not. I never saw, or at the time heard of, these interesting relics, and now they are irrecoverably lost.

In the Lady Chapel, the wall arcades had been much tampered with by Wyatt, and plaster buttresses and pinnacles had been introduced, having no reference at all to the original design. This was made sufficiently clear by the jointing of the masonry, and has since been restored as closely as evidences would permit or guide. The eastern bay was occupied by a sort of reredos made up by Wyatt, partly out of old details (probably from the choir or altar-screen) and partly in cement from his own design. I did not wish to remove this, but the chapter had it taken down; when it was found that this bay had been a plain wall without arcades, intended no doubt to leave a space for some rich retabulum.[3]

The west window was an odd affair, put up, I think, by James II., when Duke of York. This has been replaced by a window more in character, though possibly a little too late in detail.

The interior of the nave has been cleared of

---

[3] The removal of Wyatt's reredos has rendered necessary the completion of the fine flemish renaissance glass with which the eastern window (as are also the side windows of the apse) is filled. This work has been carried out with great care by Mr. Thomas Grylls.—ED.

whitewash and repaired. I always hold this work to be almost absolute perfection in design and detail. It is parallel in style to the eastern part of Lincoln Minster, the Chapter-house at Salisbury, Bishop Bridport's tomb there, and the ruined front of Newstead Abbey. The exterior of the south side of this exquisite nave had been renewed some years before my connexion with Lichfield, under Mr. Sidney Smirke. The north side remains nearly untouched (at least in modern times), including the northern return of the north-western tower. This part is in a very sad state of decay, yet it is such a precious gem of architecture that I, some years back, urged that instead of restoring it, the chapter should have perfect drawings and photographs made of its details, so that if these should eventually perish, records would be kept of them. This was pretty fairly effected.

More recently, a monument to Bishop Lonsdale has been erected to the north of the altar, and sedilia formed of some of the old canopies, formerly belonging to the choir-screen, have been constructed to the south; at the back of which, in the aisle, is erected a monument to Dean Howard, with a canopy formed from the same source.

The effigy of the bishop is by Watts, and that of the dean by Armstead.

The woodwork of the choir was executed by Mr. Evans, of Ellaston, who will be known to the admirers of "Adam Bede" and its authoress.

Lichfield necessarily reminds me of dear old Mr. Louis Petit. I always regret that I was not on more intimate terms with him. I opened acquaintance with him (in 1841, I think), by a controversy about St. Mary's, Stafford; and the odd, and somewhat perverse, line which he frequently took, in parallelism with his more natural and congenial vein, led him always to fancy me to be an opponent; whereas I really had a sincere affection and an immense admiration for him. He was of a noble, generous nature, with fine gifts, both as a scholar, as a gentleman, and as a most original artist; and though, as an architectural critic, he was too much led away by a talented but less genial friend (also departed), he was nevertheless a grand creature, and as noble-hearted a man as ever lived. His very face was a charming picture.

PETERBOROUGH CATHEDRAL.

Here I have done comparatively little. I had many years back, in Dean Butler's time, underpinned the foundations of a part of the church towards the north-east. At a later period I did the same to the eastern aisles of the transepts, which were giving way, and added buttresses to them. About the same time some decoration was carried out in the ceiling of the choir, and generally the whitewash has been cleaned from most of the interior.

A few years back my attention had been called to some unquestionable evidences of continued, and increasing, subsidence all along the north side of the church. These parts had long since shown signs of considerable sinking, but these new proofs were of an alarming character. I strongly advised that the north aisle of the nave should be securely shored, and this was done, but for a very long

time the chapter, with one brilliant exception,
did all in their power to shut their own eyes, and
those of the public, to the truth. They called in
another architect, who preached " Peace! peace!"
They then sent for a third, who at the first was
almost " carried away with their dissimulation,"
but was obliged at last to admit the danger. This
aisle has, therefore, been thoroughly underpinned.
Still the central tower, which had been affected by
the general movement northwards, and also the
north aisle, of the choir are in a very sad state, and
nothing is doing. Some of the chapter, when
their eyes were unwillingly opened, wanted to go
beyond me, and to have flying buttresses built
against the north aisle wall. I did not like this,
because it would so seriously affect its aspect. I
trust that what we have done may prove effectual.

My knowledge of Peterborough Cathedral had
begun in 1831 during my first considerable architectural tour. Blore had then just completed the
rearrangement of the choir. My visits to Boston
brought me in frequent contact with it. When I
used to go down by the Boston mail, if it were
summer, I always had a run round the cathedral,
while the coach stopped for half an hour. The
view as we came from the east, along the north
side, used to charm me more than almost any
other that I know of. There were at that time a
few lofty poplars, and trees of other forms, which
added a wonderful charm to the remarkable group
forming the north-west angle of the cathedral, as
seen from the east. These have disappeared,
perhaps from natural decay; and partly perhaps
from a strange prejudice against Lombardy pop-

lars, which, though possibly well grounded where there are too many of these trees, without the relief of other kinds, is a great error where they rise from, or among, trees of other forms. I remember hearing a man say that when he came upon the view of this group he felt as if he should like to die on the spot : his more prosaic companion replied that such a sight was just what gave him the strongest desire to live.

I often wonder that the interior of Peterborough Cathedral does not excite to stronger expressions of admiration. It seems to me, next to Durham, to be the finest Norman interior that we have. Not only the nave, but also the transepts, with the remarkable variation between their eastern and western sides, have always filled me with the highest admiration, and this is renewed by every visit.

SALISBURY CATHEDRAL.

I was appointed to this work, I think, about 1859. I have made several reports upon it, to which I refer.

The first work undertaken was that of external repair. The stone, though generally in fair preservation, was partially decayed, and the whole building was gone through carefully and conservatively, replacing only such stones as were irrecoverably perished.

I made a very careful survey of the Chilmark and Tisbury quarries, and selected nearly all the stone to be used from what is called the " trough bed " at Chilmark, which is a bed but little used in the old work, though superior in strength and durability to any of the others. It is almost a pure limestone, very shelly and hard, and was left unused by the old masons simply because the quarries were subterraneous, and this bed formed their ceiling. There is a corresponding bed in one of the quarries at Tisbury (that nearest to the village), but it is not so hard or good as that one bed at Chilmark. The quarries at Teffont I do not know, but I believe that they also contain this bed.

The foundations were extensively examined all round the church, and underpinned or repaired where found necessary. They have been throughout defended by a mass of concrete surrounding them, with a channel formed above it.

Our next great work was the strengthening of the tower. The original thirteenth-century builders had erected a central tower, rising sufficiently high to receive the roofs of the four arms of the church. The storey against which these roofs abutted is a very light structure, and was intended to be visible from within. It is perforated in its thickness by a triforium gallery, leaving externally a wall of little more than two feet in thickness, while the interior consists of a light arcade with Purbeck marble shafts. The corner turrets have each a staircase, rendering them mere shells.

On this frail structure the fourteenth-century builders carried up the vast tower, some eighty feet high, with walls nearly six feet thick, and upon this a spire rising 180 feet more. It need not then be wondered that the older storey, so unduly loaded, should have become shattered. Subsequent builders have bolstered it up by flying buttresses, and by every form of prop that they could invent, till, as Price calculated, the sectional area of the added supports exceeded that of the original structure. Still, however, the crushing went on, and when I examined it, it had proceeded to very alarming lengths. I proposed to bond it together (in addition to the numerous ties it already had) by diagonal iron ties, and then gradually to insert new stones in place of those which were shattered.

The Chapter, for further satisfaction, called in the aid of an engineer eminent for iron construction, Mr. Shields, whose opinion very much coincided with my own. To him was confided the arrangement and construction of the iron-work, which was admirably carried out under his direction by Messrs. James of London. It consists mainly of two heights of diagonal ties, branching out towards their ends and passing round the stair turrets, and so grasping them firmly, through a height of several feet, in which space they are connected by vertical irons placed upon the exterior faces. When this system of ties was once firmly fixed, I felt that we could safely proceed with the reparation of the stonework. This was carried out under the direction of my excellent superintendent, Mr. Hutchins. Nearly all the steps of the four staircases were shattered, and had to be taken out and renewed, and the same was the case with a very great amount of the stonework. This was effected almost stone by stone, so that small parts only were disturbed at once : a very lengthy process, but the only safe one. It spread over many months, till at last every crushed stone had been replaced by one stronger than the old one had ever been, and set firmly in cement, so that by the time we had done, the work was stronger than it had been when new.

Reparations of a minor kind were effected through-out the tower and even to the top of the spire, where I had the satisfaction of inspecting them up to the very vane.

We dare not do anything to the bent piers which carry the tower. Their curvature seems to have arisen from two causes, first, from the pressure of the arcades upon their flanks, and secondly, from their backs or flanks not consisting, as do their fronts, of Purbeck marble closely bedded, but of compressible rubble walling. These two causes acting together would almost necessarily produce flexure. This had been remedied in the north and south arches at an early date by building arches across them at (say) half-height. The same might have been effected by a stone screen in the eastern arch, but in the western it would produce an inconvenient obstruction. I have advised the authorities to keep a watch over the piers, and if any increased curvature should be observed, to take some precaution, such as the insertion of iron beams from pillar to pillar.

On the death of Bishop Hamilton (in 1869) a fund was raised for the restoration of the interior of the choir as a memorial to him. With this fund, and amounts otherwise obtained, the stonework of the choir and its aisles has been thoroughly re-paired, and the choir fittings brought back, as closely as possible, to what may be supposed to have been their original state. All the desk-fronts were modern, and no traces of the old ones remained. The canopies were of modern deal. The reredos was the gift of Lord Beauchamp; the choir-screen of Mrs. Lear.

During the restoration of the choir, the colouring discovered under the coating of yellow wash was in part restored. That of the Lady Chapel was repainted in the winter of 1870-1, while I was laid up by serious illness. I do not think that it was very faithfully reproduced from the old remains. I was able, in the spring of 1871, to go and examine the evidences of the painting of the choir ceiling. This, as was always known, was decorated with medallions containing busts of prophets. These had been visible until the time of Wyatt, who covered them with yellow wash, which nevertheless allowed them to be slightly seen. There is an interesting correspondence about this in the *Gentleman's Magazine*, at the time that they were being washed over.[4]

We very carefully removed the colour-wash and disclosed a considerable part of the paintings, together with the legends that accompany them. The rest of the subjects we selected as well as we could to continue the series. They represent prophets, with legends from their several books, relating to the coming of our Lord. Those in the crossing of the eastern transept show our Lord in Glory (a " Majesty "), together with the Apostles and Evangelists. Eastward, over the presbytery, are depicted the employments proper to the several months of the year.

---

[4] Cf. *Gentleman's Magazine*, 1789, pp. 874, 1065, 1195.—ED.

In the eastern transepts are other medallions which have not yet been investigated.

The arches and walls of the whole choir and presbytery were richly decorated. Messrs. Clayton and Bell made a tentative restoration of some parts, but not (as I now find) very accurately. I have quite recently (1877) made a careful investigation of these decorations with the help of my talented assistant Mr. S. Weatherly.

An interesting controversy arose last year (1876) respecting the true position of the high altar. It was started by the Rev. H. T. Armfield, an antiquarian, who laid great stress upon the falling off in dignity in the decorations of the vaulting after passing eastward of the crossing, as being inconsistent with the assumed position of the high altar, eastward of that spot. I refer to papers on the subject, and to a printed report by myself and my eldest son, which showed that there were so many arguments for the received position, that the contrary arguments were outweighed; though the difficulties which they suggest have never been fully explained.

The whole of these lengthened works have been carried out under Dean Hamilton, assisted by the chapter and by a general committee. Dean Hamilton deserves all possible praise and gratitude, both from myself and from all lovers of the cathedral. I do not know how to speak of him as he deserves, and it would be simply impossible to speak of him too highly. Beginning this great work when he was entering upon old age, he has continued it with unflagging energy, liberality, and devotion, to, I believe, the venerable age of eighty-three, and though his bodily health has all along been feeble, and has sometimes wholly failed him, he has never for a moment shrunk from the work, nor has the clearness of his insight into all its bearings for a moment abated. Personally I feel the highest and most sincere gratitude to him for his uniform kindness and support. His latest act has been a new subscription of 3000*l.* towards the repairs of the interior of the nave. The whole may most literally and truthfully be called Dean Hamilton's work.

He has, I fear, been sadly galled by the want of pecuniary support from many of the great men of the diocese, but these great names, so conspicuous by their absence, it is not my place to enumerate.

The two bishops of this period, Bishop Hamilton and Bishop Moberly, I must refer to with admiration and regard. I will also mention a humbler name, that of the late Mr. Fisher, a retired professional man, who devoted several years of his life to collecting and administering funds for the restoration of the cathedral. Next to the Dean, he really claims, as I think, the highest place among its promoters. One of his especial works was the collecting of gifts for figures to be placed in the niches of the west front, which were executed, at, I fear, too low a price, by that very promising sculptor, Mr. Redfern, whose early death we have such deep cause to lament. This artist was of humble birth, a native of the hills above Dove Dale, where his talent, while he was but a boy, became known to Mr. Beresford Hope, who brought him to London, and placed him with Mr. Clayton. He subse-

quently studied at Paris.   I had thought him a
successful man, but it turns out now that his
spirits were broken by pecuniary distress, and that
he had fallen into the hands of cruel usurers, who
made his life a torment to him, and this so undermined his health that he fell a victim to some,
otherwise slight, attack of indisposition.   He was
one of four sculptors whom I have known to die in
poverty within about two years.

I may mention two small works at Salisbury, in
which I took an especial interest.   One of these
was the restoration of the screens which part the
smaller transepts from the choir.   These had originally been plain walls with very high copings (as
was the case with all the early surroundings of the
choir and presbytery) and were each pierced by a
good early english doorway.

That on the south side had been enriched
externally in the fourteenth century, at the time
when the transept arches were strengthened, by a
series of very elaborate niches.   These niches had
been built up solid, and the doorways so far
destroyed that no trace remained of their original
form.   By removing modern work we found traces
of the design, both of these doorways, and of the
niche work, which by long and careful study was
developed into certainty, and they have been now
restored to their true forms.   I have some idea
that the niches had at one time been arcaded
towards the choir, but this was not proved with
certainty.

The other was the restoration to its original
place of the effigy attributed to Bishop Poore.
This had occupied the position of a founder's

tomb to the north of the high altar, under a part
of the thick screen-wall, which was arcaded to
receive it : as is shown by Carter, both in his
architectural book, and by his sketch made in
1781, which was published by Dr. Milner. Wyatt
swept away the whole of this, and placed the
effigy in the north-east transept upon a fifteenth
century altar-tomb belonging to some one else.

I have had the pleasure of retranslating it to its
old position, and of re-erecting the arcaded screen-
wall over it ; in doing which I was aided by some
beautiful fragments recently discovered, which,
though probably not parts of the tomb, very much
resemble Carter's sketch.

Where Wyatt deposited the body found in the
tomb no one knows. As to the question whether
this was or was not Bishop Poore's tomb, I would
refer to a correspondence between myself and
Canon Jones, of Bradford, as also to a letter
addressed by me to the Secretary of the Society
of Antiquaries in 1876, and to the report already
referred to upon the position of the high altar.

I may mention that the tablet described by
Leland states that Bishop Poore was buried at
Durham. A document in the " Fœdera " says, I
believe, the same. Matthew Paris, Matthew of
Westminster, and a document in the hands of
Canon Jones, all say that the bishop was buried
at Tarrant. Bishop Godwin says the same, but
his editor states that Poore desired to be there
interred, but that the Salisbury people claimed
his body and left only his heart at Tarrant. Dr.
Milner adopts this view. A body was, anyhow,
found by Wyatt in the tomb.

CHICHESTER CATHEDRAL.

I was called in after the fall of the central tower[5] to reconstruct what had fallen; but not wishing to displace Mr. Slater, the architect in whose hands the work had previously been, I voluntarily associated him with myself, and shared the payments with him. He was not, however, acknowledged by the restoration committee.

The work was carried out under a general committee, of whom the Duke of Richmond was chairman. It was, I think, the finest committee I ever worked under; extremely numerous, and consisting of an admirable set of men, among whom I may mention Bishop Gilbert and Dean Hook. I at once made most careful examination of the remains, and stationed my son Gilbert at Chichester while the vast heap of débris was removed. His task was, by the help of prints and photographs, to " spot " and identify every moulded and carved stone found among the débris, and to label and register them so that we might have every detail of the old work to refer to, and, if sufficiently preserved, to re-use. He executed this task most admirably, so much so that we were not left to conjecture for any detail of the tower, and much was refixed in the new work.[6]

We should, however, have been uncertain as

[5] This took place on February 21, 1861, at 1.30 p.m.—ED.

[6] Of this work I had the satisfaction of superintending every detail, from the foundations which I set out myself, to the weathercock (the old one) which I refixed with my own hands, on June 28th, 1866, upon which day the completion of the spire was celebrated by a solemn Te Deum, sung in the presence of the Bishop.—ED.

to some actual dimensions, had it not been that a former resident architect[7] had made perfect measured drawings of the whole, which drawings had come into the possession of Mr. Slater: these my association with him had given me the use of. This was a most happy circumstance, and enabled us to put together upon paper all the fragments with certainty of correctness: so, one thing with another, the whole design was absolutely and indisputably recovered. The only deviation from the design of the old steeple was this. The four arms of the cross had been (probably in the fourteenth century) raised some five or six feet in height, and thus had buried a part of what had originally been the clear height of the tower, and with it an ornamental arcading running round it. I lifted out the tower from this encroachment by adding five or six feet to its height; so that it now rises above the surrounding roofs as much as it originally did. I also omitted the partial walling up of the belfry windows, which may be seen in old views.

The new work was carried out with great solidity. The foundations were sunk to a considerable depth; in doing which we found many Roman remains, fragments of mosaic pavements, pottery, &c., and also several boars' tusks.

The foundation of each pier was a square bulk of masonry surrounded by stepped buttresses and immense footings, all built of great blocks of Purbeck stone, and laid on a mass of cement concrete.

The piers to some height above the floor of the church are wholly of Purbeck stone set in cement,

[7] Mr. Joseph Butler, surveyor to the chapter property.—ED.

but as this was found ruinously costly they were carried up above that level with dressings of Portland stone, but the mass of Purbeck. The superstructure was partly of Chilmark stone and partly of the rag from Purbeck.

No part of the piers or other portions bearing concentrated weight have any rubble walling, but are wholly of block stone; that of the piers and a good deal more being laid in cement.

The tower was carried up to the base of the spire independently of the old structure, being steadied by massive shoring. When we had reached that height, the arches, walls, &c., connecting the four arms of the cross were completed, thus uniting the new tower with the old structure. This done, the spire was carried up. I do not think that a settlement of a hair's breadth shows itself. This is as admirable a piece of masonry as ever was erected, and as faithful a restoration.

The foundations and the lower part of the piers were built by Mr. Bushby, of Littlehampton; the rest of the work by Messrs. Beanland, of Bradford, in Yorkshire. The clerk of the works was Mr. Marshall, now in business at Chichester.

I have since, in conjunction with Mr. Slater, carried on the restoration of the Lady Chapel, and of a chapel to the east of the south transept.

The fitting up of the choir, &c., were wholly Mr. Slater's work. I had nothing to do with these.

St. David's Cathedral.

I had visited St. David's before I was called in there, and had sketched most of its details. I had also read and reviewed Basil Jones and Freeman's history of it, so that I was fairly prepared for my work, which has been a very interesting and arduous one.

My first report will show in what condition I found the church, and my second, addressed to Bishop Thirlwall, the nature of the principal works. The most difficult of these was the reparation of the tower, which involved little short of the reconstruction of its two western piers. This was carried out with admirable care and energy by the builder, Mr. Wood of Worcester, under my very excellent clerk of the works, Mr. Clear, who had just completed a similar work for me on a smaller scale in Darlington Church.

The cathedral had been erected by Bishop De Leia in the latter years of the twelfth century, but the tower had fallen, through the failure of its two eastern piers about 1220. In rebuilding it the two western piers were left standing, so that the tower was supported on piers of unequal strength.

During the six centuries which have passed since this, the height and weight of the tower had been vastly increased; and while the two eastern piers have borne it well, the two western ones had gradually become crushed literally to fragments. At one time a vast wall had been erected between the piers, displacing half the width of the choir screen, but the abutment was insufficient. One transept-arch had also been walled up, as I think had been the nave arch, though this had been re-opened before I was called in. Not only were the two older piers thus shattered, but very much of the superstructure also, while the later storeys above were split from top to bottom by gaping cracks of vast width. I trust the tower is now perfectly sound.

Besides this great work, the church has been put into substantial repair throughout, excepting a part of the south transept and the porch. The aisles of the eastern arm, once in ruins, have been roofed, repaired and re-united with the church.

The east end had originally a fine triplet of lancet windows of very early style and over these four lancets of somewhat later date. The former had been blocked up by the addition in front of them of Bishop Vaughan's chapel. The latter had (excepting their outer jambs) been replaced by a perpendicular window embracing the width of the four older lancets. This perpendicular window was of inferior stone, and was so decayed as to need renewal. I discovered when I came to deal with it, that the sills of the four lights remained beneath the later sill, and that the internal comprising arch was formed of the internal arch stones of the older lancets. I further discovered that a certain heightening of the side walls, added in the fifteenth or sixteenth century, contained the débris of the original east windows. I determined on a bolder course than usual, and took down the added walling for the treasure buried in it, and, having secured that treasure, rebuilt it. This gave me the details of the eastern lancets perfectly, as to design, and in a great measure the actual stonework fit to be re-used, so that the lights are now replaced, in part with their old material, wholly of their old design.

We found that the rafters of the flat roof of the eastern arm had belonged to the high roof of early times. I determined, however not to replace them as a high pitched roof because the later roof was of good design and capable of reparation. Mr. E. A. Freeman says he would either have retained the perpendicular window or else have "gone the whole hog" and restored the high roof. I reply, 1. The perpendicular window was rotten, and I had found the older one. 2. The perpendicular roof was handsome and susceptible of reparation, and the old one was of plain square timbers. 3. I knew what the east end had been up to the foot of the gable, and thus far I could restore it with absolute certainty, and in a considerable degree with its own actual material and workmanship, but I knew nothing whatever of the design of the older gable. I therefore took the intermediate course, preserving and replacing all I knew of the earlier work, and beyond this preserving the later.

One thing that I did was non-conservative. The two stories over the tower arches had formed an open lantern, of the twelfth and thirteenth centuries below, and of the fourteenth above. Timber groining had however been introduced in the sixteenth century, cutting across the windows and spoiling this fine feature. I lifted this groining to the top of the lantern, and by doing so at once preserved it, and exposed to view the lantern windows.

The whole of the church had been prepared for stone groining, but none of it erected, excepting in the eastern chapels (now mostly ruined). The

north transept roof being very rough and un-
sightly, I have ventured to complete the groining
beneath it, but only in oak. I should wish to do
the same in the south transept. The beautiful
oak ceiling of the sixteenth century in the nave has
been thoroughly repaired.

I should have mentioned above that the walled-
up eastern triplet has been filled with enamel
mosaic, and the four lancets over it with stained
glass, at the expense of my late dear friend the
Rev. John Lucy of Hampton Lucy, as a memorial
to Bishop Lucy.

I am now preparing to restore the west front
(which was mainly rebuilt by Mr. Nash), as a
memorial to Bishop Thirlwall.

This work has been carried on under a general
committee of which the Bishop has been chairman. The secretary has all along been Mr.
Charles Allen of Tenby, a very talented and
business-like gentleman, who was formerly in
India and was private secretary to Lord Dalhousie
when Governor-General. The Dean has taken but
little part in it.

The leading Canon when I undertook the work
was a most eccentric man, aristocratic and gentlemanly by nature, but, as one must suppose,
somewhat touched in his mind. His mono-
mania was hatred of the Dean and of most of
the Canons, which he carried to a most amusing
extent. Next to that came hatred of all that is
Welsh, though a Welshman himself; and lastly, a
general hatred of the human race: sentiments,
however, expressed with the greatest amount of
bonhomie and joviality; which made him an

amusing, though tiresome companion, but a man little suited to promote a great work like this. Indeed, he sometimes used to say that he wished the whole Cathedral was pulled down and a new one built. Happily we have a canon now in his place who is the very reverse, a thorough promoter of the work not only by his influence but by his example, as he has undertaken the north transept at his own cost.[8]

When we have restored the west end and the south transept, the work still remaining will be the recovery from a state of ruin of the eastern chapels: and a most important work it will be.

Bangor Cathedral.

Never was so dreary a work undertaken as this looked at first sight. I used to say that Bangor Cathedral contained nothing worth seeing but three buttresses.

I saw it first some seven or eight and twenty years ago, when travelling in Wales, in search of green slate, with Mr. Moffatt. These noble buttresses struck me so much that I obtained leave to excavate round one of their bases, which had been deeply buried by the accumulation of soil.

When a few years since I was appointed architect to the restoration I again felt a desire to see this buried base, forgetting for the moment that I had taken measured sketches of it more than twenty years before. There chanced to be a crowd in the churchyard owing to the funeral of some person of note, and my excavation was mobbed. When standing between the crowd and

---

[8] Canon Allen, now Dean of St. David's.—Ed.

the hole, I heard a Welshman behind me exclaim, "I—mind—Scott—and—Moffatt—digging—there —before," which called to my mind my former researches which I had so strangely forgotten ; though I had often referred to and made use of my sketches then made.

On more careful examination I saw reason to hope that a careful search would bring to light more work of the age of these buttresses, and this hope has been amply realized.

The cathedral seems to have been built (so far as concerns its oldest existing remains) about the time of King Stephen. It was probably damaged during the Edwardian Wars, and its eastern part, or rather perhaps its transepts, rebuilt wholly or in part after their termination. A century or more later it was burnt by Owen Glendower, and lay in ruins for most of the fifteenth century, till restored during the reign of Henry VII.

Since that time it has passed through a course of gradual degradation, up to the period of the commencement of the works still in progress.

We soon found that the more modern walls, whether of Henry the Seventh's time, or of later date, contained vast quantities of the débris of the church partially destroyed by Glendower, and as the state of repair of these parts demanded the removal of much of the work of this later date, we were enabled to exhume these remains. We found among them enough to complete the design of the two great transept windows, and to reconstruct them, in part, with their own materials. We found also portions of, I think, seven other buttresses of nearly the same design with the original three, besides very numerous other details, such as the corbel-tables of the transepts and chancel, the jambs, bases and caps to the arches of the crossing, and of the other arches opening into the transepts, &c., &c., most of which have been followed, and often the stones themselves re-used.

Nearly the only exception is the design of the crossing-piers, which were originally too weak, and these, though following in part the ancient design, have been increased in size.

We found also much of the tile pavement; also the plan of the earlier Norman piers of the crossing, and generally of the central portion of the Norman church. The south transept is carried out exactly according to the evidences found, but we were obliged to raise the level of the floor of that on the north, owing to its having been, for some reason, placed impracticably low.

The transept-crossing, with preparations for a central tower, are complete, as also is the structure of the chancel; in which I have retained the work of Henry the Seventh's time, though I have added the earlier buttresses which we discovered.

I beg to refer to the second report which I made when the work had attained a certain degree of forwardness. It is still going on, thanks mainly to the liberality of Lord Penrhyn.

ST. ASAPH CATHEDRAL.

This has not been an interesting work. It is one of a minor class, consisting of (1) The re-arrangement of the choir; (2) The external re-modelling of the eastern arm of the church;' (3) The opening out of the clerestory of the nave and the internal improvement of its roof; with a few other smaller matters.

The chancel, with the exception of its late decorated east window, had been externally renewed in costly stone but horrid architecture, early, I suppose, in this century; not the smallest trace of its old design being left. There were extant early prints of it, and from these I made a design for its restoration, but accompanied it by earnest advice, not to act upon it until the whole work had been stripped of its modern concealment, and evidences of its original design searched after. This the Dean and Chapter ignored, saying that they could not have their cathedral disturbed earlier than was necessary, and I, in an evil moment of weakness, yielded. I introduced two couplets on either side, designed as closely as I could from the prints; when at length, as the work approached the central tower, to our dismay the old details made their appearance. Whether to welcome their apparition, as I am wont so heartily to do, or to deprecate it as the nemesis I so fully deserved, I did not know. I could not well ask for money to re-do all I had done, and yet I could not repeat it in the face of facts such as these. I therefore restored the remaining windows on either side correctly, and left the others to take their chance: monuments of weak compliance, and beacons to warn others against such foolish conduct. There ought to be a brass plate set up recording our shame and our repentance.

I found the old stalls arranged in the structural chancel, and wretched deal-grained copies of them placed under the crossing. I removed the real stalls into the crossing; but, I regret to say, seated the eastern arm, a step which was pressed upon me against my wish.

I think it might have been better to have kept them where they were, and to have thrown the crossing into the nave as I am doing at Bangor. Both had originally their stalls in the crossing; but at Bangor they were removed (or placed) eastward in the re-arrangement under Henry the Seventh.

The nave had a modern roof with plaster ceiling of an arched form hiding the curious clerestory. The roof itself was substantial, and as it lent itself well to a form which would show the windows (a form founded on that of the transepts of York), I adopted that treatment, and I think with fair success.

ST. ALBANS ABBEY,
August 8th, 1872.

IT was many years ago—I forget how many—that I was first appointed architect to St. Albans Abbey, and it was many years before that that I had first visited it, and still longer since I had begun to entertain a romantic interest for it. It was while I yet lived at Gawcott that my enthusiasm was first stirred up towards St. Albans by Henry Rumsey, my father's pupil. He promised to get my uncle King to take me there from Latimers; but this never came off. Still earlier I can recollect hearing from my old aunt Gilbert the nursery rhyme,—

> "When Verulam stood
> St. Albans was a wood;
> Now St. Albans is a town
> Verulam's thrown down;"

and later my interest was excited by hearing that two places in our neighbourhood had to send their children there for confirmation, because they were peculiars of London, and, as I now know, because Offa had granted them to St. Albans Abbey.

When I first turned my attention to architecture I almost dreamed of St. Albans. I so inspired my fellow-pupil, though not much of a gothicist, that he walked there with his brothers and saw it before me. He was, however, punished for his temerity by being apprehended as an incendiary. It was in the days of " Swing."[9]

I forget whether it was in 1827 or 1828—my first or my second year in London—that I planned with my brother John, then articled at Chesham, to meet him at St. Albans, and to walk on to Gawcott (for our holiday) together. I recollect well the romantic feeling I attached to the concluding clause of one of his letters :—" Adieu! till we meet at the ' Woolpack ' "—that being a hostelry at St. Albans. However, by some shifting of the cards, we met in London, and got to St. Albans, part of the way on foot, and part by coach. It was, I know, on the 27th of May, as I remember the oak-apples worn two days after, but I forget the year. I well remember the intensity of my delight at this visit.

What, however, I referred to at starting was my

[9] This was a period of great discontent among the agricultural labourers, owing in part to the introduction of machinery, and in part to the severity with which the Game Laws were enforced. Incendiary fires were common, and threatening letters were employed as a means of coercing farmers and landlords. These letters usually bore the signature of a feigned " Captain Swing."—ED.

being called in to report on the Abbey many years
back.   The immediate cause of this was the hope,
then entertained, that St. Albans would shortly be
erected into a see.   Subscriptions were raised on
the condition of this taking place, and on the
failure of the scheme were returned; all but a
portion which had been given unconditionally,
which was expended on some ordinary repairs,
mainly of the north arcade of the nave, and on
some parts of the north transept.

My report was printed, and is extant.   I shortly
afterwards gave a walking-lecture at the Abbey:
this was in part written, but is now lost, excepting
such fragments as Dr. Nicholson gathered for his
guide-book (since greatly amplified).   I was called
in again last year to report afresh, owing to a new
movement for the restoration of the church.   A
public meeting was held in London, and funds were
raised to somewhere about one-quarter of what
was needed.

The present work commenced about 1870-1,
owing to the dangerous condition of the central
tower.   I may refer to Mr. Chapple's printed
paper, giving an account of the reparation of the
tower.   The tower was giving way seriously at
its north-eastern corner, and also in the walls
abutting upon that angle.   This angle especially,
but also the tower generally, was thoroughly
shored.   I was laid by at the time with the illness
I was attacked with at Chester, and could not go
at first to inspect the system of shoring, but communicated my views to Chapple through my eldest
son, who was of great service in arranging the
system of shoring.   Early in the spring I was able

to go myself and inspect it; also to attend a public meeting at Willis' Rooms for the furtherance of the work.

We had first to apply a vast system of shoring, and then carefully to remove the defective parts, replacing them with hard brickwork in cement and running the pier everywhere full of liquid cement; we, at the same time, made good the orders of brickwork which had been cut away : some parts are said to have been cut out to a depth of seven feet. On the opposite side we had to underpin the foundation, which had been undermined by burials, and to sustain it with a vast mass of cement concrete.

The same process in a minor form was applied to the other piers, though we did not restore the inner orders to the western piers, inasmuch as we supposed that they had been cut away to allow the stalls of the monks to be carried past them.

We found under the south-east pier the evidence of a marvellous fact. Its foundations had been excavated into a sort of cave, some five or six feet in diameter, which was filled in with rubbish (mere dust, with some timber struts among it). I can only conceive that this had been done with the intention of destroying the building by setting fire to the struts, but that the process had been suspended.[1]

The superstructure, which was much shattered and rent, has been carefully and substantially

---

[1] It appears that when the work of destruction was countermanded, no pains were taken to make good the mischief already done, and the tower has remained propped up on short oaken struts from the " Reformation " until the recent repair.—ED.

repaired and bound together by iron rods. The north transept had been affected by the general failure, and is now being repaired: its north-east angle has been underpinned to a considerable depth. Its abutting walls eastward have also been strengthened; so that I trust the old tower is now safe and sound again.

We are now engaged in the repairs of the choir and the restitution of the two very curious entrances to the sanctuary from the choir aisles with the very remarkable tabernacle work which they once sustained. This I had discovered on a former occasion, having found the fragments of the tabernacle work of the southern entrance made use of to block up the entrance itself. This I and my assistant, Mr. Burlison, had put together and found nearly perfect. It is now being erected in situ.

On the other side, though we have found no fragments, we have discovered the traces, on the wall, of similar tabernacles.

I ought to have mentioned that, previous to the commencement of the present movement, the eastern chapels, so long alienated, had been recovered to the church, by making over the old gate-house, long used as a prison, to the grammar school, which had hitherto occupied the Lady Chapel. They at present remain desolate, and the footpath still perforates them, but surely this cannot continue.[2]

Our great discovery I have now to relate. I one day directed the removal of the blocking up of a recess under one of the windows of the south

---

[2] This scandal has now ceased.—ED.

choir aisle; this was followed up after I had left, and a number of fragments of the substructure of the shrine of St. Alban were found.

I will here mention that, very long ago, Dr. Nicholson had removed the walls which blocked up two of the five arches formerly opening into the eastern chapels, and had found (among other things) a number of beautiful purbeck marble fragments which we concluded to belong to this structure. I bargained with him that when he held such another field-day I should be sent for, but he died before it occurred, and I was cheated out of this piece of archæological sport by my zealous assistant, Mr. Micklethwaite, who, like William De Valence in Hatfield Park,[3] killed the bucks during my absence, so that when I went down thirsting for the chase I found it over and the quarry taken.

Nearly the whole of the marble shrine (erected early in the fourteenth century) was recovered, and is now, by the ingenuity of the foreman and the clerk of the works, set up again, exactly in its old place, stone for stone, and fragment for fragment: the most marvellous restitution that ever was made. The old site was marked by the impressions of the feet and knees of the pilgrims, and by the sockets of the pillars, and to these marks the veritable stones are now fitted as if they had never been removed. It is a magnificent piece of work, and its recovery is one of the most wonderful facts of modern archæology. It is fair to all parties to say that I got snubbed by the committee because a little of their money was spent on the discovery,

[3] Cf. Matthew Paris (Bohn's tr.), ii. 534.

and was ordered to make no more such researches at their expense. Several special subscriptions have, however, been made, and Mr. Ruskin, on hearing of the discovery, guaranteed the whole cost, if needful: so that now pilgrimages may be made again to the shrine of the proto-martyr of Britain.

This, however, is not all; we have also found, and in part set up, the shrine of St. Amphibalus.[4] This is of a little later date, and of common stone, and it agrees with the old description discovered by Mr. Mackenzie Walcott.

Numerous other fragments were also discovered which are not yet appropriated to their places and objects.

May the work prosper.

I ought to pay, in passing, a tribute to the memory of Dr. Nicholson, the late rector. No man has been more zealous for the conservation and restoration of the church than he. During a long period he not only preserved the church from increasing dilapidation, but carried on many efficient reparations and restorations out of the scantiest resources. To him, too, we owe the discovery of the extensive and most interesting wall-paintings, and of many other objects of interest.

[4] The priest, for concealing whom St. Alban was arrested, and to whom he owed his conversion. — ED.

CHAPTER VIII.

August 9th, 1872, *Portsmouth.*—I have been this day to Osborne to be knighted.

I have had a very agreeable day. I was summoned to Osborne to the council, and was invited to go down by the special train at nine o'clock. At the station I met Lord Ripon, Mr. Cardwell, Mr. Childers, the Lord Advocate of Scotland, and Sir Arthur Helps. We went down together to Gosport, where we adjourned to a large man-of-war's boat of twelve oars, and were rowed, under the command of an officer, to the mouth of the harbour. Here we embarked on a fine steamer, and proceeded towards the Isle of Wight. After a little time our attention was called by an officer to a mass of smoke far ahead. It was the American fleet, which had been for some time lying in the Southampton water, saluting the Queen in passing Osborne. We presently met them, one after another, five vessels. On coming off Osborne, we were landed in the ship's boat, and found carriages in waiting to take us up to the house. The Prince of Wales's two boys were at the waterside on their ponies.

On reaching the house, after a little walking about, I was asked to go with the ministers towards the presence chamber. Among them was Lord Bridport with a sword, which he informed me was to be used on me. We waited on a staircase a long time, while Lord Ripon, as the President of the Council, and I think Sir Arthur Helps as the Secretary, were with the Queen, and while we waited there the Prince of Wales passed through the staircase. He shook hands with and congratulated me.

Presently Lord Ripon came out and told me that my business would come on last : then the council were called in, but their business did not occupy more than a few minutes, and, at length, I was summoned. Having made my bows, the sword was handed to the Queen. She touched both my shoulders with it and said in a familiar gentle way, " Sir Gilbert." Then she held out her hand, I kneeled again and kissed it, and backed out, the whole taking something less than half a minute.

I should say that, previously, Mr. Cardwell had come out and asked me which of my names I chose to be called by, when I chose " Gilbert."

I thank God for the honour.

We then adjourned to luncheon with some of the ladies and gentlemen of the Court.

I had been there once before, and had lunched there then in the same way : this was some nine years ago, when my design for the Prince Consort memorial was first adopted. Excellent Sir Charles Phipps was there then ; now Sir Thomas Biddulph took his place. Sir John Cowell, one of the gentlemen of the Court, and a member of our committee, treated me with much kindness. Mr. Doyne Bell was also there.

We returned to the water's edge, and went back to Gosport as we had come. I then took leave of the members of council, and crossed over to Portsmouth on my way home, the twelve-oar with its officer taking me over.

I had not seen the Prince of Wales since his illness. He looks stouter and fairly well, yet showing traces of the attack in a more languid tone and manner, but I hope this will soon pass off.

All the members of council were very kind and agreeable.

February 21*st*, 1877.—It is four and a half years since I wrote anything in this book.

Since that time I have returned from Rook's-nest to my old house at Ham, and have lived there three years with my son John, and his wife and family, beside my two younger sons.

I had a severe attack of illness six months after my return, which led me to make a long stay abroad. I went with my son Dukinfield, and my good servant Pavings to the Engadine. I had just before been elected President of the Institute of British Architects, and waited in England in order to perform some preliminary acts of hospitality and good fellowship. We started on July 10th (or rather on the 11th, for it was at one in the morning), from Harwich and went by Rotterdam, Cologne, and Heidelberg to Freiburg, and thence through the Black Forest to Schaffhausen, then by the Lake of Constance to Chur, and on by the Albula pass to Samaden, whence we moved to Sils, and stayed there some five weeks.

Here my brother John and his son, and my own son Alwyne, joined us, and we travelled by the Splugen to Andermatt and Lucerne, thence to Interlachen and eventually to Evian on the lake of Geneva. Here I was strongly recommended to extend my tour and to go to Rome; so, being left by my sons, I went first to Lyons, then to Le Puy, Nismes, Arles, and Avignon, and thence to Genoa and on by Piacenza, Parma, Bologna, Ravenna, Pistoja and Lucca to Florence, and again by Perugia and Assisi to Rome.

Here I spent five weeks very agreeably, being very much in the company of my old friend John Henry Parker. I went thence to Naples, and to Pompeii, Herculaneum and Baiæ, returning by water to Genoa and from there by Marseilles and Paris, to London, reaching home on New Year's Day, 1874.

The next year my son John and I had a trip first through Normandy, and afterwards to Hamburg, whence I went with my youngest son (who had joined us at Brussels) to the Hartz, the Saxon Switzerland, Vienna, Saltzburg, Munich, &c., and home by way of Strasburg and Rheims.

During the autumn of this year I determined to remove to London, whether wisely or not God knows! We did not actually leave Ham until a year later.

CHESTER CATHEDRAL.

I commenced this work, so far as related to the interior of the Lady Chapel, many years since in conjunction with Mr. Hussey, who was then architect to the cathedral. I think so far as we went the work was fairly successful, and it was well decorated in colour by the late Octavius Hudon.

We did not at that time do much external work, but I commenced a careful study of its probable design, which I afterwards continued with great earnestness for a very long time.

The exterior had been so cut to pieces that it was only by study, spread over several years, that its beautiful design was at all recovered.

I will here refer to my report, drawn up at the time when I was appointed successor to Mr. Hussey, upon his resignation, and also to a paper read before the local architectural society and printed (now very scarce), which contains a statement of what had been done up to its date.

The most interesting part of the work is that already alluded to, the Lady Chapel. The connexion between this part of the cathedral and the eastern parts of Bangor, will be found detailed in the paper I have mentioned. This was made clear by the bases of the buttresses, and more so by a fairly complete buttress, which was found embedded in the wall of the later chapel on each side: that on the north side still remains. The beautiful cornice existed under the roofs of these chapels. Portions of the open parapet were discovered, and were fitted into sockets found cut in the cornice, and into sinkings in the east walls of the choir. Other details gradually developed themselves, the marks of the buttress-gables remained against the walls, breaking through the cornice; and, eventually, nearly every iota was discovered, up to the top of the cornice, as well as the parapet over it. The eastern gable and pinnacles were worked from conjecture. The curious mode in which the roof springs from an inner wall behind the parapet is genuine, that wall having remained. The windows gave themselves almost perfectly.

The paper alluded to details the discovery of the spire-like roof of the south-east apse of the choir-aisle. This was proved beyond all question by portions still remaining in place, and by very numerous fragments found embedded in the walls.

The same paper gives my reasons for departing from my customary rule in removing one of the side chapels, which had at a late date been added to the Lady Chapel, while I left the other. It was horribly decayed, it spoiled that side of the beautiful Lady Chapel, it had destroyed the apse of the choir-aisle, and its walls were the burial place of the details of the finer work which it had displaced ; while its design was the same as that of the north chapel which I left.

In its walls were found the windows of the apse, and almost every detail of its design, many of which were put up in their proper places. I leave others to judge of the result, only adding that the structure is exact to the old design, except the scaling of the spire-like roof, of which no evidence was found ; but it was so strongly pressed, that I ventured upon it. The buttress which severs the apse from the aisle, and the pinnacle upon it, were merely conjectural.

The external stonework of this cathedral was so horribly and lamentably decayed, as to reduce it to a mere wreck, like a mouldering sandstone cliff. The most ordinary details could often only be found in corners more protected, through accidental circumstances, than the rest. I can assert for myself, and for my able and lamented clerk of the works, Mr. Frater, that not a stone retaining anything like its old surface has been wilfully displaced, nor a single evidence of detail disregarded. I am the more specific on this point, because the frightful extent of the decay forced upon me, most unwillingly, very considerable renewal of the stonework. I can aver, however, that this was unavoidable, unless, indeed, I was willing, and my employers too, to leave the cathedral a mere ruin. The present state of the south-west angle of the south transept will show how matters stood : though this is not nearly so much decayed as was the tower, and some other portions. Other parts were better, and have been left to speak for themselves. We rebuilt the south walk of the cloister exactly on its old lines. It had long since been taken down, but was essential as an abutment to the aisle of the nave. I have noticed that a newspaper scribbler speaks of my having " destroyed the cloister." Any one would suppose from this, that I had pulled down the three remaining sides ; but what this man means by destruction, is the re-instatement of the part which had been destroyed, the other sides not having been so much as touched.

We added the stone vaulting to the nave aisles, which had been prepared for, but not carried out. The same was the case with the nave itself. I did not venture upon adding stone vaulting here, but completed the work in oak upon the lines given by the stone springers.

The choir had been groined in timber and plaster by my predecessor, upon the old springers. I advised merely to substitute oak boarding for the plaster, as the ribs were of wood, but the chapter pressed its entire reconstruction in oak, owing to its lines not being quite perfect. It has been decorated by Clayton and Bell. The beautiful stall-work has been carefully restored. It was essential to the scheme that the choir should be opened out. I felt averse to this, because the stone screen, though not beautiful, was ancient, excepting its doorway. I, however, consented to remove it, and set up its old portions in the side arches behind the stalls, and without further disturbance of the canopies of the return stalls than opening out their panels, I have applied to the western side an open screen founded on their own design.

The substructure of the shrine of St. Werberg had been made into a bishop's throne. We have removed it into the south choir aisle, adding to it some parts recently discovered, and have made a a new throne.

The arches of the presbytery are at present open, but will eventually have metal grilles.

The whole of the interior has been carefully denuded of its coatings of yellow wash, without disturbing the surface of the stone.

The old sedilia have been completed according to their own evidence, and one, which had a modern canopy (though far from new), has been replaced by the original one, strangely discovered among the ruins of St. John's Church. This seems to prove that all of them came from thence.

The groined chambers to the north-east of the cloister, which had been subdivided and applied to mean purposes, have been thrown together and appropriated as the priest-vicars' vestry.

The fine Norman crypt on the west side of the cloister, once the substructure of the abbot's hall, has very unhappily been made over to the grammar school, a very ill-judged proceeding.

The site of the abbot's, and more recently the bishop's, residence has also been made over to the grammar school, now built anew.

The great work still crying out to be undertaken is the restoration of the vast south transept, known as St. Oswald's Church. The sides of this have already been externally repaired, but the beautiful south front was refaced with most barbarous work early in this century.

I have made a design, founded on the remains of its aisle fronts and on old prints, for its restoration—a noble work for any wealthy neighbour to undertake. Its interior waits to be dealt with like that of the nave.

The whole of these works, excepting the interior of the Lady Chapel (and not excepting the whole of this) have been carried out under the zealous and energetic direction of Dean Howson, whose never-flagging labour has raised some 80,000*l* for the work. May he live to see it nobly completed.

Another suggested work is the addition of a spire to the central tower. This was intended and prepared for by its builders, early in the fifteenth century. I do not propose to venture on stone, but have designed a spire of timber covered with lead. This is sadly needed to render the cathedral conspicuous from the surrounding country, whence it is either invisible or marked out only by the dull and heavy outline of its tower.

I had here been represented for several years by the most faithful and laborious of clerks of the works, Mr. Frater, whose early decease we have all had to lament with very deep sorrow. A better, more talented, or more conscientious man could not be found for such a position. He was justly respected, and is sincerely regretted by all who knew him.

In the course of our works we made many discoveries relating to the Norman church. Mr. Hussey had long since discovered the bases of the pillars of the Norman apse (though unfortunately he removed them). We found parts of the walls and the responds of the apses to the aisles, and also the lower courses of the apsidal chapel projecting from the north transept; also one of the pillars of the Norman choir and some parts of the outer walls of the choir aisles, which as far as possible we have left exposed to view. We also found very numerous fragments of all periods, some of them very interesting, all of which have been preserved.

The restoration of the south-east angle of the south transept involved immense study, and though it is no doubt as correct as practicable, what we had to work from was a mere wreck.

GLOUCESTER CATHEDRAL.

This cathedral was formerly under the management (as to its repairs, &c.) of Messrs. Fulljames and Waller, architects of Gloucester.

I was long since called in to report upon the general scheme for its reparation drawn out by those gentlemen, and especially by Mr. Waller, a man of considerable talent. At a subsequent date, Mr. Waller having retired owing to ill-health, I became associated with Mr. Fulljames, and, later still, upon that gentleman's retirement, I took his place. These works were gradually carried on under a clerk of works (Mr. Ashbee) and a staff of masons; but subsequently the larger work was undertaken of the internal reparation and partial re-arrangement of the choir. This was carried out with all due regard to the beautiful woodwork which remained. The stalls and canopies have been carefully restored, and as there were no old desk-fronts, &c., these were designed anew, making use of some remains which had been removed to the lady chapel, both as guides, and also as a part of the work.

The side galleries were removed. The choir-screen (a modern one) remains untouched, with the organ upon it. The Dean objects to opening out the screen, and as the return-stalls are complete, I am not at all anxious to do so. The organ is a good seventeenth-century one, and I am very desirous to retain it, though, as is usual, all parties there condemn it.

Among other things we ascertained, by removing the floor eastward of the beautiful encaustic tile-floor of the altar space, the position of the inner altar screen, which had been long since done away with. On this site a new reredos was erected,

z

leaving a space between the two screens, as in old times. Of the actual reredos little trace remained, except fragments of details, and the outer jambs of its two doorways. We discovered the curious sunk area behind the reredos (with steps leading into the same) from which was an entrance to the space beneath the high altar. This is now exposed to view.

In making these investigations we found the bases, and lower parts of the shafts, of two great round pillars of the Norman apse, which still remain beneath the floor.

The canopies of the beautiful sedilia have been restored, mainly from their own evidence.

About this time Mr. Waller, having happily been restored to health, resumed practice, and his aid was of very important service in the restoration of the porch, of which he had, years before, made careful measured drawings, since which time the progress of decay had obliterated much which had then existed. He was also very useful in respect of the sedilia. He has now for some years been reinstated in his position of resident architect, I retaining that of consulting architect. His investigations of the history of the church have been carried on with much care and success, and he exercises a wise and important guardianship over the fabric, in which he has, since resuming office, carried out some very important works of reparation.

The choir vaulting has been decorated by Messrs. Clayton and Bell, as I think, very judiciously and successfully, though Mr. Gambier Parry thinks the reverse.

This gentleman had decorated a chapel adjoining the south transept, and had reported upon the system to be adopted for the choir vaulting. As it would have been too much to decorate both the ribs, and the intervening spaces, while the walls below remained uncoloured, he had recommended that the spaces should be decorated and the ribs left plain. I thought this wrong, because this vaulting is an intricate system of ribs, an absolute net-work, in which the figure of the ribs is everything and the forms of the intervening spaces nothing. I therefore recommended to decorate the ribs and leave the spaces, for the most part, plain. This has been done, the only exception being the star-like arrangement of panels over the altar, and another over the choir proper: these two portions have decoration in the spaces. To my eye the effect is most satisfactory.

RIPON CATHEDRAL.

As to this work, I refer to my reports and also to my paper on it in the *Archæological Journal* of 1874. This cathedral is of transitional work, altered at several periods. The choir unfortunately had long been converted into a parish church, which greatly embarrassed our work. It could not be opened out to the nave, having a massive ancient screen, serving perhaps as a buttress to the tower piers. The altar-screen, once (as at Selby) a bay in advance, had been removed and the altar pushed back to the east wall.

The choir was galleried and had beneath the galleries a set of boxes or closets for leading families, though remains of the side screens still existed. A part of the beautiful stall-work had been injured, and repaired in an heterogeneous style when the central spire fell.

The choir had been prepared for groining in the fourteenth century (or late in the thirteenth) when it was lengthened. I think it received oak groining then, though at a late date this had been renewed in lath and plaster ; but this late groining had magnificent oak bosses with figure subjects carved on them.

The transepts had been groined in plaster and papier-maché some thirty or forty years back by the Ecclesiastical Commissioners. The nave had a flat deal ceiling. The nave-aisles were prepared for groining, but it had never been carried out.

We substituted oak groining for the plaster-work, re-using the ancient bosses. We raised the choir roof and the eastern gable to its old pitch. We removed the papier-maché groining from the transepts, and exposed and restored the old oak roof. We (at a later date) added oak vaulting to the nave, adapted to the old corbels and imitated from the transepts at York.

They could not afford to raise the roof to its proper pitch, but I hope that this may one day follow.

The arrangement of the choir was difficult and unsatisfactory. The old rood-screen remaining, I acted on my principle of not disturbing it, but as the cathedral is also a parish church, the whole parochial congregation has to be crammed into the eastern arm. I found this effected, as I have said, by side galleries and a kind of stage-boxes, but now all are seated on the floor.

We cleared away the galleries, &c., from the choir, and did what we could for it, considering the serious hindrance of its being used as a Parish Church, and we restored the damaged stall-work. The organ retains its old place, but is now being rebuilt (too big, I fear, as usual).

The altar had formerly stood one bay in advance of the east wall, as at Selby, but had been moved back. This modern position we retained, and removed the sedilia to suit it.

Our greatest work, however, was the strengthening of the three towers, all of which were dangerous. The western towers had sunk dreadfully, and were split from top to bottom on three sides (if not four). The cracks were nearly a foot wide. We underbuilt the walls for some twelve feet below their old foundations, propping them up meanwhile with an enormous mass of timber shoring. The danger was terrific. At one time a perfect avalanche of rubble roared in upon the men engaged below from the centre of the wall over their heads. Thank God, however, it was effected in safety. Each tower was tied with iron in every storey, the cracks built up and bonded across, and the towers are now sound and strong.

The central tower was, and is, a curious union of twelfth and fifteenth century work, two sides of each date. It had given way from this strange union, the older work falling away from the later. We have, I think, succeeded in making it strong again.

In some places my over-zealous clerk of works introduced too much new stone. One ought to be always on the spot effectually to prevent this.

This, however, I may say, that had we not taken

it in time, the building would probably not have stood long.

I have been blamed for my treatment of the five western early english windows, which, with the flanking towers and portals, form a perfect façade of the thirteenth century. These five wide lights had been turned into two-light windows (each) in the fourteenth century. The mullions and tracery then added (and which may be seen in any old view of this front) were of an inferior stone, and had decayed and given way so as to be only prevented from precipitating themselves into the nave by beams of wood placed across them. I found them to be beyond the reach of repair, and having once taken them out, the beauty of the earlier design was so apparent, that it seemed barbarous to introduce new ones, so the windows now retain their original design. Persons may differ as to this. I have the satisfaction of finding, unasked for, the full approval of that eminent antiquary Mr. Edmund Sharpe, whose death we have just now to deplore.

The main works were carried out under Dean Goode, to whom it is just to say that he zealously promoted them. The contractors were Messrs. Ruddle and Thompson of Peterborough, the clerk of works, Mr. Clarke, who so entirely lost his health from his exposure there, that for several years he was laid by, and supposed to be so for life; but happily he has recovered, and has now been two or three years at work again.

WORCESTER CATHEDRAL.

This work was in the hands of Mr. Perkins, the

local architect, a pupil of Rickman. I had been occasionally consulted by the Dean, but not to any great extent, so that the entire structural reparation and restoration was Mr. Perkins's sole work.

When, however, the internal work of the choir was taken in hand, I was called in, and I acted, so far as that was concerned, jointly with Mr. Perkins.

The structural work was in the main already done, including some things which I regretted, such as the removal of the perpendicular screens. I fear I am jointly responsible for the removal of the Jacobean and Elizabethan canopies, and of the choir screen, but I forget now how this was.

The ancient stalls remain. Strangely, as an effect of divided responsibility, I forget whether the returned stalls were ancient.

My work comprised the stall-fronts and desks, the screens behind the stalls, the choir screen, the presbytery-screen, the reredos, altar-rails, &c., and the decoration of the vaulting. Subsequently to Mr. Perkins' death, or partly so, I carried out sundry works in the nave.

I had proposed to make a double open screen to the choir, and to place on it the key-board of the organ, and the choir organ itself, drafting off the heavier parts to the blank walls on either side, east of the tower-piers, but this, though recommended by Sir Frederick Ouseley, was foolishly overruled, and the organ has been placed in the aisle, in the usual awkward position.

The paving of the aisles of the choir was Mr. Perkins' work, that of the choir and nave was mine. The decoration of the choir vaulting I both designed and drew out full size, to a great extent, while laid up by long illness in the winter of 1870-71. I unluckily left that of the choir-aisles to Mr. Hardman, who made it too monotonous. I did not volunteer the decoration at all, but Mr. Perkins had stripped off the plastering of the choir-vaulting, and by doing so had exposed some very rough rubble-work of reddish tufâ. This Lord Dudley very much disliked, so the groining was replastered and decorated in colour. I aimed in designing this at a non-perspicuous effect, which should allow of a slight difficulty in discerning the pattern at first sight, which I thought would tend to enhance the effect of height, as it unquestionably does. I confess I think the choir ceilings very successful.

The great organ in the south transept I opposed as useless and obtrusive, but I believe that my letter on the subject was suppressed, for want of courage to withstand the munificence of Lord Dudley, a feeling in which I sympathize, from a sense of his grand generosity.

This work, though carried out at first under the dean and chapter, was made over, early in its progress, to a general committee, of which the dean was chairman, Lord Dudley, Lord Lyttelton, and Sir John Packington (now Lord Hampton) being among its leading members.

I have to regret the removal of the elegant sounding-board from the choir-pulpit. I much desired its retention. With it, unknown to me at the time, was removed the interesting representation of the New Jerusalem below it. Owing to divided responsibility, my colleague being the practical agent, and very timid, this was done, and the column, into which it had been inserted, restored, long before it came to my knowledge— all the more stupid I !

I actually sent a carver to study it as an example for another object, when he found it conspicuous only by its absence.[1]

I may mention that the perpendicular screen, which occupied the place now taken up by the new reredos, did not belong to that position, but had been placed there within the memory of man, having been removed from the north-east transept.

The woodwork was executed by Farmer and Brindley, and the grilles, &c., by Skidmore.

EXETER CATHEDRAL.

I had been consulted here many years ago, upon some matters by the then architect, the late Mr. Cornish of Exeter, a very kindly and excellent old gentleman, and a thorougly practical man ; but at a later period I was appointed architect to the internal restorations, my commission being limited to these.

Immense opposition arose to what was proposed on the ground that I retained the choir-screen.[2] The architectural society and two local architects were furious about it, but I held hard and fast to it. At length we so far yielded as to pierce the backs of the altar recesses on either side of the screen, which, without sacrifice of any

---

[1] It is figured in Pugin's " Specimens," vol. ii.—ED.

[2] My principle is not to destroy an old close screen nor to erect a new one.

architectural feature, has in some degree opened out the choir to the nave.

In the choir nothing remained of the old fittings, except the bishop's throne, the sedilia, the side screens of the presbytery, and the misereres. The stall elbows were of some semi-modern date, and the rest of the work of the last century.

The screen-walls behind the stalls were of brick plastered, but were finished by a beautiful four-teenth-century, double-embattled, coping and freize, not unlike those of D'Estria's screens at Canterbury. I suppose that they had been taken down in Queen Elizabeth's time (possibly owing to some sculpture which they contained) and rebuilt in plastered brick, the old copings being re-used. I substituted for the brick wall an open screen, with the oak canopy work of the stalls attached to it, and re-set the beautiful coping. The stall-work, all but the misereres, is new, with return stalls against the great screen. The doorway of the screen towards the choir is the old one, restored even to its colouring, much of which is original. The modern parapet of the screen has been removed.

There was a great discussion about the age of this screen. Archdeacon Freeman, who sympathised with the opposition, wished to prove it to be of late date, arguing from the old accounts, which contain extensive entries for iron-work and tiles, that there had originally been an open iron screen; but I found all the iron thus described to exist in the present structure, used for ties, and the tiles also, used as the floor of the loft, so that at length the Archdeacon admitted that it was Bishop Stapledon's screen of 1320.[3]

We found evidences that the original reredos, or altar-screen, had gone as high as the arches of the side arcades. It had been destroyed after the Reformation, and the screen which was existing when we commenced work was of the present century. We could not think of reproducing, from imagination, the old altar-screen, which would have blocked out the arches at the east end, but I was overpressed in the contrary direction, and made the reredos too inconsiderable, though not so much so as to disarm opposition. I need not go into the history of the " Exeter Reredos " case: suffice it to say that the common-sense decision was come to, that the injunctions of the sixteenth century for the destruction of imagery were at first directed against such imagery as had been abused to superstitious purposes, and were only rendered general on the ground of the difficulty found in deciding as to which had, and which had not, been thus abused, and therefore could not be applied to new sculpture intended for no such purposes. I subsequently rather increased the height of the reredos, which was a very great gain.

The restoration of the throne was carried out with the utmost care and study of the evidences. The lower part was nearly all modern, and much of it was in plaster. Evidence existed of the old design of this portion : indeed, some important parts of the old work remained, and these indications have been precisely followed, excepting that I yielded to pressure in making the front open. There were

[3] The style is quite that of Bishop Stapledon's date.—ED.

no evidences one way or another, but it had most probably been close. This front is magnificently carried out, in exact imitation of the old work at its angles, which still existed : the sides and back are simpler, and follow evidences attached to the several angle buttresses. The whole of the old work was cleansed of its paint and varnish, but where it had been decorated in colour this was preserved and restored.

This work is attributed in all the histories to the fifteenth century, but Archdeacon Freeman found proof that (as its style evinces) it was contemporary with other works in the choir.

The decoration of the vaulting of the Lady Chapel is an exact restoration of what was found. In the side chapels, Mr. Clayton weakly departed from the old design, so far as to add some foolish patterns to the mouldings, otherwise it would have been correct.

Of the decoration of the choir-roof very slight indications were found, excepting on and around the bosses. The painting of the ribs is imitated from that of the Lady Chapel, counterchanging the colours.

In all this work I was greatly thwarted by the Dean, but I think the result is good.

The stonework generally has been carefully divested of its coatings of yellow wash without disturbing its surface. The Purbeck marble-work, however, demanded very extensive reparation, being sadly decayed and mutilated.

The pavement of the fifteenth century was found, in part, beneath the modern flooring, and has been useful in determining levels, though I am inclined to think we are a step too low as regards the altar platform.

I think the interior of this cathedral will, after all is done, be as charming as any in England.

The organ retains its old place, and is only altered in appearance by a moderate increase in depth from front to back. It is, however, vexatious that, in renewing the pipes of the choir-organ which were decayed, they have not reproduced the embossed patterns. I fear now they will never do it.

ROCHESTER CATHEDRAL.

I had been called in once before on some minor matters, but was commissioned in 1871 to undertake the greater work.

Externally the work consisted, in the first place, of the restoration of the north side and east end of the choir and presbytery. This part was terribly decayed, mutilated, and altered, but by careful study it has been brought back to its old state with a great amount of certainty. At the east end a perpendicular window had been inserted, and the lower range of lancets had been filled in with tracery of late date. These parts had been renewed some forty years back, and the question arose whether it would not be best, as the old design was evident, to bring it back to its original form. The great argument in favour of this step was the extreme ugliness of the great perpendicular window, which was very offensive to the Dean and others. This course was determined on, and carried out.

A question then arose as to whether the roofs and gables, which had all been lowered, should be raised to their ancient pitch. There was not money enough to raise the roofs, but I persuaded the chapter to raise the gables, hoping that the roofs might follow, but as yet they have not. The design of the gabled roof, which formerly existed over the east side of the eastern transepts, was discovered by my son Gilbert, and has been restored to the north transept. There is a confusion of design in the windows of this transept, owing to my having left the jambs of some later windows which had been inserted there.

The levels of the choir and presbytery have been regulated by clear evidence which remained beneath the modern floors. The tile paving is founded largely on portions of the old tiling then discovered, some of which have been preserved. The position of the high altar was ascertained and followed.

The decoration of the walls behind the side stalls, and of the screen behind the returned stalls, followed exactly evidences clearly found, excepting that the shields of which we did not discover the bearings, have been filled with the arms of the Bishops of Rochester, worked out by the kind aid of the herald, Mr. S. T. Tucker, Rouge Croix.

There was also another curious exception: at the back of the sub-dean's stall there was a patch of some older decoration of a very singular kind, a sort of plaid pattern. This the Dean would not permit to remain, but it has been taken out and preserved in a frame, I think in the chapter-room.

The painting on the wooden screen had been covered over with renaissance decoration, but some parts had been left uncovered, and all was traceable.

The screen itself is of the thirteenth century, and of oak. The original panelling is visible on its western side, that toward the east is of the fourteenth century. The stone screen in front is also of the fourteenth century, the two together supporting the rood-loft.

The great transept on each side (south and north) has been restored externally. It had been most monstrously "transmogrified," yet parts of the old work remained, though in an advanced state of decay: in fact it had almost perished. The design has been recovered from these remains, aided by old prints. The interior of the south transept, with its timber groining, has been repaired, as has a projecting building on its eastern side. The clerestory and triforium of the nave, which were becoming seriously dangerous, have been strengthened.

The north and south walls of the nave aisles are almost wholly of the date of some 150 years back. They, no doubt, had gone over so much that they were then rebuilt. Their foundation was of loose chalk and had given way. This is now banked up (underground) with concrete.

Mr. Irvine, the clerk of works, discovered many interesting matters underground, and has constructed theories on them which I feel unable to explain. I think he supposes Bishop Gundulph to have begun to build the nave, and that some of the bases are of his work, but that the superstructure is nearly three-quarters of a century later.

WINCHESTER CATHEDRAL.

Here I have done nothing but the opening out of the screen. I was called in about this several years back, but declined the task, thinking it impossible to effect it without altering old work.

In 1874 I was again called in, and on close examination, I found that the work forming the back of the returned stalls, and practically the east side of the screen, terminated precisely in a plane, flush with the back of the stalls, this plane bisecting all the mouldings as if they had been sawn down their axes; so that it was quite possible to open out the choir by simply removing the stone screen, which was modern, and the rough timber framing against which the boarding behind the stalls was fixed.

This at once formed an open screen, and needed little more than the repetition of the same features on the west, which already existed on the east, to make it a sightly and consistent design. The screen, being thus bisected by a plane, wanted only the other half supplied to make it complete, and that without touching the existing work.

This is a rough definition of what was done. It is not an exact or exhaustive one, but I may state that no old work was disturbed, and that the new western face is, in all parts which applied, an exact reproduction of the work on the eastern side. Its use, however, has been stupidly marred by filling in the openings with plate glass.

DURHAM CATHEDRAL.

I was only engaged here on internal work in or about the choir.

The stalls and screen were of Bishop Cosin's time. The screen had been removed twenty-five years back, and the canopies of the stalls divided into lengths, and pushed back between the columns. The side stalls are now set right, and a very open screen placed where the old one stood. There is also a new pulpit and pavement, for which I am responsible.

The altar-screen had formerly a Purbeck slab, as a sort of retabulum, on which we know that rich embroidery was hung. This had been covered over by a piece of very bad sculpture twenty-five years back, which we removed, and have placed needle-work there again.

I suspect that the floor between the stalls (which rises two steps above that of the nave) is a step too high, as it leaves no " Gradus Presbyterii."

The lectern is also new. The organ-case and the repairs of the stalls are the work of Mr. C. H. Fowler, the chapter architect.

A violent opposition was raised against this work by certain of the canons, who thought thereby to curry favour with the bishop. The Dean and Archdeacon Bland were the great supporters of the work.

ST. ALBANS.

To return to St. Albans, much has been done since I last mentioned it. The repairs of the eastern part of the main building are generally completed, and the Marchioness of Salisbury having undertaken to raise funds towards the restoration of the eastern chapels, much has been done to them also : I may refer here to my report addressed to Lady Salisbury.

At the present moment the work is in abeyance, but no doubt it will soon be resumed, as the new see is nearly established and fresh funds are being raised.

I gave a dinner at St. Albans in 1875 to the Council of the Institute, and many other friends, and we had a delightful field-day in the abbey.

The tower had been thoroughly repaired and strengthened in 1871, as had been also its two abutting walls to the north-east and north-west. The openings made in modern times in these two eastern walls as I have already mentioned, had been walled up, and the two ancient entrances reopened ; that on the north side, however, being strengthened by reducing its width, though without concealing its earlier dimensions. The opening in the south wall had been investigated as to its internal design many years before, when we had found its materials pulled down and used to wall up the opening.

These details had been carefully stored up during the long interval, and were now built up in their original places with exact precision : thus recovering, and, to a large extent, with its own materials, a very curious feature, a projecting doorway surmounted by a range of three tabernacles, in a style very similar to that of the Eleanor crosses, though probably a little earlier in actual date.

On the opposite side of the presbytery a careful examination showed the traces of a similar arrangement to that of the south doorway, though not precisely opposite to it. Here, however, we had not the copious stored-up fragments which enabled us to reconstruct, so largely with its own materials, the southern one. There was in fact but one small fragment of the doorway, but there were considerable marks of the rest, marks which would have been of themselves unintelligible, but with the aid of the other side quite clear and indisputable. As we were compelled to reopen this doorway, owing to the necessity of walling up its modern supplanter (one bay eastward) for security, I copied the north doorway.

Later on we discovered the veritable pinnacles of the tabernacle work over this doorway, and we then removed those which had been copied from the work on the opposite side, and substituted the true ones, with their coloured decorations upon them. They differ in design from those of their opposite neighbours, showing that, while doing two things substantially alike, the builders indulged in variety in the details.

A doubt has suggested itself to me since then as to whether the doorway itself was not different in design. The circumstances are these.

In the north aisle of the presbytery there were two external doorways: one of early perpendicular character, clearly introduced at the time which its style indicates, the other as clearly of modern introduction, but made up extensively of old details, mostly of a style agreeing with the date of this eastern arm of the church, 1280-90. This latter doorway was, as I have said, clearly a modern insertion, though strangely enough inserted at a point where a small original doorway had always existed. In fact, when in modern times this main approach to the church from the town had been made, the place of this old small doorway was found to be more convenient than that of the later perpendicular one, so the latter was walled up and the former enlarged. Oddly enough they had a doorway of the thirteenth century date on hand, and this they inserted, making up some of its ornamental details from fragments of the nave-screen. I fancied at the time that the doorway thus used had been an outer doorway of the eastern chapels, and I thought that if its place could be found, we might re-insert it. Unluckily while thinking aloud, in presence of the clerk of the works, he took me too hastily at my word, and removed the inserted doorway, before I was aware of it. We afterwards found precisely the inner design of the old doorway, which formed an opening in the wall-arcading. This we have restored, but, finding no trace of its outside form (excepting that the base-moulds returned to make way for it) I did not make any attempt at restoring the actual opening.

Meanwhile we examined—by excavation—the walls of the eastern chapels, only to discover that there never had been any doorway to them, and thus we were left with a fine contemporary doorway on our hands, and so remain to this day.

Suspicions have grown upon me that this was in reality the doorway of the north side of the presbytery, far richer and somewhat larger than its southern neighbour. This has not yet been sufficiently investigated. I mention it with some shame as an antiquarian failure, arising from going on too fast, and ahead of full investigation. I repent and confess.

The great triumph of our work has been, of course, the recovery and the putting together of the sub-structure of the shrine of St. Alban. The second has been the like discovery of that of St. Amphibalus, which I hope will also be soon set up in its old place.[4] Careful descriptions of these shrines ought to be written.

I forbear to say anything of our operations in the nave, till they are more advanced, and the difficulty occasioned by the leaning of the five western bays on the south side of the nave is passed. God grant us success.[5]

I am in this, as in other works, obliged to face right and left to combat at once two enemies from either hand, the one wanting me to do too much, and the other finding fault with me for doing anything at all.

The leader of the latter party is Mr. Loftie, whom I have answered twice in the *Guardian*, in 1875, and also in *Macmillan's Magazine* in this year (1877). He seems irrepressible, for no matter how often a statement of his is refuted, he reiterates it just as if no such refutation had been made. Happily he is an Irishman, and his own bulls are his best refutation.

The leader among those who wish me to do what I ought not to do is Sir Edmund Becket.

[4] This has been done. It now stands in its original place in the ante-chapel of the Lady Chapel.—Ed.

[5] This great engineering work, to which my father had devoted immense pains, and all the details of which he had most carefully contrived, was carried out with complete success only a few weeks after his death.—Ed.

CHAPTER IX.

The Anti-Restoration Movement

(*October*, 1877).

I CAN hardly say that this movement expresses a sentiment which is new to me, for in the case of the first considerable restoration placed in my hands, that of St. Mary's Church at Stafford, I was assailed nearly on the same principle by Mr. Petit. My correspondence with that highly-gifted gentleman was lithographed, and I would refer to it as a very early discussion of this question, dating as it does about 1840 or 1841. The expression which I see has been made use of in the latest deliverance of opinion on the subject, to the effect that more harm has been done by modern restoration than by three centuries of contempt, &c., was originated by myself during that correspondence thirty-six years ago.

Some seven years later I wrote my paper on faithful restoration, wholly on the side of conservatism; but in a note, added in 1858, I combated the extreme views of Mr. Ruskin against any form of restoration. Much later I wrote a paper on restoration, again wholly on the side of conservatism, which was read before the Institute of British Architects and printed. I have drawn up directions to builders and clerks of the works employed on such works, have helped in framing those of the Institute, and in my three opening papers, delivered while President of that body, I have expressed myself, as strongly as words would enable me, on the same subject, nor have I failed on all possible minor opportunities to do the same.

It is therefore rather hard to bear that I should now be made the butt of an extreme party, who wish to make me out to be the ring-leader of destructiveness.

I have said enough in every paper I have written, and on every occasion on which I have spoken on the subject, to show that, whatever view one may take of the anti-restoration movement, I cannot for a moment assert that it is unprovoked. On the contrary, I hold that there never was a case of more intense and aggravating provocation.

The country has been, and continues to be, actually devastated with destruction under the name of restoration. For years and years the vast majority of the churches to be restored have been committed to men, who neither know, nor care anything whatever about them, and out of whose hands they have emerged in a condition truly deplorable, stripped of almost everything which gave them interest or value; while it must be admitted that the best of us have been blameable, and that even our conservatism has been more or less destructive.

The three great grounds of complaint against

the new party are—(1) That they have remained absolutely silent while all this destruction and barbarism has been perpetrated, never giving one word of encouragement to the few who, though inadequately, have been for years raising their voices against it: (2) That now, after having stood silently by, witnessing all this devastation without complaint or protest, they suddenly turn round and visit it all on those whose protests they have all along refused to support : that they do not scruple to load with false accusations and to hold up to execration, as the authors of all the mischief, the very persons who have (however feebly) endeavoured to mitigate it, and who have never received the smallest expression of sympathy from those who now, when all the mischief is done, raise their voices to vilify the men whose efforts they had throughout declined to aid : (3) That they now take, what they must well know to be, an impracticable line, advocating, not any reasonable mode of treatment of ancient buildings, but the mere abstaining from doing anything whatever to them beyond the barest sustenance.

This long-continued silence on their part has made them in truth *participes criminis :* this treatment of those who have all along protested is the most culpable injustice : and this impracticability of view makes one doubt the sincerity of the opinions thus tardily proclaimed. Yet, if they would adopt a reasonable and practicable line, they might even yet effect great good.

I have at this moment to fight a double battle. I have, as throughout, to be fighting against those who would treat old buildings destructively, and I have, on the other hand, to defend myself against those who accuse me of the principles against which I contend, and who oppose one's doing anything at all.

The last paper I had occasion to write, and that not a month back, was in opposition to Sir Edmund Becket, who argues that we ought to deal with old buildings as the mediæval builders themselves did; in point of fact, to treat them as we should do any modern building, doing to them just what is right in our own eyes. On the other hand, we are told by the anti-restoration party that we have no right to do anything to them beyond the barest reparation. Thus everything which, previous perhaps to the present century, was done to them has become sacred as a matter of history, and claims as much regard as the noblest architecture of their earlier days.

These conflicting views are to my mind almost equally mistaken.

My answer (written the other day) to the first view is that these old buildings have become, by the general consent of those best able to judge, antiquarian and historical monuments, which fact severs them from the merely common-sense treatment, to which other buildings are subjected.

But surely there must be a limit to this severance. The principle can hardly be supposed to extend to alterations so modern, as to be contemporary with buildings which have no claim to such exception.

If, for example, a house of comparatively modern date, standing by the side of an ancient church, needs alteration or enlargement to suit it to its present uses, not even our critics would affirm that no such alterations should be permitted. They would only say, if the house has any character, the better parts of it should be spared, and the alterations which may be necessary should be carried out in reasonable harmony with them. Why, then, if the church has features in it of only the same period with the house, should those features claim any greater respect? More than this, these features may be not only altogether out of harmony with the rest of the church, but may be at variance with its uses, may disfigure the original structure, and may be the result of abuses which by common consent should be abolished. Surely, then, the fact, that the church itself has become an historical monument, cannot reasonably be pleaded in favour of its comparatively modern disfigurements. True, these more modern features may have merits and claims of their own, and these should be respected, but their claims are wholly different from those of the ancient fabric itself.

Take for instance the case of Ely Chapel (St. Etheldreda's) in Holborn.

The palace to which it belonged was destroyed in 1776, after which houses were built against either side of it towards the east, blocking up two of its side windows. The east and west windows only suffered from some minor vandalism, but the rest of the side windows were deprived of their mullions and traceries, galleries were built on each side of the chapel, and two at its west end, and the area was pewed in the most wretched manner.

The blocked-up windows were some years back

partially opened out, and the beautiful tracery discovered.   The Anti-restoration Society now protest
against that of the remaining side-windows being
replaced according to the design thus discovered.
Whether they disapprove of the removal of the
galleries and pews, I know not, but they oppose
any of the mutilated architecture being reinstated,
proclaiming the execrable wooden window-frames
of the end of the last century to be just as historical as the charming tracery of Bishop de Luda ;
and, as I suppose, blaming the removal of the
historical lath and plaster which had concealed the
two remaining ancient windows.

This is a fair example of the lengths to which
this new society will go, and I do not hesitate to
say that the palm for sound sense lies with the
architects employed, who are replacing the lost
traceries, while avoiding the reparation of features
which have only suffered from decay.

There are, however, many questions connected
with the treatment of ancient buildings which are
far more reasonably open to discussion, and I wish
that some really judicious men would take these,
fairly and dispassionately, under consideration.   I
have long and often urged that such doubtful cases
should be submitted to the decision, in each case,
of some independent and competent body, which
should unite the archæological and the ecclesiological elements in due proportions, not neglecting
the claims of architecture and good taste.

November 19th, 1877.

The promoters of this hue and cry against all
restoration, seem to direct themselves especially

against the architects, as if they were the prime movers in the matter: they go so far as to lay it to our charge, as if it was our love of employment which led to our engagement in such works.

The case, however, is quite otherwise. In no instance do I remember acting as prime mover in a restoration: on the contrary, I am sent for by others who feel its necessity, or are so convinced of its desirability that they apply to me to report on the condition of the building. True, if I were convinced that restoration were in itself wrong, I ought at once to say so, and to decline to report, or to do anything to further such wish or intention; but not having this conviction, my aim has been to recommend the course which I feel to be the best, and if the work is carried out, to do it in the best manner which my experience and judgment suggest to me.

I have not read Professor Colvin's article, but in an extract which I saw the other day in a newspaper, I see, that in speaking of me, he says that I proclaim, Conservatism, Conservatism, and again Conservatism, to be my principle, but that he sees no real difference between my principle, and that against which I declaim.

I was almost going to say that if there is no such difference, " Then I have cleansed my heart in vain, and washed my hands in innocency." I do not however say this; for though this has been my aim, bad judgment, the urgent influence of clients, the constant endeavour of those who work under me, whether as clerks of works, builders, or workmen, the tumbling down of portions of ancient buildings which I most wished to preserve, and a thousand other circumstances cut the grounds of this all too boastful claim from under one. Yet surely there must be a great difference between the works of those who long, and who labour, to act conservatively, and those of men who have no such desire, or if they had, are too ignorant to know how to carry out their own aims. If Mr. Colvin does not see such difference, surely it is owing to his own want of knowledge of the subject rather than to the absence of such a distinction.

Is there no difference forsooth between stonework, gently cleansed of its coating of whitewash, leaving every mark of the old mason's tool as distinct as when first wrought, and work rudely scraped or re-tooled, so as to leave no trace of its original surface ? These critics see none.

Is there no difference between a restored roof which retains all its ancient timber, excepting the rotten parts which threatened its speedy ruin, and whose existence has been indefinitely prolonged, by most careful and only needful reparation ; and a roof entirely destroyed, whose place is occupied by a new one, perhaps of deal, and probably having no reference whatever to the old design ? These men see none.

Is there no difference, again, between a building carefully and learnedly studied, and its parts investigated with the most anxious and studious care, and one ignorantly dealt with, without investigation, without anxiety, without knowledge. These people see none.

I should care less for this wilful blindness, were it not for its mischievous result ; and here again these critics will—and are welcome to—accuse me of vulgar selfishness. The result I refer to is this. Seeing that pretended judges proclaim that no difference exists between the work of devoted and earnest-minded men, and that of the ignorant herd who have usually to deal with ancient works—seeing that, on the contrary, the works of the former are held up systematically to execration, while those of the latter are passed by unnoticed—the public who are utterly careless of the whole matter, will place future works in the hands of ignorant tyros, in preference to employing men who have devoted themselves to the earnest study of the subject.

An advocate of the "do nothing" system of medical treatment declaims equally against the most eminent physician and the most ignorant quack; both alike doctor their patients, and both alike are wrong in doing so. The public, not quite convinced that nothing should be done, are thereby encouraged to employ the first doctor that may turn up, instead of the learned and judicious physician. But here we have a wholesome safeguard, "all that a man hath will he give for his life," and the folly of the critic falls harmless to the ground. Such safeguard, however, does not exist in the case of ancient buildings.

On the contrary, the majority of men prefer the worst architect, and the most slap-dash way of dealing with the work, and would give anything to be rid of the restraint which a conscientious architect imposes upon their wishes. I can truly say that my life is burdened with the constant outcry made against me for endeavouring to keep a check upon the vandalism of my employers, and upon the earnest pressure on all sides to destroy or alter something which this, that, or the other man, has a fancy against; and I feel no doubt that the practical result of this outcry against doing anything will be the encouragement of destructiveness. I would here refer to my speech and to a long paper in reply to Mr. Stevenson in the transactions of the Institute, also to my reply to Mr. Loftie in *Macmillan's Magazine*,[1] and to the following letter to Sir Edmund Lechmere respecting an attack on me by Mr. Morris (all in 1877) :—

My dear Sir Edmund,—I thank you for sending me the number of the *Athenæum*.

I have been told that I am systematically and very bitterly traduced by writers in that paper; but as I know that I do not deserve it, I never seek to see these articles, much less to answer them.

You, my dear Sir Edmund, know whether I am "destroying" the church,[2] or contemplating such treatment of it as is intended by that term. You know whether I am "hopeless, because interest, habit, and ignorance bind" me. Nay, you know whether I have obliterated a single chisel-mark of the old masons, and whether I have not, lovingly and carefully, traced out the almost obliterated evidence and relics of much of their work, and shown by every possible means, my love of a building of the class, of which "the newly invented study" is "the chief joy" of my life.

Nevertheless, painful and galling as it is, I

[1] Both these papers will be found in Appendix C.—ED.
[2] Tewkesbury Abbey.—ED.

rejoice in such letters and protests : for true—most dreadfully true—it is that what " modern architect, parson, and squire call restoration," *has* wrought wholesale ruin among our ancient buildings. I have lifted up my voice on this subject for more than thirty years, and, though not faultless, have striven with all my might to avoid such errors, and to prevent their commission by others. I feel more deeply on this subject than on any other, and never lose an opportunity of protesting against barbarisms of this kind, in season and out of season.

I am, therefore, willing to be sacrificed by being made the victim in a cause which I have so intensely at heart.

I do fear, however, that these indiscriminating letters defeat their own object ; for I observe that they rarely attack any but the works of those who strive to act conscientiously ; and most of all attack me who, I am bold to say, am amongst the most scrupulously conservative of restorers, and have the greatest conceivable love of ancient remains. Thus, by abusing the architect who more than others has lifted up the standard of conservatism, and by sparing those (whose name is legion) who have filled the country with havoc and destruction, they encourage the increasing disposition to commit these works to the hands, not of conservatives but of destroyers, by thus assuring " squires and parsons " that the latter will be dealt with mercifully, or winked at, while the former will have to suffer in their stead.

I dare say people may be low-minded enough to

say that my protests against the destructiveness of others is self-interested. I leave such minds to enjoy their own fallacies.

Anyhow, restorations or reparations are *necessary*, but I think it wholesome that those who carry them out should live in constant danger.

Herodotus (I think) tells us that the Egyptians, while religiously scrupulous as to having the bodies of their relations embalmed, so soon as the process was over, pursued the unhappy embalmer, and if they caught him, slew him. This is somewhat like the lot of the embalmers of ancient monuments : so if I suffer among those who deserve it, I only trust it will impel me to strive not to deserve it. If so, " all's well that ends well."

Yours very faithfully,

GEORGE GILBERT SCOTT.

It seems to be the opinion of some, in whose ranks I may place Sir Edmund Becket, (who, however, puts himself out of the pale by boasting that he is no antiquary, and by condemning persons who are so, and who bring their knowledge to bear upon restoration, as steeped in antiquarianism), that the rule of action in dealing with mediæval buildings is, to act as the mediæval builders themselves did ; in fact precisely in the same manner as that in which we treat modern buildings. We ought, they consider, freely to make such alterations in them as we deem best calculated to suit them to our own convenience, and even to our own taste, without showing any special respect for their architecture, beyond what harmony and good sense suggest ; much less any special regard for them as links in

B b

the history of art, or in history of any kind. We should not, as they think, bring to bear upon their treatment any of that class of feeling which we call "sentiment," unless it be some slight tribute of respect for a noted architect, founder, or benefactor.

Now I view this theory applied to ancient monuments as wholly wrong. As regards modern buildings it is obviously (within certain reasonable limits) right; and it is natural that persons who eschew antiquarianism, historical associations, and "sentiment," should apply it equally to the treatment of ancient buildings still in use, especially when their object is the defence of some favourite scheme of their own.

The anti-restoration party, on the contrary, take the extreme reverse of this view; claiming for all ancient buildings and works, and for some which are not very ancient, so intense an amount of veneration as almost to forbid even reparation, and absolutely to forbid anything approaching to restoration or any treatment calculated to render them fitter for their present uses.

I infinitely prefer the last named view, though I believe it to be such an exaggeration as would defeat its own objects; but the former I hold to be a most dangerous error.

I have recently met in an old pamphlet on Restoration by Mr. E. A. Freeman, written in 1852,[3] with the following passage, in which he defines well the difference between the claims of old and modern buildings :—

[3] The pamphlet is entitled "The preservation and restoration of ancient monuments."—ED.

" Antiquity is the science of the past ; it is the study of things
and events sufficiently removed from us to have acquired an
extrinsic value, as witnesses to a state of things no longer existing. We look upon an ancient church or castle, not merely as
a work of art, but as the relic and witness of a former age, of
sentiments, institutions, and states of society which have passed
away. Feelings like these could not have existed in the
middle ages with regard to any of the great works of Romanesque or Gothic architecture. For in the first place, they did
not represent a past state of things but a present; all the
forms of Gothic architecture, and, for this purpose, we may
add, of Romanesque also, were parts of one living whole, continually changing, developing, improving, or corrupting, but
never becoming completely extinct. So too with those religious
and political sentiments and circumstances of which those forms
of architecture were the material expression ; the building to
be destroyed did not at any period speak of an entirely past
state of things. The age of William the Conqueror and the
age of Henry VIIIth were indeed widely different, more
widely different, in some important respects, than the latter is
from our own ; but the change between them was gradual and
imperceptible ; no one period was separated from any other by
the same impassable gulf which separates us from the whole
they constitute ; no single event from the Conquest to the Reformation ever produced the total revulsion of taste and sentiment, which, speaking widely, we may call the result of the
latter. Had William of Wykeham devoted himself to archæo
logical research, the works of Poore or even of Gundulf could
not have appeared to him in the light of antiquities. They
were merely modern erections, claiming no respect beyond
what intrinsically belonged to them as works of art, and which,
if he thought he could improve upon them, he would sacrifice
with as little scruple as we should any structure of the last age.
The venerable rust of antiquity had as yet hardly gathered even
upon the swords of the crusaders ; its consecrating mould had
still to settle upon the frowning towers of London and of
Rochester, upon the massive arches of Southwell and St. Albans.
Had a past existed to him, in the sense in which his age is the
past to us, that past could hardly have been looked for in any
remains more recent than the camps and walls and gateways,
which remained then probably in far greater abundance than
at present, to bear witness to the universal sway of the Imperial
City."

THE " QUEEN ANNE " STYLE.

January, 1878.

The movement in favour of this style, or family of styles, has been no doubt a vexatious disturber of the Gothic movement.

The ardent promoters and sharers in the Gothic movement had fondly flattered themselves that theirs was a preternatural heaven-born impulse; that they had been born, and by force of circumstances trained, and led on, by a concurrence of events wholly apart from their own choice and will, to be instruments under Providence in effecting a great revival. They viewed that revival as in part religious, and in part patriotic.

For myself, I felt conscious of having been led to love Gothic architecture in my youth spontaneously, without any external inducement, and without any selfish, or even hopeful aim. I followed up Gothic architecture from every book I could find, and every old building I could meet with, just as practically and just as much in detail, while I had no thought of ever using, or aiding in reviving it, as I have done since it became the employment of my life. So that the sketches which I made, and the details and measurements which I took, while I had no practical object in view, are as useful to me in my professional work, as those I have since made with a direct view to practical use.

I did not attempt in my early practice to use what I had thus gathered, but while working contentedly in modern styles, continued, as time and opportunity would permit, to sketch and take details, for the mere love of it, from ancient buildings.

Later on I took to designing churches, and then found my acquired knowledge useful, though in a state little serviceable, from my never having thought much of it from a practical point of view.

I was awakened from my slumbers by the thunder of Pugin's writings. I well remember the enthusiasm to which one of them excited me, one night when travelling by railway, in the first years of their existence. I was from that moment a new man. Old things (in my practice) had passed away, and, behold, all things had become new, or rather modernism had passed away from me and every aspiration of my heart had become mediæval. What had for fifteen years been a labour of love only, now became the one business, the one aim, the one overmastering object of my life. I cared for nothing as regarded my art, but the revival of gothic architecture. I did not know Pugin, but his image in my imagination was like my guardian angel, and I often dreamed that I knew him.

In later years I fully thought that my experience, and that of some, perhaps many, others pointed to a special interposition of Providence for a special purpose, and often have I expressed this in writing, as in a paper entitled the " Gothic Renaissance,"[4] in my first R.A. lecture, and in my inaugural address in 1873 as President of the Institute of British Architects.

The course which the revival was at one time taking was first disturbed by the Italian mania, arising from Mr. Ruskin's writings; then by the

[4] Published by Saunders and Otley, in 1860.

French rage, coming in with the Lille Cathedral competition ; and later on by the revulsion against this, which might have set things right again, had not many who had been most ardently French—so much so that no moderate man could hold his own for their gallomania—become as furiously anti-gothic; and to carry out their new views turned round in favour of seventeenth-century work, and finally of " Queen Anne."

I have no right to expose this frivolity, for I was myself, in a measure, carried away with some of the earlier rages ; and also because when beaten out of my gothic by Lord Palmerston in the matter of the Government Offices, I felt compelled, in the interests of my family, to succumb, and to build them in classic, for which my early training had fairly fitted me. It did, however, seem hard that the very men who had once goaded me for not being Gothic or French enough, should be the very men to forsake gothic (for secular buildings at least) at the moment when its success was the most promising. I had always resented my classic opponents calling our mediæval enthusiasm a mere " fashion," but this change did really appear no better than a tailor's change in the cut of a coat, and the trifles which gave rise to it seem to be evinced by the strange vagaries in dress, &c., by which it was accompanied.

When, however, one considers the results, the case is not so bad. Though many buildings may be erected in the so-called " Queen Anne " style, which would otherwise have been gothic, the majority of such would, no doubt, have been erected in the ver-nacular style of the day, and so far the change has been an unquestionable gain : we have rich colour and lively, picturesque architecture in lieu of the dull monotony of the usual street archi- tecture, and more than this the style is half-way between gothic and classic in its effect, and goes all the way in its use of material.

The style of Queen Anne's time was really the domestic variety of the architecture of Sir Chris- topher Wren, and a very good style it really was ; but the style now known by that name embraces all varieties, from the close of the Elizabethan period to the middle of the eighteenth century, with a preference for that most resembling Eliza- bethan, so that it really brings in very much which is highly picturesque and artistic in character such as no " Gothic man " would fail to appreciate.

Again, it has the advantage of eluding the popular objections to gothic, when used for secular pur- poses. It meets the prejudices of the modern halfway, and turns the point of his weapons. When first taken up it was really more like the true Queen Anne, than it has since become : its use of common sash windows was one of its popular points, and the difficulties, assumed to be felt in accommodating gothic windows to modern use, were urged as an argument in its favour. Once, however, in the saddle, the Queen Anne-ites soon threw off this disguise, and freely adopted lead lights, iron casements, and all kinds of old fashions which a gothic architect would have hardly dared to employ, so much so, indeed, that a so-called " Queen Anne " house is now more a revival of the past than a modern gothic house.

In my book, written about 1859, my object was

to show that gothic would admit of any degree of modernism. The aim of the Queen Anne architects now seems to be to show that nothing can be too old-fashioned for their style.

I heartily wish them all success in this, and when they have succeeded, I trust we Goths may be allowed to pick up a few crumbs of their revived old fashions, and to use them in our style, without being taunted as the revivers of obsolete customs, or with making our houses look like churches.

EXPLICIT.

APPENDIX A.

———— ◆ ————

THE latest date which appears in the "Recollections" is January, 1878. My father departed this life on the 27th of the following March. A few words seem needed to complete the story.

The following works of importance were in progress at the time of his death, beside those which are referred to in the "Recollections:"—

The refitting of the choir of Canterbury Cathedral, as to which some controversy has arisen, as will be seen from certain passages in the papers on the subject of restoration printed as Appendix C ; the restoration of Tewkesbury Abbey ; the erection of the Great Hall of Glasgow University, for which the plans had been prepared, and which is now about to commence ; the Cathedral of Edinburgh, the nave of which has just been consecrated. The restoration of the nave of St. Alban's Abbey, still in progress, is a work which has on several accounts excited general interest. The great work of forcing back to the perpendicular by mechanical means the south wall of the nave for some 105 feet of its length, a wall 66 feet in height, which in the centre of the length to be dealt with overhung its base to the extent of 2 feet 3 inches, is an example of architectural engineering upon a large scale, which has attracted much attention ; the more so, perhaps, since he who had devised the whole plan, which has been carried out with such complete success, did not live to enjoy the satisfaction of it. The repair of John De Cella's magnificent portals, and the restoration of Abbot Trumpington's nave roof, were also pending at the time of Sir Gilbert's death, and have given occasion to warm controversies. The choir screen at Beverley Minster, the Hook Memorial Church at Leeds, and the restoration of the Parish Church of Halifax, may also be mentioned; as well as the restoration of the west fronts of Lichfield and St. David's Cathedrals, and of the nave of Salisbury. The restoration of the Chapel of New College was also in progress, and that of St. Margaret's Church, Westminster; while in the Abbey itself the work of bringing back the noble portals of the north transept to their original design had been commenced, and is still in course of execution. Among many other works of more or less general interest, which were similarly in progress at the time of Sir Gilbert's death, and which it has been left to his sons to carry on to completion, may be mentioned the Cathedral of Graham's Town in South Africa.

Of the last few days of my father's life, a very minute account has been preserved by John Pavings, who had long acted as his valet, and for whom, from his constant and faithful service, my father had a high regard. Although of his four sons then living two resided under the same roof with him, and the others but a few miles away, yet so little anticipation was there of any danger on the part of the medical men or of others, that only one of us—my brother John—was with him at all during the last days of his life, and he, from one cause and another, saw but little of him.

It was on Tuesday the 19th of March that my father first began to ail. He had long suffered from varicose veins in the left leg. On this day they caused him much discomfort, and Dr. Westlake, who was called in, ordered him to keep to his bed. So little, however, was thought of this, that on Wednesday morning my brother and his wife, who resided with my father, left town for four days, and on the Saturday following my youngest brother, who also lived at home, went down into Suffolk for some fishing, intending to return on the 27th, and leaving no address. On the Friday Dr. Westlake saw my father again, and said in answer to an inquiry, " Sir Gilbert will be about again in a week." On Saturday he felt well enough to leave his bed for the sofa.

On Sunday he suffered somewhat from rheumatism, situated, as Dr. Seton, his regular medical adviser, ascertained, in the muscles between the ribs. In spite of this, he was, as usual, full of fun. A nephew, a medical student, happening to call,

my father sent out word, " Ask *Doctor* Alfred to come in."
" Is there a guinea ready ? " was the reply ; to which my father
sent back, " Ask him for his diploma." On this day he kept
his bed, but on the Monday he got up and had an interview
in his study with two members of Glasgow University on the
subject of the Bute Hall. He had acted against medical
advice in leaving his bed while suffering as he was from the
veins in his leg ; and now, instead of returning to it, he
decided to sit down to lunch with Dr. Allan Thomson and his
companion. To his man, who ventured a remonstrance, he
said, " I feel perfectly well ; why should I be mewed up here ?
I shall enjoy lunching with them, and it will do me good."
There is reason to fear that this imprudence cost him his life,
the exertion bringing about that disaster against which his
medical advisers had distinctly warned him,—the detachment
of a blood-clot from the inflamed vein, and its passage into the
circulation, and eventually to the heart. Still, although, as his
man expresses it, " done up," he was in good spirits. " I am
going," he said to Pavings, " to the Academy meeting for
the election of ————." " What shall you do with your
leg, then, Sir Gilbert ? " " Take it with me, I hope," was the
reply. " If you go, I shall go to take care of you," said his
man. " So you may," rejoined my father. " Sir Francis always
takes his butler with him, and he tucks him up. You shall do
the same for me." A little later, speaking with Pavings of
Cromwell and the Roundheads, " round-heads," he said,
" like yours ;" and calling for his rule he measured his own
and Pavings' heads. Sir Gilbert's was an inch the longer, but
his man's was the wider by one finger-breadth.

This evening Dr. Seton saw him for the last time. Though
strongly urging the necessity of perfect rest, he yet thought so
favourably of the case that he did not call on the following day.
The next morning (Tuesday the 26th) my father recounted
to his man a quaint dream which he had had, over which they
had a good laugh together. " In the course of it," said my
father, " I saw my dear wife ; I never saw her more plainly
in my life," and he seemed quite to brighten up on thinking
of it. All this day he lay in bed, but saw several persons on
business in his bedroom, and enjoyed his meals as usual.

After dinner a letter arrived from one whom my father had
often assisted, a Roman Catholic architect who had had great

misfortunes and was lying ill. Pavings was disposed to blame the man, but Sir Gilbert said, "It is very wicked to speak harshly of poor people," and wrote out a cheque at once. This was the last time that my father put pen to paper. Some seven hours later he was called to his account, and by a touching coincidence he, on whose behalf he last employed his pen, survived his benefactor but a single day. After this an allusion to a person of humbler position, whose necessities my father had constantly relieved, led him to remark upon the law of Moses concerning the jubilee, and to apply to the case of such pensioners the passage in Deuteronomy (xv. 13, 14), "Thou shalt not let him go away empty : thou shalt furnish him liberally : of that wherewith the Lord thy God hath blessed thee thou shalt give unto him." This led to a long conversation upon the story of the Exodus, in the course of which Sir Gilbert answered many difficulties which had occurred to Pavings. On his saying, "How did Moses get up to the top of that mountain ? " my father laughingly replied, "Moses had not such a game leg as I have."

Between nine and ten that night my brother John was with him, but stayed only for a short time, as Sir Gilbert seemed tired and wished to go to sleep.

A little later his leg appeared to trouble him, for remarking that the doctor had not called that day, he said, " My leg is no better ; if it does not soon get better, it will do for me." Still he was cheerful, chatting with Pavings about Stowe at the time that the present Duke was christened, and about his native village, which led to his telling the following story :— Mr. Law was a pious but absent-minded farmer, who was occasionally invited to dine at the parsonage on sundays. On one occasion—my grandfather being away—Mr. Law had to say grace, which he did at great length. He also happened in the course of the same meal to get confused among the various cruets on the table, and sprinkled the sugar upon his meat. After he had gone, the eldest of the brothers was laughing at his long grace, when Miss Gilbert, his aunt, reproved him, saying, " My dear, Mr. Law's grace was ' seasoned with salt.' " " Yes," he replied, " and his meat with sugar." I give this story not for its own sake, but as illustrating the almost child-like love of fun which my father exhibited to the very last. An allusion in the course of conversation to the old stage-coachmen, recalled to his mind a song they used to sing forty years ago : " All round my hat I wear a green willow," and he sang a line or two of it to give Pavings the tune.

He talked cheerfully until about eleven p.m., when his man handed him his Bible and hymn-book, and left him for a little. He returned for a few minutes. "It is pleasant," said my father, "to see your fat face. Good night. Schlafen Sie wohl."

About four o'clock in the morning his bell rang. Pavings finding him coughing violently gave him some brandy, and at Sir Gilbert's request prepared a poultice. While thus engaged, my father said to him, " Your had better make up a bed on the sofa; for if you leave me, you will find me gone in the morning." The instant the poultice was placed over the region of the heart, my father called out, "Oh, it is come again ! Lift me up." My brother John was summoned at once, but my father never recovered consciousness, and died some twenty minutes afterwards. A little before he died he opened his eyes, and lifted them upwards, as though in prayer. This was the last gesture he made : the eyelids fell, and after a few heavy moans all was over.

He was interred on Saturday, the 6th of April, in Westminster Abbey. The Dean of Westminster, anticipating the application from Sir Gilbert's colleagues of the Institute of British Architects, intimated to us immediately after my father's death the wish that his body should be laid to rest within the walls of the Abbey, by the grave of Sir Charles Barry, and beside the great nave pulpit which he had himself designed.

The Abbey Church of Westminster was, of all others, the place in which, even apart from the honour of such a resting-place, my father would have desired to be laid. Of all the great churches of England with which he had been connected, this was the one which he best loved. The works upon which he was from time to time engaged about the Abbey, and the investigation of its antiquities in their minutest detail, was to him a source of unfailing delight. He one day remarked to his valet, "When I get old and past work, I shall take a house near the Abbey, so as to be able to attend the daily service there, and to wander about the dear old place," and, he added, "I think that I shall be very happy." But a still happier lot was to be his. A kindly Providence spared him the sad consciousness of failing powers, the weariness of enfeebling old age, and the slow misery of a lingering sickness. Too soon, alas ! for those to whom he was most dear, but for himself, in truest kindness, not too late, he was called away, and where he had thought to wander as a worn-out old man he now lies at rest, taken from us in the fulness of his powers, which years had ripened to maturity, and age had not commenced to wither.

The coffin bore the following inscription : —

> Georgii Gilberti Scott, equitis
> viri probi architecti peritissimi
> parentis optimi reliquiæ hic
> in fide Jesu Christi resurrectionem
> expectant. Obiit xxvii⁰. die Martis
> anno Salutis MDCCCLXXVIII⁰. ætatis LXVII⁰.

By order of Her Majesty, one of the royal carriages attended the funeral procession. In the church the pall was borne by Mr. A. B. Mitford, who represented the First Commissioner of Works; Lord John Manners, M.P., the Postmaster-General; Mr. R. Redgrave, R.A., representing the President of the Royal Academy; Mr. Charles Barry, the President of the Royal Institute of British Architects; Mr. Frederic Ouvry, the President of the Society of Antiquaries ; and Mr. A. J. B. Beresford Hope, M.P., President of the Council of the Architectural Museum. The Royal Academy, the Institute of Architects, the Society of Antiquaries, and the Council of the Architectural Museum were further represented by numerous deputations, as were also the Archæological Institute, the London and Middlesex Archæological Society, the Ecclesiological Society, the Architectural Association, the Turners' Company, of which Sir Gilbert was a member, and many other public bodies connected with art and learning. On the Sunday following the interment, the Dean of Westminster preached in the Abbey Church the funeral sermon, which by his kind permission is reprinted in the following Appendix.

I am also happy to be permitted to close this story by an extract from a lecture delivered before the Royal Academy in January last, by Mr. Edward M. Barry, R.A., who succeeded my father in the chair of architecture :—

" In Sir Gilbert Scott a great movement has lost a representative man, intent on the reproduction of the forms of old English architecture. Few advocates of change, amounting almost to revolution, have experienced as large an amount of practical success, and he lived to see the Gothic revival, of which he was a leader, to a great extent triumphant. Heartily identified, however, as he was with the revival, Sir G. Scott was not an artistic bigot. He could spare some of his admiration for the architecture of Greece and Rome, of which he expressed in his Academy lectures 'no stinted or cold-hearted eulogy.' With the calmness of judgment which distinguished him, he admitted that the Renaissance style had many merits, and that it possessed at least one feature, the dome—the noblest and 'most sublime' achievement of architecture—which had found no abiding place in English mediæval art. His remarks on the internal treatment of this crowning achievement of Renaissance architecture have a special interest at the present time, when a renewed attempt is being made to induce some of our best painters to devote themselves to the glorious task of decorating the dome of St. Paul's. Identifying himself with the revival of the Gothic architecture of his own country, Sir Gilbert Scott distrusted the introduction of principles of composition and details borrowed from abroad, and thus remained, as he began, an essentially English architect. The Albert Memorial in Hyde-park may be described as an exception to Sir Gilbert Scott's usual practice in this respect. At the commencement of the present century an age of no architecture had supervened on the first classical revival of Inigo Jones and Wren, and had brought us to what may be called the Dismal Period : the era of Bloomsbury streets and Batty Langley's gothic. When men demanded something better, they were invited to choose between two renaissances —the Classic, and the Gothic. Then arose the battle of the styles, a conflict which cannot be said to be yet over, and which, perhaps, may never be decided. Sir Gilbert Scott adopted the latter, and became the principal church architect of his day. The Gothic revival was not, however, only, or even chiefly, an architectural movement, being warmly supported by the clergy, who rejoiced to see the national interest awakened in its sacred buildings. Atonement was demanded for past days of ecclesiastical carelessness, and the Cambridge Camden Society arose, with its suggestive motto, '*Donec templa refeceris.'* A great impetus was given to the new taste by the erection of the Houses of Parliament in the Gothic style, and by the labours of Pugin and others in the education of workmen in the old mediæval traditions. Sir Walter Scott had previously paved the way by entrancing a nation (already, alas! half forgetful of him) and turning their thoughts to the history, customs, and architecture of olden times. New Gothic churches and other ecclesiastical edifices arose throughout the country, and the cry for restoration increased in volume. Cathedrals were repaired and thrown open to the people, services were multiplied and rendered more attractive, and it was found that our old buildings could once more be filled with overflowing congregations. In the architectural part of this great movement Sir Gilbert Scott occupied the foremost place. To effect so great a change, enthusiasm is necessary, and when men are much in earnest, enthusiasm may easily lead to extravagance. So-called revivals are often difficult to distinguish from practical innovations, and many a fierce theological conflict has been waged over architectural details in our churches. Sir Gilbert Scott was neither by taste nor temperament an innovator. In the midst of controversy his works showed sobriety of design, and moderation of judgment. The Tractarian movement and the Gothic revival went, indeed, hand in hand; but he was too earnest a champion to wish his cause to be identified with any single party. Like many High Churchmen, he desired to tread the '*via media,*' very much as did the late Dean of Chichester; so that Sir Gilbert Scott may almost be termed the Dr. Hook of the Gothic revival. In the early stage of the latter, it was by a design for the parish church at Camberwell, that the name of Scott attracted notice, and at a subsequent period he had the satisfaction of distancing all competitors at Hamburg, thus winning for English architects conspicuous international distinction. In his own country, he secured an amount of employment scarcely paralleled in professional annals. In a few years great changes had arisen in the public taste. A time of architectural carelessness had been followed by an era of activity, an age of neglect by an outburst of restoration. Complaints have lately been much urged against restorations; doubtless with truth in certain cases. Sir Gilbert Scott had too much to do, to expect to escape criticism. An architect's deeds are never hidden, and all can have their say upon them. Few, however, have dwelt more than Sir Gilbert Scott on the necessity of a conservative spirit of reverence for the past. In so doing, he carried out the teaching of his predecessors at the Royal Academy, and particularly that of Professor Cockerell. In regard to restorations, it should be remembered that architects have serious responsibilities from which their critics are free, and however great may be their reverence for the past, they must recognize the practical requirements of their own time. Our old buildings must not be allowed to fall, while we are discussing, as an abstract principle, the propriety of restoration. Architects, nevertheless, should be jealous of unnecessary change, and the question is well dealt with in the following sentence from one of the discourses of Sir Joshua Reynolds :— ' Ancient monuments, having the right of possession, ought not to be removed unless to make room for that which not only has higher pretensions, but such pretensions as will balance the evil and confusion which innovation always brings with it.' The Gothic revival has now attained a respectable age, and we may begin to inquire as to its results. It has apparently settled the question that, for the present at least, our ecclesiastical architecture is to be Gothic. For secular buildings, no such decision has been accepted. Important works are daily carried out in both the rival styles, and there are not wanting signs of an increasing feeling in favour of the classic Renaissance or certain developements of it. Sir Gilbert Scott erected his most important civic building, the Public Offices, in the latter style, although under protest, at the bidding of Lord Palmerston. This was probably the greatest disappointment of a long and successful career, and to be regarded as an episode only, as his name will ever be indissolubly associated with the Gothic revival of the reign of Queen Victoria. His memory will live, not only in stately cathedrals, but in many a lowly village, as the great ecclesiastical architect of our time. Too learned to be over-confident, he was ever a student, and conspicuous for a modest and unassuming manner. Architect of his own fortune, his mortal remains were fitly interred in that famous Abbey which he loved so well—the national Campo Santo of Westminster. His grave is side by side with that of Sir Charles Barry, to whose place he succeeded in the Royal Academy on the death of the latter in 1860. The career of Sir Gilbert Scott was in some respects unique, and the exact circumstances of

C C

the revival, under which it was possible, can scarcely recur. It may, however, supply encouragement to architectural students. Great reputations are not indeed to be lightly won, or easily supported; but every young student may at least determine that the noble art of architecture shall not suffer in his hands by any lack of devotion, hard work, and perseverance. All may follow, though it may be at a distance, in the steps of the great men who have passed before, and thus may endeavour to deserve, if it be not given to them to achieve, success which may compare with theirs."

APPENDIX B.

———◆———

FUNERAL SERMON ON THE DEATH OF SIR GIL-
BERT SCOTT, PREACHED IN WESTMINSTER
ABBEY, APRIL 6TH, 1878,

By ARTHUR PENRHYN STANLEY, D.D.,
DEAN OF WESTMINSTER.

"I was glad when they said unto me, Let us go into the house of the
Lord."—PSALM cxxii.

"THE house of the Lord." It is an expression which we at
once recognize as *figurative*. "Behold the heaven of heavens
cannot contain Thee; how much less this house that I have
builded!" So it was said even in the Jewish dispensation.
In the Christian dispensation it is still more strongly expressed
that the only fitting temple of the Most High is the sacred
human conscience, or the community of good men throughout
the world, or that vast unseen universe which is the true tabernacle, greater and more perfect than any made by hands.
Nevertheless, like all familiar metaphors, the expression "the
house of God" has a deep root in the human heart and mind.
Our idea of the invisible almost inevitably makes for itself a
shell or husk from visible things. This is the germ of religious
architecture. This is the reason why the most splendid buildings in the world have been temples or churches. This is the
reason why even the most spiritual, even the most Puritanical,
religion clothes itself with the drapery not only of words, and
sounds, and pictures, but of wood, and stone, and marble. A
Friends' meeting-house is as really a house of God, and therefore as decisive a testimony to the sacredness of architecture,

C C 2

as the most magnificent cathedral. The barbaric artificers of
the rude tabernacle in the desert were as really inspired in
their rude manner as the Tyrian architects of the temple of
Solomon. Who is there that does not feel a glow of enthusiasm, when coming back after long absence, it may be like
him who addresses you to-day, long illness, he finds himself
once more in the old familiar, venerable sanctuary, which has
become the home of his affection, the outward and visible sign
of his country's and of his own hopes and duties? Who is
there that, having grown with the growth and strengthened
with the strength of an institution like this, does not feel that
it is part of himself—that its honour or dishonour is his own
glory or his own shame? That which a sentiment usually
ascribed to the witty Canon [1] of a neighbouring cathedral, with
singular humour, treated as an impossibility, is in fact the simple truth. We who live under the hull or framework, the
vaults or the dome of a building like Westminster Abbey or
St. Paul's, are conscious of a thrill of satisfaction when the hand
of an approving public is placed on our outward shell ; a
thrill which penetrates to our inmost souls, because we within,
and that superb shell without, constitute but one and the same
living creature. It is the consciousness of this intimate connexion between the spiritual and the material temple, between
the grandeur of religion and the grandeur of its outward habi-
tation, which gives a living interest to the thought which I
would this day bring before you—the religious aspect of the
noble science and art of the architect. We yesterday laid
within these walls the most famous builder of this generation.
Others may have soared to loftier flights, or produced special
works of more commanding power; but no name within the
last thirty years has been so widely impressed on the edifices of
Great Britain, past and present, as that of Gilbert Scott. From
the humble but graceful cross, which commemorates at Oxford
the sacrifice of the three martyrs of the English Reformation,

---

[1] It is told of Sydney Smith that he once said to a child who thought
that it was pleasing a tortoise by stroking the shell, "You might as well
hope to please the Dean and Chapter of St. Paul's by patting the dome."
("Memoirs of Sydney Smith," vol. i. 324.) It would seem, however, that
the story had an earlier origin. The remark was made, at least in the first
instance or simultaneously, by the present Sir Frederick Pollock to his
brother.

to the splendid memorial of the prince who devoted his life to the service of his Queen and country ; from the Presbyterian University on the banks of the Clyde, to the college chapels on the banks of the Isis and the Cam ; from the proudest minster to the most retired parish church; from India to Newfoundland —the trace has been left of the loving eye and skilful hand that are now so cold in death. Truly was it said by one, who from the distant shores of a foreign land rendered yesterday his sorrowing tribute of respect, that in nearly all the cathedrals of England there must have been a shock of grief when the tidings came of the sudden stroke which had parted them from him, who was to them as their own familiar friend and foster-father. Canterbury, Ely, Exeter, Worcester, Peterborough, Salisbury, Hereford, Lichfield, Ripon, Gloucester, Manchester, Chester, Rochester, Oxford, Bangor, St. Asaph, St. David's, Windsor, St. Alban's, Tewkesbury, and last, not least, our own Westminster, in which he took most delight of all buildings in all the world, are the silent mourners round the grave of him who loved their very stones and dust, and knew them to their very heart's core. But it is good on these occasions to rise above the personal feelings of the moment into those more general lessons which his career suggests.

I. It was the singular fortune of that career that it coincided with one of the most remarkable revolutions of taste that the world has witnessed. That peculiar conception of architectural beauty which our ancestors in blame, and not in praise, called Gothic, was altogether unknown to Pagan or Christian antiquity. It was unknown alike to the builders of the Pyramids and the Parthenon, to the builders of the Roman Basilica, or the Byzantine St. Sophia. Born partly of Saracenic, partly of German parentage, it gradually won its way to perfection by the mysterious instinct which breathed through Europe in the Middle Ages. It flourished for four centuries, and then died as completely as if it had never existed. Another style took its place. By Catholic and Protestant it was alike repudiated. By the hands of English or Scottish prelates, no less than by English or Scottish Reformers, its traces wherever possible were obliterated. Here and there a momentary thrill of admiration was rekindled by the high-embowed roof, or by the stately pillars of our ancient churches, as in the " Penseroso " of Milton, or as in the " Mourning Bride " of Congreve. But as a general

rule it was regarded as a lost art—and our poets of the sixteenth century make no more allusion to it than if they had
been born and bred in the new world of America.

" Look through the popular writers of the sixteenth century, the unconscious exponents of the sentiments of the age that followed the Reformation ;
examine the writings of Spenser, for instance, and Shakespere, the many-
sided, to whom all the tones of thought of all ages seem to have been
revealed and familiarized ; of Chapman and Marlow and the rest, and I
question whether you will find a line or a word in any one of them indicating the slightest sympathy with the æsthetics of ecclesiastical architecture,
which exercise such a fascination over ourselves. Not one line, not one
word, I believe, of the charms of cloistered arcades and fretted roofs, and
painted windows, and the dim religious light of the pensive poets of our
later ages. No wail of despair, no murmur of dissatisfaction reaches us
from the generation that witnessed the dire eclipse, in which the labour of
so many ages of artistic refinement became involved. Their children have
betrayed to us no remembrance of the stifled sorrows of their fathers. As
far as regards its taste for ecclesiastical monuments, the literature of Elizabeth might have been the production of the rude colonists of the Antilles or
of Virginia." [2]

Here and there an antiquarian, like Gostling at Canterbury
or Carter at Westminster, allowed the genius of the place to
overpower the tendencies of the age. And if a protest came
at last against the indiscriminate disparagement of mediæval
art from Horace Walpole, it was more in deference to his rank
than from conversion to his sentiments, that the authorities in
church and state consented to preserve what else they would
have doomed to destruction. At last, in the first half of this
century, a new eye was given to the mind of man. Gradually,
imperfectly, through various channels—in this country chiefly
through the minute observations of a Quaker student—the
visions of the strange past rose before a newly awakened
world. The glory and the grace of our soaring arches, of our
stained windows, of our recumbent effigies, were revealed, as
they had been to no mortal eyes since the time of their erection. To imitate, to preserve this ancient style in its remarkable beauty was the inevitable consequence, we might say the
overwhelming temptation, of this new discovery. The hour
was come when the ecclesiastical architecture of the past was
to be roused from its long slumber, and with the hour came
the man. We do not forget that splendid if eccentric genius

[2] Sermon preached on the Founder's Day, at Harrow, October 10, 1872,
by Charles Merivale, D.D., Dean of Ely.

who gave himself, though not with undivided love, to the service of another communion. We cannot but remember the gifted architect who raised the stately halls and the commanding towers of the palace of the imperial legislature, and who was laid long years ago—in fit proximity to his own great works—within these walls, and where he has now been followed by him of whom I now would speak. For there was one who, if younger in the race, and at the time less conspicuous than either of them, was destined to exercise over the growth of Gothic architecture in this country a yet more enduring and extensive influence.

When in this Abbey the first note of that revival was struck by the erection of Bernasconi's plaster canopies in the place of the classic altar-piece given by Queen Anne,[3] a boy of fourteen years old was in the church watching the demolition and the reconstruction with a curious vigilance, which from that time never flagged for fifty years. That was the earliest reminiscence which Gilbert Scott retained of Westminster Abbey: that was the first inspiration of the Gothic revival which swept away before its onward progress not only the plaster reredos of this Abbey, but a thousand other crudities of the same imperfect period. He impersonated the taste of the age. Antiquarian no less than builder, he became to those fossils of mediæval architecture what Cuvier and Owen have been to the fossils of the earlier world of nature. It may be that others will succeed on whom the marvellous bounty of Providence shall bestow other gifts of other kinds. But meanwhile we bless God for what we have had in our departed friend and his fellow-workers. The recovery, the second birth, of Gothic architecture, is a striking proof that the human mind is not dead, nor the creative power of our Maker slackened. We bless alike the power which breathed this inspiration into the men of old, and which even from their dry bones has breathed it once again into the men of these latter days.

II. But it is not enough that a great gift should be resuscitated or a great style imitated. We must ask wherein its greatness consisted, and in what relation it stood to the other gifts of the Creator. There are many characteristics of the mediæval architecture, as of the mediæval mind, which have

---

[3] "Memorials of Westminster Abbey," p. 530.

totally perished, or which ought never to be revived, which
represent ideas that for our time have lost all significance, and
purposes which are doomed to extinction. The Middle Ages
have left on the intellect of Europe few, very few, enduring
traces. Their chronicles are but the quarries of later historians :
their schoolmen are but the extinct species of a dead theology.
Two great poems and one book of devotion are all which that
long period has bequeathed to the universal literature of mankind. But their architecture still remains

> Of equal date
> With Andes and with Ararat,[4]

and the reason of this continuance or revival is this, that in its
essential features it represented those aspirations of religion
which are eternal. As in mediæval Christianity there were
elements which belonged to the undeveloped Protestantism of
the Western churches, so also in mediæval architecture there
are elements which belong to the churches of the Reformation
as well as to the churches of the Papal system. Its massive
solidity, its aspiring height, its infinite space, these belong not to
the tawdry, trivial, minute, material side of religion, but to its
sobriety, its grandeur, its breadth, its sublimity. And therefore
it was that when this revival of Gothic architecture took place,
it was amongst the Protestant churches of England, rather than
in the Catholic churches of the continent, that its first growth
struck root. The religious power of our great cathedrals has,
as has been well remarked,[5] not lost, but gained, in proportion
as our worship has become more solemn, more simple, more
reverential, more comprehensive. There is a cloud of super-
stition doubtless which, with the latter half of the nineteenth
century, has settled down over a large part of the ecclesiastical
world ; but the last places which it will reach will be the
magnificent architectural monuments which defy the introduction of trivial and mean decorations, or, if introduced, condemn
them for their evident incongruity with other portions of the
buildings. The great antiquaries, the great architects of this
century, are but too well acquainted with the differences
between the loftier and the baser aspects, between the golden
and the copper sides of their noble art, to allow it to become

[4] Emerson.
[5] Dean Milman's "History of Latin Christianity," vol. vi. p. 91.

the handmaid of a sect or party, or the instrument of a senseless proselytism.

And this leads me to one more point of the marvellous revival of which he who lies in yonder grave was the pioneer and champion. For the first, or almost for the first time in the history of the world, the architecture of the nineteenth century betook itself, not to the creation of a new style, but to the preservation and imitation of an older style. With perhaps one exception,[6] every age and country down to our own has set its face towards superseding the works of its predecessors, by erecting its own work in their place. The Normans overthrew the old Romanesque churches of the Saxons. Henry III. in this place "totally swept away, as of no value whatever," the noble abbey of the Confessor. Henry VII. built his stately chapel in marked contrast to all the other portions of this building. The great architects of the cathedrals of St. Peter at Rome, and St. Paul in London, adopted a style varying as widely from the mediæval, which they despised, as from the Grecian, which they admired. But now, in our own time, the whole genius of the age threw all its energies into the reproduction of what had been, rather than into the production of what was to be. No doubt it may be said that there is in the original genius which creates something more stimulating and inspiring. Yet still the very eagerness of reproduction is itself an original inspiration, and there is in it also a peculiar grace which, to the illustrious departed, was singularly congenial. If one had sought for a man to carry out this awe-striking retrospect through the great works of old, to gather up the fragments of perishing antiquity, it would have been one whose inborn modesty used to call the colour into his face at every word of praise—whose reverential attitude led him instinctively to understand and to admire. And yet in him this very tendency, especially in his maturer age, took so large and generous a sweep as to counteract the excesses into which, in minds less expansive and less vigorous, it is sure to fall. Because the bent of his own character and of his own time led chiefly to the restoration of mediæval art, he was

---

[6] The continuance of the Pharaonic style in Egypt by the Ptolemaic princes and Roman emperors. There are also a few rare examples in Mediæval Architecture, such as the completion of the nave in Westminster Abbey.

not on that account insensible to the merits of the ages which
had gone before, or which had succeeded. With that narrow
and exclusive pedantry which would fain sweep out from this
and other like buildings all the monuments and memorials
of the three last centuries, he had little or no sympathy. He
regarded them as footprints of the onward march of English
history, and whilst, with a natural regret for the inroads which
here and there they had made into the earlier glories of the
Plantagenet and Tudor architecture—and whilst willing to
prune their disproportionate encroachments, he cherished their
associations as tenderly as though they had been his own
creations; and he would bestow his meed of admiration as
freely on the modern memorial of Isaac Watts as on the
antique effigy of a crusading prince or of a Benedictine abbot.
It was this loving, yet comprehensive care for all the heterogeneous elements of the past, this anxious, unselfish attention
to all their multifarious details, which made him so wise a
counsellor, so delightful a companion, in the great work of the
reparation, the conservation, the glorification of this building,
which, amidst his absorbing and ubiquitous duties, it is not
too much to say was his first love, his chief, his last, his
enduring interest.

Such is the loss which the whole church and country deplore, but which we of this place mourn most of all. We
cannot forget him. Roof and wall, chapter-house and
cloister, the tombs of the dead and the worship of the living,
all speak of him to those who know that his hand and
his eye were everywhere amongst us. But these very
trophies of what he did for us must render us more alive
to do what we can for him. His memory must stimulate
us who remain to carry on with unabated zeal those works
in which he took so deep a concern: the completion of
the chapter-house by its long-delayed and long-promised windows of stained glass; the northern porch, which he desired
above all things to see restored to its pristine beauty; the
new cloister, which he had planned in all its completeness
as the link for another thousand years between the illustrious
dead of the generations of the past, and those of the generations of the future. So long as these remain unfinished, his
grave will continue to reproach us. When they shall be accomplished, they will be amongst the noblest monuments of him

whose ambition for his glorious art was so far-reaching, and whose requirements of what was due to this national sanctuary were so exacting.

But there is yet a more sacred and solemn thought which attaches to the immediate remembrance of so faithful a servant of this State of England, of so honoured a friend of this church of Westminster.

It has been sometimes said that it was by a strange irony of fate that the great leader in the revival of mediæval architecture should have been the grandson of that venerable commentator who belonged to the revival of evangelical religion. Yet in fact, from another point of view, it was a fitting continuity. It is always useful to be reminded that the revival, or, as we may better put it, the increase, of sincere English religion, belongs to a generation and a tendency long anterior to the multiplication of those external signs and symbols of which our age has made so much; and in the deep sense of that inward religion, that simple faith in the Great Unseen, the grandson who multiplied and disclosed the secrets of the visible sanctuaries of God throughout the land, was not an unworthy descendant of the grandfather who endeavoured, according to the light of his time, to draw forth the mysteries of the Book of books. We in this place, who knew him and valued him, who leant upon him as a tower of strength in our difficulties, who honoured his indefatigable industry, his childlike humility, his unvarying courtesy, his noble candour, we who remember with gratitude his generous encouragement of the students of the rising generation, and who know how he loved and valued the best that we also have loved and valued, we all feel that in him we have lost one of those just, gentle, guileless souls who in their lives have lifted, and in their memories may still lift, our souls upwards. And when we speak of the work which such a career bequeaths to those that remain, let us remember that although, as we said at the beginning of this discourse, the shell, the framework, of a great building like this, is an inestimable gift of God, its creation and preservation one of the noblest functions of human genius and national enterprise, yet on us who dwell within it, to whose charge it is committed, depends in no slight manner its continuance for the future, its glory and its usefulness for the present. There

are some eager spirits of our time, in whom the noble passion
for reform and improvement has been stifled and suspended
by the ignoble passion for destruction, who have openly avowed
their desire to suppress all the expressions of worship or of
teaching within this or like edifices, and keep them only
as dead memorials of the past—better silent with the solitude
of Tintern or of Melrose, than thronged with vast congregations, or resounding with the music of the Psalmist, or the
voice of the preacher. It is for us so to fulfil our several
duties, so to people this noble sanctuary with living deeds, and
words of goodness and of wisdom, that such dreams of the
destroyer may find no place to enter, no shelter or excuse from
our neglect, or ignorance, or folly. The grave of our great
architect is close beside the pulpit, which he erected to commemorate the earliest establishment of services and of sermons
in the nave, which for the first time were then set on foot by
my predecessor, and which have since spread throughout the
whole country. That reminds us of the kind of support which
we, the guardians and occupants of abbeys and cathedrals, can
give even to their outward fabric. It has been well said by a
gifted author, who, if any of his time, has been devoted to the
passionate love of art, that in the day of trial it will be said
even in those magnificent buildings, not " See what manner of
stones are here," but " See what manner of men." [7] Clergy,
lay-clerks, choristers, teachers, scholars, vergers, guides, alms-
men, workmen—yes, and all you who frequent this church—
every one of us may have it in our power to support it, by our
reverence and devotion, by our eagerness to profit by what we
hear, by our sincere wish to give the best that we can in teaching and preaching, by our honest and careful fulfilment of the
duties of each day's work, by our scrupulous care to avoid all
that can give needless annoyance or offence, by our constancy
and belief, by our rising above all paltry disputes and all vulgar
vices. In the presence of this great institution of which we
are all members, and in the presence of the Most High God,
whom it recalls to our thoughts, and in whose presence we are,
equally within its walls and without them—every one of us has
it in his power to increase the glory, to strengthen the stability,
to insure the perpetuity of this abbey. That is the best memo-

---

[7] Ruskin's " Lectures on Art," 118.

rial we can raise, that is the best service we can render, to all those, dead or living, who have loved, or who still love, this holy and beautiful house, wherein our fathers worshipped in the generations of the past, and wherein, if we be but true to its glorious mission, our children and our children's children shall worship in the generations that are yet to come.

APPENDIX C.

——◆——

REPLY BY SIR GILBERT SCOTT, R.A., TO MR. J. J. STEVENSON'S PAPER ON "ARCHITECTURAL RESTORATION : ITS PRINCIPLES AND PRACTICE."

(Read at a Meeting of the Institute of British Architects, 28th May, 1877.)

GENTLEMEN,— I have to apologize for again addressing you, after having spoken once on the subject of Mr. Stevenson's Paper ; but, on consideration of that Paper, and having observed from what was said by several speakers that it was viewed by them as being especially directed against myself, I have thought it right to crave your kind indulgence in not resting satisfied with what I said on the spur of the moment, and in reading a written comment on the Paper.

Why *I*—who have laid myself out to protest against the havoc which has been made through the length and breadth of the land under the name of Restoration—should be singled out as the special butt of this yet stronger protest, it is not easy to say. In accepting this challenge, I may claim a somewhat back-handed compliment. When Napoleon III. was told that a prophetic authority had pronounced him to be Anti-Christ, he replied, " *He does me too much honour !*" Much the same is the honour intended to be conferred on me. Yet—be it honour or affront—I feel it incumbent on me, as its selected recipient, to state carefully how far I agree and how far I differ from the sentiments expressed in that Paper, and the more especially as—whether formally or not—it is actually the manifesto of the Society recently formed for the prevention of restoration.

It is but fair, at the outset, to say candidly that there has been every possible provocation to the line taken by this new Society ; and that—up to a certain point—I heartily sympathize with their views. I wish this to be thoroughly understood ; or, while only finding fault with the views promulgated by the Society on the ground of exaggeration and unfairness, I may be supposed to be taking a side in the argument wholly at variance with my own known sentiments. No over-statement on their part, no personal accusations against myself, will, I trust, for a moment betray me into disloyalty to the side which I have for years advocated, or into ceasing to protest against the course of vandalism, which has justly made the very word " *Restoration* " a by-word and a reproach, and which has robbed England of a large portion of her antiquities. So far, then, from objecting to the general aim of Mr. Stevenson's Paper, if purged from certain excesses and over-statements, I will at once say that a very large number of the sentiments and remarks contained in it are simply reiterations of those which I have, for not less than thirty-six years, expressed; though so exaggerated, and pressed to such an extreme, as greatly to destroy their practical value, and then adroitly turned against myself and those who have similarly protested. This is no doubt a somewhat annoying form of warfare, but others have had to bear it before us. William Wilberforce lived to be viewed by his over-ardent disciples as the great clog in the way of negro emancipation, and Wilkes was constrained to proclaim himself to be no Wilkesite ; and so it is a mere truism to say that, although I have protested against unfaithful and overdone and ignorant restoration, I have myself largely transgressed what Mr. Stevenson enunciates as the correct view—*i.e.*, that there should be no restoration at all.

I have myself (as he quotes me) said I could wish the name were expunged and "reparation" substituted : but, whether called by one name or the other, it is clear that I should have been wasting my breath in attempting to suggest rules and limitations, if no such thing at all were to be permitted! I therefore at once admit that, notwithstanding all my outcry against bad restoration, I have somewhat largely infringed the new rule which forbids any restoration, good, bad, or indifferent. I will now, at the risk of egotism, show by a few extracts from my own poor writings what have been my sentiments at different periods of my professional life.

In a letter written to Mr. Petit in 1841, I said,—

" It has often struck me that, viewing an ancient edifice as a national
monument, as an original work of the great artists from whom we learn all
we can know of Christian architecture, and as a work which when once
restored, however carefully, is to a certain extent lost as an authentic example, it is hardly right that the fate of such a building should be left wholly
to the local committee or their architects, but that it would be well if they
could call in to their aid two or three non-professional and disinterested
parties, well known to understand the subject," who, on hearing arguments,
&c., would " be able to give such opinion as would set all questions at rest,
and would ensure our doing justice to the subscribers and the public."

Again—

" I do not wish to lay it down as a general rule that good taste requires
that every alteration which from age to age has been made in our churches
should be obliterated, and the whole reduced to its ancient uniformity of
style.   These varieties are indeed most valuable, as being the standing history of the edifice, from which the date of every alteration and repair may
be read as clearly as if it had been verbally recorded ; and in many cases
the later additions are as valuable specimens of architecture as the remains
of the original structure, and merit an equally careful preservation.   I even
think that if our churches were to be viewed, like the ruins of Greece and
Rome, only as original monuments from which ancient architecture is to be
studied, they would be more valuable in their present condition, however
mutilated and decayed, than with any, even the slightest degree of restoration.   But taking the more correct view of a church as a building erected
for the glory of God and the use of Man (and which must therefore be kept
in a proper state of repair), and finding it in such a state of dilapidation that
the earlier and later parts—the authentic and the spurious—are alike decayed
and all require renovation to render the edifice suitable to its purposes, I
think we are then at liberty to exercise our best judgment upon the subject, and if the original parts are found to be ' precious ' and the late inser-
tions to be ' vile,' I think we should be quite right in giving perpetuity to
to the one, and in removing the other.   As, however, an erroneous judgment might lead to unfortunate results, this is just one of those points on
which the opinion of a kind of Antiquarian Commission might advan-
tageously be taken."

Again—

" I have long and most painfully felt that the modern system of radical
restoration is doing more towards the destruction of ancient art than the
ravings of fanaticism, or the follies of churchwardens have succeeded in
effecting.   The existence and authenticity of these invaluable relics is
invaded on both sides : on the one by neglect, mutilation, and wanton
destruction ; and on the other, by the extreme to which well-meant restorations are too frequently carried."

It is difficult to say from which side the greatest danger is to
be apprehended, but between the two I feel convinced that

greater havoc has been made among sacred edifices in our own time—boasting as we do of a revived taste for their beauties—than they had experienced from three centuries of contemptuous neglect. It is desirable for the sake of guarding against both these sources of danger, that those who have a true feeling for the subject should endeavour to come to an understanding among themselves, and to compare their own views; so that their differences of opinion may not be taken advantage of by those who are glad of any excuse for withholding their contributions, or those, on the other hand, whose love of change is equally on the watch for an opportunity of indulging itself. With this object I have used my humble endeavours " to show the necessity for some such ordeal as I proposed." For, " while acknowledging the dangers to which others are exposed, we are too apt to fancy that we are ourselves individual exceptions."

In 1848 I wrote a Paper on " The Faithful Restoration of Ancient Churches," in which I entered an earnest protest against Radical Restoration, and urged the most Conservative treatment, winding up with a quotation from a poetical friend of Mr. Petit's—

> " It were a pious work, I hear you say,
> To prop the falling ruin and to stay
> The work of desolation. It may be
> That ye say right ; *but, O! work tenderly !*
> Beware lest one worn feature ye efface ;
> Seek not to add one touch of modern grace ;
> Handle with reverence each crumbling stone,
> Respect the very lichens o'er it grown ;
> And bid each ancient monument to stand
> Supported e'en as with a filial hand.
> Mid all the light a happier age has brought,
> We work not yet as our forefathers wrought."

While this Paper was in the press, two years later, Mr. Ruskin's "Seven Lamps of Architecture" came into my hands.

On his condemnation of all restoration (a notion which, as you see, I had anticipated and answered eight or nine years earlier), I added in a note as follows :—

" Were our old churches to be viewed merely as monuments of the architecture of bygone days, I confess that I should cordially agree with him ; for who would dream of restoring the sculptures of the Parthenon, or the

hieroglyphics of Thebes? Again, were it possible by present care to nul-
lify the effects of past neglect, I would heartily fall in with his advice. I
would 'watch an old building with an anxious care.' I would 'guard it
as best I might, and at any cost, from the influence of dilapidation.' I
would 'count its stones as you would the jewels of a crown; set watches
about it as if at the gates of a besieged city; bind it together with iron
where it loosens; stay it with timber when it declines,' or do anything and
everything I could to preserve it from the influences of time or the hand of
the spoliator. But, alas! the damage is already effected; the neglect of
centuries and the spoiler's hand has already done its work; and the building
being something more than a monument of memory, being a temple dedicated
—so long as the world shall last—to the worship and honour of the world's
Creator, it is a matter of duty, as it is of necessity, that its dilapidations and
its injuries shall be repaired; though better were it to leave them untouched
for another generation than commit them to irreverent hands, which seek
only the memory of their own cunning while professing to think upon the
stones, and take pity upon the dust of Sion.''

> .   .   .   .   " Yon ancient wall—
> Better to see it tottering to its fall
> Than decked in new attire with lavish cost,
> Form, dignity, proportion, grace, all lost ! "

In 1863 I read my Paper before this Institute from which
Mr. Stevenson has largely quoted, and, he will forgive my saying,
the spirit of which he has most ingeniously misinterpreted. Of
this I will only say, Read it and judge for yourselves.

In my inaugural address as President of this Institute in
1873, after some remarks on the marvellous inequality in merit
and demerit of the architecture of our own day as compared
with its uniformity of merit in previous ages, I add :—

"There is, however, a yet sadder inequality to be recorded—sadder
because irreparable in the injury inflicted. The million ugly houses, or
even the majority of them, may go to decay, or be rebuilt; but a single
ancient edifice destroyed or ruined by ignorant '*restoration*,' can never be
recovered. It is unquestionable that the ancient structures, from the study
of which a knowledge of our mediæval styles has been resuscitated, had
suffered for the most part so severely from neglect, ill-usage, and decay,
as to demand the aid of a loving and careful restoration; and this they
have happily, in very many instances, received. The knowledge and skill
of our neo-mediæval architects has often been devoted with admirable
success to this grateful work, and from among the restorations of ancient
buildings may be instanced many of the most happy results of the Gothic
revival. But here, again, the unhappy diversity I have alluded to, as
existing in new works, is found to exist in its most aggravated form. Our
old buildings too often—nay, in a majority, I fear, of cases—fall into the
hands of men who have neither knowledge nor respect for them, while,
even amongst those who possess the requisite knowledge, there has too
often existed a lack of veneration, a disposition to sit in judgment on the

works of their teachers, a rage for alteration to suit some system to which they had pledged themselves in their own works, and even the preposterous idea that the ancient examples they were called upon to repair were a fitting field for the display of their own originality.

"Nor have the official guardians of our ancient buildings exercised much restraint upon these vagaries : on the contrary, they have too often been most culpably careless as to the hands to which they have committed their trust, and are usually the inciters to ignorant tampering, the needless removal of valuable features, and even the condemnation and destruction of the buildings under their charge. The result has been truly disastrous ; so much so that our country has actually been robbed of a large proportion of its antiquities under the name of ' restoration ;' and the work of destruction and spoliation still goes on merrily ; while at the public festivities by which each *auto-da-fé* is celebrated, we find ecclesiastical dignitaries, clergy, squires, and architects congratulating one another on the success of the latest effort of Vandalism. Our Institute has done itself infinite honour by appointing a standing committee to investigate and protest, and by publishing a code of excellent suggestions as to the mode of dealing with ancient remains ; but still the work goes on, and the equivocal motto of the *Ecclesiologist—'Donec Templa refeceris'*—seems likely to prove well-nigh the death-knell of our ecclesiastical antiquities."

In my second opening address in 1874, the same subject was brought forward by Mr. Ruskin's refusal of the Gold Medal, on the ground of the prevalence of destructive restoration. On this I offered the following remarks :—

"Now, all this may be viewed from two very different points. We may, on the one hand, very fairly protest against the injustice of being made in any degree responsible for acts in which we have had no hand, over which we had no control, and against which we should protest as loudly as Mr. Ruskin : but, on the other hand, we, being the incorporated representatives of architectural practice, may, in a certain sense, be held to represent its vices as well as its virtues, and in the eyes of a self-constituted censor, and one who from his first appearance before the public has devoted himself wholly to protest and warning, we can hardly wonder that, if he holds us thus responsible, he should not think it a time for us to be playing at compliments with our censor.

"Read for a moment his expressions of righteous indignation uttered nearly a quarter of a century back, and imagine what must be his feelings wherever he directs his steps. If he travels in France, he finds restoration so rampant that nothing which shows much of the hand of time is considered worthy of continued existence, but must be re-worked or renewed, cleverly, artistically, and learnedly perhaps, but nevertheless as new work taking the place of the old, or old work re-tooled till scarce a vestige of the surface on which the old men wrought so lovingly is allowed to remain. If he goes into Italy, much the same meets his eye. In his own Venice the Fondaco dei Turchi, the most venerable secular Byzantine work, is rebuilt. At Rome he would observe an area of some half a square mile excavated and carted away, which contained—discovered only to be in great measure destroyed—the ancient wall of Servius

Tullius, twelve feet thick, of solid masonry, and against it a second
Pompeii of antique Roman houses, hardly explored, but merely disinterred
and carted away as rubbish. At Assisi he would find the works of Cimabue
and Giotto in the hands of the restorer, though, as I trust, with better
promise. In Belgium he would find ancient buildings chipped over and
made to look like new; or, as is the case with the wonderful church of the
Dominicans, at Ghent, deliberately destroyed. And is the case much
better in our own country? Has not the hand of a false and destructive
restoration swept like a plague over the length and breadth of our land,
and are not those churches which have been treated with veneration and
care a mere gleaning among those which have been dealt with in careless
ignorance of any value to be attached to them? To Mr. Ruskin's eye the
best of our restorations are mere vandalisms, for he protests against them
root and branch; and to him all the difficulties and disappointments met
with in carrying them out would be only so many reasons for reproaching
us for having undertaken them at all. Anyhow, he would find in England
far more than one half of our ancient churches to have been so dealt with
by ignorant and sacrilegious hands that one is ready to curse the day when
the then youthful Cambridge Camden Society, all too sanguine and ardent,
adopted for their motto the ominous words so sadly realized, '*Donec
Templa refeceris.*' But restoration has not laboured alone in the work
of Vandalism: deliberate destruction has been rife amongst us. Has not
one great cathedral body deliberately pulled down its ancient hospital hall
of the fourteenth century, and another its stupendous tythe barn of the
thirteenth? Near another cathedral, where the episcopal palace is formed
out of a vast Norman hall (the sole remaining instance of a hall of that
age supported by original timber pillars and arcades), I have only just
now seen some of these timber arches lying as old material in a builder's
yard, having been turned out, I fear under the eye of a Fellow of this
Institute, for the purpose, to use Mr. Ruskin's own words, of 'temporary
convenience.'"

In my third annual address in 1875, I was dwelling especially
on a duty that I would commend to the Society which Mr.
Stevenson represents—the duty of making and preserving
accurate drawings of perishing architectural remains—and, I
added :—

"We, as an Institute, do a great deal by means of the competition for
our Pugin Studentship (which usually take the form of measured drawings
of some of these perishing art treasures), but we should aim at, and strive
after, some more systematic method of dealing with this most urgently
pressing object. I know many remains whose details every time I visit
them, seem to get dimmer and dimmer, from the yearly falling away of
their surfaces in impalpable dust, and which another generation will find
utterly unintelligible. Such is the case with the remains which surround
the cloister court of Fountains Abbey; such, too, is the case with that
invaluable remnant the sanctuary of Tynemouth Priory, with its accompanying fragments, perhaps unequalled in their architecture by any
cotemporary building in England; such is the case in a still more distressing degree with Kelso Abbey, and such is the destined fate, sooner or

later, of most of the ruined structures which remain throughout our land as proofs at once of the glorious art of our forefathers and our own heed-lessness. We need not suppose that the admission that this duty is incumbent on ourselves involves the consequence that the cost must necessarily fall upon us. There can be no doubt, that if we take the initiative, funds will be supplied by the very many who take an intelligent and zealous interest in the subject ; but, if we hold our peace, who ought to be the first to speak, how can we expect others to bestir themselves ?

" When we come to buildings still in use, and especially to churches, we have a truly mournful and disgraceful scene presented to us.

"Our churches had, during the three centuries between the extinction and the revival of Gothic architecture, for the most part been allowed to fall, step by step, into a state of sordid and contemptuous neglect, decay, and dilapidation ; while they become encumbered with galleries, pews, and all manner of incongruous interpolations :—nothing being, in many cases, considered too mean in character for an old Gothic church. People became conscious of this before our architects became fitted to correct it ; and, like Jack, in Swift's ' Tale of a Tub,' set about ridding their churches of disfigurements before they knew what to substitute for them, and, with every blemish which they removed, tore off some fragment of the original fabric, and mended the tear with work of their own, if not quite as incongruous, certainly far more nauseating. Soon, however, they got to think they knew all about the matter ; and boldly set about restorations, as if the old art had been beyond question revived. They even disputed among themselves as to whether restorations should be ' conservative, destructive or eclectic ;' great authorities not being wanting to defend even the destructive system.

Meanwhile,—even with those best disposed,—knowledge was imperfect, and the difficulties of careful and well-considered treatment immense. The promoters of the work were more impressed, perhaps, with the axiom of the first church restorers—that the house of God ought not to be less carefully dealt with than our own houses, than with the equally indisputable fact that they had a treasure of ancient art and of ancient church history to deal with, which demanded the most earnest study for its conservation. Walls and roofs were found decayed, and their entire renewal was urged ; changes in our ritual, it was argued, demanded corresponding changes in arrangement ; clerks of the works, builders and workmen vied with each other in opposing conservative measures ; and—fight as they would—all kinds of influences continued, in addition to their own short-comings, to check or frustrate the efforts of conservative architects, so that the result was, at the best, a mixture of successes with failures, of right decision with compromise.

" This has now been going on for years, so far as concerns the best among us, but many well-meaning restorers, from imperfect knowledge and want of firmness, come yet worse out of their work. Beyond these, however, is a very different set of restorers (so-called), a host of men not always architects even in name, though occasionally such, men justly respected in other branches, and who ought to know better than to touch this ; but, for the most part, men who have taken to Gothic architecture, as being a style in vogue, and merely as a part of their stock in trade ; and into their hands a very large proportion of our churches fall. They may be likened to a herd, before whom our precious pearls are cast, and who trample them under their feet, and turn again and rend all objectors.

We receive, from time to time, appeals to our Committee for the Conservation of Ancient Monuments against vandalisms which one would have thought incredible ; and only within the last few days I have heard of one clergyman selling to a grocer one of the old chained-up books which he thought would disfigure his 'restored' church ; and of another expelling a famous series of brasses to secure the uniformity of his encaustic tile floor ; while one hears of noblemen of the highest names who make over the nomination of architects for the restoration of the churches on their estates as a piece of patronage which is the perquisite of their agents.

"Taking a review of the results of this sad history, one may say that a certain proportion of our churches have been carefully dealt with ; another proportion treated with fair intention but less success ; but that, as I fear, the majority are almost utterly despoiled, and nine-tenths, if not all, of their interest swept away. Nor is a word of remonstrance raised against this by those whose position would enable them to prevent it ; indeed I can with confidence assert that more objection is raised against those who labour hard to do their duty carefully, than against the whole host of those who have so ruined our old churches, as to render a church-tour one of the most distressing and sickening of adventures. Yet, happily, a remnant remains : a few churches in each district are still left unrestored ; and for the preservation of these, like the remnant of the Sibylline books, it is worth while to pay any price. I saw one such church recently, on a little tour in the eastern counties, as if in the still water missed by the tide of destructive restoration : its roof still retaining the thatch which once prevailed through that district, but admitting the rain in torrents ; its timbers the veritable old ones, though partially decayed ; its quaint and beautiful seating remaining almost entire, though preyed upon by the worm ; its floor retaining beautiful tiles, of varied geometrical form and unique design, though loosened and displaced; its windows still containing extensive remnants of the most beautiful fourteenth-century glass, exquisite in design and colouring, but ready to drop out of its leading ; the walls, happily, nearly as good as new, and with windows, arcades and niches of the most perfect design ; the whole just wanting that tender, loving handling which would preserve all which time has spared, and give it a new lease of existence. Oh, that we could search out these last gleanings from the harvest of destruction, and save them from the destroyer's hands."

I now come to the Paper of suggestions relative to ancient buildings which was issued twelve years since by our Institute, and which Mr. Stevenson has so boldly held up to ridicule and reprobation.

This Paper consists, I think, of contributions from different members of a sub-committee, which will account for some trifling inconsistencies. I was myself a contributor, though — strange to say—I do not know that I have till recently examined it with care in its completed form. I really feared, from Mr.

Stevenson's alarming description, that I should find it to be something which we have just cause to be ashamed of. The reverse is the case ; for, subject to some few inadvertencies of which he has not failed to take full advantage, to the extent—I will not say of misrepresenting—but of absolutely reversing its real aim, I do not hesitate to say that I have never met with a document more creditable to the great Society from which it has emanated, nor one more truthfully and more wisely advising on the course to be taken by those whom it addresses.

It is a plain, unvarnished and unpretending document. Mr. Stevenson's Paper—on the contrary—is graced with literary and rhetorical beauty ; yet I am bold to say that the manifesto of the Institute is worth a thousand of that which holds it up to ridicule and traduces its suggestions. The only point of importance which Mr. Stevenson has fairly made good against this document is that in its first clause it, strangely enough, leaves the clearing away of modern incumbrances which conceal ancient work to the employers instead of their architects. This is a manifest mistake, and it ought at once to be corrected. Personally I also object to the clause about stripping off plastering to show the junctions of parts of differing date. This, however, is inconsistent with other clauses which direct the careful examination of old plastered surfaces in search for colouring—directing that "plastered surfaces of ancient date should be preserved if possible ;" and that, "as a general rule, ancient plastering should *not* be removed, but only repaired where necessary." The clause in question was, then, only intended for exceptional cases. Subject to the correction of such inadvertencies and of some minor details as well as to a few verbal corrections, I boldly aver that I have rarely read a document more characterized by experience and wisdom, or more diametrically the reverse in its tone, of the colouring which its critic has laid upon it. I would further assert that were these suggestions (subject to the minor corrections I have alluded to) faithfully followed, our churches would be models of all which is excellent and to be desired.

As truthful would it be to attribute the defects in our Constitution to Magna Charta ; what still remains of the slave-trade to Wilberforce ; or of small-pox to Jenner, as to saddle the guilt of the barbarisms committed on our old churches upon the admirable code of suggestions which was drawn out for the express purpose of arresting the tide of vandalism. To hold up such a document to ridicule is not only grossly and absurdly unfair, but it tends to give unbridled licence to the evils it sincerely professes to deplore; for, as the intended deduction, that we are to do nothing, is one which can never be acted on, it follows that the holding up the rules of action, and the protests of those who offer them, to contempt, is simply throwing the reins upon the neck of vandalism. All honour, then, to the Institute, which has (even with a few imperfections) pro- mulgated such a code of rules; but what honour can we award to those who seek to turn its wisdom into folly?

Imagine any one quietly stating that "the Institute Paper advises the destruction of Perpendicular work," backing it by a reversal of the meaning of what it does say, which is dia- metrically the contrary, and which really goes too far in urging the exposure to view of alterations in the later styles, and is in another place called to account for doing so.

Imagine, again, the statement that it advises the getting rid of "the flat roofs of perpendicular times," and that the "new roof should be made of the same steep pitch as the original roof," when what it really says is "if it be found absolutely necessary to construct a new roof, owing to the existing roof being entirely decayed or modern, one of the two following courses should be adopted: either the old roof where it exists should be carefully copied, or the new roof should be made of the same pitch as the original roof." It further suggests that, "where there is a clerestory, it will be well to keep the pitch of the roof erected at the time it was built," and adds, "flat roofs are by no means to be condemned." Again, imagine any one saying of the beautiful western porch at Peterborough "that, as the Institute Advice puts it, it is a modern addition put up without regard to architectural propriety;" while at the same time he criticizes, and with more justice, the suggestion "that the whole of the old work should be preserved and exposed to view, so as to show the history of the fabric with its successive alterations as distinctly as possible."

This system of misrepresentation seems unhappily held to be essential to the anti-restoration movement. As a small example of it, our friend, though two days before reading his Paper he made a special journey to Canterbury to see what was really contemplated, nevertheless stated in his Paper that I contemplated the removal of the screen which separates the choir from the nave; while the fact was that we were only talking of the removal of some comparatively recent fittings, for the sake of bringing that screen into view.[1] He has since modified that statement, so I only notice it to show that we are viewed as lawful spoil.

The statements of writers in newspapers merely follow out the same principle, actually bristling with inaccuracies of the grossest kind, and, unlike Mr. Stevenson, they usually refuse to correct them. I have recently met with a signal instance of this, reminding one of a story told by Lord Brougham in the House of Lords to show the uselessness of attempting to correct such statements. A grave and correct parishioner had complained at a parish vestry meeting of the state of the church, declaring that if not bettered he would not continue to attend that *damp* church. The local paper reported his words correctly excepting the word "*damp*," which they changed for a strong word of somewhat similar sound. The respectable parishioner protested, but the editor annotated his protest by saying that, having consulted his reporter, he felt it due to him to say that the speaker had not said "*damp*," but *had* used the objectionable word attributed to him.

The question, however, before us is not the truth of particular statements and criticisms (no doubt they are meant to be true, but things by superabundant zeal are seen through a distorting medium), but rather what is the true course to be followed? We are all agreed as to the calamity which the country has suffered; we differ as to the remedy. We do not differ widely as to the premises, though we may as to the conclusion to be drawn from them. Mr. Stevenson's view has an unquestionable *primâ facie* advantage. It is certain that, if restoration were from this moment stopped, no new mischief would be done by it! Many persons have died from bad doctoring. If all medical treatment were prohibited, such disasters would unquestionably cease. Nor is this illustration imaginary, for a few years since a medical (or anti-medical) sect was founded, which, abhorrent of old allopathy, and discontented with the infinitesimal treatment, styled itself the "*do-nothing*" party. Their general acceptance would have done

---

[1] This statement was afterwards corrected in Mr. Stevenson's Paper at the author's request.

away for ever with deaths from overdosing, and who knows but that disease itself would have fled before their frown? But the movement unfortunately failed, because misguided and impatient patients would not be persuaded to allow themselves to be let alone.

Such doctors would not have been content with crying down incompetent practitioners, and would have condemned Hahnemann himself as a tamperer with the human constitution—they would forbid all such meddling; and, had they succeeded, we might have become a race of Methuselahs; but human nature is blind, and the proffered boon was refused! *O, fortunati nimium, sua si bona nôrint!*

I could almost wish myself that the " do-nothing " system could be applied to old buildings, if only as an experiment; but I fear it would meet with the same fate as when proposed to human patients; and then, perhaps, after all it might be found the best course to call in good doctors (if there be any), and for them to stick to such prosaic rules as those of the Institute of British Architects—reasonably revised, and rendered as much more stringent as may be,—to the pious conservation of whitewash, high pews, three-deckers, and other bequests (if Mr. S. will have it so) of the Reformation, or (as I should say) of the yet more blessed days of Queen Anne and the Georges.

I confess to having tried this in some degree myself; but I have been circumvented by the prejudices of my clients. I uniformly succeed as regards Jacobean pulpits, and I think altar tables; but am less successful in my attempts in favour of seventeenth-century pewing, unless it be indisputably fine—such as we find at Brancepeth, St. John's Leeds, or Halifax. By the way, I can claim a share with Mr. Norman Shaw (who actually carried out the work) in the credit of saving St. John's, Leeds,—probably the most interesting church of the Jacobean period—from destruction. It was referred to me, and on taking leave of a leading Leeds architect as I was starting to inspect it, his last exhortation was, " Paint it black enough." I painted it in the most brilliant colours I was master of, and it was saved, all but its pew doors, the loss of which I deplore, for they were beauties. Sounding-boards I strive after, but often fail. I preserved one, however, recently in spite of the incumbent, the parishioners, and an archbishop.

I set off against this the loss of another—a beauty—by the casting dictum of a bishop, a weakness of which I am ashamed.

Returning to the consideration of the *do-nothing* system, I will mention some cases bearing upon it. Mr. Stevenson has sketched a charming picture of an unrestored church. His exquisite language and touchingly pathetic tone carried one quite away. Certainly such a church it would be sacrilege to touch! I cannot help flattering myself that he founded this beautiful picture on the lines of one which I clumsily attempted to draw in my own Paper read before this Institute ; but the charm of genius has given it such beauty that one can hardly recognize the resemblance to the rude original. I confess that when I sketched it I was conscious of allowing my imagination to congregate, into one fancied church, charms which were culled from several ; but my friend has gone far beyond this. A whole rural deanery would scarcely supply the raw material for such a church as his. Would that he would tell me of its whereabouts, under oath that I would not restore it!

This is far different from what we usually find. Sordid neglect, barbarous mutilation, and ruinous dilapidation are the most frequent characteristics of an unrestored church, united, it is true, with the charm of its traditional and untouched condition.

I made a survey of such a church a few weeks back ; no architect had ever touched it ; only unsophisticated country builders, innocent of archæology and even of the word "restoration." What was its condition ? The tower looked sufficiently old and rubbishy, having no architectural features whatever. The clerk, a man of sixty, declared it had not been meddled with in his day, or within his hearing of ; but an octogenarian whom we found, told us that he had himself worked at the rebuilding of it during the first years of the century. The windows of the church seemed of doubtful age, and I found that they had been tinkered out of shape and style by a neighbouring mason some thirty years back. The octogenarian told me that he remembered a chancel screen, through which poor people "peeked" at the parson—and old oak seats "with a kind of ornament at the top of the ends," but these had been replaced with high deal pews, and he said with a humourous leer that he supposed the old ones were burnt. The roofs, on the other hand, were in a good traditional state ;

lowered in the seventeenth century, and containing many fragments of older work mingled with later parts, some by no
means bad. There were also a beautiful pulpit, desk, and altar
table of the same period. One clerestory had fourteenth-
century round windows, the other mullioned ones of the seventeenth. Now, is it best to let such a church wholly alone, or to
preserve all old work, down to the seventeenth century inclu-
sive, and try to improve the rest?

But I will take a stronger case. Llandaff Cathedral had
been allowed, from the Reformation downwards, to fall into
something more than a semi-ruinous state: in the middle of
the last century, with just as good intentions as the man mentioned by old John Evelyn, they set to work to redeem it.
Their system was as follows: they sent for Mr. Wood, of Bath,
who had just erected the Pump Room there. He seems to
have advised that so much of the eastern part as they thought
needful should be cut out from the rest and internally converted, so far as might be, into a double of his Pump Room.[2]
He found the arcades, projecting strings, labels, &c., in the way;
so he walled up the arches, and chopped off projecting mouldings, and, as the old walls might prove to be damp, he battened
them over, cutting the grounds to which his battens were nailed
deep into the walls. By this clever device, he was able to shut
out from view all that was "gothic;" and an enthusiastic
clergyman writes at the time: "The church, in the inside, as
far as it is ceiled and plastered, looks exceeding fine, and when
finished, it will, in the judgment of most people who have seen
it, be a very neat and elegant church."

The rest he happily left a ruin, of which the architecture is
as fine as anything in this country.

Now when our friends Messrs. Prichard and Seddon were
called in to advise, what ought they to have said? An echo
answers "*nothing.*" They did not think so, but following the
dictates of common sense, they did away with the Pump

[2] Since this Paper was in type I have received a letter from a friend
stating that it was the Hot Baths—not the Pump Room, which Mr. Wood
erected. Mr. Freeman's and Mr. King's accounts of Llandaff Cathedral
give particulars as to Mr. Wood's works at Llandaff. My information
about his having imitated at Llandaff his own work at Bath was oral and
may have been mistaken. The present Pump Room is of far more recent
date. It may have been his Assembly Room to which the statement
referred.

Room, re-roofing and repairing the entire church, and thus recovered a noble and most charming interior. I am not pledging myself to all that was done, my knowledge of it is insufficient; but I confidently assert that they took the only right course. I offer no opinion on the added south-west tower, for I have not seen it; I speak only of the manner in which they rooted out the barbarism of the eighteenth century and reinstated the beauty of the thirteenth.

I am tempted to speak of St. David's. I knew it well, long before I was professionally connected with it, and most truly sordid was its condition. Not to mention the eastern chapels which were, and still are, in ruins, the choir aisles were walled off and unroofed; the roofs throughout dripping water into the church, the walls, pillars, arches, &c., running down with wet, and everything evincing the most abject and contemptuous neglect.

When called upon to advise, I found two of the four piers of the central tower crushed in the most fearful manner, so as to threaten destruction to the whole building; was this, I would ask, a case for doing *nothing?* What I have done has saved the existence of this most noble church, rendered the structure safe and strong, made the interior dry and wholesome, brought to light many most interesting features before nearly lost. The choir aisles have been re-roofed, and their arcades re-opened; and all this without the loss of a single ancient feature, unless it be one quite decayed Perpendicular window of whose early English predecessor we found and largely re-used the actual details. In the same way very many noble churches have been saved from utterly perishing, by careful treatment applied only just in time.

I will take another instance. The first considerable church entrusted to me was placed in my hands some thirty-six years back, almost in that golden age when restoration was unknown. It was a grand cruciform church; the nave and crossing being of noble Transitional work, one transept of developed Early English of the finest kind, the other of exquisite Decorated; the choir and its aisles of Early English passing on into Decorated. The clerestory of the nave, with its roof, were very good Perpendicular, and some other parts had more or less changed their style. No ancient fittings remained, all having undergone that honest traditional transformation so romantically pourtrayed by Mr. Stevenson as the legitimate out-spring of the Reformation. Here, surely, was a case for nobly declining to interfere. But let us look a little further into the condition of the church : the nave was severed from the rest of the church, not by the magic lattice-work of screens, but by partitions dividing the interior into two separate buildings. The nave was so deeply be-galleried on the north, south, and east, that the galleries enclosed the pillars of the arcading, so as wholly to box up their capitals, which being found rather in the way as well as invisible, no scruple was felt about cutting away their noble transitional foliage and mouldings to make better room for the timbers ; their outer faces had, consequently, undergone amputation. I have mentioned that the cross gallery was at the east; the glorious three-decker was, consequently, placed westward, and in that direction were the pews made to face. The available church being reduced to less than half its size, no room was to be lost, so wherever pillar or pier or arch came in the way of a sitting they had been hollowed and mined into without remorse.

Partly from such causes and partly from others, the piers of the central tower—most noble works of the end of the twelfth century—had given way alarmingly, and the crushing process continued to increase. The transepts, usefully occupied by gallery stairs of great commodiousness, had been most beautiful structures, especially that to the south, but the lofty spire having fallen across it in Queen Elizabeth's time, it had been patched up in true Reformation style; and aided by subsequent neglect and decay, its "comeliness" had (as I should say) been "turned into corruption," or, as Mr. Stevenson might perhaps say, into historical picturesqueness. The exterior was much marred by decay. Now was this a case for doing *nothing?* In my simplicity I thought not; so I swept away high pews, galleries, three-decker and partition walls—works, it may be, of the days of good Queen Anne, but more probably of much later date. Thinking it a case for more than usual care, I engaged as clerk of the works, a talented young friend, a son of old George Gwilt, the most zealous antiquary I knew, and conservative almost to the level of the anti-restoration Society. We had to lay out, I think, some 1500*l.* to make the tower safe ; and, some important antiquarian questions arising, we referred them to the decision of the Oxford and Cambridge Societies.

Another church I remember, also a cruciform church, but with aisles only to its chancel. Its nave and transepts were completely filled up with a gallery in each, whose front crossed each arch of the central tower, while each chancel aisle was similarly filled by other galleries. What would the *do-nothing* theory say to this? In another case – a cathedral— the choir was cut off to the very crown of its arches on all sides by partitions of lath and plaster with a little glass, and absolutely severed from the rest of the church.

No trick was so commonly played with a large church in the two last centuries as cutting off a large part of their length by a wood and glass partition reaching to its very roof, and gallerying the remainder in every possible way that could be contrived. Very many noble churches have I had the pleasure of redeeming from such degradation, and reinstating them to their original size. One of these I have seen so re-opened since our last meeting. It had been chopped in two as late as 1798, but no one could remember ever seeing the whole interior until now, or had the smallest conception of its grandeur. One poor man, a dissenter, was melted to tears at the first sight of it. The consequence of such restoration is always a vast increase in the number of worshippers; for while, as Mr. Stevenson says, "Men believed in the preaching of the Word, and the church had been arranged with this view," by a strange inconsistency the "better classes" monopolized that preaching to themselves, and, boxing themselves up in their high pews, left their poorer neighbours to hear as they could, or not at all.

In one glorious monastic church, of which only the nave has been spared, not only was the church cut in two, by such a partition, but the remainder was interspersed with private galleries, each containing the special pew of a reputable family, approached by its own private staircase. I recollect nearly forty years ago being invited to sit in the pew of one of these magnates, and on failing to see where it was, and finding another place, I at last spied out my friend sitting with his sister in a glazed gallery which seated only three, the third seat being kindly reserved for myself. In the same church, being near a watering-place, each parishioner took the key of his pew in his waistcoat pocket. I recollect being told by an aged lady visitor that, after waiting near a large empty pew, a young man came and unlocked it, locked himself in alone in the pew, put the key again into his waistcoat pocket, leaving her out in the cold! These were the men who "believed in the preaching of the Word," and these were the churches "arranged with this view." I was at this church only last Wednesday, now long since opened out and filled with open sittings from end to end, "just as if the Reformation was a mistake."

In another church, a noble family held an octagonal glazed pew, hung like a bird-cage from the chancel arch, and so well contrived that, by facing about east or west, his lordship could attend either the nave or chancel service. Many of these aristocratic pews had fireplaces, before which the noble occupant was wont to stand with his coat-tails hooked over his arms, as if in a coffee-room. But time would fail to tell of these monstrosities, which I do not wonder that the new enthusiastics should venerate, being the productions of the days of Queen Anne and the Georges.

In the north of England the high pews, whether in galleries or below, were usually lined with green baize; and where they cross pillars or windows the stonework was *painted green* to match, up to the same level with the baize!

The parish in which I was born had once a noble church, with a central tower which swayed so much in the wind as to cause certain cracks to open and shut so conveniently that the boys are said to have cracked nuts in them. One fine night— the *do-nothing* system having prevailed too long—the tower fell and destroyed the whole church. In another, the parish vestry at length became alarmed, and invited an eminent engineer who was in the neighbourhood to meet them. He declined because the vestry where they met was too near the tower. It fell the next week, and destroyed the church. Brunel is said to have been similarly consulted about a tower, and reported that the only reason he could give why it should not fall to-morrow was that it did not fall yesterday.

I have had the happiness of saving several noble towers imminently threatened with destruction, among which I may mention St. Mary's at Stafford, St. Mary's at Nottingham, those of Aylesbury and Darlington churches, the central towers at St. David's, and St. Alban's, and the western towers at Ripon. Two which I was desirous to save, were, after much anxious thought, found to be past recovery, having been neglected too long. I do not covet such work :—one sleeps more quietly without it. I have surveyed three towers within the last few weeks ; one I pronounced to have nothing the matter with it, two to be in very serious danger.

I will only trouble you with one other case, and that a more agreeable one. It is that of a church dearly loved by me, as that which first called forth my reverence for architecture. It was, when I first knew it, more than half a century ago, almost equal to Mr. Stevenson's poetical *beau-ideal.* Hard by there had once been a mediæval mansion belonging successively to the Giffords, the De Veres, the Bolbecks, and the Courtenays. The oldest part of the church—the unpretending tower—was only of early perpendicular date, but the exquisite decorated churchyard cross showed the church to have been cared for at an earlier period. The Courtenays had forfeited the Manor during the Wars of the Roses, but had recovered it after Bosworth Field ; when they and a little Abbey, which held the great tithes, rebuilt the church about 1493 in architecture just as good for a village church as the chapel of Henry VII. is for a royal burial-place. The Courtenays were again attainted, and the manor went into another highly respected family, which (excepting the time of the Commonwealth) held it till the present century, when it lapsed by the female line into another noted family, who sold it within my own memory. There had not been a resident incumbent for many centuries, and the resident proprietors had passed away, but the church as yet remained as they had left it, saving only the effects of damp, decay, and neglect. The exquisite screen and roodloft still secluded the beautiful chancel. The old seating remained nearly throughout ; but, of later ages, there were the long succession of tombs, the stately family pew, a small gallery in the tower, and Moses and Aaron depicted in gorgeous array over the rood loft. All the windows seemed to have been filled with painted glass of the very highest merit ; but only the upper range of lights of one window remained entire, containing beautiful illustrations of the legend of St. Nicholas; others had fragments of noble figures of abbots, &c., while the heads of the lights in the chancel and its side chapel contained most charming scraps, like some of Van Eyck's, or Hans Hemling's backgrounds, giving views of mediæval cities, so faithfully drawn that, if we knew them, we might recognize the individual steeples. Here I used to spend much of my time, when I hardly knew that there was such a profession as ours ; and later on I used during my holiday-time to make measured drawings of the details.

Well, nearly half a century passed away, and I was called upon to survey the dear old church with a view to its restoration. During the interval decay, neglect, and mutilation had been silently doing their deadly work. The panelled ceiling had almost all disappeared, and all sorts of things were much worse for half a century's neglect. I undertook the work, not professionally, but as a labour of love, and set myself to preserve all which was old, to restore some parts which were lost, and to put the whole in so substantial a state as indefinitely to prolong its existence.

Some of the mouldings of the lost ceilings remained stowed away in a corner ; and with these, and the help of sketches which I had made when a boy, I had the happiness of reinstating them. Some fragments of stonework which had fallen from their place I had myself stowed away during my youth, and they came out now, ready to guide the restitution of the fallen parts. I had a terrible fight for the family or "great house" pew, put up by a chief justice in the last century, and condemned as a symbol of human pride, though the family to whose pride it had ministered had passed away. I saved it by the compromise of a little of its width to reopen the way into the chancel aisle— the older scene of family worship—which it had closed.

I was circumvented about Moses and Aaron—the too canny vicar having unshipped them before I was aware of it. He also got rid of the sounding-board, the red rag of the modern cleric, but it was only Georgian. I plead guilty to the sacrifice of a gallery of a like date. I saved with difficulty the worm-eaten door, studded with the bullets of Cromwell's soldiers who besieged and burnt the castle. I was defeated in the next fight for the non-removal of two effigies and their altar tomb, shattered by the Cromwellians, which stood upon the altar platform, the vicar declaring them (not without reason) incompatible with the due performance of the service. My defeat, however, was due to his proving that it was impossible that this could have been their original position, and that there was no burial beneath them. It was clear, therefore, that their fragments had been collected and placed here after the Common-

3

roughly strong and permanent without the insertion or loss of asingle piece of glass, and all shattered fragments were preserved4ir

another, the church was brought back much into the state itwas in when Cole, the antiquary, says of its distinguishedof the place, " but the best thing belonging to the place is itsmaster." For myself, who have for half a century loved it be-yond all other parish churches, I can only say that it is one of thegreatest comforts of my life to think of its present condition.

I have dwelt, all too lengthily, upon these instances, just toshow how unavoidable it is that some restorations should takeplace. Mr. Petit, a strong anti-restorationist, used to say that,like the measles, restoration was inevitable; and, like children sovisited, he could only wish the churches safe through it. Timewould fail to tell of the necessities of enlargement, &c., to meetpresent needs. These and the desire to reinstate lost featuresare the great difficulties of the restorer; though sometimescompensated by the discovery of lost and beautiful features,such as the two shrines at St. Alban's.

In carrying out such works as I have been describing, thebest of us often err. We are too apt to be led astray by sirenvoices both from without and within. We are—it may be—weak, and open to intimidation. We are—possibly—obstinate,and adhere too much to our own fancies. We are—perhaps—insufficiently careful, and pass over things with too littlethought. We are—sometimes—not sufficiently severe with de-structive builders, clerks of the work, and workmen, whose bar-barisms—found out when too late—are often truly heart-breaking. And—one evil influence with another—we areguilty of all kinds of short-comings and over-steppings; and itis most wholesome to have such Papers as that under con-sideration to goad us into more careful dealing, and to bringour sins to remembrance: and if the New Society were toabate somewhat of what I think the exaggeration of its views,I should welcome it as a court of appeal, which we so greatlyneed in difficult cases, and which I called out for as early as

F e 2

thirty-six years back. I dare say our codes of rules are not of sufficient stringency, and should be stiffened. I know that, whatever their defects, we do not always adhere to them as we ought. I do not, therefore, complain of our critics if their little finger proves thicker than our loins ; nor when we have chastised others with whips, they chastise us with scorpions.

I will add one more word : that while wishing success to the Society in all their *reasonable* endeavours, I would suggest to them a few most useful fields for their exertions.

1. To press upon the proprietors of ruined buildings the duty of protecting them as much as possible from increasing decay by securing the tops of the shattered walls from wet.

2. To find out and oppose, while there is time, the contemplated destruction of ancient buildings, down even to those of the last century. The losses we are constantly sustaining by the actual destruction of old buildings is truly appalling ! Of timber buildings, which are constantly being taken down as ruinous, I assert that timely and judicious reparation is the only possible means for their preservation.

3. To have measured drawings made, systematically and constantly, of all the unprotected architectural antiquities of our land, that when, in the course of nature, their architecture perishes, authentic drawings may remain behind.

4. I am ready and willing to take my share, where I deserve it, in the protests against bad restoration, but I beg the Society to recollect that (as I have elsewhere said) the great majority of ancient buildings are committed to the mercy of a herd who trample them under their feet and turn again and rend all objectors. Let this herd at least have a share of censure, or their patrons will conclude that they have done rightly in casting their pearls before them.

I will only add, as regards churches, that it will be useless to endeavour to persuade seriously thinking people that it is wrong " to restore churches from motives of religion." They were built from such motives, and must ever be treated with like aim. It is equally useless to persuade them that it is wrong from " religious sanction " to redeem them from " their present state of mutilation," that it is right to preserve the high pews which, added by the rich like " field to field till there be no place," have driven God's poor from their own churches. Mr. Stevenson talks of the " dreary ranges of low benches," and truly they do often look dreary enough, but I do not know that they are more so than high pews which half bury the pillars. Let us not, however, judge of churches only when empty : " empty benches " are proverbially dreary : let us rather see them when thronged by devout worshippers, and the dreariness of the seat-backs will not much trouble either eye or memory. Better see the people than have them buried to the neck in Georgian " dozing pens." Let the Society make up their minds at once that any attempt to banish religious motives from the treatment of churches is suicidal ; and let them rather aim—this being taken for granted—at making us do this necessary and religious work with the smallest possible sacrifice of history and antiquity.

By the bye ! I have good news for the Society ! A clergyman whom I met the other day, and who confessed to the *malice prepense* of contemplated " restoration," told me that he had found his parishioners " too conservative to part with their money—too anti-ritualistic to part with their square pews."

THOROUGH ANTI-RESTORATION.

SIR,—On reading Mr. Loftie's article on " Thorough Restoration," in last month's *Macmillan*, my first reflection was that I had never felt more pointedly the truth of the injunction, "Judge not, that ye be not judged ;" since, after having for years been amongst the most earnest of protesters against the system he condemns, I find my sentiments, and almost my very words taken out of my mouth, and adduced to my ow n condemnation.

This is the more excruciating, when I find in a list of damaged churches one, which had filled me with such wrath as to provoke me (though without expressly naming it) to introduce a most pungent paragraph into my inaugural address, when elected President of the Institute of British Architects ; and—then find one of my own (which I had rather plumed myself upon) introduced in the same list. This, however, is, after all, a mere flea-bite ; but, while Mr. Loftie does not think it worth while to say much about the common run of restoration (such as those which have provoked my most earnest protests) he devotes himself with a special *gusto* to writing down some of my own which I had flattered myself were unassailable, or to which I had at least devoted special love and earnest anxiety.

Now, how am I to account for this? Am I really such a self-deceiver as to fancy my own works to be honest and conscientious, while in fact they are just as bad as those against which I have been crying out "in season and out of season" for so many years?—or do I look at matters from a different stand-point from Mr. Loftie?—or is that gentleman's perception warped or obscure? I cannot answer these questions. There is only one test that I can think of. It is clearly useless to discuss the abstract merits or demerits of works. I can, however, examine into questions of fact, and by inference from these it is possible that some aid may be obtained in judging of questions of opinion. Anyhow, it will be the better for the general subject that it be divested from any palpable errors of this nature.

Mr. Loftie lays great stress upon the restoration, ten years back, of the church of St. Michael, near St. Alban's. "A very bad case, indeed," says he, "where one of the oldest churches in England has been deliberately ruined." The excellent incumbent, who is absolutely devoted to his church, and well knows every stone and brick of it, says on the contrary, "I consider the restoration of the church as thoroughly conservative, and often point out to visitors evidences of your great anxiety that every old feature should be distinctly shown. . . . . Pray accept my best thanks for your true and careful restoration of the dear old church of St. Michael's."

Another competent person, who watched the work throughout, says:—"I have no hesitation in saying that a more careful restoration was never carried out, special care to preserve every portion of the building being taken by Sir Gilbert Scott." For my own part I can assert the same. I took a very particular interest in the building and its conservation: and even walls which it seemed at first impossible to save, were bolstered up and embalmed, one may say, against the common decay of nature, by being saturated internally with cementing matter; so that their surface remained identically as I found it, with all its strange intermixture of flint, stone, and Roman tile. In this course of laborious conservation, work, apparently Saxon, constructed in Roman brick, has been discovered throughout the church. An arch and doorway on the north of the chancel, and windows on either side the nave, of this age and material, have been discovered and carefully opened out to view, cut through and ignored by the Norman arcade, itself so old that Clutterbuck says of the arches, that " they bear a striking resemblance to those in part of the nave in the Abbey Church." The old roofs of the nave, the north aisle, and the south chapel of the nave have been cleared from the lath and plaster which largely concealed them, carefully repaired, without in the least disturbing their antiquity, and exposed again to sight. The half-timber work of the south chapel has also been opened out to view : while not a wall or a bit of wall has been disturbed or renewed, beyond a small amount of reparation imperatively demanded for safety. Windows of later date, long walled up, have been opened out again and, where necessary, repaired. None, however, have been renewed excepting the east window of the chancel, which had fallen out and had been replaced by a wooden frame : and, even in this single renewal, the jambs, &c., are the old ones, and the arch contains the only old stone which could be found of it. In fact, the loving pains taken to preserve and hand down in its identity this ancient fabric, with all the changes in its history not only retained, but rediscovered and brought again to light, was beyond what I can describe. And this is what Mr. Loftie calls being "deliberately ruined ! "

Hitherto, however, difference of view may be pleaded. Let us come, then, to more palpable questions of fact. He says— still speaking of St. Michael's—" the Elizabethan entrance, ceiling, and pews were all relics of his (Lord Bacon's) time, and are all swept away, and the chapel reduced to the level of an ordinary chancel aisle." These expressions evidently took their rise from Mr. Thorne, who probably trusted too much to his memory, and similarly speaks of the " Elizabethan porches, ceilings, and fittings " as " strengthening Baconian associations ;" and further says : " the Verulam Chapel opposite the tomb, with its Elizabethan entrance, ceiling, and pews, had quite a Baconian character before the recent restoration when . . . . the chapel was reduced to an ordinary chancel aisle." I learn also that Mr. Loftie speaks of a " ceiled pew," as being the very seat in which Bacon sat, " alluded to in the touching epitaph "—the epitaph containing the words, *Sic sedebat.*

Now, all this is most perplexing. In the first place, the "ordinary chancel aisle" into which I have succeeded in reducing the "Bacon chapel" or "ceiled pew" neither exists nor ever did exist. The chancel has not and never had an aisle. Clutterbuck correctly describes the church, as it was then and now is, as consisting (besides the tower), of "a nave, north side-aisle, a south chapel of the nave, and a chancel;" but no chancel aisle was there. Again, there was no ceiled pew or anything of the kind; nor was there any form of "Elizabethan ceiling" whatever. The chancel, it is true, was ceiled—but how? Let us hear from the clerk of the works. "The roof was for the most part fir, some of the rafters were chestnut. The whole of it is in such a rotten state, it was found impossible to do anything with it; and but for the modern ceiling shaped in fir to form the same it must have collapsed." This "Elizabethan ceiling" was probably put up "during the repair of the church," which Clutterbuck mentions "in the year 1808." Mr. Thorne mentions "new roofs." The only new roof takes the place of this, which was so rotten as only to be held up by a modern ceiling.

Let us come, however, to the "Bacon chapel" or pew. I never heard of its having anything to do with Bacon, nor did any one I have inquired of, and I utterly disbelieve it. Even Mr. Loftie can hardly believe it to be identical with (hardly that it contained) the handsome arm-chair referred to in the "*Sic sedebat!*" It was a common, ordinary pew, bearing no signs of antiquity, and was about one-third of it in the chancel, and two-thirds in the nave: as a consequence, if it is older than 1808, it was severed in two by the chancel screen, which it seems was only removed in that year. Besides this *frustum* of the Gorhambury pew, the main portion of which (with its fireplace) was in the nave, the chancel contained "three ordinary square seats for the Gorhambury servants," of which the incumbent says: "My own opinion is that the pews were made by some of the members of the family of the present owners of Gorhambury, the Grimstons."

In corroboration of this opinion I have (in addition to my own memory and that of a most trustworthy assistant) the testimony of the clerk of the works that "no remains of posts were found which could have supported such a covering [or 'ceiling'], but only a curtain on brass rods: that the framing was in part of deal, and some few panels on the sides of wains-cot, but quite modern : not small, square panels, with moulded styles and rails like Queen Anne's period, but simply of a very coarse moulding." He gives the section, which is of quite modern character.

So much for the "Bacon chapel," which I, for one, never till last month heard of. The "Elizabethan porch" or "entrance" consisted of jambs and lintel of Portland stone, in section like the nosing of a stone step, which the clerk of the works from its own evidence, states to have been "re-used"—that is re-moved here from some place where it had been previously employed. "The insertion of it," he says, "caused the de-struction of one half of the decorated canopy of a tomb found in the south wall of the chancel," and now opened out to view. I do not know that Portland stone was brought into the neigh-bourhood of London till Inigo Jones's time,[3] which hardly allows of these pieces having been used and re-used before Bacon's decease in 1626. The fact is that this entire Baconian theory is a mere *mare's nest*. Neither "chapel," "ceiled pew," "porch," "entrance," nor "ceiling" of Bacon's time, existed, save in the fertile imaginations of these zealous gentlemen. Nor had the church ever exhibited its antiquities so profusely or so plainly as has been the case since (in Mr. Loftie's lan-guage) it has been "deliberately ruined."

I now come to the glorious abbey church (now happily the cathedral) of St. Alban.

I may begin by saying (at the risk of egotism) that for scarcely any church have I so strong and earnest a love as for this. It was the day-dream of my boyhood to be permitted to visit it, and on the earliest opportunity which offered—only a year less than half a century back—I made, with a palpitating heart, my first pilgrimage there. This was before the repairs were undertaken by Mr. Cottingham, and while the small leaded spire, so characteristic of the district, still crowned the central tower. Ever since that time I have been a not unfre-quent visitor and student, and my various reports, as well as—to those who recollect them—my many peripatetic lectures, will show how earnest have been my feelings towards this, probably

[3] Mr. Hull, the geologist, in his *Treatise on Building Stones*, says of Portland stone : "previously to 1623 this stone does not appear to have at-tracted any attention."

the most interesting of all English churches; and I can scarcely think it possible for any one to believe (whatever may have been my errors of judgment) that I should have purposely injured a building so dear to me.

Mr. Loftie begins by saying that " the works, as carried out, have already been the subject of controversy." No one knows this better than himself, for it was he who raised that controversy, in which he was, as I think, signally discomfited.

He begins with a thrice-told tale about the tower having been "stripped of its original plaster." This has been more than once fully explained, but is too good a stone to remain unthrown. Mr. Loftie has, however, in the interval of fight, forgotten his tale. It is clear that he now thinks that it was internal plaster which was thus stripped, for he goes on to say of the exterior of the tower that "the exquisite weathering of the old bricks" has been "rudely removed;" and, again, that "there was a venerable bloom on the bricks." Now, will it be believed that this "exquisite weathering" and "venerable bloom" are ascribed to brickwork which I was the first to expose to view, and which had never known what weather was since the days of Henry I., when the walls were coated with the mortar with which my critic accuses me of having " daubed " them " every-where"? I can hardly be blamed for destroying beauties which existed in Mr. Loftie's brilliant imagination—and nowhere else.

The facts of the case are these : the tower, like the rest of the Norman structure, was built of Roman bricks from Verulam, and coated all over with plastering. This plastering had often gone out of repair, and been patched again and again in a not very slightly manner. It was once more in bad order, and was falling off in large flakes when I was repairing the tower, so much so that it was found necessary to remove it, with the full intention of repeating it. Here I suppose came in what he alludes to as "the wishes of the townsmen," for I recollect arguing against some one's wishes, and urging that the tower was always meant to be plastered. So far, however, was I from being "led by them," that I obstinately persisted in my own way, and began to replaster the walls, when on my next visit I was so horrified at their hideousness, that I at once restripped my own plaster, and exposed to view the entire structure of Roman brick. The "pointing" alluded to was simply to protect the decayed mortar-joints. I do not ask Mr. Loftie's opinion as to its necessity, he has no means of judging—while I have. Whether the Roman brick, or the plastering which covered it, be the best looking, I leave to others : but this being the largest structure in England of the Roman brick, the interest attached to that material, and the fact that the construction is now visible, at least make some amends for the loss of its coating of mortar.

As a matter of taste, pure and simple, there is room for two opinions. Sir Edmund Becket likes it, Mr. Stevenson does not, and while Mr. Loftie is not quite sure what we have done (whether plastering or unplastering) he dislikes it, whatever it may be. We find the editor of Mr. Murray's *Guide to St. Alban's Cathedral* saying that "the tile-work, which is the great feature of St. Alban's, is thus shown in its integrity, and the tower has infinitely gained in beauty of tone and colour," and the editor of his *Handbook to the Environs of London* (Mr. Loftie's text-book for St. Michael's) saying that "lastly, to the great improvement of its appearance, the remaining cement was stripped from the exterior, the mortar repointed, and the structural character fairly exposed to view."

Mr. Loftie next attacks the interior, which he says has been "simply gutted." By this he means that the pewing, galleries, &c., have been removed. He omits, however, to give the reason for their removal. This was not done, in the first instance, with any notion about the incongruity of such fittings, but simply because the central tower, under or near which most of them were placed, threatened to fall, and the space occupied by them was imperatively required for the timber shoring, excavations, and new foundations requisite to render it secure. Mr. Loftie mentions the "Georgian oak panelling." Any one who looks at Neale's view of the interior of the choir, will at once observe that this panelling enclosed the two eastern piers of the tower, in which the chief danger existed. How, then, let me ask, were these pillars to be repaired (one of them was crushed for seven feet deep into its substance) without removing the panelling? The same was the case with the adjoining walls of the presbytery. One, at least, of them was crushed throughout its length beneath the casing of this "Georgian panelling." How was it to be rendered safe while this remained? It was as much as we could do to save it at all.

If the panelling had remained, the tower would probably not now be standing.

" But," it will be asked, " why not have refixed this panelling when the work was done ? " One reason was this, that it had covered up on either side the ancient doorways into the presbytery, the beautiful tabernacle-work over which had been ruthlessly hewn down, probably to make way for it. New openings had been rudely cut through the walls to the eastward of these, and it became necessary to security that these should be solidly walled up, and consequently that the older ones should be re-opened just where the wainscoting was. But " why not refix the old pewing, galleries, &c. ? " Our work had been begun for the safety of the building, but it had grown into restoration. A bishopric was hoped for and even promised. The galleries, &c., had already partly disappeared before we began, and the organ shown at the west end of the choir in Neale's view had yielded to one (on a sufficiently absurd design) in the transept. But what need is there of explanations ? Let any reasonable being take a glance at Neale's or Clutterbuck's views, and ask himself whether, when the Abbey Church should become a cathedral, it would be possible to retain such fittings ? They dated, I believe, from 1716 to 1801, with other parts erected within the last fifteen years. I know of no " Elizabethan " work or " traces of the Stuart period " earlier than Queen Anne's time. The pulpit and its sounding-board will, no doubt, be retained.

I may add that Mr. Loftie speaks of the oak as " black with age." He is not perhaps aware that oak does not get black with age, but with oil and varnish. The " Watching Loft " is of far greater age than the work he laments, but shows more disposition to become white, than black, with age.

Mr. Loftie winds up his remarks on this most venerable building by saying that " it would have been impossible, three years ago, to believe that it could be made to look so new by any expenditure of thought or money."

I write while fresh from St. Albans, and I simply meet this statement by denying it. True, that where the tower piers have been repaired to save the building from destruction their new plastering necessarily "looks new." True, that where stone details of windows had so perished that it had for many years been thought hopeless to glaze[4] them, the renewal or repair of such portions must necessarily look in part new. True, that where dirt has given place to cleanness, it may look newer for the operation, just as any other building, when repaired, looks fresher than before. But I assert that not only the real antiquity, but the old look of the building has been thoroughly respected. Wherever the whitewash is scraped off old paintings and inscriptions appear; and, contrary to what is usual, where stonework is divested of its whitewash, its darker colour gives it a look of even increased age. The building was in a degree a ruin, and must be repaired. Five whole bays of the nave clerestory had scarcely a square yard of old stone surface remaining, while the aisle roof below them was, after each successive winter, strewed thickly with the débris annually brought down. Is this state of things to remain because, forsooth, some can be found to prefer ruin to reparation? This glorious temple must not, and so far as I am concerned shall not, be left to crumble on to its destruction, but I hope to redeem it at the smallest possible cost of real, and even apparent, antiquity.

I will not, however, further defend my own course as regards this building. Mr. Street, in recently addressing the Institute of British Architects, said that as to St. Alban's Abbey he (Mr. Street) could only say that the work which had been done there under the direction of Sir Gilbert Scott was the opening to us of what was practically a sealed book, and he could hardly conceive that anybody, who at all cared for mediæval art, could object to what had been done there.

The rector of St. Alban's, in writing to express his "admiration" of "the ingenuity displayed" by Mr. Loftie, goes on to say: "I can positively affirm that Mr. Loftie's statement, that the exquisite weathering of the old bricks has been rudely removed, is absolutely untrue. The only external portions of the building in which they were exposed to the weather have not been touched, while the tower, where they had been plastered over, and could by no possibility have gathered any bloom, now reveals them; and even the last three winters have given them a weathering which will grow

---

[4] The glass had been replaced by open brickwork which Mr. Loftie has, I believe, elsewhere called Elizabethan lattice-work, but which has been shown to have been put in by a man now living.

more charming as years roll on. So far from the tower looking 'modern' (as it did when it was stuccoed) the course after course of the tiles of old Verulam now exposed to view impart an appearance of unique antiquity, and tell even the chance beholder the story of the pile. I shall never forget Charles Kingsley's enthusiastic admiration when I had the pleasure of pointing this out to him." After saying what I have already stated about the old pulpit, he suggests that Mr. Loftie "might have told his readers of the finding of the shrine of St. Amphibalus; of the discovery of the charming perpendicular doorway and stone screen in the south presbytery aisle; also of the lovely fourteenth-century choir ceiling; of the restoration of the old levels, adding to the height of the interior of the building in some places as much as two feet; of the discovery of the foundations of the old choir stalls, whereby you have been able to replace their temporary successors on the old lines." He mentions also the ancient tile pavements and wall paintings, the presbytery entrances, &c., but adds " only this would not have agreed with the indictment."

Mr. Ridgway Lloyd, the great local antiquary of St. Albans, who has done so good a work in elucidating its history, writes to me also to express his indignation at the attack. After telling me that watching the progress of the work had been one of his greatest pleasures for several years, he says:—

" With your permission I will give a few instances to show the conservative character of your work.

" The Georgian (not Elizabethan) oak panelling in the presbytery was of no great merit, and its removal was most fortunate, since it served to hide the fractures in the north-east pier of the lantern tower, which so nearly led to the destruction of the central tower, and a great part of the eastern limb of the church. It also concealed from view the presbytery doorways as well as the canopied structure over the southern of these doorways. That over the north door is certainly new [though following old indications], but soon after it was finished, some finials [pinnacles] belonging to its predecessor were found in the Saint's chapel, and at once the new finials were cut off and the old ones substituted.

" It is true that after the two eastern piers carrying the lantern tower had been partly rebuilt with brick and cement, they were plastered over to match their fellows on the western side, but who would wish it otherwise?

"In the Lady Chapel, in almost every instance. in which the wall-arcading has been renewed, old and new work may be seen side by side, the former by its presence attesting the faithfulness of the latter.

"One most valuable of the many discoveries made during the restoration is that of the ancient paintings on the ceiling of the choir. This was until recently adorned with a series of seventeenth-century paintings indifferently executed, but it was discovered that the panels bore an earlier design beneath. The later painting having been carefully removed, a splendid series of thirty-two heraldic shields (date *circa* 1370) was disclosed, showing the mediæval arms assigned to the saints Alban, Edward the Confessor, Edmund, Oswyn, George, and Louis; to the emperors Richard (Earl of Cornwall) and Con - stantine; to the kings of England, Scotland, Man, Castile and Leon, Portugal, Sweden, Cyprus, Norway, Arragon, Denmark, Bohemia, Sicily, Hungary, Navarre, France, and to the Crusader king of Jerusalem; as well as those of several of the sons of Edward III. There are also several sacred devices, including the coronation by our Lord of St. Mary, and, in addition, nearly the whole of the *Te Deum* in Latin, and a number of quotations from the Antiphons at Matins and Lauds from the Sarum Antiphoner. This discovery, which is entirely due to the work of restoration, it is impossible to estimate too highly. Among lesser 'finds' may be mentioned the two pits for heart-burial, one in the Lady Chapel and the other in the south transept: both have been most carefully preserved."

Of the entire work of restoration, reparation, or whatever we may call it, I may say that it has been replete with the most important discoveries; that it has been characterized by the most studious conservatism; that it has saved the building from destruction; and that it is gradually fitting it for its advance to the rank of a cathedral, without the loss of any object of antiquity.

Passing over a number of less important matters, we will now proceed to Canterbury Cathedral.

Mr. Loftie introduces the subject by giving an account of all the things done to the Cathedral for the last half-century, including the erection of the south-west tower, which, with the reparation of its fellow tower, he mysteriously describes as being "in the style now universally recognized as that of Camberwell;" an expression I do not understand, unless it be a means of connecting it with myself, I having, thirty-five years back, built a church at Camberwell, though as far as possible from being in the style of this tower. I beg, however, to clear the ground by saying that I have never carried out any structural work in connexion with Canterbury Cathedral. The question at issue, however, relates to the proposed refitting of the choir, and I have elsewhere stated it as follows :—

We do not know what were the fittings of the choir at Canterbury after its restoration in 1180. Very probably they were only temporary. "We have, however, records of their having been renewed by Prior De Estria about 1304. He is especially said to have decorated the choir with beautiful stonework, a new pulpitum (or rood loft), and three doorways. The fittings, &c., then introduced continued undisturbed till after the great Rebellion. It is probable that they had been much injured during that period ; and we find that Archbishop Tenison, in 1702, removed all the old stallwork; concealed the beautiful side screens of De Estria by classic wainscoting ; and substituted pewing for the side stalls; but, to the west, erected new return stalls with very rich canopies, concealing entirely the pulpitum or rood screen of De Estria. The wainscoting of the sides was removed about 1828, leaving the pewing backed up by De Estria's side screens. The Dean and Chapter now desire to substitute for these pews as near a reproduction as may be of De Estria's stalls. We have found parts of them below the flooring, and trust to find other fragments from which their pattern may be recovered. The difficulty, however, is with the western or return stalls : for behind them we find De Estria's pulpitum or rood screen with its original and rich colouring, apparently complete, except-ing the stone canopies of the Priors' and Sub-Priors' stalls, which were rudely hewn off when Tenison's stalls were erected. We want to preserve both the stalls and the more ancient objects which they conceal. I love Tenison's stalls well, but I love De Estria's pulpitum more. Some probably take the contrary view. Why should not both be gratified?"

Now this is a very fair subject for discussion and difference of opinion ; and the more so as this is practically "*Queen*

Anne " work, and to the special lovers of that style its removal would naturally be exasperating. For myself I do not in the least degree wish its removal on account of any discrepancy between it and the surrounding architecture. Some have gone so far as that ; for my part I have no sympathy with that feeling, but the reverse. My own leanings entirely arose from my excitement at the discovery (or re-discovery) of De Estria's pulpitum, hidden behind Tenison's stalls, which I do not hesitate to say filled me with an enthusiasm with which the devotees of Queen Anne cannot be expected to sympathize. That work is described by those who desire to minimize it as small in quantity and greatly mutilated. I have devoted much time to it, and have to state that it is almost entire, having only suffered from the mercilessness of Archbishop Tenison's workmen, who, while putting up the stalls, chopped away the two canopies and much of the mouldings of the central doorway. The necessity for restoring the inner face of the side screens in 1828, when Tenison's wainscoting was removed, no doubt arose from its like barbarous treatment by the same men. It is droll to find the enthusiastic advocates of the style of the last century arguing, from the havoc made in older work by their demi-gods, that it is hopeless, to the extent of being beneath contempt, to try to recover the older work from their depredations.

Putting, however, such considerations aside, the simple question is this : having a Queen Anne work placed in front of a mediæval work, each possessing its own class of merit, ought we to be content with seeing *one*, or ought we to endeavour to render *both* visible ? I have taken the latter view, and have suggested that a worthy position should be sought for Tenison's work, and that the choir screen,—the " pulpitum " of Prior de Estria—should be exposed to view. Mr. Loftie has spoken of this idea as " a new design by Sir Gilbert Scott founded on a fragment." He speaks of " the portion of it already restored behind the altar" (which does not exist), and says "could we be certified that the stone screen exists intact behind the panelling, we might hesitate. But nothing of the kind is asserted. A small portion only remains, and from it an eminent architect is prepared to reconstruct the whole." He has elsewhere described what is proposed as "modern work in imitation of some fragments of a stone screen of the fourteenth century." Mr.

F f

Morris speaks of it as "Sir Gilbert Scott's conjectural restoration," and again, as "the proposed imitation, restoration, or forgery of Prior Eastry's rather commonplace tracery."

The *facts* are that the old screen, or "pulpitum," remains throughout its extent in very fair condition, with its ancient colouring nearly complete and exceedingly beautiful. It is true that the barbarous mutilations made in putting up Tenison's work have left a few parts in some degree to conjecture; but the evidences left *in situ*, aided, it may be fairly hoped, by fragments still to be found, will probably bring these exceptional parts into the region of certainty, just as the discovery of the two thousand fragments of the shrine of St. Alban led to the re-erection of that structure without a jot or tittle of new work or a single modicum of conjecture. Anyhow, what is aimed at is the exposure to view of an actually existant and ancient work—not its restoration, for, with few exceptions, *it is there.*

Another reason in favour of exposing to view this fine old work is that Canterbury differed from many other cathedrals in having no canopied stalls excepting those of the two great dignitaries. In this it agreed with the sister (or daughter) cathedral at Rochester, where we have evidences of the same arrangement. Tenison altered this by adding canopies to all the returned stalls, and thus ignored the traditions of the building.

It is the fashion of the critics to under-rate the screenwork of De Estria, but I find Professor Willis describing it (the side screens—he never saw the western one) as consisting of "delicate and elaborately worked tracery," and again saying of it, "the entire work is particularly valuable on account of its well-established date, combined with its great beauty and singularity." He also speaks of "the beautiful stone enclosure of the choir, the greatest part of which still remains." The ancient obituary of Prior De Estria calls it "most beautiful stonework delicately carved."

Those who seek to under-rate it also try to make the most of the restorations which followed the removal of the wainscot work in 1828; but Professor Willis speaks of it as "in excellent order." Mr. Parker tells us that he saw and studied the screen work when unrestored, and speaks of it as "a very beautiful piece of fourteenth-century work." No doubt it suffered much from the reparation of Tenison's mutilations, but if these authorities speak so strongly of its present beauty, what would they say to the parts still concealed which have never been touched by reparation ? Some parts of the side screens themselves retain their ancient colouring, so that even they cannot be so far gone from their old state as is described.

Mr. Loftie, in one of his letters, says " that very little is left of the construction of Canterbury Cathedral older than the present reign " (!) but Mr. Morris's fear is that " before long we shall see the noble building of the two Williams [of the twelfth century] confused and falsified by the usual mass of ecclesiastical trumpery and coarse daubing." Let him be assured that, whether it be of the twelfth or nineteenth century, there is no idea of touching it : on the contrary, in my paper read before the Institute of Architects in 1862, the following passage occurs, and the principles there advocated for the exterior may be supposed equally to actuate us in dealing with the interior :—

" Imagine for one moment, by way of illustration, that unequalled ' history in stone,' the eastern half of Canterbury Cathedral, so admirably described and unfolded by Professor Willis, if the hand of undiscriminating restoration had passed over it : the works of Lanfranc, of Conrad, of William of Sens, and of the English William, whose intricate interminglings now form a history at once so perplexingly entangled and so charmingly disentangled; and which together present the very best illustration existing in this country of the changes of architectural detail from the Conquest to the full establishment of Pointed architecture; and which must ever form the very textbook of the architectural history of that period, as being at once the most perfect in its steps, the most completely chronicled, and the most admirably deciphered. Imagine, I would say, this treasury of art-history reduced to an unmeaning blank by the hand of the restorer, either all indiscriminately renewed, or one half renewed and the other scraped over to look like it ; the coarsely-axed work of the early Norman mason, the finer hewing of his successor, and the delicate chiselling of the third period, all scraped down to the semblance of the new work by the same undiscriminating *drag*, or replaced by new masonry, uniting all periods into one, or else making a mimic copy of their distinguishing characteristics ! I take an extreme imaginary illustration, because the work in question, as it remains in its authenticity, forming the most precious page of our archi-

tectural history, is so well known as to place the principle I
am speaking of in a clearer light than if I took a less marked
example."

This Canterbury question is, however, as I have before said,
a fair subject for fair discussion; and I will add no more than
this—that, while I heartily sympathize with the new movement
for the preservation of ancient monuments in its leading aims,
I must protest against its being carried to the length of leaving
our ancient buildings to fall into ruin, or to retain (in all cases)
the effects of mutilation, disfigurement, and decay. And, as
quite a secondary objection, I would venture respectfully to
suggest that the legitimate aims of the movement are hardly
likely to be furthered by overstatement or misrepresentation.

GEORGE GILBERT SCOTT.

P.S.—It is rather comical to think how much more is said
about moving Gibbons's returned stalls—if indeed they be
Gibbons's—from the position they were made for at Canterbury, than about the removal of his corresponding stalls from
the position they were made for at St. Paul's. This may,
however, be accounted for on the ground of the latter being a
fait accompli; but what will be said to spending 40,000*l.* on
obliterating Thornhill's paintings in the dome of St. Paul's in
favour of mosaics of our own day, though arranged and directed
by a " Committee of Taste " ?

THE END.

GILBERT AND RIVINGTON, PRINTERS, ST. JOHN'S SQUARE, LONDON.

APPENDIX 1

This Appendix contains the readings in the manuscripts which were omitted from the printed version in 1879. The first reference is to the location in the manuscripts (five leather-bound notebooks with clasp locks, written in pencil between 1864 and 1878); the references in round brackets are to the location in the printed text. Occasional editorial comments appear in square brackets.

Vol. I [begins]: '1864 / Geo. Gilbert Scott / 20 Spring Gardens / London. Address to which it is begged that this book may be sent if lost.' [and opposite]: 'J. H. Scott / 19 Coleman Street / E.C.' [then rough pencil drawings of church tower.]

p. 1 'Personal & Professional Recollections / My motive in jotting down the following miscellaneous recollections is...'

Vol. I, p. 25 (omitted after p.9, l.9) 'I will briefly enumerate a few of the old customs of the district which I can recollect, beginning with Christmas. Besides the usual carol singers and hymn singers who went from house to house I recollect we were always visited by a *piper* a little before Xmas. This man played an instrument which few persons of the younger generations perhaps know, I mean 'the pipe and tabour' which consisted of a small flat drum hung by a leather thong to the end of a wooden pipe, the drum being beaten with one hand while the pipe was played with the other, making a rude but merry kind of music (one may see a player on this instrument quaintly carved in sculpture of the 13th century on the tower at Higham Ferrars).
    The most characteristic, however, of Christmas observances was 'Mummery'. The 'Mummers' came from house to house after dark in quaint dresses and, if admitted, performed the old play of 'Father Christmas'.
    I seldom happened to see this performance (perhaps but *once*) as my father had no great love for them; and certainly what I remember is not of an elevated kind. The characters I remember as 'Father Christmas', a Turkish Knight, Prince Arthur, K. George, Beelzebub, and a doctor. Father Xmas enters with a besom [?] sweeping snow, with the sage remark
    'Here comes old F.C., ? Welcome or welcome not,
    And let old F.C. / never be forgot.'
The Turkish Knight's remark are about equally intellectual
    'Here comes I, the Turkish Knight / Come from the Turkish land to fight' etc. etc. Prince Arthur makes his debut as follows
    'Here comes I, P.A., sword in hand / and who's the man that dares bold bid me stand? / I'll cut him up as small as flies / And send him to the cookshops there to make mince pies / Mince pies hot mince pies cold' &c etc. as usual. St George informs us

'I slew the dragon with great slaughter / and won the King of Egypt's daughter'
I do not recommend any [illegible word] remark of Beelzebub who by the bye wore a very [?] sable dress and carried a blown bladder at the end of a stick; but the doctor on his introduction to aid a fallen knight romantically informs the audience

'All diseases I very well know / particularly the Mulligubs [?] in the great toe'
This is all I remember and is perhaps much more than is worth remembering of these relics of the sacred mysteries of the Middle Ages. Some further particulars, with variations, may be found in Miss Baker's Northamptonshire Glossary.

St Valentine's Day was kept not by letter-writing but by all the Boys and Girls in the Village going together from house to house crying

'Good morrow morrow Valentine'
in response to which cry they expected a scramble of ginger-bread nuts.

Easter was celebrated by fiddling and in our case this was for the most part performed by one 'Jemmy' usually called 'King of the Gipseys'. This specimen of the Gipsey race was a little old man almost as black as a negro. I have seen him fiddle, dance and sing all at once when he was upwards of 100 years old. He lived I think chiefly in Oxfordshire in the lanes and commons about Bicester and shared his sovereignty with his consort called 'Fair Nancy' from her not being of Gipsey blood – I have heard that they had sons of 70 or 80 years old.

May day was a great festival though the May pole and the Queen of the May had become obsolete. It was observed by the girls carrying about garlands and by the boys dressing one of their number in branches of box so as to look like a bush and then chairing him astride of two 'white wands' or peeled willow poles laid cross-wise on two boys shoulders. The multitude surrounding him with 'white wands'. This boy was called the 'Bumbailie' and the whole was a purely local observance in imitation of the chairing on the same day of the Bailiff or Mayor of Buckingham.

But the most amusing celebration was that of Whitsuntide. This was by means of the 'Whitsun Morris dancers'. I suppose that the custom is not obsolete, but as it is known now to comparatively few, I will describe it as well as I am able. The Morris dancers were young men perhaps about a dozen in number. They were stripped of their coats and waistcoats and wore clean white shirts, white stockings and light coloured knee breeches. They were gaily decorated with bunches of long flying bright-coloured ribbons on their hats and all parts of the person, and to their legs were attached large patches of coloured cloth covered all over with little brass bells. In their hands were short 'white wands' and they danced to the 'pipe and tabour'. In the dance each two youths always faced each other and holding their wands by both hands near the middle they contrived as they danced to strike the ends of them together so as to keep time to the tune. I well remember my intense admiration of their skill. The noise of the dozen wands keeping time with the tabour and of the jingling bells also roughly following the tune added to the lively antics of the dancers had a most merry and exhilarating effect. One character however I have not yet mentioned – I mean the 'Fool'. This worthy seemed to have the liberty of dressing as he liked, for while a perfect uniformity was observed by the others, he seemed to change his costume from year to year. For the most part, however, he was dressed most fantastically in many-coloured rags and had a head-dress betokening his calling – He carried a wand, suspended to the end of which by a long thong was an inflated bladder, which he kept continually bringing down with telling force upon the heads of the spectators which he joined in a ludicrous mimicry of the dance mingled with extemporized buffooneries of his own.

It may readily be imagined that this show had great attractions for children and that we heard with grim dissent the discouragements offered to the performers by my father who opposed them as productive of drunkenness.

The other great observance was the village feast. This in our village was of ancient date being commemorative of the consecration of old John West's church nor can I say much in its favour being marked by little else than debauchery. To this observance my father was a deadly foe and I recollect on the Sunday night he used to perambulate the village in person to put a stop to the profanation of the day.

One more odd custom I will mention: this is what was called in local parlance 'low-belling' or *loud bellowing* and was the conventional form of reprobation of the beating of a wife by her husband. When such a misdemeanour had taken place a 'low belling' was proclaimed and in the evening all the boys in the village assembled, armed with everything which would make a noise. The majority bore cow horns which they blew with almost continuous blasts; others carried tin pots and kettles which they beat vehemently with sticks, others two and two carried a dripping pan which they used as a kettle drum and sometimes an old pensioner would join them with his shrill fife. This rough band walked three times through the whole length of the village, making the most tremendous noise one can fancy and stopping each time at the door of the offender before which they threw down a large heap of chaff, in token of his having been engaged in *threshing* – a memento of his disgrace which it took some days to obliterate.

In the midst of this funny population ...'

Vol. I, p. 62 (after l.2, p. 19) 'Under the same roof with this primitive couple lived two old women sisters respectively to Mrs and Mr Warr. The former, 'Molly Adams' I think I never saw, though on this I am uncertain, for she was 'bedridden' and had been so for years yet I feel to have known her perfectly for she was the special pet of my excellent old Aunt Gilbert who was her constant and untiring visitor and religious instructor and I believe the poor woman was worthy of her care and was a truly pious person. The other old woman was called 'Molly Warr', and if one 'Molly' had become *unknown* through her maladies the other amply made up for it through hers. My village was as eccentric in its diseases as in its other conditions. Two of its inhabitants, both named Warr, suffered from a strange form of madness and poor old Molly was one of them. I have heard ...' (p. 19, 1.8...) (...1.27...) '...our dread of her was beyond description even during her lucid intervals of clear hours, when, however, the hated meridional hour approached, things assumed a more serious form – she began to walk determinedly up and down the room making a strange grunting sound at every step which constantly increased in loudness. At a certain stage in the paroxysm, which she well knew, for I believe she was as conscious as anybody else, she went out into the garden behind the house and walked up and down; her walk gradually increasing to a run and her little groans to the most violent screams, which could be heard throughout the village, but which after the clock struck twelve subsided by degrees corresponding with their rise, when she retired, by day, to the chimney corner, and by night to her bed into which (I have it on the evidence of 'Molly Adams' given through my Aunt Gilbert) she vaulted through mid air head first – and subsided to rest.

The other subject of madness was a young man of the same name – of a superior order in our village society – a noble person – tall, Herculean, and of a strong intellect (and of earnest piety [-deleted-]) he was suddenly seized with madness, not like that of his poor old namesake but coming on at accidental intervals when his cries, like hers, was audible throughout the village – his friends built a bedroom expressly for him with a window out of reach and he of his own choice went to bed every night with a chain to his ankle lest an attack should come on. During the intervals, which were long, he was one of the most excellent of men, he died under one of these strange attacks, during many of which it took four strong men to hold him though I recollect my father who was attacked by him resisting him single handed, and reducing him to quiescence. His brother is now the leading man in the village and a most excellent person.

One of the other sufferers from St Vitus' dance ...'

Vol. I., p. 74 (after p. 21, 1.6) 'Good old benignant Nanny White! How willingly would I give up any fame or advantage I have attained in subsequent life to share your blessed lot among the saints above! I wonder whether my sweet sister Mary Jane who has this day been called to her rest (Jany 22. 1864) recollects her. She too is now a blessed saint – Never did I know a character so faultless. This morning at 6 she made signs (being nearly speechless) that she wanted to write and a slate being given her, wrote on it in a strong steady hand 'Be of Good Cheer thy sins be forgiven thee'. Oh 'if the righteous scarcely be saved where shall the ungodly and the sinner appeal?' if the most blameless of the human race feel their sins such a burden what must those feel who live a life of carelessness. Oh Lord Jesus Christ, Make us all to be numbered with thy Saints in Glory everlasting!

I have been cheering myself today after the death of my dear sister while travelling by writing the above reminiscences which I know she would have enjoyed to do herself, but grief *will* return and I must stop.

A sad catastrophe happened at poor 'Mother Warr's' house during the latter part of my residence at Gawcott. A young man chanced to go to a fair at Warwick and in passing a funeral there, felt a strange sensation come over him with a conviction that he had caught an infectious disorder. On returning to Gawcott he was seized with Smallpox and died in a few days. My father buried him secretly by lantern light omitting the tolling of the Bell to avoid attracting spectators. That night poor old crazy Molly Warr remarked 'how wicked [?unkind] it were to hear the bell a tolling as I sat in the chimney corner' and on being informed that the bell had not tolled she saw at once that her time was come for she heard the bell toll in the chimney stack 'as plain as plain'. She was taken ill at once and poor bedridden Molly Adams too and both died without any distinctive symptoms to mark the disease. After their funerals 'Mother Warr' began to feel queer but her pride rebelled against saying so for she had been irate at a suggestion that the old women had died of smallpox; a suspicion which was calculated to hurt the shop. She said nothing and when a rash appeared upon her arms she put on her long gloves, till at last on her falling down from the giddiness which accompanies the disease her son who carried her to bed found out what was the matter, but it was not made known till mother, father and son were all laid up together and then no one could be found to nurse them – fortunately the old man had been a 'calf-man' and consequently had the cow pox – and being less ill than the others, he was able to help them and they all recovered – though sadly to the disfigurement of the young man who had been a handsome fellow.

Two of our favourite village characters ...'

Vol. I, p. 99 (p. 26, l.15) 'Why should not I have been a fair classic? True, he had four more years of it, and was a genius, but this did not make all the difference. He unhappily did not follow up his vantage-ground but rested on his oars, or he might have been senior wrangler and near the top in classics and would now be a Bishop I have no doubt – as it was, he was 11th Wrangler high in classics and elected Tutor of his college which however he did not accept and so (continued [– deleted]) became a plain country parson wasting his preeminent talents 'in the desert air' while I have risen in a line of my own but ever mourning my slender attainments in all else. Both of these failures arose from not working *at the right time* – I as a schoolboy, my brother as an undergraduate. I cannot recover what I lost nor can he, though he had worked intensely as a schoolboy and has done so ever since he took his degree, make up for that one bit of lost time which blighted his magnificent prospects as a man of the highest talent. It is one of the greatest wonders ...'

Vol. I, p. 125 (p. 34 after l.23) 'Here we met a number of Buckingham friends who were to join us in our lodgings at Margate. The most conspicuous amongst whom was a family of quakers – our medical man Mr Southam his wife, two grown up daughters and a son of 10 years old – we had also my dear old friend Mrs Rogers with her 3 daughters – the two eldest long afterwards married to my friends Mr Stowe and Major Macdonald, also a Mr Grade uncle to the present dean of Ripon.'

Vol. I, p. 138 (p. 37, l.33) 'Another constant correspondent was a cousin, Mr Gordon of Stocks near Tring and of [blank space here]. Poor man he corresponded ...'

Vol. I, p. 141 (after p. 38, l.26) '*Buckingham Friends* / Our local friends were chiefly inhabitants of Buckingham, most of whom took to my father on his first arrival and became many of their constant attendants at his church. Among the latter, the Bartlett family were the cheif [sic]. The Heads of this family John and Edward Bartlett were I think partners in a multifarious business. The latter died before my time but the former in my day united the businesses of Tanning and banking while the sons of the latter were great wool staplers. They were the leading people of Buckingham. Our great friend and ally was old Mrs Bartlett the widow of Edward – a thoroughly excellent person in every way and my mother's chief local friend. She had 3 sons and two daughters. Of the former, one (Robert) was a solicitor in a large practice at Chelmsford and clerk of the Dean of the Coy. of Essex (whose son is now an excellent clergyman in the East of London). Philip and Thomas were the wool-staplers, the former a talented-hearty-jovial person and the latter a very witty man. The daughters were very lady like persons and were married respectively to Major Macdonald and to my youngest [?] uncle Revd. Benjm. Scott. All of this generation are now dead.

Old John Bartlett (profanely known as 'Jack Ramskin') was a sort of little King in Buck a rough morose money-minding [?] man who took the command at everything. I think his family are also dead. His eldest son was a most pious and excellent clergyman Vicar at Bildwas in Shropshire a perfect contrast to his father – gentle and polished in the extreme.

The Bartlett family came over every Sunday en masse to Gawcott church as did others from Buckm. who held with Evangelical views and Mrs B used usually to dine with us.

Our medical man in early days was a sturdy old Quaker (already mentioned) Mr Southam – but he took his Doctor's degree and removed to Coventry shortly after which we took in his place Mr Stowe a very talented and excellent man who was at that time one of our most valued friends. He married the eldest daughter of our friend Mrs Rogers whose second daughter became long afterwards the second wife of Major Macdonald. Mr Stowe died quite recently. I would mention that his eldest son was on the staff of *The*

Times and was sent to the Crimea to administer the fund raised by *The Times* for the relief of the Soldiers when he unfortunately died of fever. He was a most promising man. Another of our great friends though not of our immigrant church comers was Mr Hearn the [blank space here] solicitor and now Banker of Buckm. A truly estimable man and still living at a great age.

I have mentioned Major Macdonald and I will only add that he was a very noble person and one of our best and warmest friends besides being a sort of half brother in law of my fathers – or rather [?] of my uncle's (Benjamin). He too has lately died at a very advanced age.

I enumerate these old friends merely that my sons if they read these memoranda they know better who they were.'

Vol. I, p. 191 (after p. 52, l.15) 'Before quitting these early times I must here [?] enumerate my brothers and sisters and a few relatives I have more or less omitted to mention.

My brothers and sisters were all of age as follows: Thomas -b- Feb 1807 I think / Nathaniel Gilbert died in infancy / John b Novr 1809 / (Myself July 13th 1811) / Euphemia 1813 / Nathaniel Gilbert 1814 / Elizabeth died in infancy / William Langstone 1817 / Anne died in infancy / Samuel King 1819 or 20 / Mary Jane 1821 / Elizabeth do not recollect / Melville Horne 1827.

My father's brothers were the Revd. John Scott vicar of St Mary's Hull and North Ferriby and the Rev Benjamin Scott of Bedford and Salford Warwickshire. His sister (Elizabeth) Mrs King – my father's first cousin Revd. Thos. Webster Vicar of Oakington in Cambridgeshire etc. and many others one of whom was my dear Mother in law Mrs Oldrid daughter of my grandfather's eldest brother John.

My Mother's brothers Mr John Lynch formerly of Dunmow died perhaps about 1819 or so several of whose family are living and Nathaniel who died young. She had a half sister. Her father's daughter by a prior marriage – a Mrs Watson who died before my time. Her most representative relation was her first cousin the Revd Nathaniel Gilbert son of the beforementioned Rector of Bledlow of the same name and proprietor of the Antigua Estate. He died a few years back but his widow who still holds the estate is living at Leamington. She also was a cousin a daughter of the Revd Melville Horne.

My father's brothers and sisters visited us (unless my father and mother visited *them*) every year at least and it was a great occasion for we usually had several of our cousins with them which we much enjoyed.

My uncle John of Hull was a most dignified man – fully as much so as any modern Archbishop. He was also a man of great ability and excellence – My uncle Benjamin was a great mechanician and a man of Science. He lost his wife I suppose about 1825, after which he married again and his widow is living.'

Vol. I, p. 236 (p.67, l.13) [for 'A builder named Moffatt' read:] 'A small builder named Moffat.'

Vol. I, p. 257 (after p. 74, l.15) 'I had formed during this period the acquaintance of Mr Sampson Kempthorne a very worthy and religious young architect and I used occasionally to follow at Mathematics with him and I kept up my friendship for Edwin Nash a very nice excellent young man and a beautiful draughtsman -
I have little recollection of my visits home ...'

Vol. I, p. 258 (p. 74, l.18) '...I lost my dear old Aunt Gilbert and my sister Euphemia was married. I remember one visit however ...'

Vol. I, p. 259 (p. 74, l.22) '...I went with him to reconnoitre I could not undertake the survey of dilapidations being so much engaged I thereupon recommended Mr Voysey - Kemthorne's old master - who did this for him most efficiently, and my father having to build a new house there ...'

Vol. I, p. 261 (after p. 75, l.10) '...by defending my representative, a state of things very typical of many subsequent experiences.'

Vol. I, p. 264 (after p. 76, l.1) 'Alas, how soon they proved far otherwise!
My youngest Uncle (Benjamin) had died some years previously and my father had damaged his health by the labours of getting up lists of subscribers to and editing a volume of his sermons for the benefit of his family and my eldest uncle (John) died while I was on this little sketching tour with E. Nash.'

Vol. I, p. 271 (p. 78, ll.5 and 13) '*action* and *decision*' and '*gone*' [underlined].

Vol. I, p. 277 (after p. 80, l.10) '...at my office! The Guardians of the former meanwhile becoming impatient at Moffatt's absence.
After these things had gone on for some time I went into a competition for a fifth union house in my neighbourhood but without success a new plan on an original system coming suddenly in to my discomfiture. On the other hand Moffatt had competed for one in *his* district with similar ill-success. This led him to come and make a formal proposal to me to this effect. There were numerous unions being formed in the West of England and he felt sure he could carry many of them were it not for his youthful appearance and this might be got over if he had a partner already in practice whose name he could use to back him. He therefore proposed that I should throw in my lot with him in the West, each keeping what we had got to ourselves and I keeping my private practice and also all union practices in districts in which I could claim any personal interest whatever. I agreed to this proposal and it became the foundation of our future partnership.' (l.12)

Appendix 1

Vol. I, p. 281 (after p. 80, l.31) '...the too hard unsentimental pursuits which at this time and still more *from* this time almost overwhelmed me, and to which I must now return.'

Vol. I, p. 289 (after p. 83, l.24) '...a host of enemies and traducers. His weaker points began to show themselves somewhat later when his early success had too much elated him.'

Vol. I, p. 295 (p. 85, l.22 reads:) '...actual partner with Mr Moffatt, I owe it to my dear wife that this partnership was not of permanent duration.'

Vol. I, p. 303 (p. 89, l.16) 'new man' [underlined]

Vol. I, p. 309 (after p. 92, l.2) '...We succeeded and from that moment Moffatt's head was turned! He used to boast that he could *afford* to make a fool of himself. His talent energy and industry remained, but he was an altered man. He cared not who he offended either by dissent annoyance or indirectly by his strange way of conducting himself. Still however he carried out the work, for it was mainly committed to him, with great ability and success only that in doing so he contrived thoroughly to alienate his employers and convert them into enemies where by a little circumspection and self control he could have made them staunch friends.'

Vol. I, p. 329 (after p. 98, l.30) '...their verdict in my favour. I have somewhere lithographed copies and the correspondence which I think is rather valuable. It is illustrated by anastatic sketches by Petit and myself. The whole case, however, is given in the account of the restoration by myself in Masfen's History of St Marys Church, to which I specially refer.'

Vol. I, p. 333 (p. 100, l.4 reads:) 'the very best Roman Cement.'

Vol. I, p. 337 (p. 101, l.11 reads:) '...a good game after dinner in his grounds – every other minute of the day being devoted to the closest work in which he and often I joined as closely as any of them.'

Vol. I, p. 340 (p. 102, ll.17 and 21) 'but *it was new*' and '*shame* and *chagrin*' [underlined].

Vol. I, p. 344 (p. 103, l.33 reads:) '... in spite of every effort on their part to put me down by misrepresentation and flippant criticism of the most galling character.'

Vol. I, p. 347 (p. 104, l.31 reads:) '...anything but honourable.'

Vol. I, p. 352 (p. 106, l.24) '...his single sin being *his independent existence.*' [underlined]

Vol. II, p. 1 '*Sir George Gilbert Scott*
    20 Spring Gardens
    London
Please if this book be found to return it to the above address.'

Vol. II, p. 2 '*Government offices competition Prize men – War office*
    H. B. Garling
    Mr B. D'Hazeville of Paris
    J. E. Rochead
    Pritchard & Seddon
    C. Broderick
            Foreign office
    Coe and Hofland
    Banks & Barry
    G. G. Scott
    Deane & Woodward
    T. Bellamy'
(this list appears as a footnote on p. 181)

Vol. II, p. 63 (after p. 130, l.27) '...and I could not muster pluck to broach it. Moffatt had, as I have already mentioned, got into a sad way of offending employers. This grew rapidly upon him till it became *most serious* and I was formally and seriously warned of its consequences. He was also extravagant, keeping four horses, and one thing with another all our practice led rather to debt than to laying by money. Besides this, the great Railway speculation mania was just then coming on and Moffatt was severely bitten, so much so as to be absolutely wild, and the line of practice he was actually getting into partook so much of a speculative character as to be decidedly dangerous.
    At length Mrs Scott "took the bull by the horns..."'

Vol. II, p. 66 (after p. 131, l.19) '...As, however, they were in their own nature and origin *his* works it did not seem unfair that he should stand the brunt of their speculative character. 1846 was to me a year...'

Vol. II, p. 66 (p. 131, l.32 reads:) '...bad management on my own part and of extravagance on that of my partner.'

Vol. II, p. 73 (p. 134 begins:) 'Moffatt's misfortunes in subsequent years have been a great sorrow to me. They have been the natural consequence of speculative practice and indeed of speculation wholly alien to his profession. He never recovered the moral damage of that year of Speculation Mania 1846, and I can never cease to be thankful that I escaped in time. I was 35 years old in the midst of my year of transition...'

Vol. II, p. 75 (after p. 134, l.31) '...to which they refused admission, and gave a worse than garbled statement of it. This I suppose was the work of *Mason Neale*, (see my defence it is lithographed and I have some copies)' [reproduced pp. 135-146, but not in MSS].

Vol. II, p. 84 (after list on p. 148) 'See my report upon Ely 1847-8 Cathedral. It contains I think the truest theory of cathedral arrangement and use. Also look up the original internal Views etc.'

Vol. II, p. 103 (after p. 154, l.27) '...of some interest and value! See also my series of annual reports – in the possession of the Chapter Clerk and of which I possess no copies.'

Vol. II, p. 113 (p. 158, l.10) [for 'a well known incumbent of Westminster' read:] 'the Revd Cyril Page of Westminster.'

Vol. II, p. 159 (after p. 173, l.12) '...was ably advocated by Mr Denison who took ample toll out of it in the shape of self-praise nor would I attempt to deny him his fair meed [?] of it. He like my friend Mr Stevens...'

Vol. II, p. 174 (p. 178, l.33) '*excellent*' [underlined]

Vol. II, p. 175 (p. 179, l.5) [for 'or nearly so' read:] '...the best ever sent into a competition or thereabouts.'

Vol. II, p. 173 (p. 179, l.31 reads:) 'The judges however who knew amazingly little about their subject were not Gothicly disposed and though they awarded premiums to all the best Gothic designs they took care not to put any of them high enough to have much chance.

The first for the Foreign Office was a flash affair by my old pupil *Coe* – The first for the War Office a not bad one by any means by Garling. Barry and Banks came second for the F.O. and I third – Barry's far from any good as I think.

I did not fret myself at the disappointment...'

Vol. II, p. 180 (p. 180, l.27 reads:) 'It appeared on the evidence of Mr Burn who had acted as one of the Architect assessors to the judges that though the assessors agreed without [?within] consultation as to the order of merit among the designs they did not agree with the decision of the judges and further that they had agreed in placing me second for *both* buildings while no one was on any showing first for both, and that they considered second for both (the two being essentially parts of the same group) to be a higher position than first for *only one ...*'

Vol. II, p. 186 (p. 183, l.4) [for 'One leading member of our profession' read:] 'Professor Donaldson.'

Vol. II, p. 186 (p. 183, l.14 reads:) 'As he had been my introducer to the Institute and to the Graphic Society and had for many years acted in a very friendly way to me I have never allowed his conduct in this matter to provoke me to any unfriendly act', the following deleted: 'but I confess it has greatly lowered him in my estimation though every man has a fair right to act on his own opinion.'

Vol. II, p. 186 (p. 183, l.24) [for 'this gentleman' read:] 'Donaldson.'

Vol. II, p. 195 (p. 186, l.6) [for 'his secret mentor's second hand learning' read:] 'Mr Donaldson's second hand learning.'

Vol. II, p. 195 (p. 186, after l.12) '...both styles. I refer however to the papers my memory not carrying it all. In all these discussion Charles Barry was in attendance and in close communication with Tite etc.'

Vol. II, p. 197 (p. 186, l.22) [for 'Mr A---' read:] 'Mr Ellyce M.P. for Coventry.'

Vol. II, p. 199 (p. 187, l.11) [for 'one of my opponents in the original competition' read:] 'Barry.'

Vol. II, p. 201 (p. 187, l.32) [for 'a leading member of the profession, a Mr B---' read:] 'Donaldson.'

Vol. II, p. 205 (p. 189, l.21, read:) 'Tite repeated his heavy commonplaces and introduced Charles Barry and Garling as the successful competitors (Barry was *not* so but poor *Coe* had no friends).'

Vol. II, p. 206 (after p. 189, l.30) '...any personal breach.
    I would here record that the "Mr Cockerell" named in the list (see the Builder) was *not* [underlined twice] *Professor* Cockerell who wrote to me directly stating that he should decline to go – but it was his son. I saw also Penrose's name among those who though not present had given their adhesion – I wish to remark on this point that when I was first appointed he had expressly volunteered a letter of congratulation, in which he expressed himself as almost a convert to the style! *See his letter.*'

Vol. II, p. 208 (p. 190, l.5, instead of list of names, reads:) '...one or two who exerted themselves in the most generous way / R. Brandon / look to document signed by some 18 or 19.'

Vol. II, p. 212 (p. 191, l.30, read:) 'To resign would be to give up a sort of *property* which Providence had placed in the hands of my family and would be simply rewarding C. Barry for his unprecedented attempt to wrest...'

Vol. II, p. 216 (p. 193, l.16 read:) 'About this time a friend (I forget who) [deleted] called and told me he was sure that something secret was going on about Mr Garling for he had casually in conversation, mentioned the Foreign Office to him when so extraordinary an expression had come over his countenance that he was convinced that some mischief was brewing. Some time later another friend told me that he had found out that Garling was preparing a design for the Foreign Office! He also asked me if Lord Palmerston had not once proposed to make Garling my coadjutor in the matter and I had refused! I now saw how matters stood. The introduction of Garling by the deputation of architects had by some means ousted Barry and placed Garling in his stead as my rival. Ld P. had hoped to thrust him upon me as a colleague...'

Vol. II, p. 220 (p. 194, l.27) [for 'the competitor to whom I have referred' read:] 'Garling.'

Vol. II, p. 234 (p. 200, l.1, reads:) 'The India Office was wholly my *design* though I had adopted an idea as to its grouping and outline suggested by a sketch of Wyatt's and which I thought very excellent though in his own sketch he had done but little justice to the idea. Lord Palmerston highly approved the design...'

Vol. II, p. 238 (p. 201, l.9) '*quite right*' [underlined].

Vol. II, p. 240 (after p. 200, l.22) 'I am ashamed to have occupied so much space in detailing these heartless and almost heartbreaking vexations and will leave the subject merely referring back to a voluminous mass of written evidence on the subject among my papers and which I think should be examined.

(I must however privately warn my sons against publishing what may get them into ill odour with authorities).'

Vol. II, p. 243 (p. 203, l.2) '*late* decorated' [underlined].

Vol. II, p. 244 (p. 203, l.15 reads:) 'In my own office Mr Street and his then implicit follower Mr Bodley used to view every one as a heretic...' [see Introduction, p. 11].

Vol. II, p. 247 (p. 204, 1.14) [for 'Others took a contrary view, as Mr Bodley in his design for the memorial church at Constantinople' read:] 'Others took a contrary view.'

Vol. II, p. 266 (p. 211, 1.19) [for 'days of mere eccentricity' read:] 'days of wildness.'

Vol. II, p. 299 (p. 220, 1.27) [for 'muskets' read:] 'guns.'

Vol. II, p. 300 (p. 221, 1.8 reads:) 'He was succeeded by his brother – educated as a sculptor – who has fallen with considerable success into his elder brother's groove.'

Vol. II, p. 308 (p. 224, 1.3 reads:) '...when a firm [deleted] society of painters of a higher class had been formed with the express intention of *introducing* [deleted?] uniting high art with true principles, to find them producing works yet still more strange than those of any of their predecessors. *Let us hope against hope!*' [underlined].

Vol. II, p. 319 (after p. 232, 1.22) 'My Uncle King died in Jersey in 18--. He had sustained severe pecuniary losses for his property lay in the hands of a city firm who failed. This my aunt's health had led him to settle down in Jersey. Here again I feel a pang of remorse at not having acted in so affectionate a part as I ought. My business so absorbed me throughout these years as to leave hardly a shred of time for anything else! I most deeply regret this. My dear Aunt King followed him within a year I think and thus nearly the entire generation had passed away which had been the guides and guardians of my youth, and here I would again say *Make me to be numbered with thy saints in Glory everlasting!* The only remnant of this generation is the second wife and widow of my youngest uncle – Benjamin. She was much younger than her husband who died I think within the year of their marriage. She is still living though I regret that I seldom see her. My life is filled with this species of regret. On my Mother's side...'

Vol. II, p. 320 (p. 233, 1.10 reads:) '...with a remainder to her Sister Miss Horne and after her to the Bible Society! I dare say the reversion could be purchased off them for an old song. Mrs Gilbert and Miss Horne are now living at Leamington. The estate has been so much reduced...'

Vol. II, p. 323 (p. 233, 1.26) '...delicate health – May God of his infinite Mercy bless her and my sons and continue to them and me the happiness He has so long given us and at last bring us to his Heavenly Kingdom through Jesus Christ!'

Vol. II, p. 327 (after p. 235, 1.22) '...which they say *must* be fatal and is of the most painful nature!

Oh My God, Spare her if it is consistent with the laws Thou hast given to nature and, if not so, Oh give her strength to endure what thou sendest and fill her heart with such earnest love to thee and such spiritual consolation and support as may make her sufferings seem but a light affliction and bringing about an eternal weight of Glory! The letters I get from her are of *exquisite beauty*. Nothing could be more touchingly beautiful ...' (after p. 235, 1.31) '...these grievous trials! Lord grant it me for Jesus Christ's sake! Sunday March 20th 1864.'

Vol. II, p. 330 (p. 236, 1.13) [for 'to St Johns Wood' read:] 'to the Avenue Road.'

Vol. II, p. 331 (after p. 236, 1.24) '...was very remarkable, usually taking the form of short sermons and essays written wholly for his own pleasure. Many of these were really remarkable, and one written when he could not be more than 10 years old his tutor Mr Weldon introduced into one of his own sermons. For a short time...'

Vol. II, p. 332 (after p. 236, 1.32) '...for the University under tutors. His disposition one may say was *faultless*; indeed none of us can remember ever seeing him angry or ever ruffled in temper or known him act otherwise than with the most perfect consideration for others and his modesty and humility were among the leading qualities of his disposition. His intellectual tendencies, though at first tending towards mathematics, took eventually more distinctly the direction of classics, logic &c to which he added a most ardent love of natural science. At one time he followed photography with great success doing all the chemical work himself: but, finding it clashed with his studies, he relinquished it. He went to Exeter College...'

Vol. II, p. 335 (after p. 237, 1.16) '...far stronger brother! We took great delight during his absence in fitting up a bedroom for him, his brother John joining with great zeal in making it comfortable (our house being rather deficient in bedrooms) and our dear boy on his return was quite pleased with what we had done – He had been excessively charmed with the place...'

Vol. II, p. 338 (p. 238, 1.19 reads:) '...but a medical man who was attending Gilbert saw him...'

Vol. II, p. 339 (p. 238, 1.28 reads:) '...hardly able to walk and the Doctor coming to see Gilbert at once said it was rheumatism...'

Vol. II, p. 339 (after p. 238, l.33) '...unable to move hand or foot – I had to be out that day at Salisbury to attend the first meeting of the restoration committee (alas that it should have so happened!!!) At night I found him very bad and the next day the same. We then with great difficulty carried him down to a larger room.

On Saturday he seemed better the rheumatism having left his limbs in a considerable degree but the Doctor announced that his heart was (as he said slightly) affected and now suggested our calling in a physician – foolishly, I doubted and hesitated and lost this day (Alas! Alas! Alas!) – Meanwhile Leeches [?] were applied to the heart – On Sunday morning I went to town for a physician who came in the afternoon and pronounced the heart to be *very much* affected and prescribed a blister and nourishing food. He did not suffer from pain but chiefly from rapidity of respiration. Now commenced the hours of serious alarm, for hitherto we had not thought very seriously of the attack. He had been somewhat delirious at times but during Sunday night he came more so. I had several times directed his thoughts a little to religious subjects when he always answered me in a quiet and cheerful manner without showing any alarm. On Sunday night he expressed a desire for me to read a service with him which I did, selecting portions of the Litany, the confession from the Communion and portions of the Service for the Visitation of the Sick – He joined in a fervent though not impassioned manner and I afterwards found that he thought he was in a Chapel.

All the earlier half of the night he was extremely rambling though not distressed, nor did his wanderings take a religious form. About six in the morning, however, on waking up from a short sleep he spontaneously showed an extraordinary intensity of religious fervour. Praying aloud and with *great earnestness* both for himself and his brothers &c suiting his prayers to what he supposed to be their needs and expressing many religious sentiments and the vanity of earthly pleasures and pursuits etc. I was asleep during most of this, which I deeply regret, but I was awakened at last by his earnest prayers – the first of which I heard was 'Oh Lord Jesus Christ have mercy on my body and soul', which was followed by several others.

After this he went to sleep again for a time and during this the nurse left the room asking me to watch him. Then commenced a scene which I can never forget though its very intensity and its stunning nature has in part driven its details from my memory!

He seemed to wake from some fearful dream, and with the fullest conviction that he was in the world of Spirits. He told me he had seen the torments of the lost, and he was filled with the most intense horror. The whole character of his countenance was changed and his diction, his voice and manner had become more solemn and impressive than anything I ever heard. He in the most intensely solemn manner desired to confess to me everything he could think of that he had done wrong – and poured forth the most earnest entreaties for forgiveness – his words being eloquent beyond description, his mode of diction intensely forcible and precise, and his whole manner that of a person under some preternatural influence. I doubt not that God had made up for our neglect in not calling his mind to his religious state by preternaturally revealing to him his danger and exciting his mind to every process of preparation for death. First his asking overnight for short service next his fervid prayers earlier in the morning and held this by the terrors of 'the valley of the Shadow of Death' exciting him to the most earnest repentance and conviction of Sin – with the most agonizing crys for forgiveness and for 'holiness' accompanied by formal and distinct confession. Still, however, no comfort as yet came, and after being with him for some time I asked if he would like to see our excellent clergyman Mr Hough, which he at once most earnestly fell in with though clouded with a delusion as to his being in the world of spirits, which led him to pray that the 'Spirit of Mr Hough' might be sent to him. While I was away the same terror kept possession of him, his brother John was with him and had even to hold him to prevent his hurting himself as he had some notion of attonning [sic] his Sin by causing himself pain.

When Mr Hough arrived he at once began to apply to him the Consolations of the Gospel but he long resisted them as inapplicable to himself protesting his sinfulness and crying out for *holiness*. He once said that he would wish to be crushed to atoms if '*one attom* [sic] could be made holy as God is holy.' He also said that he had often for hours together entreated God for *holiness* – which we have other reasons to think was literally true as his brother Gilbert who slept next to him when at Hampstead tells us he had often heard him praying aloud in the middle of the night. Once when John was with him he chanted part of the De profundis in latin. Every expression which was though distressing excitement was devout though he in the most clever manner answered every argument of consolation and threw it off from *himself* [sic].

At length Mr Hough kneeled down and prayed over him most beautifully but even then he argued against the applicability of what was prayed for to his own case. Finally, however, Mr Hough solemnly invoked the Holy Spirit upon him – When, as if by a Miracle, the whole scene was changed, – his terror and distress were instantly dispelled and he joined with quiet trustful earnestness in Mr Hough's prayers and in taking some refreshment he became placid and comfortable. The only thing he said afterwards bearing upon the scene which he had passed through was after we had left the room when he said to his nurse 'Don't you see those spirits there?' And when she said he must have been dreaming about them he said 'Oh! thats jolly then it must have been a Vision' after which he went to sleep.

It seems to me and several persons to whom I have narrated the circumstances, seem to think it probable that there was in all this an antagonistic influence. This Divine influence exciting him to what was needful to his salvation and the enemy attempting to counteract this by suggesting feelings of despair – but that this adverse influence was suddenly and semi-miraculously dispelled on the invocation of the Holy Spirit. Certainly the whole scene was the most solemn and the most tremendous I have ever almost heard of and I cannot doubt that it was ordered by the allwise God to perfect his preparation for what was so soon to follow. And therefore I thank God for it, and under God I shall ever feel grateful to Mr Hough for his ministrations at this time of extreme need when flesh and heart were failing.

After this his remaining hours were a blank. He slept a little – and his mind wandered a good deal but not in a manner to indicate any mental distress at all – And even when a paroxysm of violent delirium came on later in the day so that we had to hold him it did not take a distressing form or indeed show any feelings even of discomfort. After this paroxysm he sunk into a state of exhaustion and insensibility which we at first mistook for sleep but which to our indescribable distress and anguish soon showed itself to be the precursor of dissolution. Even the medical attendant who was with him within half an hour of his death had no idea of his state and was to meet the Physician in an hour or two. He departed without pain and apparently without consciousness at about half past three in the afternoon of Monday January 30 1865 (p. 239, 1.12) and was interred in Petersham churchyard on the following Saturday.

I earnestly pray God never to let his image be dimmed in my memory but to keep it ever fresh in my thoughts. I doubt not that our Gracious God will make his dear soul an object ever precious in his sight – and train it to ever higher and more exalted happiness. He was a choice spirit and one among ten thousands for the truest amiability united with very high mental powers.

I will endeavour to state in another volume a little of what we received as the testimony of those who knew him at college and than which nothing could be more *consoling and cheering.*

Laus Deo March 24 1865.' [end of volume]

Vol. III [begins with letter to the Editor of *The Times* from Scott about 'The Designs for the Law Courts,' 1st July 1868, pasted in.]

Sir, – Might I be permitted, without a thought of entering into the controversy on the relative claims of competitors, to offer a few words in correction of an opinion expressed in your article on the subject in your impression of yesterday, which was, I think, formed in the absence of full information on one point, and which might, if uncorrected, tend to injustice towards my profession, and to the prejudice of future competitions for the erection of public works?

You express an opinion that "to the architects it (the Government) has no obligation at all" that "they have been requested to exhibit designs, for which designs they have been well paid," and that "the architects, having been remunerated for their labour, had then no claim whatever legal or moral, upon the nation," and you draw from this the inference that the Government might have refused to employ any of the architects whom they had invited to devote their labours to this almost herculean work.

As they have not acted on this principle, it is the less important to controvert it in this case, but, as such a view would tend to deter architects from responding to future invitations of this kind, it may be important, in the public interests, to inquire into its correctness.

Now, it is frequent, in inviting a select number of architects to complete, to stipulate that each shall receive a sort of honorarium as an acknowledgement of his services, and in aid, at the least, of the actual outlay incurred. This honorarium, however, is in no degree intended to represent the value of his design, though, in some instances, as in the present, that design may remain in the hands of the party inviting the competition.

In the present case, I have heard several competitors say that the amount offered fell short of the outlay in actual money, leaving the entire labour and study of the architect without any remuneration.

What that labour was I may describe, from my own experience, as almost continuous study for three quarters of a year, involving absence for fully half my time from ordinary business, and the almost entire absorption of my thoughts from other subjects. Of this time and study at least five-sixths were devoted in my case to the arrangement of the plans.

What, then, is the inducement to enter upon these most laborious undertakings? Surely none but the confidence that the competitor whose work should be most approved would be appointed to carry it into execution.

The competitors, however, in the present instance, did not leave it as a matter of mere personal and honourable confidence. The work was too herculean to be left in any degree in doubt, and they accordingly, before accepting the invitation, made a direct stipulation that he who might be considered to have acquitted himself best should be appointed architect to the building.

The words of their communication to the Commission, dated the 2d of March, 1866, are as follows:-

"On the second point" (viz., the reservation of the power of not engaging any of the selected architects) "we take the liberty of remarking, firstly, that by the selection of six architects" (afterwards increased to 11) "the Commissioners have virtually expressed their confidence in any one of them as the one whom they would commission to carry out the work – the selection of that one is the natural object of the competition; for it is unreasonable to suppose that any one of the designs submitted will be actually adopted. Such is never the case, either with or without competition, as the designs actually adopted are, or ought to be, not the result of a single impulse, but of the united and studious labours of the architect with his employers, and with the help, in such a case as this, of those practically conversant with the actual working of every department and with every practical detail. We, therefore, respectfully submit that the architect who is thought by the judges to have acquitted himself best in the competition should be the one to be intrusted with the carrying out of the work, though his actual design may be deviated from, no matter how widely, in the actual execution."

This stipulation was agreed to by the Commission and the Treasury.

Having said thus much in the public interests and those of the professors of my art, I wish to add that I am in no degree personally interested in the result of the recent competition, having as long ago as the 18th of December, 1867, formally withdrawn myself therefrom. My reason for doing so was this:- I had suggested to the Treasury some doubts as to the accordance of a divided award with the terms of the competition, but had stated that if the judges should, after hearing these suggestions, reaffirm such award, I would abide by their opinion, as being the parties to whose judgment we had all voluntarily submitted. When, then, I heard that the judges had re-affirmed their award, I wrote a formal letter to the Commission withdrawing myself from all further participation in the competition, and consequently at the time of the final decision I had ceased to be a competitor.

Having thus become "an outsider," I may perhaps be allowed to add, in justice to myself, that though the assessors, in reporting on the internal arrangements, had awarded the greatest number of first marks to Mr Barry and the second greatest number to myself, they did so before receiving the returns from the heads of the law offices, who awarded the greatest number to myself and the second greatest number to Mr Waterhouse.

I am aware of some important faults in my arrangement (as judged by the instructions), which arose from my imprudently acting, in one instance at least, on my own convictions rather than on the views of the Commission, and Mr Barry was rather specially strong on points where I was considered deficient; having, in fact, made some very clever and original arrangements for which he deserves full credit. Nevertheless, I believe there were not wanting some who viewed my design – taking arrangement and architecture jointly – to have claims to the first position.

Such claims, however, whether good or bad, I voluntarily withdrew; and whether or not the final decision be logically correct, I cannot but rejoice that this great work has fallen into the hands of an architect of the highest claim of talent, and in whom, without derogating from the talents of his competitors, we may feel full confidence that he will produce a building worthy of our age and country.

I have the honour to be, Sir, your obedient servant,
Geo. Gilbert Scott

31, Spring-gardens, July 1. 1868'

Vol. III, p. 5 'April 21 – 1865. What I have stated of the religious circumstances which accompanied the last illness of my dear son Albert is amply backed by the testimonies we receive as to the state of his mind while in health. His two tutors while at home (Mr Probert and Mr Surridge), his College tutor (Mr [gap in original]) and several of his college friends all bear witness to the religious

456

tone of his mind and conversation. But I would especially mention the statements of one of his friends – Mr Ward. I will endeavour to annex copies of several letters from these gentlemen but will mention in addition to what is contained in them a little of what I have personally heard from Mr Ward.

I find that Albert had frequent and lengthened conversations, sometimes amounting to friendly discussions with this gentleman on various abstract subjects. On these occasions Mr Ward tells us that Albert always selected subjects of a high class such as justice, goodness and the moral Government of God – and other religious topics which he describes him as discussing with a very high tone of thought and feeling and in a manner which showed that they were the chosen subjects of thought with him. He speaks of his conversations on such subjects being in a very high degree interesting and improving and at the same time characterised by a remarkable degree of humility and self-negation. He was (says Mr W) evidently seeking in all such conversations for truth, and the moment he saw reason to think he had been mistaken in any line of argument he had been following, he instantly yielded without an attempt or thought of pressing it a moment longer...' [and more in the same vein to p. 9:] '...All these noble testimonies on the one hand tend to add poignancy to our grief but on the other minister to us unspeakable consolation. To have lost *such* a son is a blow most hard to bear yet that a son thus lost to us has shown such tokens of preparation for an infinitely higher destiny than he could have aimed at in this life is an alleviation for which we have infinite cause for thankfulness! We may well say with a certain nobleman who had lost a son of great promise and excellence 'My dead son is more to me than any living son I know of.'

I will mention that...' (p. 239, l.20).

Vol. III, p. 22 (after p. 240, l.27) '...alas too little consulted. I was present at her funeral in the churchyard of K--- church Alford and united [?] parish [?] with her dear Brother in Law Henry Oldrid. Thus have I recorded three losses during a space of only about 12½ months! Oh My God! I entreat thee long to spare any repetition of such visitations! Bless those which thou hast seen good to send us to our souls, to drawing us nearer to thee and to making us dear to ourselves, heart and soul, to thy service! but visit us not again as thou hast lately visited us! spare to us the remnant of our dear family that thou hast left us and bless them with every temporal and spiritual blessing in Christ Jesus. Let them and us feel that the very object of our existence is to serve obey and honour thee, purge out of us every thing that offends thee and breathe into us by thy Holy Spirit every Christian grace and virtue. Thou hast made severe break up in our family both of our own generation and that which is rising. Oh do thou now bless both! Spare the brothers and sisters and others of our own generation to serve thee to a good old age in happiness and comfort and Oh spare the rising generation to live long in thy service and long to enjoy every blessing at thy hands while they devote their lives and the abilities which thou givest them to thy service and the good – spiritual and temporal of thy creatures and Oh let the memory of them whom thou hast in thy mercy taken from us be ever precious to our souls as all trust that their souls are to thee! Let thy mercy lighten upon us, oh Our God, and let our trust ever be in thee! But never let us forget our duty towards thee our God! Let us oppose every corrupt influence both from without and within, let us mortify every sinful affection and tendency and wage daily and hourly war against our corrupt nature. Oh that thou wouldst rend the heavens, oh our God and come down and wouldst destroy the corruption of the heart of man! Till then, however, send us thy Holy Spirit to chase out of us every sin and to enable us to serve thee and to uphold our faith in thy word and in the one and only means thou hast provided for our safety! Hear this oh our God for ourselves our children and all we love for Jesus Christ's sake Amen!'

Vol. III, pp. 29-39 'Thoughts on the present position of the Gothic Revival April 1865' (pp. 225-229).

Vol. III, p. 37 (p. 228, 1.26) [for 'a slight infusion' read:] 'a smacking.'

Vol. III, p. 47 (after p. 243, 1.15) '...and subsequently his successor – Being without capital this arrangement though very advantageous entailed for many years a pecuniary burden which was followed by others arising from the necessity of buying off undesirable partners, so that though he fell into most active practice it was *very long* clogged with a constant drain upon its returns. About 1846 he married ...'

Vol. III, p. 56 (after p. 246, 1.20) '...not far divided. Again, again I say Make *me* to be numbered with thy Saints in glory everlasting!
    (after 1.26) '...glory in his strength! He leaves 13 or rather 14 children who with his admirable and most excellent and pious widow, I make no doubt will be blessed by that God whom he and she have so faithfully and constantly served.
    He was followed to the grave by I believe *all* the medical men in Brighton. His clerical friend Mr Smith – declared after the funeral that he had never met with a more thorough going consistent Christian and a man more estimable in any relation of life and that he never expected to find his equal. 'The Memory of the just (righteous) is Blessed!' I hope that his different friends will contribute [illegible word] from their own knowledge to a sketch of his character, conduct and course of Christian life. All his brothers were present at the funeral and *many* others both friends and relatives. Oh Lord withdraw now thy hand and spare our family from further bereavements – Let it repent Thee concerning thy servants for Thou hast afflicted us *very sore*!'

Vol. III, p. 59 (p. 247, l.3 reads:) 'March 10th 1872

I have neglected this little chronicle now for nearly seven years. Years of mercy and prosperity in most respects. The Prayer with which I closed it was answered for some few years, so far at least as related to our more immediate circle. My Brother Thomas lost his third son, Nathaniel Gilbert, a few years back – an excellent youth – and my Brother William lost very recently a daughter – both of consumption, – My Brother Melville, too, lost his eldest boy a few years back, an admirable child. Death came nearer to us on Oct 19th 1869 when my Eldest Brother lost his wife, my own Dear Wife's eldest sister, a most admirable and pious person.

Just a few years later, October 19th, 1870, I was myself threatened with fatal disease ...' p. 60 (p. 247, l.15) '...my usual engagements. Lord spare me and forgive my great unworthiness and unprofitableness!

Now, after yet another year, a terrible blow has fallen upon me...'

Vol. III, p. 62 (after p. 248, l.10) '...snatched away from us during sleep!!! How did I, and do I still, blame myself for a thousand little things I might have done but did not think to do! How many things I might have said but did not think to say! Oh! if I could have but one more year more of her dear companionship, how much more affectionate, considerate, kind and studious of her happiness would I be! but oh! It is now too late – Oh! Lord forgive my thoughtlessness, my ignorance and my negligences! Oh my dearest wife, if thou canst hear me now forgive the faults which thou knowest but too well!

Oh! Lord God, bless my sons, both those who are now established in their profession and the younger two of whom one, Dear Alwyne, has done little more than select his profession and the other, Dear Dukinfield, has hardly though of what his calling is to be! Oh Lord Bless this terrible affliction to me and to them and, if it be thy blessed will, spare me to see my sons well established both in the earthly pursuits and also in the pursuit of heavenly things and devoted – heart and soul – to thy blessed service. Amen.

Among my dearest wife's recent papers written apparently on the Saturday night (or rather the Sunday morning) immediately preceding Xmas day I find the following:

Xmas 1871, Saturday 12.40

'There they are all three and one (John) away – Gilbert tells me tonight Dr H(ayman) did not think he would live when he was so ill at Eastbourne – and John has been almost as ill and who can tell what may occur – and oh when I am gone and Dear G(eorge) may not live very long – who will pray for them – who will ask for God's tender mercy for them. I know they pray for themselves, but D(ukinfield) is very young, Oh may he and all be kept in the narrow path which leads on safely to God's throne in heaven – and may we all meet in bliss and joy there through the tender love of Jesus and the Holy Ghost Amen.'

It is clear from this as it is from many other evidences that my dearest wife did not share in the encouraging opinion of her Physician, but anticipated a speedy removal. I find a memorandum on a slate written a year before while suffering similarly, directing several little matters to be attended to in case of her decease – and again, only some three weeks before it occurred, she wrote other directions and told her maid to inform me where to find them and several times she had said things to the same purpose to myself. I fear that my illness, already alluded to, that of my son Gilbert last summer, and that of my son John this winter (the latter being at the same time with that of the Prince of Wales about which she felt intensely) had together a serious effect on her health and tended to aggravate this last attack.

Her loss is to me that of one of the wisest and best of earthly companions...'

Vol. III, p. 68 (after p. 248, l.34) '...None came to her and went away empty handed. At St Johns Wood, at Hampstead, at Ham, and finally at Godstone – this characteristic is well known. Nor did she forsake the poor of the district she had left. Even at the watering place where circumstances at one time compelled her to reside much the same practice was continued.

She was a truly devout and pious person – Her diaries and papers are full of devotional and pious expressions and sentiments. She took a great delight in the compilation of prayers for family use. So much so that, as a rule, we customarily made and still make use of her prayers – I find her memoranda and papers full of the materials of these compilations. They are very excellent – They are taken from all sources within her reach. Mainly, perhaps, from Jeremy Taylor, but largely from different portions [?] of old litergies [sic] &c and which she could meet with. I hope to print some of these admirable and useful compilations. To be continued D.V. GGS!'

Vol. III, p. 70 'March 12 – I do not recollect whether in the earlier portions of these notes I have gone into any particulars as to my marriage. My dearest wife was my second cousin; her mother being the daughter of Mr John William Scott of Grimblethorpe Hall and subsequently of – Lincoln. This the elder brother of my grandfather. My mother in law married an excellent man, Mr J. Oldrid of Boston. She had known my father in their youth...' (p. 249, l.5)

Vol. III, p. 73 (after p. 250, l.2) '...happiness together. Now of these four, *three* are in the grave! As indeed are several others of our party old and young. My Grandfather and Aunt Gilbert as well as my dear parents are gone in the course of nature. Dear Nathaniel Gilbert died only a year and a half after our happy meeting – Euphemia 37 years later Sam and Mary Jane were children but they have departed now these 7 or 8 years and now my darling Carry – the life and soul of the party – has followed at a distance of about 43 years. Helen is still living and is kindly helping me in my sad bereavement.

I well remember...'

Appendix 1

Vol. III, p. 75 (after p. 250, l.14) '...greatly fostered. On my return to Gawcott, however, my Mother discovered my feelings with a woman's instinct – as did my sister Phimy – then engaged to Henry Oldrid – and my Mother rather scornfully dissuaded me from encouraging them, saying that Mr Oldrid would think we had laid a scheme to get his property &c – so I exerted myself to forget my feelings and the more so as I was not 20 years old, with no prospect of providing for myself. I saw my dearest Carry again...'

Vol. III, p. 77 (after p. 250, l.19) '...about 1833. Two years later, however, just after my dear father's death, I was at Wappenham, when my dear Mother called me aside and told me that I should meet my cousin Carry at Gawcott, where my sister then married and Henry Oldrid lived and that if I found my old feelings return I might consider that her objections were removed. This hint gave new life to my old love which instantly resuscitated and in the course of the summer of 1835 we were engaged...'

Vol. III, p. 81 (p. 251, l.10 reads:) '...we removed (I think in 1844) to the Avenue Road, St Johns Wood ...'

Vol. III, p. 81 (p. 251, l.16) [for 'straitened' read:] 'close.'

Vol. III, p. 82 (after p. 251, l.19) '...very prosperous.
Wisdom, charity, purity of heart and piety were her great characteristics.'

Vol. III, p. 86 (after p. 252, l.22) '...to be haunted! I cannot speak from my own experience as I was only occasionally there but all the rest of my family were tremendously troubled with the unearthly visitants, and another year we found that a friend who had taken the same house was still more annoyed by them, and we then discovered that it was noted as a haunted house and that a murder had been once committed there of an heiress by her own uncle!
I recollect on one occasion I had driven my dear wife a long distance inland; so far that it became a question whether we should return by the same way or round by St Lawrence and Ventnor. My wife was for the former – I for the latter. She evidently had a special objection to going on to St Lawrence while I had an instinctive dislike to turning on our own track. While the question was pending, we saw an eccentric looking man dressed in white before us and we agreed to stand by his decision. So driving up to him we asked his advice. He replied to this effect: 'You may go back as you come or you may go on to St Lawrence, if you do so – you will have to drive down a steep hill called St Lawrence's Shoot where a great many people have been killed as you may see by their gravestones in the church yard; so, if you ask me I would advise you to turn your horse's head and go back by the same way that you came.' Seeing that he had produced an impression on my dear wife's mind,

461

he proceeded to say 'When I saw you at a distance I said to myself "there's evil in the road," so if you take my advice you'll turn your horse's head and go back by the way you came.'

My dear wife viewed it as a more than natural intimation, and always believed that some ill would have happened had we gone counter to this strange man's advice.

I remember telling the story to the late Lord Yarborough when he recognised our second sighted monitor saying oh it was old so and so, a half crazed man and went on to say that it was quite right about the grave stones, and that among them was one to an old Gentleman who 'came to an untimely end at the age of ninety one' – This I have since verified. Our last visit...'

Vol. III, p. 94 (after p. 254, l.21) '...life-long sorrow to my dearest wife. I find among her memoranda, a lamentation, a year earlier, on our dear son Albert's leaving us for Oxford. She describes him as her greatest resource and comfort, always ready to consult and advise with her and of kindred tastes loving hard reading on mental subjects as she herself did. What then was her grief when she lost him! I believe she never got over it. I find Dear Albert's papers stowed away as her choicest treasures and truly they deserved it for they were remarkable for both intellectual and religious character.

The very same year, 1865, she was threatened with another sorrow, though it was mercifully averted. We drove down to the Isle of Hayling near Portsmouth to witness the arrival of the French fleet – while there our next son, Alwyn, was suddenly seized with violent fever caught, as we thought, from passing through the hospital of the French Ship Solferino. His attack was *tremendous* but by God's mercy he recovered after a stay there of 6 weeks.'

Vol. III, p. 103 (after p. 256, l.2) '...the deterioration of the Inns.

In 1869 we fancied that Ham did not suit our younger boys and tried long to get a nice furnished house elsewhere: feeling vexatious, at length however we took a gaunt place called Parkhurst high up in Leith Hill. While we lingered at home my dear wife and Dukinfield were simultaneously attacked by scarlet fever and our stay (when we could so) at Parkhurst was a Melancholy and solitary time though in the midst of noble scenery.

We never returned to Ham...'

Vol. III, p. 106 (p. 256, l.14 reads:) '...shortly afterwards she was herself attacked in the heart, our eldest son Gilbert and subsequently our Second Son John were ill and then came our greatest trouble her own illness and departure! brought about mainly I think by her sollicitude [sic] for others.

(after l.19) 'May Almighty God bless us who remain. May He overrule this sad, sad trial for our Souls' Good! May He spare and bless my dear Sons! May He spare me to see them well established in life! May He make us all truly His servants – preserving us from error from temptation from worldliness and every evil way and guiding us in His Service, averting from us all misfortune and all evil, spiritual and temporal, – and may we all make it one of our most special objects in life, after the service and fear of God, to cherish and honour the memory of her who has so long cared for us and to whom our dear Sons owe their religious and moral training and the careful watching over their health and comfort from their birth to the present moment!

Oh God, hear and answer this prayer through Jesus Christ our Lord! AMEN'

Vol. III, p. 111 (after p. 257, 1.8) '...wherever met with. We have many fragments of an irregularly kept diary beginning previously to our marriage and breathing devoted and earnest piety throughout. Her writing rather contrasts with her personal manner of conversation – the latter was full of cheerfulness and hilarity and humour always ready for and looking out for a good joke and keenly alive to wit. The former was melancholy and subdued overdwelling in the gloomy side of what passed. I attribute this to two causes. I think she viewed her diary as a sort of penitential musing in which all the troubles of the soul were to find vent and 2. she was so much alone, owing to my best hours being at business and on journeys that I have no doubt she frequently did feel melancholy and when I returned home jaded with work and often disturbed by severe anxiety and disappointment I fear I did little to enliven her spirits. Still however, we did enjoy much happiness and indulged in many innocent enjoyments and amusements. I always wish I had been musical – She was eminently so but my deficiency led this to lie fallow in a way I deeply regret.'

Vol. III, p. 114 (after p. 257, 1.24) '...devoted friends.

My wife was opposed to Calvinistic views in predestination &c and was most practical in her opinions. She never leaned to High Church views yet much approved many of their practical modes of acting and was never prejudiced against them. Her most intimate friend when at Ham was a Romanist – Lady Huntingtower – an excellent and deeply injured lady...'

Vol. III, p. 116 (p. 258, 1.15, reads:) '...bosom of your God. My *dear* uncle" (the Honbl. Frederick Tollemache, M.P.) "Unites with me in the expression of his sympathy and I feel I cannot thank you sufficiently...'

Vol. III, p. 117 (after p. 258, 1.23) 'In a postscript thanks for photo she speaks of her as one of the most Christian women she has known.

Again she writes:

My Dear Mr Scott

I will not harrow your feelings unnecessarily with a long letter, but I must thank you for the touching note you have exerted yourself to write to me in the midst of your own overwhelming grief. If the prayers...' (p. 258, l.26)
(p. 259, l.17) '...His Kingdom. Oh! I do feel for you so much God be with you. Ever yours sincerely, G.W. Weldon.'

Again he writes (March 9 1872)

My Dear Mr Scott,

Your letter has I assure you deeply affected me. You and your dear wife were among the few friends who had always a secret spot in my memory. The concerns of human life are so varied and entangled and subject to such rapid and complicated changes that friends are not permitted to meet or mature their friendship as they would wish.

You have asked me to put down anything I can remember about her. In general terms I may say that she possessed a mind far superior to the majority of either men or women whom one meets in ordinary life. Her simplicity of character and her thoroughly domestic disposition were very prominent. There was an air of sincerity and sensitiveness of character about her, I have never in my varied experience met with. She was one of those persons whom none knew unless they knew her *well*. There are many little things in themselves mere nothings which I can remember about her, but which in the aggregate make up a rare character. Her personal kindness to me and the touching letter she wrote to me when my dear wife was taken from me, cause me now to call to mind many traits of her character which make me feel more grieved at the sad tidings than perhaps you can well comprehend.

I did not know that your son was so near me, I shall have much pleasure in calling on him after Easter.

With my kindest regards believe me, yours very sincerely, G.W. Weldon.

A poor man who knew her mainly through reading [?] a tract of hers on the destitute poor writes of her as follows:

'I have every reason to believe that Her you know so well is safe within the fold of God, for it could have been nothing less than His infinite love that moved her heart and bosom to feel such love and pity and tenderness for others as her little pamphlet she sent me testified. That love was the love of God so ? free expansive and wide as the ocean billows, free as the winds of heaven that knew no rest until her kind gentle heart had embraced all mankind and any creature she would call her brother or her sister until the time that the fruit was ripe and the harvest was to be gathered, remembering only that the image of God was stamped upon those the world forsook and upon the orphan and him that was ready to perish. She was ever ready to ? Your loss is her gain, you shall go to her but she would not return if she could leave her bright crown of Glory that shall never fade and the saviours side by the throne for such a world as this. Grieve not for them but dry your tears and strive manfully to the end that you and I may also join the crown of never-fading glory.'

I wish I could give extracts from her diaries but they are so melancholy and distressing for me to read that I cannot undertake it at least at present.'

Vol. III, p. 120 [out of sequence in MS: 'THIS to come further on']: 'Our house at Ham belonged to Lord Dysart and was very near to Ham House. We were on very friendly terms with the Tollemache family several members of which resided there.

My wife during a part of her stay there introduced a Scripture reader and subsequently founded a reading room, which has done much good, her charity then as usual was extensive. Our residence there was an old Georgian house founded on one of much earlier date. It has extensive and beautiful gardens and my dearest wife much enjoyed it and regretted leaving on very many accounts.'

Vol. III, p. 127 (after p. 259, l.30) '...very agreeable friendships especially with Mr and Mrs Lane at the Rectory and with Lady – and her family – also with a visitor at the Rectory, Lady ---. We had delightful drives there and back though the latter were very rainy [?] My dearest wife was then attacked, I will not deny for the first time but more seriously than before with symptoms connected with the heart.

Oh! that I had appreciated the danger of these attacks and had taken more precautions. Oh! – that I had taken occasion from then to be more demonstrative in my affection to have been more tender and considerate and to have more carefully avoided my natural fretfulness and irritability and watched every opportunity of showing my love! How sadly and bitterly I repent having got into the way of behaving to the dear companion of my life in a matter of course manner of not restraining in her presence as I should in that of people I cared nothing, for the peevishness [?] and impatience of my temper – not valuing her as I ought and not showing my value and my admiration of her, I feel as if were I to have her back again – were it only for one week or one month or one year, how I would strive to evince my love in every way I could invent but alas! it is too late. Neglected opportunities are gone not to be recalled and I can only grieve and repent and blush at my neglectfulness and indulge in the fruitless amends of cherishing her memory and her virtues and her noble qualities now I have lost her and in showing in any ways I can think of my devotion to her memory and her love.

She had a noble mind – was devoted to reading...'

Vol. III, p. 130 (after p. 260, l.2) '...and read with much avidity. The world of the future shared its intensity in her mind with the world of the past. She believed wholly apart from modern science, in previous races of man – holding that the 1st and 2nd Chapters of Genesis recorded two creations of man. She had a strong conviction of the bodily existence of angels as distinguished from a wholly spiritual existence.

She was much addicted to mental study, a faculty which her sons Gilbert and Albert seem to have inherited from her. Alwyn also possesses it.

She took much interest in my profession and often aided and encouraged and corrected me in its pursuit. Her criticisms to my designs were always true and as I usually followed them, were very serviceable.

My profession and its overbearing and perplexing demands on my time and on my thoughts, though blessed as a means of especially in later years providing her with the means of living in great comfort, were also a cause of much loss of happiness...'

Vol. III, p. 133 (after p. 260, l.27) '...for their material well-being.

My dearest wife had a nice income of her own, which I did not interfere with but left at her own entire disposal. She paid out of it, however, a great deal that I ought to have borne, besides exercising much charity, and yet always had plenty of money at her command often several hundreds of what may be called pocket money.

In appearance my dearest wife was...'

Vol. III, p. 134, (p. 261, l.1) '...She was peculiarly dignified and stately in her deportment and always dressed very handsomely and in the best possible taste. She was perhaps too stout but this added to the importance and dignity of her appearance.

I deeply regret that I never had any portrate [sic] beyond photographs made of her – we always talked of getting Richmond to do this but her constant absence from London interfered. I now want him to do one from the many photographs we possess. His eyes at present prevent this.

My dear wife was fond of drawing and had a great taste for water colours – Had they been fostered she would have been quite an artist but her health interfered much and though we often talked of getting her some high-class professional aid we never did. At her death she had numerous sketches in water colour in hand. She only once ventured in any formal way into print – I wish I had encouraged her to do more. It was a little pamphlet on the state of the lower orders especially in London and is in many and most respects exceedingly good' (p. 261, l.6) 'She was very severe on the economies of the present ministry in their bearings on the poor.'

Vol. III, p. 136 'I ought to have mentioned among our Summer trips one in (I think it was 1856) to the Manchester Art Treasures exhibition. It was one of the most agreeable we ever had.

We went with our two eldest sons by railway to Rugby and Derby and then next day to Matlock. Then we posted through Derbyshire looking at Chatsworth and Haddon on our way to Buxton and then by Staleybridge [?] to Manchester.

We were obliged to be content with plain lodgings wh. were near the Exhibition where we spent our whole [?] days. My dear wife in- [illegible] had a chair and was wheeled from picture to picture. Her delight in the objects of art was unbounded and untiring. Nor were we satiated with our week's inspection. Among smaller enjoyments we had always a most merry luncheon in the open air and the provisions were very good though plain and our party always merry and geneal [sic]. We enjoyed even these interludes most thoroughly. We returned by Lichfield where we stopped a night.

To go back to earlier days I may name the only two occasions on which my dear Carry visited mountainous districts. The first was a little trip into North Wales about, I think, 1845.

We went by railway to Wolverhampton and then posted to the house of our friends Mr and Mrs John Bartlett at Longwood [?] on the south slope of the Wrekin. Mr Bartlett was vicar of Bildwas but being a man of ample means he lived in a house of his [illegible word] in a most exquisite position cut out of a lengthy wood and commanding a noble view of that charming reach of the Severn – with the ruins of the abbey – and in the distance Wenlock Edge and Caer Caradoc.

Mr and Mrs Bartlett were most excellent and delightful people. He is now gone but she, I hear, still living. We spent Sunday there in company with them and some of their friends and on Monday Mr B drove us to see Wenlock Abbey [sic] with which as well as the country round it we were much delighted. The visit was quite a bright spot in our memories.

Whence we next morning took the old Holyhead stage [?] through the Vale of Langolen [sic] to Capel Curig. I persuaded my dear Carry to ride outside through the beautiful Vale and again when we approached the Snowdonian mountains. We had however a severe fright there and incurred much real danger from a madly kicking horse.

My dearest wife was perhaps charmed with the scenery, all through our course went [?] by Capel Curig Bangor Beaumaris Carnaevon Llanbeblig Beddgelert Tan y Bwlch Harlech to Barmouth where she joined her sisters and I left her and where she spent a very agreeable time. I met her at the close of it at Chester.

In 1847 we made a visit to the Lakes with our second son John then 6 years old. We went on the way to see Dukinfield in Cheshire from the interest my wife felt in the old Hall there as the ancient seat of Sir Henry Dukinfield's family.

But our tour was not a fortunate one for she was taken ill at Low wood [?] and was laid up a week there thus losing nearly all the pleasure of her trip. We were there when I heard of my first cathedral appointment – Ely.'

Vol. III, p. 143 'I have designed what I trust will be a beautiful monument to my ever dearest Carry – It is to be a low altar tomb, parts of white marble and in part of polished granite. The upper stone which is of marble will have a very richly floreated cross, the foliage being partly conventionalised and partly natural, the latter carrying out her intense love of flowers and of botany. On

either side of the cross two of the beatitudes will be inscribed which especially characterized her two more prominent virtues:
BLESSED-ARE-THE-*PURE-IN-HEART*-FOR-THEY-SHALL-SEE-GOD
BLESSED-ARE-THE-MERCIFUL-FOR-THEY-SHALL-OBTAIN-MERCY

Purety [sic] of heart and commiseration with the unfortunate were her pre-eminent characteristics though both exercised in especial connection with the cross or with holy religion.

Round the dado will be medallions also symbolizing her special virtues by emblematic figures – *FAITH* – her belief in our holy religion being the one object of her mind; HOPE as illustrating her constant dwelling of her thoughts on the unseen world: CHARITY her great practical virtue; COUNSEL indicating her great practical wisdom; MERCY and PURITY OF HEART is already explained and lastly THE-FEAR-OF-GOD not only as the very guide of her life but as illustrated by her favourite study, the compilation of PRAYERS.

These moral and Christian virtues – I have not taken at random or as a matter of routine, but I can safely aver that they were in a pre-eminent degree the leading features of her character. I might have added to them FORTITUDE as she was gifted with an amount of moral courage which falls to the lot of few. I am [illegible word] preferred to dwell upon her most gentle characteristics and I am sure that in these she was exceeded by but few if by any.'

Vol. III, p. 148 'I write miscellaneous matters as it occurs to me, and I will first mention that my dear wife wished us to understand clearly that our family including her own were derived from the Kentish Scotts.

All members of it who have borne arms, bore these of the Scotts of Kent. I cannot trace them directly into Kent or from Kent but one of the oldest members of the family told us they always heard that they went in early times (from Scotland) into Kent. My wife's grandfather who was father to the Gentleman just alluded to, always urged his sons to remember that they did not belong to certain Lincolnshire Scotts who had lived near them – and it is a tradition among such of our family that remain in Lincolnshire I believe that we are of *Royal* descent – This arises from the Kentish Scotts being in fact *Baliols*. I hope to insert an account of this family. Thus we are related to Baliol who founded the College at Oxford of that name and to John (Scott) of Rotherham, Archbishop of York, who contributed largely to buildings at Cambridge with the University Church and the Schools.

I may mention that my uncle King impaled the Kentish Scott Arms with his own. Mr Burgess of Leicester who married a sister of my Grandfather did the same, as also did, as I have strong reason to believe, Mr Ford who married another sister, I have not had opportunities of tracing it with previous generations, but I think this is proof enough in conjunction with family traditions to prove us to be *Baliols*.'

Vol. III, p. 151 'March 21, 72 / I have probably stated that my dear son Albert from an early age amused himself by writing short sermons, these my dear wife treasured up as his most precious possession.

I fancy she had a good number of them but by some mischance in the short interval since her departure most of them have I fear disappeared to my great distress though I am sure no one did this wittingly.

I can now find only 6 of these little productions of which I hope to give copies. The earliest dated March 53 when he was between 8 and 9 years old.

It is as follows:
'John XXth. 24L 25V
But Thomas (one of the twelve) called Didymus was not with them when Jesus came.   25 The other disciples therefore said unto him we have seen the Lord but he said except I see in his hands the print of the nails and thrust my hand into his side I will not believe.

Here is a proof of unbelief. Thomas would not believe unless he saw Jesus, behold blessed are they which have not seen and yet believe Thomas because he had not seen him would not believe that Christ had risen though he had declared to his disciples that he must be killed and the third day rise again. But the disciples could not understand him and so Thomas could not believe Jesus when he appeared unto them (and) said Peace be unto you and the 2nd time he said to Thomas reach hither thy finger and behold the print of the nails and thrust thy hand into my side and be not faithless but believing – Thomas said My Lord and My God.

If John is the only Evangelist that mentions these things but in St Luke XIV and the 30th V it says that Christ appeared unto his apostles and rebuked them for their unbelief. Now, this proves that other apostles as well as Thomas doubted that the Lord had risen. Therefore he rebuked them and in St Mark L16 V9 [sic] it says that he appeared with the apostles as they sat at meat and upbraided them for their unbelief.

Thomas was one of the 12 who said that he would not be offended at Christ yet he did not believe that he had risen. It was like Peter who said he would follow him wherever he went yet he denied him.'

Left apparently unfinished.

Another is dated Feby 25. 1855 when he was between 10 and 11 years old and is as follows:
'Paul at Antioch or The Model Sermon Acts XIIIth – 16th – 41st
Paul having gone from Antioch in Syria came to Antioch in Pisidia and coming into the synagogue (the place for common worship and the Jews who I suppose had settled there in sufficient numbers as to build themselves a synagogue) he after the example of his divine master taught these on the Sabbath day.

His congregation being of a mixed kind both Jews and Gentiles he addressed himself to them in a manner which would suit both classes that is to say (as Paul himself demonstrates there) "Men of Israel and ye that fear God" by telling them God's mercy and loving kindness towards Israel but how that when that God came among them in human form, how they then took him and nailed him to the Cross although the judge himself declares "I find in him no fault at all" (John XVIII 38th).

To show the Jews and reprove them for their ungrateful conduct and to warn the Gentiles not to abuse the mercies of God; he proceeds to add the narration of Christ's resurrection and proves that David prophesied of this where he says "thou shalt not suffer thine holy one to see corruption." He next proceeds to show that Christ justifies those that believe from which (he adds) ye could not be justified by the law of Moses and in these two verses is contained the form and substance of the Christian faith (38 and 39).

Next comes a warning taken from the Prophets to those who despise the atonement of Christ and with this end a speech which (next to our Lord's discourse) I think is one of the best ever spoken on earth and which may be truly called The Model Sermon

Albert Henry Scott, Febry 25. 1855'

'Mark XIII part of the 37th V "watch"'

In the text before us is contained one of the most important and necessary maxims one of (the) least attended to in the Holy Scriptures: it contains a warning it contains a promise and it contains an encouragement when fighting against the temptations of the world the flesh and the devil. Yes! all these are contained in this one small word "watch".

It warns me from entering the paths of wickedness and from doing anything which might cause us to fear for the salvation of our souls when we shall be judged on that day which might arrive even at this very instant the time of which "knoweth no man" we must not deviate from the path of duty in the least we must not think that we can just depart and afterwards return blinding and shifting our conscience by thinking that *perhaps* we may afterwards be reconciled to God in his mercy. No, he knows not when "the master of the house cometh" therefore we must "watch".

We must not listen to the evil whispering of the devil or our own fleshly lusts which try to persuade that there is no harm in it and that it cannot be wrong to enjoy these pleasures which it says prevent our minds from getting heavy and dull; but which truly poison our souls and unfit us for the service of God, so we must not listen to these persuavments, do wrong, we must "watch". Our text thus gives us a warning and it also contains a promise, for if we watch and resist the devil we know that he will flee from us and we shall confess "and to him that overcometh will God give to eat of the tree of life which is in the midst of the Paradise of God," let us therefore if we wish to gain this, "watch".

However, besides a promise it also contains an encouragement to bear us wh. in the battles between good and evil, when we are ready to fall from exhaustion let us be borne up with the thought of that Glory which awaits us in (the) Kingdom of heaven to which we cannot enter but through much tribulation, and let us act up to the high calling and remember that if we would be ready when the Lord cometh we must "watch".

Let us strive to enter in at the strait gate even by a crucified Saviour, and let us watch that saviouring coming, for the day of our Lord Jesus Christ, to whom with the Father and the Holy Spirit be ascribed glory, honour, majesty and dominion now and for ever. Amen.'

'Isaiah 1 (2-3)

Hear o heavens and give ear o earth for the Lord hath spoken. I have nourished and brought up children and they have rebelled against me. The ox knowether his owner and the ass his master's crib but Israel doth not know my people doth not consider.

Whenever we consider (and it is a thought that will occur at least sometimes to all of us) the natural state of fallen man, the state of man by nature, its wretchedness, its misery and its hopelessness; the feeling or no, that we are of ourselves utterly undone and without hope, that of ourselves we are unable in the least degree to help ourselves or in any way to ameliorate [?] our condition, not only make to be truly happy in this world but also unable to free ourselves from dread of what will be our fate in that other world, of that lake of fire that cannot be quenched and those torments which shall never cease. To men (in) such a state of wretchedness the tidings of a saviour who is willing and able to deliver them from their state of misery, and to lead them on to blessed immortality should have been received with universal joy and thankfulness and when they were told that it was their father whom they had so grievously offended who had sent them this saviour, this should have filled their heart with joy and thankfulness.

The truths of the Bible though frequently conveyed to other individuals and nations yet they are equally applicable to ourselves as well as to those to whom they were first addressed. Has not God ample reason to complain that we whom he has made his children by baptism when he has treated as his sons, that we have rebelled against him and that when the tidings of the Gospel were first made known to us, we turned from it a grievous and heavy thing instead of clinging to it as the only means whereby we can be saved. In our physical life we do not act so. If anything happens which tenders the amputation of an arm or a leg necessary to the preservation of our temporal life, which at the longest can endure but a few short and troubled years, do we not willingly undergo a most painful operation rather than enjoy a few hours of ease and then die? But in spiritual affairs where our spiritual life is at stake we think it too grievous a thing to repent and amend our lives but desire to live on in our old courses and reckless of the future. Ought this to be su. ought we poor miserable sinners utterly make of ourselves to help ourselves [sic]. Should not we eagerly and anxiously cling to that one hope of salvation set forth by Christ Jesus? The drowning man eagerly clutches a plank as a means of assistance, but those in a state of spiritual ? refuse the hand held out for their deliverance. Has not God these just reasons for this accusation – I have brought up children but they have rebelled against me! The ox knoweth his owner and the ass his masters crib but Israel doth not know, my people doth not consider! Even the brute animals of creation know those who treat them with kindness, their instinct teaches them that, but we all who are endowed with reason and abilities will act as though we knew not that God was our father or considered not what was due to him as such and should the case be so. Should man, whom God made Lord over all brute creatures, should then lie outdone in faithfulness by dumb animals who act upon instinct alone? Certainly not. But why is this the case? One might ask why does not man know God as his father? We have the answer in our text. Simply because he does not consider. The ox and the ass and other animals act entirely by instinct, they cannot reason with themselves why and wherefore, but man is endowed with an understanding heart. He can reason ought to reason, and the cause of his disregard for God is simply that he does not make use of his reason.

We do not mean to say that man is at all of himself by the exercise of his reason to turn to God, but I do mean to say that man, as a free agent has the power to turn to a certain degree which way he thinks fit. I will not enter upon the difficult point how God can order man's heart and yet man be a free agent for that question does not bear on our subject, and what is the greater importance it is one of those questions which no human knowledge can answer, but while we believe we shall be able to understand when our glorified spirits shall enter into the realms of eternal bliss. Let me now lastly deduce from what has been already said a few practical lessons for our admonition and instruction. And first, the former part of my text should teach us to examine our own hearts to see if we are rebellious children, let us ask ourselves are we now leading a life of sin? Now, I would have it clearly understood what I mean. I do not mean by my question do I still continue to sin? Such a question would be presumptuous for there is no man that liveth and sinneth not. But what I mean is am I living a life of habitual sin? Am I still without God in the world? And we should never rest till we can conscientiously answer: I hope to believe that through God's grace I am endeavouring to live a regular [?] life, that I pray God for his mercy to forgive my failings for his Son's sake.

The second part of my text should teach us not to act in religious matters only upon the momentary impulse but to consider before we determine on any matter, will God approve of this? When we have accustomed ourselves to this we shall find that our religion will be more genuine and proceeds more from the heart than before and may God of his infinite mercy grant that in the day of his coming you may find grace in his sight through Jesus Christ our Lord.'

The only two more little sermons I have found are prefaced by a "litany".

"Litany.

In the name of the Father and of the Son and of the Holy Ghost. Lord have mercy upon us *Christ have mercy upon us* Lord have mercy upon us. Jesus the Almighty God and Saviour of Men.

Have mercy upon us our Father.

Thou Lord art in the patterns of meekness; of innocence and simplicity; of truth and sincerity; of chastity and purity of heart; of submission and obedience; of mildness and Gentleness; of charity and goodwill towards men and all other virtues;

Be merciful to us oh Lord Jesus and help us to imitate thee.

From all lying, deceit, cheating and hypocrisy; for all hatred malice and illwill, from ill nature, spitefulness and revenge

Good Lord deliver us. O Lord Jesus deliver us. We Sinners beseech thee to hear us.

Make us to love thee above all things that we may keep thy commandments.

We beseech thee to hear us.

Make us to love our neighbours and companions as ourselves that we may do to them as we will them to do to us; and never deceive them by fraud, lying or deceit.

We beseech thee to hear us.

Keep our thoughts, words, and actions from all impurity and sin, and make them pleasing to thee.

We beseech thee to hear us.

Keep us from being ungrateful to thee the Giver of all Good things we have,

We beseech thee to hear us.

Lamb of God who takest away the sin of the world

Spare us O Lord Jesus

Lamb of God &c

Hear us O Lord Jesus.

Lamb of God &c

Have mercy upon us O Lord Jesus

The Grace &c.

John XVII – 14. "I have given them thy word and the world hath hated them, because they are not of the world, even as I am not of the world."

People are too apt to think that religion and the world can be combined so as not to clash, although if they were told "ye cannot serve God and Mammon" they would not think of denying it; in fact their professions and lives are at variance one with another, they are deceiving themselves. These people forget that the friendship of the world is enmity against God, they forget our text for it seems to imply that because God hath given them his word therefore the *world hath* hated them.

As to Jesus giving his disciples his "word" we see in the eighth verse "For I have given unto them the words which thou gavest me and they have received them". All his sayings, sermons, teachings, had been given him of the Father. Besides the disciples having the word given them it all implies that they receive it or else it would have no effect. Judas heard the word; but he was still by trade a thief, and finally betrayed his Master; yes, we must "receive with meekness the engrafted word which is able to save our souls."

We must follow the pattern of our Lord, for he was not of the world, and the world hated him; he denied himself the pleasures and enjoyments which the world has and profusely scatters around those who offer themselves to her, but she is only an engine of the devil which he employs to execute his wickedness; she offers no hope for the future, she only attempts to blind the eyes of her victims, but on the contrary Christianity shows a bright future and says that these present sufferings are not to be compared to the eternal weight of Glory; but not only does religion give hope for the future but also pleasures and hence even now for its religion that can give sweetest pleasure while we live. Its religion can supply solid comfort when we die.

To be out of the world in a spiritual sense we must deny ourselves all those pleasures which tend to draw off the heart from God, though perhaps there may be no harm in the amusements themselves.

We must give our whole hearts to God. No lurking hankering after the pleasures of this life must be left. We must be ready to say that with us "to live is Christ and to die is gain." God will not take half our hearts though the world may for she knows that if she has any place with us she will soon be able to gain the whole unless we make a bold stand and pluck her out and cast her from us.

Let us resolve this year if we are spared from death to resist the world, the flesh and the devil with all our might through looking to the Captain of our salvation for aid, for he will aid us if we set heartily to work, and if we wish to succeed we must ask his assistance for he is strong though we are weak and though high yet he condescends to stoop to us, let us therefore ascribe to him – even to Jesus Christ with the Father and the Holy Ghost.

Albert H. Scott Jany. 4. 1857   The Grove'

'Isaiah XL. 3. "Prepare ye the way of the Lord and make straight in the desert a highway for our God."

The solemn season of Christmas is drawing near and the Church is as it were watching for the appearance of the bright star in the East: and we had better think how to prepare our souls for the ushering in of the great anniversary of the birth of the Saviour of men.

His first coming was very unlike what his second will be; he came lowly and humble as a helpless infant, born of parents though rich in heavenly gifts, poor and despised with regard to earth: He left his Father whom he loved and reverenced he left his crown of Glory, he left his power, his worship from angels and arcangels [sic] to inherit the sins of the world to bear their punishment, to experience the anger of his Lord Father, to be despised and scorned by those whom by the smallest use of his power he could lay dead at his feet. He – the type of purity came to die the death of the basest malefactor to (be) scourged, mocked and insulted, he left the Glory of the equal with the Father and he counted for the vilest imposter. He left the joy of heaven to

474

become "a man of sorrows and acquainted with grief"; in fact he left the height of happiness for nearly the depth of woe.

But at his second coming he will judge the world on his throne, he will weigh the lives of men and award Glory or punishment.

The four collects for the Sundays in Advent show how we must prepare the way of the Lord: we must gird ourselves to the battle by casting away the works of darkness and putting on us the armour of light, for the Lord will set up his standard and all must enlist either under his banner or under that of his rebellious subject the fallen angel Satan. The reward for the soldier of Christ if he faithfully serves is a crown of glory which fadeth not away; but for the follower of Satan, fire and misery and iron! When therefore ye have equipped yourself stand hopefully, faithfully, lovingly and boldly so that ye may be accounted good and faithful servants fit to enter into the joy of their Lord. We must study God's word which he has given us by praying for his holy spirit and looking for help with faith and patience that we may be strengthened to run the race that is set before us and to fight the good fight of faith. We must attend God's messengers given to us by our fellow men though sinners like ourselves we must pray for them that they may be helped in understanding and preaching this word remembering that for our opportunity of hearing his word we shall have to give account at the day of judgement.

Above all we must seek God's help and assistance by earnest prayer and supplication for we can do nothing without him to keep us from the dangers and trials and temptations of the world the flesh and the devil.

Our hearts are indeed deserts unless they are cheered by the light of the gospel; they are pathless and fruitless and it must be our care to form a way for the approval of our God; we must prepare a goodly light on which the Sun of righteousness can work with pleasure; we must carefully extract all weeds and plant good seeds so that at the Last Day we may be formed an acceptable people in the light of Jesus Christ who with the Father &c &c."

(I think this must have been within a few days before the last, a little before Xmas 1856.)

Alas! That I can find no more. Where oh where are they gone?

Vol. III, p. 185 'I have since found two of the fragments apparently *early* Mark V. 19.

"Howbeit Jesus suffered him not, but saith unto him. Go home to thy friends and tell them how great things the Lord hath done for thee and hath had compassion on thee".

One of the greatest temporal mercies that our Lord performed when on earth was the curing of a species of insanity prevailed in those times. This kind of madness seems to have been one of the greatest curses there were – Through an unseen agency the mind of a man seems to be entirely in the possession of an evil spirit which excites him to all kinds of acts.

Having thus regarded the nature of this malady we will now proceed to the case before us.

The man alluded to in the text seems to have been in a worse state than many, for when our Lord asked the Spirit his name, he replied Legeon [sic] for (he adds) we are many.

Neh. 13th – 16 – 18.

Some people seem to think that this earth is their home, they know it is not and even profess to look forward with joy to the world to come, but this is hypocrisy, for if you look at their lives you can see that though this is but a resting place they live as if they were to be here for ever.

We are placed here to try our hearts by God we are given some commandments which if we obey we shall live in light and glory, but if not in misery and darkness. If we had been left in this state in spite of the glorious promise and dreadful punishment Satan would have had very nearly all of us but God did more than this for he sent his ...''

I have since found another sermon.' (p. 188)

Vol. III, p. 189 'March 26th / The more I reflect on my dearest Carry and the whole history of our married life and of the years of our acquaintance which preceded it, the stronger grows my sense of her great and unusual merits and of my own debt of gratitude to her, first for her friendship towards me, then for its ripening with love and at length for a long course (33½ years) of devotion to me and our dear family. I do not believe I could have been half so prosperous without her continual advice and encouragement and her correct discretion and quick perception of what was right in each emergency.

Her religious life must have affected this deeply, though of itself it was a separate matter – for externally she was usually merry, jocose and full of the enjoyment of ordinary matters and ordinary conversation. Mentally she was devoted to deep thinking and difficult reading – but her religious life was another matter, as it was behind a screen which severed it in great measure from her external life. It is only by her posthumous papers that I have become fully aware of its depth and devotion. I cannot read these papers – they are so touching, but I see in them a wholly different phase of my dearest wife's character and one which shows me more than ever her merits and my own utter unworthiness of her GGS.

Oh My God forgive me for my deep, deep unworthiness! Fill my heart with thankfulness for the inestimable blessing thou granted me – fill it with shame for my neglect and want of appreciation of it and my want of due sense of my duties to her – and now that thou hast taken her from me, her most unworthy husband, enable me to devote the rest of my life thou mayest grant me find [?] to thy fear and to obedience to thy commandments and the rules of thy blessed Gospel and then to the enshrining of her memory in my heart to showing it honour and to doing just what under thy guidance she would have wished me to do – Grant this Oh Blessed God for Jesus Christ's Sake AMEN.'

Vol. III, p. 199 (p. 262) 'July 11 – 1872 / I resume after an interval of some seven years that statement of my personal and professional reminiscences...'

Vol. III, p. 220 (after p. 268, l.1) '...wholly irrespective of the merits of the case. I have some years since had one great attack made upon me of this kind. I believe that Mr Beresford Hope though nominally friendly, is only too glad to promote these attacks and it was, I dare say, he who set upon me one of the most vindictive and unscrupulous writers of the age.

I believe I had offended that man a few years before – by perfect accident and that he has always remembered it against me.

I have last week been the subject of an equally virulent attack in another print and I am told that I have to expect another probably this week in the Saturday Review. [in margin:] It did not appear.

I must trust in God and take Courage.

I need not enumerate the criticisms. Most of them are groundless...'

Vol. III, p. 257 (after p. 277, l.17) '...I have already given my reasons for not doing so – The work had been mine – and being mine belonged equally to my wife and family – and to give up what represented in the end about five and twenty thousand pounds which was placed by providence in my hands as a trustee for my family, seemed to me to be an immoral act. The claim of party had grown up artificially...'

Vol. III, p. 271 (after p. 280, l.23) '...by my pupils, assistants, my sons and myself. If I do not live to publish these, I trust my sons *will* and I will also publish a series of my reports on cathedrals and other ancient buildings and my papers read before societies etc. from 1841 onwards.'

Vol. III, p. 277 (after p. 282, l.18) '...passing trackers upwards. *There was no ancient choir screen remaining.*

Subsequently I refitted St Mary's Chapel as a church...'

(p. 283, ll.12-16) [not in MSS at this point]

Vol. III, p. 284 (p. 285, l.3 to 286, l.17 reads:) 'The chapter house has during this interval been restored I think with much success. All details up to level of cornice with few exceptions were found above this nothing except a single fragment of an octagonal pinnacle. The western window was found to have been like the others originally in its tracery but to have been altered to a 5 light window by Abbot Byrchesten.

The cloister has been partially restored, with much care...'

Vol. III, p. 288 (pp. 287, ll.23-28 read:) 'I am now planning the restoration of Northern Portals.'

Vol. III, p. 289 (pp. 291-298 reads:) 'Lichfield / My work here was mainly the opening out and rearrangement of the choir.

This had been wholly altered by Wyatt to the extent of absolutely severing it from the church by partitions and glazing! So that in our generation no one had seen the nave and choir together.

The arcade of the choir proper – i.e. so far as the stalls extended – was internally early decorated like the nave, though the back of the same arcade towards the aisles was transitional and all the Eastern bays *late* decorated. This seemed little short of miraculous but on removing the plaster which enveloped this arcade (and which was done or begun before my appointment and under my predecessor Mr Sydney Smirke), it was found that the early decorated work was a mere sham in *Roman cement, spikes and tar cord* and that the real arcade was of two dates transitional with late decorated engrafted upon it. The unravelling of this cost me infinite study and it was the happy survival of one or two stones which were the sole clue to the inigma [sic] but by their help, the whole was at length unravelled and accurately restored. It was the greatest puzzle I ever had to solve. We brought back the altar from the east end of the Lady Chapel to its old place and erected behind it a rich [?] reredos. We made to the west a [illegible word] screen of Iron. Iron grilles were to have backed the stalls but have not yet been executed, so that this from being the *closest* of choirs is now the *openest*.

The stonework of the whole interior was cleansed from yellow wash and restored where needful. The west win. given by James, Duke of York has been renewed – in character with the west front. More recently a monument to Bishop Lonsdale has been erected to the north of the altar [?] and sedilia formed of some old canopies formerly belonging to the Choir Screen erected to the north. At the back of which in the aisle, is erected a monument to Dean Howard with a canopy formed from the same screen. The effigy of the Bishop is by Watts and that of the Dean by Armstead. My dear friend the Precentor Hutchinson was the Prime Mover and the very soul of this work. He was supported by Dean Howard and followed up by Archdeacon Moore.

A wretched foreman of masons who accompanied Professor Willis in his inventory and with him discovered in the triforium of the transept the setting out of the early English triforium – deliberately destroyed them without any communication with me to my intense disgust.

I have had made a [?] of drawings [?] of the decayed work of the side of the nave as a *help* to future restorers.

(The woodwork by Mr Evans of Ellaston)'

Vol. III, p. 296 (pp. 298-300 reads:) 'Peterborough / My works here have been slight, and having mainly safety as their object – much should be done but there are no friends and little zeal. The decoration of the Choir ceiling might [?] be [?] mentioned [?]'

Vol. III, p. 297 (after p. 288, l.4) 'Hereford / The western tower having fallen about 1798, the nave had been wretchedly dealt with by Wyatt. In our own day Cottingham had undertaken extensive works including the almost entire reconstruction of the piers of the central tower and choir. The rebuilding of the eastern end of Lady Chapel, the reroofing of the same, opening out of the central lantern, the decoration [!] of the vaulting of the nave etc. etc. He had entirely removed all the choir fittings which had been for 20 years I believe, stowed away in the crypt.

My work was to continue his and complete the restoration of the Eastern parts of the church. I did it as conservatively as possible though the excessive decay of the stone presented serious difficulties. I refer to the work rather than describe it.

The choir had gone through the central tower into the nave but having been long dismantled and reduced to its mere *elements*, I felt at liberty (I am not sure how justified) to adopt an arrangement founded rather upon utility than history. I limited the choir to the (short) Eastern arm (using the old stalls and canopies) and erected [?] there [?] an open screen of metal.

I do not think that Cottingham had found...' (p. 291, ll.3-17) '...Octavius Hudson. I found there a monument to one of the Dentons of Hillesdean – a progenitor of Lord Leicester. I put it up but subsequently found the true fragments of the altar part and applied to Lord L— to restore it but as yet in vain. Cottingham had removed the majority of the tombs but with the help of the Revd Mr Havergal we restored them to their places.

I carried out this work with my excellent friend Dean Dawes for whom I conceived a sincere friendship.

The tower is in a very bad state...' (p. 291, ll.22-28)

Vol. III, p. 305 (pp. 300-38) 'Salisbury / I think I was appointed in 1858.

I made several reports on the state of the Cathedral and at length its restoration was set about. It mainly consisted of renovation of such stones as were severely decayed, a work carried out with the utmost possible care, besides this the foundations were throughout the exterior [?] with concrete etc.

The shafts where marble had disappeared in favour of stone, were retranslated into marble (Devonshire) externally.

The great work however, was the interior of the tower which was crushed in the most frightful manner imaginable. We first introduced a splendid system of diagonal ties (designed by and constructed under Mr Shields) and then proceeded to replace the shattered stonework stone by stone till at length the tower was as strong as when first built – *see my reports* – It is a very fine engineering work. We dare not, however, touch the piers below which buckle inwards at mid height. They must be *watched* and strutted [?] if needful. I trust *not*!

More recently we have restored the interior of the Lady Chapel and choir, restoring the old colouring to a certain extent. That to the Lady Chapel was done while I was ill and is not to my mind at all. That to the Choir has given infinite trouble and is only partially satisfactory. I think it is a comfort that the medallions covered in 1789 are now restored, or recovered (or *un*-covered).

The stallwork etc. is still un-done. We found some carved things at [?] the screen 14th century in S. aisle [?] in E. transept, a very rich work.

See my reports. Builder Mr White clerk of works Mr Hutchins both *first-rate men.*'

Vol. III, p. 311 (pp. 309-311) 'Chichester / My connection with this cathedral arose from the catastrophe which befell the tower in 1863 [sic, it was 1862].

I consider this misfortune due absolutely to the folly of the clerk of the works.

There was much indignation against the architect Mr Slater, but I voluntarily associated him with myself in the work.

The first work was to collect photographs and views – and to search the heap of debris so constantly, perseveringly and diligently as to find and appropriate to its place every detail.

This was ably carried out by my eldest son Gilbert, who worked 6 weeks at it labelling and registering every detail as it was recognised. Happily Mr Slater had in his possession a measured elevation to a large scale drawn by the late resident architect Mr Butler. This was a most happy circumstance – and enabled us to put together all fragments (upon paper) with certainty of correctness, so – One thing with another the whole design was absolutely and indisputably recovered. The work was commenced from its very foundations anew and carried out to the top of the tower without correcting it with the old walls. The connections were then made and the spire subsequently carried up. No settlement has ever shown itself. The piers had been of marble cased with very soft stone. They are now of solid Portland and Purbeck stone set in hard cement. The foundations are on a vast mass of *cement* concrete upon which are cross form piers of Purbeck stone almost meeting one another. The Tower was made 5 to 6 feet higher than the older – because in the 14th century the clerestories and roofs had been raised so as to bury the tower, to that extent I have recently restored the beautiful Lady Chapel, as a memorial to Bishop Gilbert.

The Builder at first was Mr Bushby of Littlehampton. He laid the foundations and carried up a pair of the piers. The contract from that point onward was taken by Messrs Beanland of Bradford, Yorkshire. Clerk of Works Mr Marshall. This is as admirable a piece of masonry as ever was erected, and as faithful a restoration.'

Vol. III, p. 320 (pp. 336-339 read:) 'Gloucester / I had reported on Gloucester many years back while it was under Mr Waller (Fuljambes & Waller) – but that gentleman being obliged to retire for some years owing to ill health and

Mr Fuljambes subsequently retiring, I was appointed. The work has consisted of repairs of stonework carried out under the clerk of the works Mr Ashbee by their own masons and – of the restoration internally of the choir mainly by Mr Brindley. Mr Waller now recovered, has helped me in respect of the porch of which he had detailed measured drawings prepared before the decay had been so complete. We have erected a new reredos on the site of the original one destroyed – a very curious sunk space was formed beneath it communicating with a space under the altar, no doubt for relics.

The stalls and canopies have been carefully restored and as there were no old desk fonts etc. these were designed anew, making use of some remains which had been removed to the Lady Chapel – both as guides and also as part of the work.

The side galleries were removed. The choir screen (a modern one) remains untouched with the organ upon it. The Dean objects to opening the Screen and as the return stalls are complete I am not anxious on this subject. The organ is a good 17th century one and I am anxious to retain it though all parties there condemn it.

We have decorated the vaulting of the choir modernly/moderately [?]. In my opinion successfully and in that of Gambier Parry the *reverse*. He wanted to decorate the panels rather than the ribs – I say the ribs are the very essence of the design and the panels mere accidents and have acted accordingly and *I am convinced rightly*.

The Sedilia had been sadly mutilated but are being restored according to evidence and my best judgment.'

Vol. III, p. 326 (pp. 339-342 read:) 'Ripon / The work here has been chiefly structural reparation.

The two western towers had given way fearfully and have been underbuilt to I think some 12 feet deep, the towers also repaired and restored [?] of all points [?] with iron and made perfectly strong. This was a very difficult work. The towers had to be almost wholly supported by timber shoring and even then the work was difficult and dangerous in a high degree. The central tower was also in a dangerous state but has been rendered substantial – two of its sides (and 3 arches) had been rebuilt in the 16th century while the others remained of the transitional period. The early parts were very infirm and terribly shattered, most of the remainder of the work was ordinary reparation which has been done in a most careful and conservative way. We newly roofed the choir raising the E-Gable to its true pitch – and introducing oak vaulting. The eastern bays had been prepared for stone vaulting, but not so the western ones, we have however continued it throughout and have removed Blore's plaster vaulting and found that its bosses were original oak bosses of the 14th century which seems to show that it *had* oak vaulting. These were reused. The vaulting is slightly decorated.

We restored the canopy work of the stalls much of which had been replaced with 17th century work. The arrangement was difficult and unsatisfactory. The old rood screen remaining, I acted on my principle of not disturbing it, but as the cathedral is also a parish church, the whole parochial congregation has to be crammed into the eastern arm. I found this effected by side galleries and a kind of stage boxes but [?] is now all on the floor. The altar had formerly been a bay in advance as at Selby – but had been carried back, this we retained and removed the Sedilia to suit it.

We removed some horrid papier maché vaulting introduced by the Eccles Commissioners into the transepts and restored (or nearly so) the 15th century roofs.

I am now removing a horrid modern flat ceiling from the nave and introducing oak vaulting founded on that of the transepts at York. They could not afford to raise the roof to its proper pitch, but I hope that this may one day follow. The mullions and tracery introduced in the 14th century into the western lancets were ready to fall and only kept up by cross timbers, we have therefore elected to remove rather than replace it. The stonework which concealed gables of the western portals has also been removed.

The builders were Messrs Ruddle & Thompson, Clerk of Works Mr Clark who ruined his health by his close attention to the work.'

Vol. III, p. 332 (pp. 342-345 read:) 'Worcester / I came in at Worcester as a colleague and backer up to Mr Perkins, the cathedral architect *and* my work has been limited to the fitting up etc. of the choir with some very trifling exceptions. The general restoration and reparation of the church I do not approve but found effected to my hand.

I am using the old stalls but without returns, adding book desks and front seats. I am introducing an open Screen – and grilles over the stalls. I have erected a new reredos, the open screen which occupied that position had been merely a parclose and belonged to the north east transept.

The ceiling of the choir has been decorated under my direction by Mr J Hardman Powell.

The woodwork by Brindley, Grilles etc. by Skidmore.'

Vol. III, p. 335 (pp. 345-349 read:) 'Exeter / My work here has hitherto been wholly *internal* and consists largely of cleaning and repairing stonework. The misereres are old here as is the Bishop's throne but all other woodwork was modern.

We are carrying out new woodwork including canopies, deskfronts, stalls, elbows, front seats etc. new. The wall behind the stalls was of brick but capped by a beautiful cornice of the 14th century. I [?] [?] a stone [?] pierced behind each stall (of which Canterbury in some degree offers a precedent.)

The ancient reredos was destroyed at the reformation, we are introducing a new one. There has been a tremendous agitation to make me take down or pierce the wood Screen. For this I refer to my reports etc.

My principle is not to destroy an *old* close rood screen, nor to erect a *new* one.'

Vol. III, p. 338 (pp. 311-316 read:) 'St Davids / This has been a very interesting and arduous work.

The Tower was actually threatening to fall and two of its pillars were shattered to fragments. These had to be rebuilt and the whole rendered safe. The interior has been or is being, put in thorough repair, the ruined aisles of choir roofed and restored. The fittings of Choir put in thorough order etc. The lower East windows of choir had been walled up owing to the erection of a beautiful chapel behind them in the 16th century. These have been filled at the expense of my friend Mr John Lucy, with glass mosaic. The windows over this had been converted into a large perpendicular window, but this being decayed and the design of the early work perfectly discovered – and extensive portions of the actual windows found, they have been reproduced on their old design and in part of their old materials. They have been filled with stained glass by Mr J. Lucy. His gift was a memorial to his ancestor Bishop Lucy. The vaulting of the N Transept planned in transitional [?] times and marked clearly on the walls but never executed is being carried out in oak at the cost of Canon Allen.

My two reports on the cathedral – one previous to the commencement of the work – the other after it had progressed to a considerable extent, (*both printed*) give the best account of what has been contemplated and to a certain point effected. The work has since gone steadily though slowly on and is still progressing. It is a most interesting work and has been effected so far under great disadvantages and I may say wholly through the energy of the Bishop.

The Dean has taken but little part in it. The leading Canon when I undertook the work was The Revd Chancellor Sir Erasmus Williams, a most eccentric man ...' (p.315, l.25 – p. 316, l.9) '...at his own cost.'

Vol. III, p. 343 (pp. 330-336 read:) 'Chester / This cathedral offered exceptional difficulties owing to the thorough decay of its stonework rendering restoration nearly synonymous with renewal. Hitherto we have gone quietly on underpinning foundations and renovating thoroughly decayed or destroyed work according to the best evidences we could obtain.

I wrote in 1870 a report or paper on it which has been published by the local antiquarian society and to which I refer. It will be found to explain a deviation we have made from the form of the east end as it had come down to us owing to the discovery of evidences as to what had been there before – a most marvellous stone-roofed apse. We have discovered certain evidences of the plan of the Norman east end.

We have since rebuilt the Southern walk of the cloister which had been long since destroyed – partly as an abutment to the vaulting of the north aisle of the nave.

The great South transept, a sad wreck of a once beautiful decorated structure, still remaining to be undertaken but with the energy of Dean Howson I do not despair of its completion.

The interior of the nave has been cleansed, repaired and groined in oak. The cleansing and reparation of the choir will soon be undertaken and as it has already been vaulted (some years back) in wood and plaster, this vaulting will probably be decorated in colour.

See my report at the commencement, my paper published by the local society and a letter recently written to the Dean in reply to certain criticisms.'

Vol. III, p. 348 (as pp. 316-318) 'Bangor...'

Vol. III, p. 356 (pp. 318-320 read:) 'St Asaph / This has not been an interesting work. The chancel with the exception of its late Dec. E window had been externally renewed in costly stone but horrid architecture, I suppose early in this century not the smallest trace of its old design being left...' (p. 319, l.3 – p. 320, l.10) '...rearrangement under Henry VIIth.'

Vol. IV, p. 2 'May God bless what I have [?] to record in this book GGS Aug. 8. 1872.'

Vol. IV, p. 3 (pp. 320-326) 'St Albans Abbey...'

Vol. IV, p. 6 (p. 322, l.11 reads:) 'My report was printed and is extant (*I refer to it*).'

Vol. IV, p. 7 (p. 322, l.19 reads:) '...of what was needed. Our great work at the commencement was to provide for the security of the central Tower – which had shown unmistakable symptoms of giving way – mainly towards the North East – we had to apply a vast system of shoring and then carefully removed the shattered parts replacing them with hard brick work in cement...'

(p. 322, l.21 to p. 323, l.3, not included here.)

Vol. IV, p. 13 (after p. 324, l.30) '...cannot continue! The committee seem very inert on the subject and to incline to the self seeking policy of repairing the ordinary parts such as the neighbourhood can be obviously called upon for. *This* must be *abated*! Our great discovery however, I have to relate...'

Vol. IV, p. 17 (after p. 327, l.2) 'August 9th 1872 / *Portsmouth* / I have been this day to Osborne and been Knighted! Oh that my dearest Carry was here to share this honour and that on reaching home I could salute her as *Lady Scott,* but she is in greater honour by infinite degrees – 'Thou hast set my feet in a large Room' said David when relieved from some of his troubles. I too can say this, but oh what a glorious Room does *She* inhabit! Oh that I may share that Glorious place with her and *all* our dear children!

I have had a very agreeable day...'

Vol. IV, p. 20 (p. 328, l.14 for 'summoned' read:) 'called for'.

Vol. IV, p. 20 (after p. 328, l.22) '...when I chose *Gilbert* – My dearest wife would have chosen it as she used to tell me to call myself 'Mr Gilbert Scott'. I thank God for this honour!'

Vol. IV, p. 23 (after p. 329, l.18) '...two younger sons. I had at my dear wife's decease at one time thought that my sister in law Helen Oldrid, might keep this house for me – but my sons thought it would be dull for them and the other arrangement was made.'

Vol. IV, p. 27 (p. 330, ll.23-28 read:) 'During the autumn I became painfully [?] impressed in the costliness of my mode of living and the falling off of my practice – and as my son and daughter in law did not care for Ham, determined to remove to London whether wisely or not God knows! We did not finally [?] move till a year later – I am now a Londoner and have much [?] lost [?] in position. May God bless the change! I fear it was not quite well considered.'

Vol. IV, p. 29 (as p. 353, l.27 to p. 354, l.9) 'To return to St Albans ... I gave a dinner there in 1875 to the Council of the Institute and many friends and we had a jolly Field day in the Abbey – The next work [?] D.V. will be the nave.'

Vol. IV, p. 31 'List of cathedrals and other large churches of similar class which I have been by God's permission engaged upon / Ely Cathedral / Westminster Abbey / Hereford Cathedral / Lichfield Cathedral / Peterborough Cathedral / Salisbury Cathedral / Chichester Cathedral / Chester Cathedral / St Davids Cathedral / St Asaph Cathedral / Bangor Cathedral / Gloucester Cathedral / Worcester Cathedral / Exeter Cathedral / Rochester Cathedral / Durham Cathedral / (in prospect) Canterbury Cathedral / St Albans Abbey (partly done) / Tewkesbury Abbey / Ripon / Beverly / Bridlington / Selby.'

Vol. IV, p. 33 'Ely Cathedral / I have I think said a good deal about this work already since that when [?] ended in the restoration of the fabric of the octagon as a memorial of Dean Peacock, the interior of the timber lantern has been decorated by Mr Gambier Parry, but I had nothing to do with it. I am now completing the great turrets and pinnacles of the octagon. I have made a strong move towards...' (as p. 283, ll.10-16) '...I wrote a paper on Ely while abroad in

1873 which was read at the Millenary festival of St Etheldreda in my absence by my son Gilbert (see this)...'

Vol. IV, p. 35 'Westminster Abbey / I have written much on the Abbey in the paper called the *Gleanings* etc. but very many things have turned up since. I may mention the discovery of the curious opening at the South west of the Refectory – that of a part of the architrave of the shrine misfixed [?] in its place (see notes of mine in my copy of Dart). I have since that time thoroughly restored the Chapter House. I have given lectures about this but I fear have written nothing. I had almost immediately...' (as p. 285, l.4).

(p. 286, l.16 to p. 287, l.23, not at this point)

Vol. IV, p. 42 (p. 287, l.28 reads:) '...them all perfected. Mention Deans I have worked under etc. Buckland (Lord John Thyn in an interval of many years) Trench [?]. Stanley – and also some curious mad individuals etc.'

Vol. IV, p. 43 'Hereford' (as p. 288, l.7 to p. 289, l.24)

Vol. IV, p. 46 (after p. 289, l.25 reads:) 'I was interested to discover one of my old friends the Dentons of Hillesden which I replaced as near its own position as I could but subsequently found to my regret that parts of its altar tomb and heraldic remains had escaped my notice – I applied to Lord Leicester the representative of the family in vain for aid to its more perfect restoration. The same want of success has since attended a like application to him to restore a sister monument of his ancestors at Hillesden. His grandmother was the last of the Dentons and through her his father obtained the Hillesden estate. He sold it to obtain funds for a family settlement at the time of his marriage with the mother of the present Earl – Lord Leicester it is true does not hold the estate but he would be less wealthy to the extent of its value if his father had not inherited it. / The beautiful stallwork...'

Vol. IV, p. 51 (after p. 291, l.2) '...now do the same. The Screen was executed in metal by Mr Skidmore from my design with as usual with him a few liberties of his own. I had the pleasure of carrying out this work under the kind and friendly auspices of my dear friend Dean Dawes. / See the report etc. on Hereford.'

Vol. IV, p. 53 (as p. 291, l.31) 'Lichfield / I here succeeded rather against my will Mr Sydney Smirke...'

(p. 297, ll.19 to 30 not included here)

Vol. IV, p. 73 'At Peterborough I have done comparatively little...'

Vol. IV, p. 77 (p. 299, after l.17) '...may prove effectual. One eminent canon Dr Westcote, was so offended with me I fancy because I was not favourable to the adding of flying buttresses, that he will hardly deign to speak to me – and when I last saw him and innocently went up to him to shake hands, he put his hands behind his back lest he should contaminate them with contact with mine! His meaning I cannot divine – as I had never uttered a word or harboured a thought which was disrespectful to him but as one lives on one finds a few such enigmas! [?] but here the question is doubled. What are these celestial minds angry about? My knowledge of Peterborough...'

Vol. IV, p. 82 (p. 300, l.19 reads:) 'Salisbury / I was appointed to this cathedral I think about 1858 (Qu). I have made several Reports upon it (at least three which see) / The first work undertaken...'

Vol. IV, p. 93 (after p. 304, l.2) '...no traces of the old ones remained. The canopies were of modern deal and as yet none have been provided for. Lord Beauchamp gave the Reredos, as unpleasant a man to do business with as I ever met with – a tyrant of the first water! The choir screen was professedly given by Mrs --- Lear as a memorial to her husband – *but was very sadly stinted* – while she assumed from her very partial gift a power of tyrannizing only second to that assumed by Lord B. I designed what I view as a magnificent screen but it was treated with no great respect by Mrs Lear, whose gift while it assumed to herself the honour of being donor of the most conspicuous feature in the church, but only required considerable outlay from the restoration fund to eke it out but I fear put the person who executed it Mr Skidmore, to loss, and infinite trouble in screwing down its expense but was the means of depriving the church of a far nobler screen. I am the more severe in my remarks because I find fault with such gifts however munificent in themselves, as saddle noble churches with comparatively unworthy objects while they assume to donors an honour, they do not allow money enough to give them a full title. Mr Skidmore has here done his *very utmost*. During the restoration of the choir...'
[Written over the above:] 'Don't publish this.'

Vol. IV, p. 105 (after p. 307, l.9) 'He was one of four sculptors whom I had known to have died in poverty within about two years! Philip, Stephens, Phyffers and Redfern. / I may mention two small works...'

Vol. IV, p. 111 (p. 309) 'Chichester Cathedral / I was appointed after the fall of the central tower...'

Vol. IV, p. 199 (p. 311) 'St Davids Cathedral / See my two reports – one made before the commencement, the other addressed to Bishop Thirlwall after the restoration of the Tower had been effected. I had visited ...'

Vol. IV, p. 130 (p. 315, 1.22 to p. 316, 1.10 reads:) '...when Govr Gen! His brother is now Chancellor of St Davids and a more admirable man could not be. His predecessor was the eccentric Sir Erasmus Williams, a most extraordinary man! If we restore the west end and the South Transept, the work remaining...'

Vol. IV, p. 131 (p. 318) 'St Asaph / This work has been of a minor class. Consisting of ...'

(p. 319, 1.2 to p. 320 1.11 reads:) 'The old stalls of the choir though made for the space below the central tower, had been transferred to the eastern arm, and modern deal stalls and canopies put in their place, but I regret to say seated the eastern arm which was pressed upon me against my wish. The Eastern arm had excepting its east window, been thoroughly modernised. No trace of its old side windows remaining – These were shown in old views – and it was pressed upon me to restore them from this sole authority. I begged to be allowed to explore the old walls first but this was not allowed. I ought to have insisted on this, but foolishly gave way and inserted Early English windows in two bays on each side. When we came to the third – that next the tower, we found the jamb of the original window – quite different to what I had done and very superior indeed. This I faithfully restored, but the others remain monuments of weak compliance – and beacons to warn others against such foolish conduct. The nave had a modern roof...'

Vol. IV, p. 135 'Bangor Cathedral / I think what I have done there will be sufficiently explained by my *two* reports aided by a printed paper on Chester Cathedral in which it is alluded to.
I am hoping to go on with the nave shortly D.G.'

Vol. IV, p. 135 (p. 330) 'Chester Cathedral / I commenced this work...'

Vol. IV, p. 136 (p. 331, 1.14 reads:) '...and printed (now *very scarce*) which contains a statement of what had been done up to its date (probably 1870). The most interesting part...'

Vol. IV, p. 155 (p. 336) 'Gloucester Cathedral / This cathedral was formerly under the management...'

Vol. IV, p. 162 (after p. 339, 1.18) '...To my eye the effect is most satisfactory, but it has so angered Mr G[ambier] P[arry], that when he undertook the decoration of the lantern at Ely, he was so oblivious of what was due to me as architect and to himself as a Gentleman, as not only not to consult me in the least but to recommend the Dean and Chapter not to do so – wh. however they saw [?] the propriety of not acting upon – though he has followed his own

488

devices and neglected all evidence of ancient decoration though not wholly unsuccessful in his result.'

Vol. IV, p. 164 (p. 342) 'Worcester Cathedral / This work was in the hands of Mr Perkins the local architect, a pupil of old Rickman. / I had been occasionally consulted by the Dean but not to any great extent, so that the entire structural reparation and restoration was Mr Perkins sole work. / I was, however, called in when the internal work of the choir was taken in hand, and acted so far as that was concerned jointly with Mr Perkins. See my several reports on this work and many important letters. The structural work ... I forget whether there were ancient return stalls...'

    (p. 345, l.11 reads:) '...being removed from another position.'

    [p. 345, ll.13-14 not included here.]

Vol. IV, p. 176 (p. 345) 'Exeter Cathedral / I had been consulted...'

Vol. IV, p. 176 (p. 348, l.25 reads:) '...in all this work I was horribly thwarted by the Dean, but I think the result is good.'

Vol. IV, p. 186 (after p. 349, l.2) '...the altar platform. The Dean was so outrageous in his interference that I was driven nearly out of my senses – over and over again all through this work and really could [?] not [?] get any part of my own way without [??] most wretched squabbling – which often made me perfectly ill and made me hate the very name of Exeter. Yet after all I believe him to be a good man at heart, though delighting in what half kills other people! He seemed as fond of bullying an architect as a hunter of running down a fox and for the mere fun of it! I think the interior of this cathedral...'

Vol. IV, p. 190 (p. 349) 'Rochester / I had been called in once...'

Vol. IV, p. 200 (p. 352) 'Winchester Cathedral / Here I have done nothing but...'

Vol. IV, p. 203 (p. 352) 'Durham Cathedral / I was only engaged here on internal work...'

Vol. IV, p. 205 (p. 353, l.22 reads:) '...are Mr Fowler's work. / A stupid idiotic opposition was raised against this work by 2 canons – who thought to curry favour with the Bishop – but I believe this ebullition of ignorant folly has subsided. The Dean and Archdeacon Bland were the supporters of the work.'

Vol. IV, p. 207 (p. 339) 'Ripon Cathedral / This ought to have come much earlier in my list (see Reports on this work). See also my paper on it in the

Archaeological Journal I think 1875 – / The cathedral was transitional work altered at several periods...'

Vol. IV, p. 211 (p. 340, l.23 reads:) '...We (at a later date) added oak vaulting to the old corbels and imitated from the transepts at York to the nave (we could not get money to restore the roof to its true pitch which I desired) – We completed the stone vaulting of nave aisles. We cleared away galleries etc. from choir...'

Vol. IV, p. 221 'St Albans / See Reports – one some 20 years back or more several of more recent date – Lady Chapel Report etc.

A certain amount of work was done some 20 years or nearly so ago. It was mainly on the North side and in a large degree for safety. The present works commenced about 1870 – owing to the dangerous condition of the central tower ...' (as p. 322, l.18) '... at Willis' Rooms for the furtherance of the work.

The tower was thoroughly repaired and strengthened – as were also its two abutting walls ...' (as p. 354, l.11...) ... (p. 355, l.11 reads:) '...I copied the South doorway. Later on...'

p. 231 (p. 356, l.32 reads:) '...I mention it with some shame as an antiquarian failure arising from going on too fast and ahead of full investigation. *I repent and confess*! I will now try to state some set offs against this.

The great triumph of our work...'

Vol. IV, p. 231 (after p. 357, l.7) '...be carefully written. My report on the Eastern chapels will be found to contain much information.

I forbear to say anything of our...'

Vol. IV, p. 232 (p. 357, l.13) 'I am in this as in other works... The leader among those who wish me to do what I ought not to do is Sir Edmund Beckett.

Turn over 3 pages here.'

[Rest of MS written from the *back* of the book. Continuing:]

Vol. IV, p. 239 'Beckett Denison!

Phoebus what a conjunction of names! That of the indomitable Archbishop of Canterbury and of the indomitable Archdeacon of Taunton! Beckett Denison unites the qualities of his archi-episcopal and his archi-diaconal namesakes with a lot of stuff [?] good and bad but always strong of his own. He can curse with either ecclesiastic. He has the determination of both – unflinching, unbending, invincible [?] as either! No conventional rules of propriety influence him, he cares less for friends if possible than foes. I said he was always strong – I mean in manner. He is not always so in fact. He sometimes reverses the 'suaviter in modo fortiter in re' for never suaviter in modo – always fortiter in re – in a sense he is nevertheless subject to be made a fool of by his own vanity and by a strange unintelligible favouritism not always guided by wisdom, though always by self confidence. Nevertheless he has many good points and kindly disposition. I once described him as a hypocrite on the reverse side – The hypocrite is bad and tries to make himself seem good – Beckett Denison is not bad but does everything in his power to make himself seem so!'

[The above, with modifications, was quoted by G. G. Scott junr in *The Sacristy*, 1881, vol. iii, p. 131.]

Vol. IV, p. 257 (p. 358) 'the Anti-Restoration Movement (October 1877)...the claims of Architecture and good taste.'

Vol. IV, p. 266 (as p. 9, l.27) 'My recollections of the period of my youth are very curious in one respect...he subsequently had to be chasséed altogether.' (p. 14, l.17)

Vol. V, p. 3 (p. 363, l.31) 'Novr 19, 1877 Anti Restoration.

The promoters of this hue and cry ... the encouragement of destructiveness' (p. 367, l.6:) 'See my speech and my long paper in reply to Stevenson in the Transactions of the Institute and my reply to Loftie in Macmillans Magazine (all in 1877). See also a copy of a letter to Sir E. Lechmere respecting an attack on me by Morris – it is in the *pressing off book* in my study.

It seems to be the opinion of some...' (p. 369, l.18 – p. 370, l.32) '...the claims of old and modern buildings 1877.'

Vol. V, p. 23 (p. 372) 'The Queen Anne Style. The movement in favour of this style...'

Vol. V, p. 25 (after p. 373, l.6) '...from a practical point of view. I had by the bye gone into a competition in the style and had once sketched a design in it, thinking to use it to obtain a studentship at the Royal Academy but these were solitary spirits/sprints [?].

I was awakened from my slumber by the thunder of Pugin's writings...'

Vol. V, p. 29 (p. 374, l.8 reads:) '...suddenly became as furiously antiGothic and to carry out their views turned in favour of Perpendicular – 17th century – and finally *Queen Anne*.

I have no right to expose this frivolity...' '...making our houses look like churches.

January 1878' (p. 376)

END

APPENDIX 2

Sir Gilbert Scott
An Appreciation by his son, George Gilbert Scott junr.
(RIBA notebook No 13, p. 76)

My Father Sir George Gilbert Scott died in the night of March 26-27 at about 4 in the morning, as is believed from the result of a blood clot passing into the heart from a varicose vein in the leg, from which he was suffering. In all other respects he was in good health and in fullest vigour of mind and in good spirits. He rang for his man John Pavings at about 4 complained of his heart and desired him to prepare a poultice. He was then out of bed. While this was being done he said he was very bad and desired Pavings to make up a bed on the sofa for himself saying 'if you leave me you will probably not see me again alive.' Pavings thought nothing of this (as when feeling unwell my Father would often speak in this sort of way) and passed it off in a jocular manner. Nor do I think my Father really meant it or he would surely have desired to see my brother John who was sleeping at home. As soon as the poultice was applied my Father called out 'Raise me up, its coming on again.' Pavings raised him in the bed but he was insensible and continued with his eyes half closed and breathing very heavily for nearly half an hour when he raised his eyelids and cast his eyes upwards as in mute prayer and then gradually life ebbed till with a heavy sigh or slight groan he expired R.I.P. John was sent for at once upon the seizure, but my Father did not appear to see or to hear him. There was no sign of pain except the heavy breathing almost gasping. He was buried in Westminster abbey on Saturday April 6. The coffin of oak bore a large brass cross having on the base the legend 'Memento Mei Domine Jesu' and on the Plate the Inscription 'Georgii Gilberti Scott Equitis viri probi architecti peritissimi Parentis optimi reliquiae hic in fide Jesu Xti resurrectionem expectant. Obiit 27° die Martis Anno Salutis 1878° – aetatis 67°.'

Of his many great qualities his strong sense of Justice and his devotion to the best interests of his children whom he loved with a deep warmth which his extreme natural reserve prevented even them from realising fully, deserve to be especially mentioned. Also his beautiful modesty and his perfect breeding and courtesy not so much finish of manner, as genuine inbred politeness. In the best sense of the word he was a gentle man. The foundation of these 'graces of character' was a sincere practical Xtian faith. He was pious in a quiet somewhat reserved manner which concealed, except at an occasional glimpse, the warmth of his feelings and the firmness of his faith. His faith was certainly not the result of ignorance of modern criticisms. He was exceedingly interested in such questions and his study of them confirmed his conviction of the Divine character of Xtianity.

He was an *Anglican* essentially and in the best sense of the term. Decidedly opposed to Roman practices on many points, principally upon the use of Images which he could not but think was *almost* if not quite Idolatrous. But he was never bitter and of late years became perhaps somewhat less unfavourably disposed. He defended the practice of praying for the departed, and practised it himself constantly. Indeed I have reason to believe that he never mentioned my Mother's name in the course of conversation without a silent prayer for her repose and when out of doors he would always raise his hat as he made this prayer on mentioning her name. The ardour of his devotion is illustrated by a fact which I have learnt since his death. His man observed one day the underside of Sir Gilbert's fore-arms to be roughened and sore-looking as he described 'like leprosy'. He asked my Father what was the cause and after a great deal of query and frequent returns to the subject my Father said 'When I am praying especially for my sons, I feel as if I could not do enough, I feel kneeling to be too little and I prostrate myself upon the floor, owing to this my arms get a little galled.' How *long* his prayers lasted we may form some idea of from this result.

His sense of Justice was very strongly exemplified in his *indignation* at the Ridsdale judgement condemning the vestments, and virtually the Eastward Position. He was exceedingly well up in the controversy and was convinced that the Judgement was utterly false. He returned to the subject again and again, gave me a pamphlet of Parkers on the point, and expressed his indignation at the injustice of the decision with a warmth unusual to him. At the same time he said 'I have never seen a chasuble worn in the English Ch: and have no wish to see one, the eastward position is not used in the churches which I usually attend. I do not sympathise with those who are fighting for these points, and many of their objects as I understand them I distinctly and strongly disapprove of, but to make the ornaments rubric forbid what every one who studies the subject knows it was intended to order and to pervert the perfectly well known history of the "position" rubrics is a grossly immoral proceeding.'

He used to add that the north end position was not so bad with the small dressing-table-like altars that used to exist in most of our churches, but that with the better proportioned altars now everywhere seen, a priest at the north end 'looked' as he said, 'like a naughty boy in a corner.'

APPENDIX 3
NOTES, MAINLY BIOGRAPHICAL
by Gavin Stamp

In this Appendix are notes which further illustrate references in the text and the first two appendices. These have not been separately indexed.

AKROYD, Colonel Edward, M.P. (1810-1887), worsted manufacturer of Halifax and builder of ALL SOULS' CHURCH, HALEY HILL, q.v., which GGS thought his finest, and of the suburb of Akroydon for his workers around the Haley Hill Mills of James Akroyd & Son.

ALAN of Walsingham (fl. 14th C.), Sacrist of Ely Cathedral.

ALEXANDER, The Revd Michael Solomon (1799-1845), first Anglican Bishop of Jerusalem, whose appointment in 1841 at the behest of the King of Prussia provoked opposition from the Anglo-Catholics; born of Jewish parents in the Grand Duchy of Posen, came to London 1820, baptised 1825, ordained 1827 and connected with the Episcopal Jews' Chapel in Palestine Place, London, q.v., and with the London Society for Promoting Christianity amongst the Jews; see also the Revd Joseph WOLFF.

ALFORD, The Revd Henry (1810-1871), dean of Canterbury after 1857.

ALLEN, Charles, of Tenby, secretary to the restoration committee for St David's Cathedral.

ANDREWES, Lancelot (1555-1626), Bishop of Winchester and Anglican divine.

ANTI-RESTORATION MOVEMENT (see LOFTIE, the Revd W.H., MORRIS, William, and STEVENSON, John James).

ARCHITECTURAL MUSEUM, a collection of casts first installed in a loft in Cannon Row, Westminster, in 1851; moved to the SOUTH KENSINGTON MUSEUM in 1857 and in 1859 to purpose-built premises for the Royal Architectural Museum in Tufton Street, designed by Joseph Clarke and Ewan CHRISTIAN, q.v. (subsequently the home of the Architectural Association); dispersed 1892. See John Summerson, *The Architectural Association 1847-1947* (London, 1947), pp. 35-37; see also L. N. COTTINGHAM.

ARMSTEAD, Henry Hugh (1828-1905), sculptor who worked with Scott on the Albert Memorial &c. and designed the sculptured historical frieze at ETTINGTON PARK, q.v. See Benedict Read, *Victorian Sculpture* (New Haven and London, 1982).

ATKINSON, Thomas Witlam (1799-1861), architect and explorer, unsuccessful competitor for the Nikolaikirche, Hamburg. See Howard Colvin, *A Biographical Dictionary of British Architects 1660-1840* (1978).

BACON, Francis (1561-1626), Lord Chancellor.

BAGOT, The Revd Richard (1782-1854), Dean of Canterbury, Bishop of Oxford 1829, Bishop of Bath and Wells after 1845.

BANKS, Robert Richardson (1813-1872), architect; assistant to Sir Charles BARRY and partner of Charles BARRY junior after 1847, qqv.

BARLOW, William Henry (1812-1902), civil engineer; consulting engineer to the Midland Railway.

BARRY, Sir Charles (1795-1860), architect of the New Palace of Westminster, &c. See the Revd Alfred Barry, *The Life and Works of Sir Charles Barry, R.A., F.R.S., &c.* (London, 1867; reprinted New York, 1973).

BARRY, Charles junior (1823-1900), eldest son of Sir Charles BARRY, q.v.; architect to Dulwich College. Became Scott's principal rival in the Government Offices controversy after his design (with R. R. BANKS, q.v.) for the Foreign Office was placed second in the 1856 competition while Scott was placed third. See Jan Piggott, *Charles Barry, Junior, and the Dulwich College Estate* (Dulwich, 1986).

BARRY, Edward Middleton (1830-1880), architect; third son of Sir Charles BARRY, q.v., competitor for the new Law Courts, 1866.

BEAUCHAMP, Frederick Lygon, 6th Earl (1830-1891).

BELL, Alfred (1832-1895), stained-glass artist who in c. 1847-53 had been a pupil of GGS, who encouraged him to join with Richard CLAYTON, q.v., to found the firm of CLAYTON & BELL. See Peter Larkworthy, *Clayton and Bell, Stained Glass Artists and Decorators*, Ecclesiological Society (London, 1984).

BELL, Doyne Courtenay (1830-1888), civil servant and writer, secretary to the committee for erecting a memorial to the Prince Consort 1862, author of *The Albert Memorial: A Descriptive and Illustrated Account...* (1873).

BELLAMY, Thomas (1798-1876), architect of the Law Fire Insurance Office in Chancery Lane, London; placed fifth in the competition for the Foreign Office.

BENTHAM, the Revd James (1708-1794), historian and canon of Ely who published his *History of Ely Cathedral* in 1771.

BERNASCONI, Francis (d. 1841), sculptor and decorator.

BIDDULPH, General Sir Thomas Myddleton (1809-1878), master of Queen Victoria's household, 1851, and subsequently equerry to the queen and keeper of H.M.'s privy purse.

BLOMFIELD, Sir Arthur William (1829-1899), architect.

BLORE, Edward (1787-1879), architect and archaeologist; GGS's immediate predecessor as Surveyor to Westminster Abbey.

BODLEY, Dr William, physician; father of G. F. BODLEY, architect, q.v., and father-in-law of GGS's brother, Samuel King Scott.

BODLEY, George Frederick (1827-1907), distinguished ecclesiastical architect; first pupil of GGS, and then assistant, 1845-1856, and relation by marriage through his sister, Georgina, q.v. Although he was best known for his use of a refined Late Gothic style, Bodley's first churches were in a severe Early French style; he later explained to F. M. Simpson, in 1901, that "St Michael's, Brighton of 1858, was a boyish antagonistic effort. Not believing in what one saw at Scott's one went in for a violent reaction. One had seen bad mouldings, and so would not have any, and inane crockets – one felt 'away with them' – which was but the weakness of youth"; see *RIBA Journal*, xv (1908).

BODLEY, Georgina (1819-1901), daughter of Dr William BODLEY, q.v., who married Samuel King Scott, GGS's brother, in 1846.

BOISSERÉE, Sulpiz (1783-1854), antiquary and a native of Cologne – along with his brother, Melchior Boisserée (1786-1851) – who was the driving force behind the rebuilding of Cologne Cathedral which he surveyed after 1808; work began on the restoration in 1823, the year he finally published his *Geschichte und Beschreibung des Doms von Köln...* and after 1833 it was under the direction of E. F. ZWIRNER, q.v., who enjoyed Boisserée's confidence; see Georg Germann, *Gothic Revival in Europe and Britain: Sources, Influences and Ideas* (London, 1972).

BOTREL D'HAZEVILLE, A., mysterious architect, of Paris, not a student at the Ecole des Beaux-Arts, who, when 'Inspecteur aux Travaux du Louvre', was placed second in the competition for the War Office; he was in partnership with Alphonse-Nicolas Crépinet – who won the competition for the Block Plan for the Government Offices in Whitehall in 1857 – and they were placed second in the first round of the competition to design the Paris Opera; in the second round each architect submitted separate designs, but the commission went to Charles Garnier.

BRANDON, John Raphael (1817-1877), architect and author, with his brother Joshua Arthur Brandon, of *The Analysis of Gothic Architecture* (1847).

BRIDPORT, Alexander Nelson Hood, 1st Viscount (1814-1904), Equerry to Queen Victoria 1858-84.

BRINDLEY, William of the London firm of Farmer & Brindley, architectural stone carvers.

BRODRICK, Cuthbert (1822-1905), architect of the Town Hall and Corn Exchange in Leeds, placed fifth in the competition for the War Office in 1856.

BROUGHAM, Henry, 1st Baron Brougham & Vaux (1778-1868), politician.

BROWN, Lancelot, known as 'Capability' Brown (1716-1783), landscape gardener and architect.

BRUNEL, Isambard Kingdom (1806-1859), civil engineer; engineer of the Great Western Railway and designer of Paddington Station.

BUCCLEUCH, Walter Francis Montagu-Douglas Scott, 5th Duke of, and 7th Duke of Queensberry (1806-1884).

BUCKINGHAM & CHANDOS, Richard Temple-Nugent-Brydges-Chandos-Grenville, Duke of (1776-1839), Marquis of Buckingham, created Marquis of Chandos and 1st Duke in 1822.

BUCKINGHAM & CHANDOS, Richard Plantagenet Temple-Nugent-Brydges-Chandos-Grenville, 2nd Duke of (1797-1861).

BUCKLAND, The Very Revd William (1784-1856), Dean of Westminster after 1846, geologist, mineralogist.

BURGES, William (1827-1881), Gothic architect, sometime partner of Henry CLUTTON, q.v., and the creator of Cardiff Castle; see Crook, J. M., *William Burges and the High Victorian Dream* (London, 1981).

BURGON, The Very Revd John William (1813-1888), writer, biographer, professor, Vicar of St Mary the Virgin, Oxford, 1863-1876, Dean of Chichester after 1875, best known as the author of the description of Petra as "A rose-red city – half as old as time!"

BURLISON, John (c.1810-1868), GGS's personal assistant.

BURN, William (1789-1870), highly successful Scottish country house architect who moved his practice to London in 1844; assessor in the Government Offices competitions; see David Walker, 'William Burn', in J. Fawcett, ed., *Seven Victorian Architects*, London 1976. See David Walker, 'William Burn' in *Seven Victorian Architects* (London, 1976), and James Macaulay, *The Gothic Revival 1745-1845* (Glasgow & London, 1975).

BURNE-JONES, Sir Edward Coley (1833-1898), artist who designed stained-glass for the firm founded by his friend William MORRIS, q.v.

BURTON, Decimus (1800-1881), Classical architect, designer of the Athenaeum Club, Waterloo Place, and, with Richard Turner, the Palm House at Kew Gardens.

BUTLER, The Revd George (1774-1853), Headmaster of Harrow 1805-1829, Dean of Peterborough after 1842.

BUTLER, Joseph, surveyor to Chichester Cathedral.

BUTTERFIELD, William (1814-1900), *avant-garde* Gothic architect, designer of All Saints', Margaret Street, and Keble College, Oxford; see Thompson, Paul, *William Butterfield* (London, 1971).

BUXTON, Charles, M.P. (1823-1871), politician and amateur architect, supporter of Gothic Revival who designed his own house, Foxwarren Park, Surrey.

CAMBRIDGE CAMDEN SOCIETY founded in 1839; refounded in London in 1846 as the ECCLESIOLOGICAL SOCIETY. Highly influential body which reinforced the Gothic Revival with theology and which was sometimes critical of GGS. See James F. White, *The Cambridge Movement* (Cambridge, 1962, 1979).

CARDWELL, Edward, M.P. (1813-1886), secretary for war 1868-74, created Viscount Cardwell 1874.

CARPENTER, Richard Cromwell (1812-1855), church architect associated with the Cambridge Camden Society and a friend of A. W. N. PUGIN, q.v.

CARTER, John (1748-1817), antiquarian and architect. A pioneer in the serious appreciation of Medieval architecture, he was a ferocious critic of the destructive restorations of architects like James WYATT, q.v. See Howard Colvin, *A Biographical Dictionary of British Architects 1660-1840* (1978).

CAVENDISH, the Hon. Charles Compton (1793-1863), 4th son of 1st Earl of Burlington, q.v., created Baron Chesham, 1858.

CAVENDISH, the Hon. George Augustus Henry (1754-1834), 3rd son of 4th Duke of DEVONSHIRE, q.v., and brother of 5th Duke, created 1st Earl of Burlington and Baron Cavendish 1831.

CAWDOR, John Frederick Vaughan Campbell, 2nd Earl of (1817-1898).

CHAMBERS, Sir William (1726-1796), architect, author of *A Treatise on Civil Architecture* (1759).

CHAMPNEYS, William Weldon, Dean of Lichfield, father of the architect Basil Champneys (1842-1935).

CHILDERS, Hugh Culling Eardley, M.P. (1827-1896), politician, Chancellor of the Duchy of Lancaster 1872-73.

CHRISTIAN, Ewan (1814-1895), Consulting Architect to the Ecclesiastical Commissioners, 1850-95.

CLAYTON, John Richard (1827-1913), stained glass artist, sculptor and decorator, who, with the encouragement and, possibly, financial support of GGS, joined Alfred BELL, q.v., in c.1855 to form the firm of CLAYTON

& BELL, stained glass makers and decorators. See Peter Larkworthy, *Clayton and Bell, Stained Glass Artists and Decorators*, Ecclesiological Society (London, 1984).

CLUTTERBUCK, Robert, county historian of Hertfordshire, 1815-1827.

CLUTTON, Henry (1819-1893), Gothic architect who, in partnership with William BURGES (q.v.) won the competition for Lille Cathedral in 1856 (unbuilt).

COAD, Richard (1825-1900), Cornish architect and GGS's clerk; in the office 1847-1864; GGS's manuscript of a 'Diary of Architectural Tour on the Continent' in 1862 begins, 'Sept 26 when by early train to Chartres and joined Gilbert and John & Coad ...' See Alan Calder, *James Maclaren, Arts and Crafts Architect* (RIBA exhibition catalogue, 1990).

COBBETT, William (1762-1835), agriculturalist, radical politician and author of *Rural Rides.*

COCKERELL, Professor Charles Robert (1788-1863), distinguished classical architect and archaeologist, designer of the University (now Ashmolean) Museum, Oxford; see Watkin, David, *The Life and Work of C. R. Cockerell* (London, 1974).

COCKERELL, Frederick Pepys (1833-1878), architect and second son of C. R. Cockerell, q.v.

COE, Henry Edward (1826-1885), architect, pupil of GGS who, with G. E. STREET q.v., in 1844 had prepared the drawings for his winning design for the Nikolaikirche in Hamburg, and who, in partnership with Henry H. HOFLAND, won the first premium in the 1856 competition for the Foreign Office; he later, with F. Peck, designed the Agricultural Hall in Islington.

COKE, Thomas William, 1st Earl of Leicester (1754-1842), agriculturist.

COLE, Sir Henry (1808-1882), Secretary of the South Kensington Museum (subsequently the Victoria & Albert Museum) who was actively hostile to the Gothic Revival and ensured that the Royal Albert Hall was not designed by GGS but by a Royal Engineer. Cole may well have been the 'prejudiced and unfriendly man' referred to by A. H. LAYARD, q.v., in the letter reproduced by GGS on p. 270.

COLLING, Mr, clerk of works for Charles FOWLER, q.v., on the Covent Garden and Hungerford Markets; his son was the architect and draughtsman, J. K. Colling, who worked for Scott & Moffatt in 1841-42.

COLVIN, Sir Sidney (1845-1927), critic of art and literature, Slade Professor of fine art at Cambridge and subsequently Director of the Fitzwilliam Museum, who published critical articles on both the Albert Memorial (anonymously: *Pall Mall Gazette*, 5th July, 1872) and Scott's restoration practice ('Restoration and anti-restoration' in *The Nineteenth Century*, vol. ii, October, 1877); founder member of the Society for the Protection of Ancient Buildings in 1877.

CONGREVE, William (1670-1729), dramatist.

COOKE, Edward William (1811-1880), marine and architectural artist and engraver, who had studied draughtsmanship with Augustus Pugin; he was a member of the Institute of British Architects and commissioned Norman Shaw to design Glen Andred at Groombridge.

CORNISH, Robert Stribling (1788-1871), architect of Exeter and surveyor to Exeter Cathedral.

COSIN, John (1594-1672), Bishop of Durham 1660-1672, who made several remarkable alterations to the cathedral furnishings.

COTTINGHAM, Lewis Nockalls (1787-1847), architect and archaeologist and a pioneer in the scholarly appreciation of medieval architecture. The author of numerous publications, notably on Gothic metalwork and ornament, he restored both Rochester and Hereford Cathedrals. In the house he built for himself at No. 43 Waterloo Bridge Road, London, he assembled a collection of medieval woodwork and carvings, together with plaster casts of Gothic details. This was put up for sale in 1851 and, thanks to GGS, subsequently formed the nucleus of the Royal ARCHITECTURAL MUSEUM, q.v. See Howard Colvin, *A Biographical Dictionary of British Architects 1660-1840* (1978)and the thesis by Janet Miles on Cottingham (de Montfort University), to be published shortly.

COWPER, William Francis, M.P. (1811-1888), later Cowper-Temple, Whig politician, President of the Board of Health 1857-1858, Vice-President of the Board of Trade 1859-1860, Commissioner of Works 1860-1866, assumed name of Temple in 1869, created Baron Mount Temple 1880.

COX, Mr, stone carver and builder.

CUNDY, Mr, mason at Westminster Abbey.

DALHOUSIE, James-Andrew Broun-Ramsay, 10th Earl of (1812-1860), Governor-General of India 1847-1856.

DANBY SEYMOUR, Henry (1820-1877), M.P. for Poole.

DAWES, The Very Revd Dr Richard (1793-1867), Dean of Hereford after 1850.

DAWES, William Rutter (1799-1868), astronomer, who resided with Thomas SCOTT, 'The Commentator', q.v., 1807-1821.

DENISON, Edmund Beckett, Q.C., M.P. (1816-1905), after 1874 Sir Edmund BECKETT, Bart., and after 1886 1st Baron GRIMTHORPE; horologist, churchman, amateur architect, controversialist, bully and the despoiler of

St Alban's Abbey; for an account of the life of this deeply unpleasant man, 'tormentor' of GGS, see Peter Ferriday, *Lord Grimthorpe* (London, 1957).

DEVONSHIRE, William Cavendish, 5th Duke of (1748-1811).

DEVONSHIRE, William Spencer Cavendish, 6th Duke of (1790-1858), 'The Bachelor Duke', who commissioned Joseph PAXTON, q.v., to design conservatories at Chatsworth.

DEVONSHIRE, William Cavendish, 7th Duke of (1808-1891), became 2nd Earl of BURLINGTON, q.v., in 1834.

DONALDSON, Thomas Leverton (1795-1885), architect and Professor of Construction and Architecture at University College, London, from 1842 to 1865; founder and first Hon Secretary of the Institute of British Architects and President in 1863-1865; an indifferent architect but well connected and regarded as 'the father of the profession'.

DUDLEY, William Ward, 1st Earl of (1817-1885).

DYSART, Lionel William John Tollemache, 8th Earl of (1794-1878), eldest son of William, Lord HUNTINGTOWER, q.v., whose seat was Ham House.

EARP, Thomas (1828-1893), stone carver who worked principally for G. E. STREET, q.v. See Anthony Mitchell, *Thomas Earp: Master of Stone* (Buckingham, 1990).

EASTLAKE, Sir Charles (1793-1865), painter and art critic, President of the Royal Academy and first Director of the National Gallery, 1855; his nephew was Charles Locke Eastlake (1836-1906), author of *A History of the Gothic Revival* (1872).

EDMESTON, James (1791-1867), hymn-writer and dim architect, to whom GGS was articled in 1827, and who later designed St Paul's, Onslow Square, London (1859-1860); his design for a 'Protestant Church' in the Free Architectural Exhibition of 1850 was ridiculed in the *Ecclesiologist*, q.v.

ELCHO, Francis Wemyss-Charteris-Douglas, Lord Elcho (1818-1914), M.P., member of the Select Committee on the Reconstruction of the Foreign Office, became 10th Earl of Wemyss & March 1883.

ELLICE, The Rt Hon. Edward (1781-1863), M.P. for Coventry 1818-1826 and 1830-1863, founder chairman of the Reform Club and critic of GGS's Gothic Foreign Office design.

EMMETT, John T. (1828-1898), architect and writer, who was a ferocious critic of 'Art-architects' like GGS in anonymous articles in the *Quarterly Review*, e.g. 'The State of English Architecture' in April 1872 and 'The Hope of English Architecture' October 1874, some of which were published in his *Six Essays* (London, 1891, reprinted with an introduction by J. Mordaunt Crook, New York, 1972). Also see T. G. JACKSON.

ENCYCLOPAEDIA EDINENSIS or Dictionary of Arts, Sciences and Literature, originally edited by James Millar, was published in six volumes in Edinburgh in 1827; GGS was therefore wrong about the date he saw this work but correct in recalling that in the section on 'Architecture' in volume I there was, in addition to illustrations of Classicial buildings, a plate showing the west front of Rheims Cathedral and another (Plate 19) depicting both the interior of the late Medieval Roslin Chapel, near Edinburgh, and the exterior of the 'New Episcopal Chapel, York Place, Edinburgh', which was St Paul's, designed by Archibald Elliott and built in 1816-18.

ESSEX, James (1722-1784), architect of Cambridge who took an interest in Gothic and repaired Ely and Lincoln Cathedrals. See T. H. Cocke, 'James Essex, Cathedral Restorer', in *Architectural History*, xviii (1975).

ETTINGTON PARK, Warwickshire – incorrectly printed as 'Eatrington Hall' – Gothic Revival house of 1858-1862 designed by PRICHARD & SEDDON, qq.v., with sculptured reliefs designed by H. H. ARMSTEAD, q.v., and executed by Edward Clarke.

EVANS, William, builder of Ellaston, Staffordshire, which was the birthplace of his relative, Robert Evans (1773-1849), father of Mary Ann Evans, better known as the novelist George Eliot (1819-1880), whose novel *Adam Bede*, published in 1859, was based partly on her father and her early experiences and in which Ellaston appears as the village of 'Hayslope'.

EVELYN, John (1620-1706), 'virtuoso', writer and diarist.

FARMER & BRINDLEY, Messrs, of London; firm of stone carvers and architectural sculptors set up by William BRINDLEY, q.v., and William Farmer.

FERGUSSON, James (1808-1886), architectural writer and pundit and author of *The Illustrated Handbook of Architecture* (1855), and *A History of the Modern Styles of Architecture* (1862); sometime architectural adviser to the Office of Works.

FERREY, Benjamin (1810-1880), church architect and the author of *Recollections of A. N. Welby Pugin, and his Father Augustus Pugin* (1861).

FITZROY, Henry, M.P. (1807-1859), First Commissioner of Works 1858-1859.

FOLEY, John Henry (1818-1874), sculptor, responsible for the gilded figure of the Prince Consort in the Albert Memorial.

FORMAN, W. H., of Pippbrook House, Dorking, Surrey, who asked GGS to alter and enlarge his house.

FOWLER, Charles (1791-1867), Neo-Classical architect conspicuous for innovative use of structure, responsible for the Covent Garden Market and the Hungerford Market, q.v., on which GGS worked for the builders,

GRISSELL & PETO, q.v. See Gavin Stamp, 'The Hungerford Market', in *AA Files*, No. 11, 1986.

FOWLER, Charles Hodgson (1840-1910), prolific architect and restorer, a pupil of GGS who became diocesan architect to Durham.

FRATER, James (d. 1875), Clerk of Works at Chester Cathedral.

FREEMAN, Edward Augustus (1823-1892), historian with a particular interest in churches, whose first book was *A History of Architecture* (1849). He wrote histories of Llandaff Cathedral and, with Basil JONES, q.v., St David's Cathedral.

FULLJAMES, Thomas (1808-1874), architect and County Surveyor of Gloucester, who entered into partnership with his former pupil, Frederick Sandham WALLER (1822-1905), and who acted as architect to the Dean and Chapter of Gloucester Cathedral in 1862-1866 after Waller had had a hunting accident.

GARLING, Henry Bayly (1822-1909), architect, whose design in the Second Empire style won first premium in the competition for the War Office.

GARRICK, David (1717-1779), actor.

GERENTE, Alfred (1821-1868), sculptor and stained-glass maker, who executed the west window at All Saints', Margaret Street, after the sudden death of his brother, Henri, from cholera in 1849.

GERENTE, Henri (1814-1849), French stained-glass painter with an English mother, who escaped from Paris during the 1848 Revolution; an honorary member of the Ecclesiological Society, he was commissioned by A. J. BERESFORD-HOPE, q.v., to execute glass and decoration in All Saints' Margaret Street.

GIBBONS, Grinling (1648-1720), wood carver.

GILBERT, Miss, GGS's aunt.

GILBERT, The Revd Ashhurst Turner (1786-1870), Bishop of Chichester after 1842.

GILBERT, Miss Elizabeth, GGS's great aunt.

GILBERT, Harriet, GGS's aunt's cousin.

GILBERT, Sir Humphrey (1539?-1583), sailor and adventurer.

GILBERT, Nathaniel, GGS's great-grandfather, speaker of the house of assembly in Antigua who, according to his son's entry in the *Dictionary of National Biography*, 'was a methodist, and in 1790, "amidst torrents of reproach, he preached the gospel to the slaves and persevered until he had formed a society of nearly 200." He died before 1778...'.

GILBERT, The Revd Nathaniel, rector of Bledlow, GGS's mother's uncle who married his parents in 1806.

GILBERT, The Revd Nathaniel, son of the eponymous Rector of Bledlow, GGS's mother's first cousin and the 'head and the last of the Gilbert family'; in his footnote on page 232-33, the editor would seem to have confused this Nathaniel Gilbert with his great-uncle (?) Nathaniel Gilbert, q.v. (scarcely surprising, given the seemingly incestuous complications of the Gilbert family tree).

GILBERT, Mrs Nathaniel (d. 1832), GGS's 'aunt Gilbert' who was the wife of the Revd Nathaniel GILBERT, Rector of Bledlow, sister of William GILBERT and daughter of Nathaniel GILBERT of Antigua, qq.v.

GILBERT, William (1760?-1825?), born in Antigua, the brother of GGS's "aunt Gilbert', and the son of Nathaniel GILBERT, qq.v., who eventually merited an entry in the *Dictionary of National Biography*, was an extraordinary man, a lawyer and poet, the friend of Southey and Coleridge, who entered an asylum in Bristol in 1787, disappeared mysteriously in 1798 but eventually turned up in Charleston, South Carolina, where he died.

GLADSTONE, The Rt Hon. William Ewart, M.P. (1809-1898), politician and four times Prime Minister. Gladstone was Chancellor of the Exchequer in Lord Aberdeen's government of 1852-1855 but was out of office at the time of the first Government Offices competition, in 1856, and he declined to join Lord Derby's government in 1858; but when GGS's 'arch-opponent', Lord Palmerston, returned to power in 1859, Gladstone agreed to be his Chancellor of the Exchequer, which he remained until 1866. Gladstone later wrote how, "about twenty years before the Foreign Office was rebuilt, the British Government, in want of a Gothic building, gave the work to one who had earned a noble reputation in the practice of Classical architecture; desiring a classical Foreign Office, the British Government employed the best known Gothic architect of the day to erect it".

GODWIN, Edward William (1833-1886), architect and designer, whose style evolved from Continental Gothic to a personal 'Queen Anne' manner. He was a regular contributor to *The British Architect* in the 1870s. See Dudley Harbron, *The Conscious Stone: The Life of Edward William Godwin* (London, 1949).

GODWIN, George (1815-1888), architect and writer, who was editor of *The Builder* from 1844 until 1883. See Ruth Richardson & Robert Thorne, *The Builder Illustrations Index 1843-1883* (Gomshall, 1995).

GOLDIE, George (1828-1887), architect, principally of Roman Catholic churches.

GOODE, The Very Revd Dr William (1861-1868), divine and Dean of Ripon after 1860.

GOODWIN, Harvey (1818-1891), Dean of Ely 1858-1869, formerly curate at St Giles', Camberwell 1845-1848, and Bishop of Carlisle after 1869.

GOSTLING, The Revd William (1696-1777), antiquary, of Canterbury.

GREY, Thomas Philip de (1781-1859), elder son of Thomas Robinson, 2nd Baron Grantham, assumed surname of Weddell 1803, became 2nd Earl de Grey and Baron Lucas 1833 and assumed surname of De Grey in lieu of Weddell, Lord Lieutenant of Ireland 1841-1844 and first President of the (Royal) Institute of British Architects, 1835-1859, rebuilt Wrest Park, Bedfordshire, in a French style using a French architect 1834-1836.

GRISSELL, Thomas (1801-1874), contractor, who was in partnership with Samuel Morton PETO, q.v., from 1830 until 1846, after which date Grissell continued with the contract for the New Palace of Westminster.

GRISSELL & PETO, contractors, responsible for erecting the Hungerford Market, q.v., on which GGS worked.

GRYLLS, Thomas J. (1845-1913), stained-glass artist who in 1868 with the help of G. F. BODLEY, q.v., joined with John Burlison, also formerly with CLAYTON & BELL, q.v., to found the firm of Burlison & Grylls, stained-glass manufacturers; see Martin Harrison, *Victorian Stained Glass* (1980).

GWILT, Charles Edwin, architect, who worked for GGS as clerk of works 1842-1845; son of George GWILT, q.v.

GWILT, George (1775-1856), architect and antiquary, responsible for the restoration of the choir and tower of St Saviour's, Southwark (now Southwark Cathedral) in 1822-1825.

HAHNEMANN, Christian Friedrich Samuel (1755-1843), German physician and founder of homeopathy.

HAKEWILL, 'Mr. T.H.' (? John Henry (1811-1880), architect).

HALL, Sir Benjamin (1802-1867), politician; First Commissioner of Works, 1855-1858; created Baron Llanover, 1859.

HAMILTON, The Revd Henry Parr (1794-1880), Dean of Salisbury after 1850 who contributed financially to the restoration of the cathedral.

HAMILTON, The Revd Walter Kerr (1808-1869), Bishop of Salisbury after 1854.

HARDMAN, John (1812-1867), designer and manufacturer, son of John Hardman, button manufacturer of Birmingham, whose firm he expanded into producing ecclesiastical metalwork and stained-glass under the inspiration of his friend and close associate A. W. N. PUGIN, q.v.

HARDWICK, Philip (1792-1870), architect of the Euston 'Arch'.

HAREWOOD, Henry Thynne Lascelles, 4th Earl of (1824-1892).

HEIDELOFF, Karl Alexander von (1789-1865), architect and early German medievalist; Conservator of City Treasures of Nuremberg in 1824 and Royal Bavarian Conservator after 1837, von Heideloff assembled a collection of medieval antiquities and restored Corburg Castle. He published *Ornamentik der Mittelalters* (1838-1855); see Michael J. Lewis, *The Politics of the German Gothic Revival; August Reichensperger* (Architectural History Foundation, New York, 1993).

HELPS, Sir Arthur (1813-1875), clerk of the Privy Council, author and editor of Prince Albert's speeches, 1862.

HIGGINS, William Mullinger, architect and surveyor.

HILL, Sir Rowland, 4th Bart, and 2nd Viscount, M.P. (1800-1875), of Hawkestone Hall, Salop, an 18th C house whose library was converted into a chapel by GGS in *c.*1860.

HOOK, The Revd Walter Farquhar (1798-1875), influential High Churchman who became Vicar of Leeds in 1837, subsequently rebuilding the parish church, and was made Dean of Chichester in 1859; All Souls' Church, Blackman Lane, in Leeds (1876-1880) was built in his memory to the designs of GGS. See Christopher Webster, *The Rebuilding of Leeds Parish Church 1837-41, and its Place in the Gothic Revival* (Ecclesiological Society, London, 1994).

HOPE, Alexander James Beresford, later A. J. B. BERESFORD-HOPE, M.P. (1820-1887), Conservative politician; son of Thomas Hope and the 'lay' leader of the Gothic Revival; patron of All Saints', Margaret Street, by William BUTTERFIELD, q.v., and Chairman of the Parliamentary Select Committee on the Foreign Office Reconstruction, 1858. See Irene & Henry William Law, *The Book of the Beresford Hopes* (London, 1925).

HOWSON, The Revd John Saul (1816-1885), Dean of Chester after 1867, editor of *Essays on Cathedrals by Various Writers* (1872).

HUDSON, Octavius, decorator, associated with the South Kensington circle, appointed instructor in Art for Woven & Printed Fabrics at the Department of Practical Art under Henry COLE, q.v., in 1852 and so came into contact with Christopher Dresser and Gottfried SEMPER, q.v.

HUNGERFORD MARKET, London, remarkable building with partial novel iron construction designed by Charles FOWLER, q.v., and built in 1831-1833 by GRISSELL & PETO, q.v., for whom GGS was then working; demolished in 1862. See Gavin Stamp, 'The Hungerford Market', in *AA Files*, No. 11, 1986.

HUNT, Sir Henry Arthur (1810-1889), architect and surveyor, employed as a surveyor by GRISSELL & PETO, q.v., on the Hungerford Market, q.v., when he probably first met GGS; later professional adviser to the Office of Works and as such a key figure in the Foreign Office saga.

HUNTINGTOWER, Lady, Katherine Elizabeth Camilla (1822-1896), younger daughter of Sir Joseph Burke, Bart, of Glinsk Castle, Co. Galway, who married her cousin, William Lionel Felix Tollemache, Lord Huntingtower (1820-1872), son of the 8th Earl of DYSART (1794-1878), q.v., in 1851, at both the Roman Catholic Church in Shepton Mallet and St John's Church, East Horrington, Somerset, and was buried in the Roman Catholic cemetery at Mortlake; their son became the 9th Earl but in 1881 a claim was made to the title by a Miss Acford (or Ackland), one of Lord Huntingtower's two mistresses, who claimed a previous Scottish marriage to Lord Huntingtower and who had children by him both before and after his marriage to Katherine Burke which, she claimed, was therefore null and the 9th Earl illegitimate; a leading article in *The Times* for 9th February 1881 wrote of the husband of the 'excellent and deeply-injured' Lady Huntingtower that, "had he died at three and twenty, it is not impossible he might have left the tradition of a life, if cruel and injurious to others, gay and brilliant and delightful to himself. Fortunately, perhaps, for moral example, an indomitable constitution, which he goaded as if it had been an enemy, preserved him to be the gaunt, dismal, needy adventurer whom the existing generation can remember. Repudiated by his parents, in constant strife with the cousin he had persuaded to marry him as a reformed rake, sued in the County Courts and by parish guardians, chained to an illiterate woman he had seduced, and whom he did not know whether to cast adrift on a pittance which he did not regularly pay, or at risk of the pains of felony, to own her as his wife in order to spite her who bore the title. He had done all in his power before he was thirty to wreck the noble inheritance of his ancestors. He had sold every expectancy, contingency or reversion upon which he could induce a usurer to lend a pound. Though his father's forty years of hoarding secured riches to the grandson whom the family of Tollemache acknowledge, it is still a question under litigation how far the ancient possessions of the house can be rescued from the inroads of the son's mad folly." Among the injuries Lord Huntingtower inflicted on his unfortunate wife was to have a black bow tied around the legs of every animal on the estate when he learned that she was returning to Ham and to have her met by a funeral cortège; for more of this see Major-General E. Tollemache, *The Tollemaches of Helmingham and Ham* (1949). See also the Hon. Frederick TOLLEMACHE, M.P.

HUSSEY, Richard Charles (1806-1887), architect, who became the partner of Thomas RICKMAN, q.v., in 1835 and who inherited his practice in 1838. Hussey subsequently became architect to Chester Cathedral.

IRVINE, James Thomas (c.1825-1900), GGS's stalwart clerk of works, born in Shetland, who worked for him 1854-78 and looked after several important cathedral restorations; a number of GGS's draft reports on cathedrals and other buildings, together with draft lectures, written in pencil on small bound notebooks, were given by John Oldrid Scott to Irvine, who presented them to the Society of Antiquaries of Scotland in 1887; these, along with letters from G. G. Scott junior, J. Drayton Wyatt, C. R. Baker King and others, together with other material including GGS's 'Diary of an Architectural Tour on the Continent' (in 1862 to France with GGS's two architect sons and Richard COAD [qq.v.] are now at the National Monuments Record of Scotland in Edinburgh.

IRVINGISM, the movement inspired by the Revd Edward Irving (1792-1834), the charismatic Scottish Evangelical preacher, who came to the Hatton Garden chapel in London in 1822 and whose apocalyptic visions resulted in his being expelled from the pulpit of the Scotch Church in Regent Square for heresy in 1832, after which his followers founded their own church which became the Catholic Apostolic Church.

JACKSON, Sir Thomas Graham (1835-1924), architect, who was a pupil of GGS, 1858-61, and who provided a valuable description of life in the office in Basil H. Jackson, ed., *Recollections of Thomas Graham Jackson* (London, 1950). 'Anglo-Jackson' became known for an eclectic Early Renaissance style and his book, *Modern Gothic Architecture*, was an early attack on the orthodoxies of GGS and his generation. Jackson's *Recollections*, p. 153, reveal that GGS "was under the impression that I was the author of a very slashing article in the *Quarterly Review* which made havoc of him and the school to which he belonged" – 'The State of English Architecture' (April 1872), in fact written by J. T. EMMETT, q.v.

'JEWS' CHAPEL', properly the EPISCOPAL JEWS' CHAPEL, Palestine Place, Bethnal Green, London, was designed by Charles Augustus Busby and George Maliphant and built by the London Society for Promoting Christianity amongst the Jews 1813-14; demolished 1895; the chapel, with its flanking schools, is illustrated in Neil Bingham, *C. A. Busby: The Regency Architect of Brighton & Hove*, RIBA (London, 1991).

JOHNSON, Mr (? John Johnson (1808-1879), architect and draughtsman, who published *Reliques of Ancient English Architecture* in 1857).

JOHNSON, Samuel (1691-1773), lexicographer, harmless drudge.

JONES, Inigo (1573-1652), architect.

JONES, The Revd William Basil, with E. A. FREEMAN, q.v., author of *History and Antiquities of St David's* (1856).

KELK, Sir John, Bart (1816-1886), contractor; builder of the 1862 Exhibition and much else in South Kensington after 1851, so that Scott was initially alarmed at his appointment to take on the Albert Memorial as he was close to Henry COLE, q.v.; at the Memorial's inauguration Kelk was annoyed that the Queen merely bowed and did not speak to him, and he then declined a knighthood (for the second time), holding out for the baronetcy which was eventually granted by Disraeli in 1874; his seat was Bentley Priory. See the *Survey of London* vol. xxxviii, *The Museums Area of South Kensington and Westminster* (London, 1975).

KEMPTHORNE, Sampson (1809-1873), architect to the Poor Law Commissioners, 1834, whose *First Report* (1835) published his model designs for workhouses; his father-in-law, the Revd Joseph Pratt, was Secretary of the Church Missionary Society and in 1841-42 Kempthorne emigrated to New Zealand.

KING, Elizabeth, née Scott (d. 1857), GGS's aunt, who married the Revd Samuel KING, q.v.

KING, Richard John (1818-1879), antiquary and author of Murray's cathedral guides, notably *Cathedrals of Wales* (1873).

KING, The Revd Samuel (d. 1856), GGS's uncle, curate of Hartwell and Stone, vicar of Latimers.

KING, Thomas (or George?), wine merchant of London and GGS's great-uncle, the father of the Revd Samuel KING, q.v., perpetual warden of the Episcopal Jews' Chapel, Bethnal Green.

KINGSLEY, Charles (1819-1875), writer and novelist.

KIRBY, John Joshua (1716-1774), architect and author of *Dr Brook Taylor's Method of Perspective made Easy, both in Theory and Practice* (1754), and other books on perspective drawing.

LANGE, Ludwig (1808-1868), German architect who entered the competition for the Nikolaikirche in Hamburg and who, with Emil Lange, won the abortive first competition for the Rijksmuseum in Amsterdam in 1863.

LANGLEY, Batty (1696-1751) architect and publisher, author of *Ancient Architecture Restored and Improved...* (1741-42), re-issued as *Gothic Architecture, improved by Rules and Proportions...* in 1747.

LAUD, William (1573-1645), Archbishop of Canterbury.

LAYARD, Sir Austen Henry (1817-1894), archaeologist, excavator of Nineveh and politician; Under-Secretary for Foreign Affairs 1861-66 and Chief Commissioner of Works, 1868-69, afterwards British minister in Madrid, then Constantinople.

LECHMERE, Sir Edmund Anthony Harley, M.P. (1826-1894), 3rd baronet, of Rhydd Court, Worcester, politician and chairman of the Tewkesbury Abbey Restoration Committee, who responded to the attacks on GGS's restoration proposals by William MORRIS, q.v., with a letter to the *Athenaeum* on 31st March, 1877.

LEEDS, ST JOHN'S CHURCH. Scott's claim for a share in the credit for saving this remarkable and rare church of the 1630s was fully justified; Richard Norman SHAW, q.v., had protested against plans to rebuild it in 1865, to the annoyance of the Trustees, but it was GGS's opinion as 'umpire' which counted, the Bishop of Ripon writing that "nothing but the respect I have for Mr Scott as the highest authority we have on Church Architecture, in connection with his strongly expressed opinion in this case, could have overcome my feeling". GGS's Report of November 1865 argued that the decayed building could be repaired, as it was "an object worthy of preservation... I do not hesitate to say that it stands alone among all the churches in this country as an instance of the old feelings for church architecture lasting on to the days of King Charles and expressing itself with the feeling of older times ..." Shaw's restoration of 1866-68 was, however, as thorough as one by GGS in that he discarded much original woodwork and removed the plaster from the walls; by 1884 he regretted what he had done, but the present appearance of the interior is owing to the 'reparation' carried out first by Shaw in 1884-85 and then by Temple MOORE, q.v., in 1890-91 at the instigation of Canon John SCOTT (1836-1907), the son of GGS's cousin, the Revd John SCOTT, q.v., who was vicar of St John's in 1883-98; see Janet Douglas & Ken Powell, *St John's Church, Leeds* (Redundant Churches Fund Guide, 1985, 1993).

LELAND, John (1506?-1552), 'earliest of modern English antiquaries'.

LE STRANGE, Henry l'Estrange Styleman (1815-1862), of Hunstanton Hall, Norfolk, "amateur of art" and decorative painter, responsible for the painted ceiling in the west tower of Ely Cathedral 1854-55 and for the first of that of the nave, begun 1858.

LEWIS, Joseph, director of the Midland Railway Co.

LOFTIE, the Revd William John (1839-1911), antiquary, art historian and journalist, born in Tandraghee, Co. Armagh; a founder member of the Society for the Protection of Ancient Buildings and author of several books on the architectural history of London; a frequent critic of GGS. His article on 'Thorough Restoration', in *Macmillan's Magazine* for June 1877, evidently caused great annoyance and GGS replied in the following issue (reprinted in Appendix 3 here).

LOGGAN, David (1635-?1700), topographical artist.

LUCY, The Revd William (1594-1677), Bishop of St David's.

LYNCH, Euphemia (1785-1853), GGS's mother, married the Revd Thomas SCOTT, q.v., in 1806.

LYSONS, Daniel (1762-1834), topographer, and Samuel (1763-1819), antiquary, who together published *Magna Britannia, being a Concise Topographical Account of the several Counties of Great Britain* after 1806.

MACAULAY, Thomas Babington, Baron (1800-1859), historian.

MACBRIDE, Dr John David (1778-1868), Principal of Magdalen Hall, Oxford, 1813-68.

MADDOX, George (1760-1843), architect and architectural drawing-master whose many pupils included Decimus BURTON and Edwin NASH, qq.v., as well as GGS. See Howard Colvin, *A Biographical Dictionary of British Architects 1660-1840* (1978).

MANNERS, Lord John James Robert, M.P., 7th Duke of Rutland (1818-1906), politician; a romantic Tory and a member of the 'Young England Party' associated with Benjamin DISRAELI, q.v., in the 1840s. He became First Commissioner of Works in Lord Derby's government of 1858-59; succeeded his brother as Duke of Rutland in 1888.

MANNERS-SUTTON, John Henry (1822-1898), M.P. for Newark 1847-1857, who asked GGS to rebuild his seat, Kelham Hall, Nottinghamshire, after a fire gutted it in 1857. See Mark Girouard, *The Victorian Country House* (1971, 1979).

MARLOWE, Christopher (1564-1593), dramatist.

MAROCHETTI, Baron Carlo (1805-1867), sculptor, born in Turin, who came to Britain in 1848 and was soon patronised by Queen Victoria and the Prince Consort; in discussing the Albert Memorial in 1865, F. T. PALGRAVE, q.v., concluded that "the choice of Marochetti for the figure of the Prince will seem simply disastrous", and when in 1867 GGS first saw his model for the figure it gave him "a severe shock"; but the problem was solved by the sculptor's sudden death soon after.

MEMLING, Hans (d. 1494), Flemish artist: here printed incorrectly as 'HEMLING'.

MICKLETHWAITE, John Thomas (1843-1906), architect and antiquary; pupil of GGS in 1862, set up in independent practice in 1869, in partnership with Somers Clarke 1876-92; author of *Modern Parish Churches* (1874), which criticised the church architecture of GGS's generation; Surveyor to Westminster Abbey 1898.

MILMAN, Henry Hart (1791-1868), Dean of St Paul's after 1849 and author of *The History of Latin Christianity* (1855).

MILNER, Dr John (1752-1826), Roman Catholic Bishop of Castabala and Vicar-Apostolic of the western district of England, archaeologist, antiquary and opponent of WYATT 'The Destroyer', q.v.

MINTON, Herbert (1793-1858), manufacturer of pottery and porcelain at Stoke-on-Trent; built and endowed schools and a church, designed by GGS, at Hartshill, near Stoke, in 1842.

MITFORD, Algernon Bertram Freeman (1837-1916) author and diplomat, secretary to Board of Works in Disraeli's government, 1874-80; created 1st Baron Redesdale 1902.

MOBERLY, The Revd George (1803-1885), Bishop of Salisbury after 1869.

MOFFATT, William Bonython (1812-1887), architect, son of a builder, met GGS while a pupil of James EDMESTON, q.v., and became his partner 1835-46, concentrating on securing commissions to design workhouses; subsequently designed the Earlswood Asylum, Surrey (1849-53), the Shire Hall at Taunton, Somerset (1855-58), and housing estates in London (Manor Villa, Norwood) and the West Country; much involved in railway speculation in the 1840s and arrested for debt of about £1,000 in 1860; incarcerated in the Queen's Bench Prison and released after six months after application for *habeas corpus*. GGS contributed £20 towards legal fees. See biography file in the British Architectural Library (RIBA) which includes 'Charles Matthew Strange (1838-1925), by his son, Charles Hilbert Strange'.

MOLLER, Dr Georg (1784-1852), German architectural historian and draughtsman, author of *Denkmäler der Deutschen Baukunst*, 3 vols (1815-51) who executed drawings of Cologne Cathedral for the *Domwerk* by Sulpiz BOISSERÉE, q.v.

MORDAUNT, Sir Charles, 10th Bart (1836-1897), M.P. for Warwickshire who asked GGS to rebuild his seat, Walton Hall, 1858-62.

MORRIS, William (1834-1896), artist, poet, writer, designer, radical reformer, who, apparently provoked by GGS's restoration of Tewkesbury Abbey, founded the Society for the Protection of Ancient Buildings in 1877 (announcing it in a letter to the *Athenaeum* on 10th March, 1877, with a further letter published on 7th April and the society's manifesto on 23rd June, 1877, under the title 'Restoration') and ferociously attacked GGS as a restorer, later describing him as "that (happily) dead dog". See Fiona MacCarthy, *William Morris: A Life for Our Time* (London, 1994). See also ANTI-RESTORATION MOVEMENT.

MORTIMER, Mr, Clerk of Works at the Nikolaikirche in Hamburg, who was killed in an accident on the site.

MÜLLER, Emilius, GGS's agent in Hamburg.

MYERS, George (1803-1875), builder, who worked mostly for A. W. N. PUGIN, q.v.; established first in Hull and moved business to London in 1842; built for GGS Loughborough Workhouse (1838), St Matthew's, Westminster (1849-51), Newfoundland Cathedral (c.1850), Christ Church, Swindon (1850-51), Christ Church, Ealing (1852), the Broad Sanctuary Houses, Westminster (1853), St Mary's, Stoke Newington (1858) and

Wellington College Chapel (1861). See Patricia Spencer-Silver, *Pugin's Builder: The Life and Work of George Myers* (Hull, 1994).

NASH, Edwin (1814-1884), architect, district surveyor for Penge and Norwood in the 1850s and 1860s.

NASH, John (1752-1835), architect.

NEALE, The Revd John Mason (1818-1866), High Church Anglican divine and author, and founder, with Benjamin WEBB, q.v., of the CAMBRIDGE CAMDEN SOCIETY, q.v.

NEALE, John Preston (1780-1847), architectural draughtsman, who published the *History and Antiquities of the Abbey Church of St Peter, Westminster* (1816-23) and *Views of the Seats of the Noblemen and Gentlemen in England, Wales, Scotland and Ireland* (1818-29).

NEWMAN, John Henry, Cardinal (1801-1890).

NEWTON, Sir Charles Thomas (1816-1894), archaeologist, Keeper of Greek and Roman Antiquities at the British Museum.

NICHOLSON, Peter (1765-1844), architect and prolific architectural publisher, responsible for, amongst others, *The Student's Instructor in Drawing and Working the Five Orders of Architecture, The Architectural Dictionary, The New Practical Builder and Workman's Companion*.

NORTHCOTE, Sir Stafford, Bart, M.P. (1818-1887), one of the secretaries of the Great Exhibition who became a politician and close associate of Benjamin DISRAELI; created the 1st Earl of Iddesleigh in 1885.

NORTON, John (1823-1904), architect; a pupil of Benjamin FERREY, q.v., who built up a large country house and ecclesiastical practice.

O'CONNELL, Daniel (1775-1847), Irish politician, known as 'The Liberator'.

OLDRID, Caroline (1811-1872), GGS's second cousin, whom he married in 1838.

OLDRID, Fanny (1806-1869), GGS's sister-in-law, who married his brother and her second cousin, the Revd Thomas SCOTT (1807-1888), q.v.

OLDRID, Helen (1810-1884), GGS's sister-in-law and second cousin.

OLDRID, J. (*c.*1778-1848), of Boston, Lincs, GGS's father-in-law.

OLDRID, Mrs J. (*c.*1787-1857), née Mary SCOTT, daughter of William SCOTT of Grimblethorpe Hall, q.v., GGS's mother-in-law and second cousin once removed.

OLDRID, The Revd John Henry (1808-1898), GGS's second cousin and brother-in-law, who married GGS's eldest sister, Euphemia SCOTT (1812-1865), q.v., and who succeeded GGS's father, the Revd Thomas SCOTT, q.v., as perpetual curate at Gawcott, then vicar of Alford, Lincs.

OUSELEY, The Revd Sir Frederick Arthur Gore, Bart (1825-1889), musician and composer, who built St Michael's College, Tenbury.

OUTRAM SHIELD, a London testimonial of silver plate presented in 1862 to Sir James Outram, Bart. (1803-1863), lieutenant-general of the Indian Army, which GGS may have confused with the Pakington Shield presented to Sir John PAKINGTON, q.v., which was modelled by H. H. ARMSTEAD, q.v., and shown at the 1862 International Exhibition.

OUVRY, Frederic (1814-1881), antiquary, President of the Society of Antiquaries 1876-78.

OWEN, Sir Richard (1804-1892), naturalist.

PAKINGTON, Sir John, Bart, M.P. (1799-1880), created 1st Baron Hampton 1874.

PALGRAVE, Francis Turner (1824-1897), poet and critic, compiler of *The Golden Treasury* (1861), whose critical articles of April and May 1863 on GGS's Albert Memorial design were republished in his *Essays on Art* in 1866 under the title 'The Albert Cross and English Monumental Sculpture'; his concluding essay, dated July 1865, expressed disappointment in the way in which GGS's conception was evolving and asserted that "his style wants originality and imagination ... The truth is that the Cross is an Italian design, imported whole into Hyde Park. It wants that first and last thing in architecture, appropriateness. It fails, not because so much is copied from older sources – for in all architecture copying holds a great place – but because it is *unimaginative* copying, and hence neither fused into harmony with itself, nor appropriate to its situation."

PALMER, The Revd William Jocelyn (1778-1853), Rector of Finmere and of Mixbury, Oxon.

PALMERSTON, The Rt Hon. Henry John Temple, Viscount Palmerston, M.P. (1784-1865), Prime Minister 1855-58 and 1859-65; GGS's principal opponent over the Foreign Office who was determined to have a building 'in the Italian style' and who, in 1861, announced to the House of Commons, "Sir, the battle of the books, the battle of the Big and Little Endeans, and the battle of the Green Ribands and the Blue Ribands at Constantinople were all as nothing compared with this battle of the Gothic and Palladian styles. If I were called upon to give an impartial opinion as to the issue of the conflict, I should say that the Gothic has been entirely defeated."

PARKER, John Henry (1806-1884), architectural writer and publisher of Oxford, who produced *An Introduction to the Study of Gothic Architecture* in 1849 amongst many other books; appointed first keeper of the Ashmolean Museum in 1870.

PARRY, Thomas Gambier (1816-1888), painter and authority on decorative painting, inventor of the 'spirit fresco' method, which he used for his decorative schemes in Ely Cathedral, Gloucester Cathedral and Tewkesbury Abbey (all done at his own expense); built the parish church at Highnam (1847-51, designed by Henry Woodyer) next to his Gloucestershire seat.

PAXTON, Sir Joseph, M.P. (1801-1865), gardener, landscape designer, railway promoter and enthusiast for iron and glass structures who created the Crystal Palace in 1851 and supervised its re-erection on Sydenham Hill in 1854.

PEACOCK, The Revd George (1791-1858), mathematician and Dean of Ely after 1839, who initiated the Victorian restoration of the Cathedral.

PEARSON, John Loughborough (1817-1897), church architect, GGS's successor as Surveyor to Westminster Abbey and the architect of Truro Cathedral. See Anthony Quiney, *John Loughborough Pearson*. (London and New York, 1979)

PEASE, Henry, M.P. (1807-1881), railway promoter and M.P. for South Durham 1857-65.

PEEL, Sir Robert, Bart, M.P. (1788-1850), Conservative politician and twice Prime Minister.

PENNETHORNE, Sir James (1801-1871), government architect, the pupil and successor of John Nash, who, despite the award of the RIBA Gold Medal in 1856, became the victim both of the desire of politicians like Sir Benjamin HALL, q.v., to reform the Office of Works, and of the Government Offices saga; after he had prepared plans for new government offices in Whitehall in 1854 and 1855, his efforts were superseded by Hall's proposals to hold competitions, although the Prime Minister, Lord PALMERSTON, q.v., attempted to reinstate Pennethorne in 1857, so provoking the successful lobbying of GGS and the Gothic Revivalists; see Geoffrey Tyack, *Sir James Pennethorne and the Making of Victorian London* (Cambridge, 1992).

PENRHYN, George Sholto Gordon Douglas-Pennant, 2nd Baron (1836-1907), M.P. for Caernarvonshire, whose seat was Penrhyn Castle, Bangor.

PENROSE, Francis Cranmer (1817-1903), architect, archaeologist and astronomer, surveyor to St Paul's Cathedral after 1852.

PERKINS, A. E., architect, of Worcester.

PETIT, the Revd John Louis (1801-1868), architectural artist and divine, who published such books as *Remarks on Church Architecture* in 1841 and *Architectural Studies in France* in 1854, amongst other illustrated books.

PETO, Sir Samuel Morton (1809-1889), contractor, in partnership with Thomas GRISSELL, q.v., 1830-46, after which he concentrated on railway building; made a baronet 1855 and retired from public life after the collapse of Peto & Betts in the financial panic of 1866.

PHILIP, John Birnie (1824-1875), sculptor, who worked for GGS on the Government Offices and the Albert Memorial frieze; his last work was the statue of Edward AKROYD outside the church of All Souls, Haley Hill, Halifax, q.v. After his death, Philip's widow arranged for his studio to be carried on by Signor Fucigna, in proof of whose ability a testimony was published signed by W. Calder Marshall, GGS and John R. CLAYTON, q.v.; his daughter married first E. W. GODWIN, q.v., and then Whistler, the artist.

PHILIPPA of Hainault (1314?-1369), wife of King Edward III of England.

PHILPOTT, The Revd Henry (1807-1892), Vice-Chancellor of Cambridge University who was made Bishop of Worcester in 1860.

PHIPPS, Sir Charles Beaumont (1801-1866), courtier, Keeper of Her Majesty's Purse, private secretary to the Prince Consort.

PHYFFERS, Theodore (d. 1872), Belgian sculptor who worked on the New Palace of Westminster and the India Office, whose death, unlike that of J. B. PHILIP, Alfred STEVENS and J. F. REDFERN, qq.v., seems not to have been noticed.

PLOWMAN, John (c.1773-1843), architect and builder of Oxford whose younger architect son, John Plowman (1807-1871), won second prize in the competition for the University Museum in Oxford in 1839.

POLLOCK, Sir William Frederick (1815-1888), Queen's Remembrancer and author.

POORE, Richard (d. 1237), Bishop of Chichester, Salisbury and Durham, who began the rebuilding of Salisbury Cathedral on its present site in 1219 and whose effigy on the north side of the high altar is now thought to be that of his successor, Bishop Bingham.

POWELL, James & Son, stained-glass manufacturers of Whitefriars, London, founded in 1834 by James Powell (d. 1844).

POWELL, John Hardman (1827-1895), designer, the son of William Powell, the partner and brother-in-law of John HARDMAN, q.v., went to work for A. W. N. PUGIN, q.v., in 1844, whose eldest daughter he married in 1850, and whom he succeeded as chief designer for John Hardman & Co. in 1852; see Alexandra Wedgwood, ed., 'Pugin in his home', A memoir by J. H. Powell, in *Architectural History*, xxxi (1988).

PRICE, Francis (c.1704-1753), architect surveyor to Salisbury Cathedral after 1737, whose *Series... of Observations... upon Salisbury Cathedral* were published in 1753.

PRICHARD, John (1817-1886), Diocesan Architect of Llandaff, Wales, in charge of restoring the Cathedral, in partnership with J. P. SEDDON, q.v., 1852-63, designed ETTINGTON HALL, Warwickshire, q.v., 1858-62.

PUGIN, Augustus Charles (1769-1832), architectural draughtsman, teacher and publisher, who worked with Rudolph Ackermann and Thomas Rowlandson on *The Microcosm of London* (1808-10), and produced *Specimens of Gothic Architecture* in two volumes in 1828-29 and *Examples of Gothic Architecture* in three volumes (two published posthumously) in 1828-36, amongst several influential architectural books. See Benjamin FERREY, q.v., *Recollections of A. N. Welby Pugin, and his Father, Augustus Pugin* (1861), reprinted with an introduction by Clive Wainwright (London, 1978).

PUGIN, Augustus Welby Northmore (1812-1852), church architect, Roman Catholic convert and polemicist, who worked for Sir Charles BARRY, q.v., on the New Palace of Westminster and who changed the course of the Gothic Revival through his example and his books: *Contrasts* (1836 and 1841); *The True Principles of Pointed or Christian Architecture* (1841); *The Present State of Ecclesiastical Architecture in England* (1843); the *Glossary of Ecclesiastical Ornament and Costume* (1844, 1846); and *A Treatise on Chancel Screens and Rood Lofts* (1851); see Alexandra Wedgwood, *A. W. N. Pugin and the Pugin Family* (London, 1985), and Paul Atterbury and Clive Wainwright, eds. *Pugin: A Gothic Passion* (New Haven & London, 1994).

PUSEY, The Revd Edward Bouverie (1800-1882), theologian who inspired the Oxford Movement within the Church of England.

RATTEE & KETT, Messrs, builders, of Cambridge.

REDFERN, James Frank (1838-1876), sculptor, who worked on the sculptures on the fleche of the Albert Memorial for GGS.

REDGRAVE, Richard (1804-1888), artist, actively involved in the government school of design.

REICHENSPERGER, August (1808-1895), influential German architectural theorist, writer and propagandist for Gothic as the national style for Germany, who met GGS on his first visit to England in 1846, became a powerful advocate for his (unexecuted) designs for the Hamburg Rathaus (1854) – 'giving a German city a German building' – and the Berlin Reichstag (1873), and had a great Gothic chair designed by GGS in his study in Cologne; see Michael J. Lewis, *The Politics of the German Gothic Revival: August Reichensperger* (Architectural History Foundation, New York, 1993).

REYNOLDS, Sir Joshua (1723-1792), painter.

RICHMOND, Charles Henry Gordon-Lennox, 6th Duke of Richmond & Lennox (1818-1903).

RICHMOND, George (1809-1896), portrait painter, who executed the crayon portrait of GGS engraved as the frontispiece of *Recollections*.

RICKMAN, Thomas (1776-1841), architect, sometime in partnership with Henry Hutchinson and with R. C. HUSSEY, q.v., and author of *An Attempt to Discriminate the Styles of Architecture in England from the Conquest to the Reformation*, first published in 1817, in which the terms 'Early English', 'Decorated' and 'Perpendicular' were proposed.

RIDSDALE JUDGEMENT, the, concerning the Catholic liturgical practices carried on by the incumbent of St Peter's, Folkestone, in the first prosecution made under Disraeli's Public Worship Regulation Act of 1874 intended to outlaw Ritualism within the Church of England; after appeal, the Privy Council in 1877 found against the Revd C. J. Ridsdale on his wearing of vestments, the use of wafer-bread and the erection of a crucifix on a rood screen, but reversed the judgement of the Public Worship Regulation Court against the Eastward Position at the altar; see Michael Reynolds, *Martyr of Ritualism* (London, 1965).

RIPON, George Frederick Samuel Robinson, 2nd Earl of and 1st Marquis of (1827-1909).

ROBERTS, David (1796-1864), Scottish topographical painter who specialised in architectural subjects, best known for views of Egyptian temples.

ROBERTS, Henry (1803-1876), architect, a pupil of Charles FOWLER, q.v., who designed the Fishmongers' Hall in the City of London, 1832-55, and the Camberwell Collegiate School (demolished) of 1834-35, on both of which GGS worked; later specialised in improved working class housing; see James Stevens Curl, *The Life and Work of Henry Roberts 1803-1876, Architect* (Chichester, 1983).

ROCHEAD, John Thomas (1814-1878), architect, born in Edinburgh and practising in Glasgow, designer of the Wallace Monument at Stirling, who was placed third in the competition for the War Office.

ROPER, David Riddall (c. 1774-1855), architect and surveyor of London, designer of the Shot Tower in Lambeth (demolished) and St Mark's Church, Kennington.

ROSE, The Revd Henry John (1800-1873), rector of Houghton Conquest after 1837, Archdeacon of Bedford 1866, brother-in-law of the Revd J. W. BURGON, q.v.

ROYAL COURTS OF JUSTICE, Strand, London, for which GGS unsuccessfully entered the competition held in 1866-67; after the usual muddle and deviousness characteristic of such competitions, GGS's old pupil G. E. STREET, q.v., was appointed architect in 1868 and the new courts, replacing those attached to the Palace of Westminster, were built in

Appendix 3

1874-82; see David B. Brownlee, *The Law Courts: The Architecture of George Edmund Street* (New York, Cambridge & London, 1984).

ROYAL INSTITUTE OF BRITISH ARCHITECTS (RIBA), until 1866 the INSTITUTE OF BRITISH ARCHITECTS, constituted 1834, Charter of Incorporation granted 1837, with Earl de GREY, q.v., as President and Professor DONALDSON, q.v., as one of the Hon. Secretaries; GGS received the Institute's Royal Gold Medal in 1859 and was President in 1873-76; see J. A. Gotch, ed., *The Growth and Work of the Royal Institute of British Architects 1834-1934* (1934).

RUSKIN, John (1819-1900), artist, art-critic and social reformer, whose *Seven Lamps of Architecture* (1849) and *Stones of Venice* (1851-53) were hugely influential on architects; eloquent opponent of the restoration of ancient buildings and founder member of the Society for the Protection of Ancient Buildings in 1877 who declined the Gold Medal of the Royal Institute of British Architects in 1874 when GGS was President because he disapproved both of restoration and of professionalism – to the Institute's embarrassment as the Queen had already been notified, while GGS took the rebuttal personally: in his first reply to Charles Eastlake, Secretary of the RIBA, in May 1874 Ruskin listed four examples of the degradation of ancient buildings – three of which were in Italy – and claimed that "For the existence of this state of things we, the members, actual and honorary, of the Institute of British Architects are assuredly answerable, at least in England ..." and in his response to GGS's appeal to reconsider, he wrote "My dear Sir Gilbert ... The primary object of all such Associations is to exalt the power of their own profession over the mind of the public, power being in this century synonymous with wealth. And the root of all the evil and ruin which this century has seen (and it has destroyed more than the French Revolution did of what *that* had left) is summed up in four words, 'Commission on the Cost'. And, from any body of architects, however small, who will bind themselves henceforward to accept a given salary ... for their daily work, and to work with their men (or at least with their own hands, on the sculpture of the building) while they take such salary, from such a body I will take a medal tomorrow ..." (see Cook & Wedderburn, *The Works of John Ruskin*, vol. xxxiv, pp. 516-6); while in a letter to Thomas Carlyle, Ruskin was more explicit and implicitly critical of GGS: "I cannot accept medals from people who let themselves out to build Gothic Advertisements for Railroads – Greek Advertisements for firms in the city – and – whatever Lord Palmerston or Mr Gladstone chose to order opposite Whitehall – while they allow every beautiful building in France and Italy to be destroyed, for the 'job' of its restoration."

RUSSELL, Lord John, M.P. (1792-1878), 3rd son of 6th Duke of Bedford, Whig politician and Prime Minister 1846-51; created Earl Russell 1861.

ST ALBAN'S, Herts: Abbey, made the Cathedral of a new diocese in 1877.

ST AUBYN, James Pearse (1815-1895), architect, in practice in Devonport and in London.

SALISBURY, Marchioness of (d. 1899), Georgina Caroline, daughter of Sir Edward Hall Alderson, married in 1857 the 3rd Marquis of Salisbury (1830-1903), who succeeded to the title in 1868.

SALTER, Stephen, model maker employed in GGS's office.

SALVIATI, Dr Antonio (1816-1890), Venetian lawyer who became interested in mosaic and the restoration of those in St Mark's, Venice; in partnership with Lorenzo Radi 1859 and executed mosaics designed by Alfred STEVENS, q.v., for St Paul's Cathedral, completed in 1864, founded the Società Salviati e Compagni in 1866 with British support, notably that of A. H. LAYARD, q.v., and worked on the Westminster Abbey reredos and the Albert Memorial for GGS; left English associates in 1876 and founded his own Venice & Murano glass and mosaic company.

SALVIN, Anthony, the younger (1827-1881), the architect son of Anthony Salvin (1799-1881), the successful country house architect.

SANDBACH, Henry Robertson (1807-1895), of Hafodunos, near Llangernyw, Co. Denbigh, who asked GGS to build his seat (not to be confused with the demolished Hafod) in 1861-66. "In red brick and stone, it is one of the most convincing demonstrations of Scott's ability to use fourteenth-century Gothic for a workable Victorian house – better even than Kelham." Elisabeth Beazley and Peter Howell, *The Companion Guide to North Wales* (London, 1975).

SANDFORD, Francis (1630-1694), herald and genealogist, author of *A Genealogical History of the Kings of England and Monarchs of Great Britain &c...* (1677).

SCHOPENHAUER, Arthur (1788-1860), German philosopher; in the *Builder* for 14th June, 1879, p. 645, the reviewer of Scott's *Recollections* (George GODWIN? q.v.) noted that "... his views and observations upon important subjects beyond the profession are disappointing. It is impossible not to smile at his account of his pleasure in talking to 'an old German philosopher named Schopenhauer', who, however, was apparently an 'Atheist', without apparently the slightest suspicion that he is speaking of a man who fills a much more important place in modern intellectual Europe than Scott or any other modern architect."

SCOTT, Adrian Gilbert (1882-1963), grandson, son of George Gilbert Scott junior, architect of Roman Catholic churches.

SCOTT, Albert Henry (1844-1865), third son.

SCOTT, Alwyne Gilbert (1849-1878), fourth son.

SCOTT, Anne (1822; died in infancy), sister.

SCOTT, the Revd Benjamin (1788-1830), uncle, vicar of Priors Salford, Bideford and of Great Harborough.

SCOTT, Caroline, née Oldrid (1811-1872), wife and cousin, married GGS 1838.

SCOTT, Dukinfield Henry (1854-1934), fifth son, palaeobotanist, hon. director of the Jodrell Laboratory at Kew.

SCOTT, Edith (1852-1871), niece.

SCOTT, Elizabeth (d. 1857), aunt, who married the Revd Samuel KING, q.v.

SCOTT, Elizabeth King (1815, died in infancy), sister.

SCOTT, Elizabeth (1824-1884), sister, married the Revd William Graeme Gibson.

SCOTT, Euphemia (1813-1865), sister, married the Revd J. H. Oldrid.

SCOTT, Sir Francis Edward, 2nd and 3rd Bart (1824-1863), of Great Barr Hill near Birmingham, for whom GGS (no relation) designed a lodge, bridge and boat-house and who published the pamphlet, *Shall the New Foreign Office be Gothic or Classic? A Plea for the Former: Addressed to the Members of the House of Commons* (1860).

SCOTT, George Gilbert: for a complete list of works by GGS, with dates where known, see David Cole, *The Work of Sir Gilbert Scott* (London, 1980).

SCOTT, George Gilbert, *homes:*

    Avenue Road, St John's Wood 1844-56

    Admiral's House, Hampstead 1856-64

    Manor House, Ham, Surrey 1864-69 and 1873-75

    Parkhurst, Leith Hill, Surrey 1869-70

    Rook's Nest, Godstone, Surrey 1870-73

    Courtfield House, Collingham Road, Kensington 1875-78

SCOTT, George Gilbert, *offices:*

    Holborn, Warwick Court, *c.* 1831-34

    Carlton Chambers, Regent Street 1835-38

    No. 20 (No. 31 after 1866) Spring Gardens, Trafalgar Square 1838-78

SCOTT, George Gilbert, junior (1839-1897), eldest son, architect and author of *An Essay on the History of English Church Architecture Prior to the Separation from the Roman Obedience* (1881).

SCOTT, Sir Giles Gilbert (1880-1960), grandson, son of George Gilbert Scott junior, architect of Liverpool Cathedral, the House of Commons, Bankside Power Station, &c.

SCOTT, The Revd John (1809-1886), elder brother, vicar of St Paul's, Cambridge; rector of Tydd St Giles; vicar of SS Peter & Paul, Wisbech, canon of Ely.

SCOTT, The Revd John (1809-1865), cousin, vicar of St Mary's Hull, son of GGS's uncle, the Revd John Scott (1779-1834), vicar of St Mary's Hull; his son, Canon John Scott (1836-1907), became vicar of ST JOHN'S, LEEDS, q.v.

SCOTT, John Oldrid (1841-1913), second son, architect, who inherited GGS's practice in 1878.

SCOTT ?(John) William, of Grimblethorpe Hall, near Louth, Lincolnshire, great uncle.

SCOTT, Mary Jane (1821-1864), sister.

SCOTT, Mary, mother-in-law and second cousin once removed, who married J. OLDRID of Boston, q.v.

SCOTT, The Revd Melville Horne (1827-1898), brother, vicar of Ockbrook, Prebendary of Lichfield, Archdeacon of Stafford.

SCOTT, Nathaniel Gilbert (1808, died in infancy), brother.

SCOTT, Nathaniel Gilbert (1814-1830), brother.

SCOTT, Nathaniel Gilbert (1840-1865), nephew.

SCOTT, Richard Gilbert (b. 1923), great-grandson, architect.

SCOTT, Samuel Hey (1856-1866), nephew.

SCOTT, Samuel King (1818-1865), surgeon, of Brighton, brother.

SCOTT, Euphemia, née Lynch (1785-1853), mother, only daughter of Dr Lynch of Antigua, married the Revd Thomas SCOTT, q.v., 1806.

SCOTT, The Revd Thomas (1747-1821), grandfather, known as 'The Commentator', son of John Scott (d. 1777), a grazier; ordained priest 1773, wrote a commentary on the Bible, *The Holy Bible, with ... Notes* (1788-92), and many other theological works, which were collected and published 1805-08, rector of Aston Sandford, Bucks, 1801.

SCOTT, The Revd Thomas (1780-1835), first perpetual curate of Gawcott 1806-33, rector of Wappenham 1833-35, father.

SCOTT, The Revd Thomas (1807-1880), elder brother, rector of Wappenham 1835, married his cousin Fanny Margaret OLDRID (1806-1869).

SCOTT, The Revd Thomas (1831-1914), nephew, vicar of West Ham, rector of Lavenham, canon of St Albans.

SCOTT, Sir Walter (1771-1832), Scottish novelist and poet; no relation.

SCOTT, The Revd William Langstone (1817-1888), vicar of Abthorpe, Northants., rector of Great Dunmow, Essex, brother.

SEDDING, John Dando (1838-1891), architect.

SEDDON, John Pollard (1827-1906), Gothic architect, designer of University of Wales College at Aberystwyth; partner of John PRICHARD, q.v., of Llandaff, 1852-63; placed third in the competition for the War Office.

SELBORNE, Sir Roundell Palmer, 1st Baron (1812-1895), son of the Revd William Jocelyn PALMER (1778-1853), Rector of Finmere and of Mixbury, Oxon., q.v.

SEMPER, Gottfried (1803-1879), German architect and theorist, designer of the Dresden Opera and unsuccessful competitor for the Nikolaikirche in Hamburg, who spent the years 1851-55 in London during his exile from Germany after the 1848 Revolution; his defeat in Hamburg by GGS, backed by BOISSERÉE and ZWIRNER, qqv., turned Semper against Gothic, about which style he was especially critical in his great book, *Der Stil in den technischen und tektonischen Kunsten, oder praktische Aesthetik*, 1860 & 1863. See Wolfgang Herrmann, *Gottfried Semper: In Search of Architecture* (Cambridge, Mass., & London, 1984).

SHARPE, Edmund (1809-1877), architect, railway engineer, antiquarian and enthusiast for terra-cotta, who published *Seven Periods of Gothic Architecture* (1851).

SHAW, Richard Norman (1831-1912), architect; see LEEDS, ST JOHN'S CHURCH; also see Andrew Saint, *Richard Norman Shaw* (London, 1976).

SHEILDS, Francis Webb, engineer, who worked on the rebuilding of the Crystal Palace at Sydenham and wrote a successful textbook, *The Strains on Structures of Ironwork; with Practical Remarks on Iron Construction* (1861); assisted GGS on the restoration of Salisbury Cathedral as described in *Salisbury Cathedral. Report on the Tower and its Sustaining Piers* by GGS (1865).

SHELLEY, Sir John, 7th Bart (1808-1867), M.P.

SHEPHERD, Sir Thomas Cotton, Bt, of Thornton Hall, Bucks, (born 1785) who was presumably the Sir Thomas Cotton Shepherd Shepherd at whose house near Uttoxeter GGS met the Revd Thomas STEVENS, q.v.

SKIDMORE, Francis Alfred (1816-1896), designer and manufacturer of art metalwork, son of a Coventry watchmaker, jeweller and silversmith, who studied historical metalwork and joined the Oxford Architectural Society and the Ecclesiological Society, q.v., published 'On the Use of Metals in

Church Building and Decoration' in the *Ecclesiologist* in 1854; joined his father as Francis Skidmore & Son by 1845 and set up on his own in 1850, contractor for the iron roof in the Oxford University Museum (1855-59) – which initially failed; in 1861 joined with six others to form Skidmore's Art Manufacturers Company which won a medal 'for progress, for elegance of design, and for excellent workmanship' at the Great International Exhibition of 1862; produced much metalwork for GGS, notably at the Albert Memorial and screens in Hereford, Salisbury, Ely and Lichfield Cathedrals – the screen in Salisbury Cathedral was removed and broken up in 1959-60, the magnificent Hereford Cathedral screen, of iron, brass, mosaic, jewels and stones, which was exhibited at the International Exhibition of 1862 and for which GGS subscribed £50, was taken out in 1967 and is now in store at the Victoria & Albert Museum; by 1873 Skidmore was failing to deliver gas fittings for the Midland Grand Hotel on time and the firm amalgamated with Messrs Winfield of Birmingham in the 1870s; Skidmore then set up in business again at Meriden and then moved to Birmingham; but again fell into financial difficulties following partial blindness and a consequent carriage accident and was assisted by charitable subscriptions in his last years; see *Victorian Church Art*, V & A catalogue (1971).

SLATER, William (1819-1873), architect, pupil of R. C. CARPENTER, q.v., with whose son, R. H. Carpenter, he was in partnership 1863-73; architect to Chichester Cathedral.

SMILES, Samuel (1812-1904), writer, railway promoter, historian of engineering and social reformer, who published *Self-Help, with Illustrations of Character and Conduct* (1859).

SMIRKE, Sir Robert (1781-1867), prolific Greek Revival architect, designer of the British Museum.

SMIRKE, Sydney (1798-1877), Classical architect, younger brother of Sir Robert SMIRKE, q.v., responsible for the Reading Room of the British Museum, 1854-57, and the additions to Burlington House, Piccadilly, for the Royal Academy 1866-70.

SOANE, Sir John (1753-1837), architect of the Bank of England and Professor of Architecture at the Royal Academy.

SOUTHEY, Robert (1774-1843), poet, writer and historian, whose *Life of Wesley* appeared in 1820.

SOUTH KENSINGTON MUSEUM, renamed the Victoria & Albert Museum in 1899, founded 1852, opened in South Kensington, 1857, under its first secretary, Sir Henry COLE, q.v.

SPENCE, Sir Basil (1907-1976), architect of Coventry Cathedral, who reacted violently to criticism of his design for the Home Office at Queen Anne's Mansions at the end of his life.

SPENSER, Edmund (?1552-1599), poet.

SPRINGBETT, Enoch Hodkinson, architect(?).

SPRY, The Revd John Hume (1778/9-1854), Bampton lecturer in 1815, rector of Marylebone after 1825, and after 1828 Prebendary of Canterbury Cathedral, where he is buried.

STANLEY, The Revd Dr Arthur Penrhyn (1815-1881), Dean of Westminster, 1864, author of *Memorials of Westminster Abbey* (1868).

STANLEY, Edward Geoffrey, M.P. (1799-1869), became 14th Earl of Derby 1851, politician, Prime Minister in 1852 and 1858-59.

STANLEY, Edward Henry (1826-1893), became 15th Earl of Derby 1869, politician, Secretary of State for India 1858-59 in his father's Conservative government.

STEINBACH, Erwin von (d. 1318), architect of the west front of Strassburg Cathedral.

STEVENS, Alfred (1817-1875) – incorrectly printed as 'Stephens', sculptor, creator of the Wellington Monument in St Paul's Cathedral and "the greatest genius of English sculpture"; see Susan Beattie, *Alfred Stevens 1817-75* (London, 1975).

STEVENS, The Revd Thomas (1809-1888), son of the rector of Bradfield, Assistant Poor Law Commissioner 1836-39, rector of Bradfield after 1843, founder and warden of St Andrew's College, Bradfield 1850.

STEVENSON, John James (1832-1908), domestic architect born in Glasgow who became a leader in the 'Queen Anne' revival and who published *House Architecture* in 1879; worked for GGS in London 1858-60 but soon became a severe critic of his restoration practice, delivering a lecture to the Glasgow Architectural Society in 1863 which complained of ill-advised and destructive restorers and who in 1877 attacked GGS in terms which shocked many of his audience at the RIBA in a lecture on 'Architectural restoration: its principles and practice' (*Transactions of the Royal Institute of British Architects*, vol. xxvii, 1877, pp. 219-235 and 256-268) which provoked the response from GGS printed here as Appendix 3; founder member of the Society for the Protection of Ancient Buildings in 1877; see 'Sir Gilbert Scott and his critics' in Wim Denslagen, *Architectural Restoration in Western Europe: Controversy and Continuity* (Amsterdam, 1994).

STORER, James Sargant (1771-1853), topographical and architectural artist and engraver who with his son Henry Sargant (1795-1837), published *The Cathedrals of Great Britain* in 1814-19.

STRANGE, Charles Hilbert, son of Charles Matthew STRANGE, q.v.

STRANGE, Charles Matthew (1838-1925), architect, who worked for W. B. MOFFATT, q.v., in 1859-60.

STREET, George Edmund (1824-1881), architect, arguably the greatest genius of the High Victorian Gothic Revival, assistant to GGS 1844-49, designer of the Royal Courts of Justice (1866-82), author of *Brick and Marble in the Middle Ages: Notes of a Tour in the North of Italy* (1855), and *Some Account of Gothic Architecture in Spain* (1865); see Arthur Edmund Street, *A Memoir of George Edmund Street, R.A. 1824-1881, by his son* (London, 1888, reprinted New York, 1972), and David B. Brownlee, *The Law Courts: The Architecture of George Edmund Street* (New York, Cambridge & London, 1984).

STUART, James (1713-1788), known as 'Athenian' Stuart (or 'Stewart', as printed here), architect and creator, with Nicholas Revett, of *The Antiquities of Athens* (first volume published 1762; second and third published posthumously 1789 and 1816).

SWIFT, Jonathan (1667-1745), Dean of St Patrick's, Dublin and satirist, whose *A Tale of a Tub* was published in 1704.

TAYLOR, The Revd Jeremy (1613-1667), Bishop of Down and Connor and Anglican divine.

TAYLOR, Sir Robert (1714-1778), architect to the Bank of England and of Heveningham Hall, who built his own house at No. 34 Spring Gardens and to whom Albert Richardson attributed the doorcase added in c. 1760 to No. 20 (renumbered in 1866 as No. 31) Spring Gardens, a Queen Anne house in which GGS had his office: see SCOTT, George Gilbert, *homes, offices*; now demolished, this is illustrated in A. E. Richardson & C. Lovett Gill, *London Houses from 1660 to 1820* (London, 1911).

TENISON, The Revd Thomas (1636-1715), Archbishop of Canterbury.

TEULON, Samuel Sanders (1812-73), Gothic architect.

THACKERAY, William Makepeace (1811-1863), novelist.

THIRLWALL, Connop (1797-1875), Bishop of St David's and historian.

THOMSON, Alexander (1817-1875), known as 'Greek' Thomson, architect of Glasgow, who condemned the choice of the Gothic style and GGS's designs for the new buildings for Glasgow University, q.v., on Gilmourhill in his lecture of 1866 to the Glasgow Architectural Society on 'An Enquiry as to whether the Character and Purpose of the University can be fully expressed in Medieval Architecture – and whether the merits of the proposed Plans have justified the University Authorities in going from home for an Architect', published in the *Builder* for 19th May, 1866 as 'An Inquiry as to the Appropriateness of the Gothic Style for the Proposed Buildings for the University of Glasgow, with some Remarks on Mr Scott's

Plans'; later met G. G. SCOTT Junior, q.v., in 1871 at dinner with J. J. STEVENSON, q.v., in London and described how "he made his appearance in black knee breeks black silk stockings high heeled shoes with large buckles, blue coat, yellow vest white neck cloth with stiffener and frilled shirt – He is one of the Queen Ann folks"; see Ronald McFadzean, *The Life and Work of Alexander Thomson* (London, 1979), and Gavin Stamp and Sam McKinstry, eds., *'Greek Thomson'* (Edinburgh, 1994).

THOMSON, Dr Allen (1809-1884), biologist, Professor of Anatomy at the University of Glasgow 1848-77 and chairman of the removal and buildings committee 1863-74.

THORNE, James (1815-1881), antiquary and author of the *Handbook to the Environs of London* (2 vols, London, 1876).

THORNHILL, Sir James (1675-1734), painter, responsible for decorating the interior of the dome of St Paul's Cathedral.

THORP, The Revd Thomas (1797-1877), Fellow of Trinity College, Cambridge, Archdeacon and Chancellor of Bristol, rector of Kennarton 1838-77, first President of the CAMBRIDGE CAMDEN SOCIETY, q.v., 1839-59.

THYNNE, The Revd Lord John (1798-1881), 3rd son of the 2nd Marquis of Bath, Sub-Dean of Westminster after 1835.

TINNEY, Colonel, M.P.: nobody of this name is cited in *Who's Who of British Members of Parliament, 1832-1885*.

TITE, Sir William (1798-1873), wealthy architect, businessman and politician who, as M.P. for Bath after 1855, opposed GGS's Gothic designs for the Government Offices; designer of the Scotch Church in Regent Square 1827-28 and the Royal Exchange 1840-44, which commission he deviously secured through his City of London connections against the superior competition winning design by C. R. COCKERELL, q.v.; President of the RIBA 1861-63 and 1867-70; knighted 1869.

TOLLEMACHE, The Hon Frederick, M.P. (1804-1888), of Ham House, son of William, Lord Huntingtower, and brother of the 8th Earl of DYSART, q.v.

TOMLINE, The Revd Sir George Pretyman (1750-1827), Bishop of Lincoln after 1787 and author of *A Refutation of Calvinism* (1803) which brought him into controversy with Thomas SCOTT, q.v.

TRENCH, the Revd Richard Chenevix (1807-1886), Dean of Westminster 1856, Archbishop of Dublin 1864.

TRIQUETI, Henri Joseph François, Baron de (1807-1874), sculptor, born in Conflans, France, of Piedmontese origins, responsible for the bronze doors and high altar of the Church of the Madeleine in Paris 1834-41, the effigy of

Duke Ferdinand of Orleans in the Chapelle St Ferdinand at Neuilly-sur-Seine 1842-43 and involved in the restoration of the Ste Chapelle in Paris in the 1840s; invited to England in 1864 to decorate St Paul's Cathedral, provoking opposition on the grounds that he was a Roman Catholic (which was denied), and to execute the sculpture of the reredos, designed by GGS, and the recumbent figure of the Prince Consort in the Albert Memorial Chapel in St George's Chapel, Windsor Castle 1863-73, where his walls of 'marble inlay scriptural panels' were bought by the Royal Family from the 1867 Paris Universal Exhibition; author of *Les Trois Musées de Londres*.

VAUGHAN, Edward (d. 1522), Bishop of St David's.

VIOLLET-LE-DUC, Eugène Emmanuel (1814-1879), French architect and theorist whose *Dictionnaire raisonné de l'architecture française du XI au XVI siècle* was published in ten volumes between 1854 and 1868.

VOYSEY, Annesley (c. 1794-1839), architect and surveyor, designer in *c.*1823 of the first building in London intended exclusively for offices; emigrated to Jamaica where he died; father of the Revd Charles Voysey, whose son was the architect C. F. A. Voysey.

WALCOTT, Mackenzie Edward Charles (1821-1880), ecclesiologist, author of the *Guide to the Cathedrals of England and Wales* (1858, 1860, &c).

WALLACE, Robert (*c.*1790-1874), architect, won competition for National Scotch Church in Regent Square 1824 but that by William TITE, q.v., was built; worked at St Saviour's Southwark (now Southwark Cathedral), 1829-30; designed Athenaeum complex, Derby 1837-39.

WALLER, Mr, surveyor.

WALLER, Frederick Sandham (1822-1905), architect, pupil and partner of Thomas FULLJAMES of Gloucester (1808-1874), q.v.

WALPOLE, Horace, 4th Earl of Orford (1717-1797), writer and amateur architect who pioneered the revival of Gothic in his house, Strawberry Hill, at Twickenham.

WATERHOUSE, Alfred (1830-1905), prolific secular Gothic architect, designer of Manchester Town Hall 1868-77 and the Natural History Museum 1872-80; see Colin Cunningham and Prudence Waterhouse, *Alfred Waterhouse 1830-1905* (Oxford, 1992).

WATTS, George Frederic (1817-1904), painter and sculptor, responsible for the monument to Bishop Lonsdale at Lichfield 1871 and 'Physical Energy' in Kensington Gardens, *c.*1883-1906.

WATTS, Isaac (1674-1748), hymn writer, whose monument of 1774 in Westminster Abbey is by the sculptor Thomas Banks.

WEATHERLEY, William Samuel (1854-1922), architect, assistant to GGS 1870-78 who subsequently worked for G. G. SCOTT Junior.

WEBB, The Revd Benjamin (1819-1885), ecclesiologist, founder, with J. M. NEALE, q.v., of the CAMBRIDGE CAMDEN SOCIETY, q.v., vicar of St Andrew's, Wells Street, London 1862.

WELDON, The Revd George Warburton (1823-1889), vicar of St Saviour's, Upper Chelsea 1869-82.

WESLEY, The Revd John (1703-1791), evangelist.

WEST, John (d.1814), builder of Gawcott church.

WESTCOTT, The Revd Brooke Foss (1825-1901), canon of Peterborough 1869-83, Bishop of Durham after 1890.

WHEWELL, The Revd William (1794-1866), scientist and antiquary, Master of Trinity College, Cambridge, and author of *Architectural Notes on German Churches, with Remarks on the Origin of Gothic Architecture* (1830, enlarged edition 1835) with *Notes during an Architectural Tour in Picardy and Normandy.*

WHITE, Mr, builder, Salisbury.

WHITE, William (1825-1900), important Gothic church architect, who worked for GGS 1845-47. See Stefan Muthesius, *The High Victorian Movement in Architecture 1850-1870* (London & Boston, 1972).

WILBERFORCE, The Revd Samuel (1805-1873), Bishop of Oxford 1845-69, then Bishop of Winchester; known as 'Soapy Sam'.

WILBERFORCE, William (1759-1833), philanthropist.

WILD, James William (1814-1892), architect, printed here incorrectly as 'Wylde', much travelled in Europe, Asia Minor and Egypt 1842-48, authority on Arab art and architecture, Curator of Sir John Soane's Museum 1878-92, designed Christ Church, Streatham, 1842 and the Bethnal Green Museum, 1872.

WILKES, John (1727-1797), radical politician, author of *An Essay on Woman* (1763).

WILLEMENT, Thomas (1786-1871), writer on heraldry and pioneer in the revival of stained glass manufacture, 'Heraldic Artist to King George IV', 'Artist in Stained Glass to Queen Victoria'.

WILLIAM THE ENGLISHMAN or 'English William' (d. 1214), mason, who succeeded WILLIAM OF SENS in the rebuilding of Canterbury Cathedral in 1178.

WILLIAM OF SENS (d. 1180), mason who designed the rebuilding of Canterbury Cathedral after the fire of 1174 until he was invalided home to France after an accident in 1178.

WILLIAM OF WYKEHAM (1324-1404), Bishop of Winchester and architectural administrator, Clerk of Works at Windsor Castle, Chief Warden and Surveyor of Royal Castles, &c.

WILLIAMS, The Revd Sir Erasmus Henry Griffies, 2nd Bart (1794-1870), rector of Rushall after 1829, Chancellor of St David's after 1858.

WILLIS, Professor Robert (1800-1875), archaeologist and Jacksonian Professor of Applied Mechanics at Cambridge University after 1837, author of numerous studies of the constructional history of medieval buildings, notably *Remarks on the Architecture of the Middle Ages, especially of Italy* (1835), 'On the Construction of the Vaults of the Middle Ages', in the *Transactions of the Institute of British Architects* (1841) and the *Architectural History of the University and Colleges of Cambridge* (completed posthumously by J. W. Clark) 1886.

WINSTON, Charles (1814-1864), lawyer and writer on stained-glass, incorrectly printed here as 'Whinston', author of *An Inquiry into the Difference in Style observable in Ancient Glass Painting, especially in England; with hints on glass painting, by an Amateur* (1847), and *Memoirs illustrative of the Art of Glass-Painting* (1865).

WOLFF, Dr Joseph (1795-1862), missionary and explorer, son of a Jewish rabbi, born in Germany, became a member of the Church of England in *c.*1820 and associated with the Revd Edward Irving; described himself as 'Apostle of Our Lord Jesus Christ for Palestine, Persia, Bokhara and Balkh'.

WOOD, Sir Charles, 2nd Bart, M.P. (1800-1885), politician, Secretary of State for India 1859-66, created 1st Viscount Halifax 1866.

WOOD, John the younger (1728-1781), architect of Bath who designed the New Assembly Rooms of 1769-71, whom GGS erroneously believed was responsible for the Pump Room (by Thomas Baldwin, 1791-92) and the Classical church built in 1734-52 inside the ruined nave of Llandaff Cathedral – in fact by John Wood the elder (1704-1754) – which was removed by PRICHARD & SEDDON, q.v., in the restoration of the 1850s.

WOODWARD, Benjamin (1815-1861), brilliant Irish architect in partnership with Sir Thomas DEANE (1792-1871), q.v., who died young after designing the University Museum at Oxford, 1854-58, and winning fourth prize in the competition for the Foreign Office; see Eve Blau, *Ruskinian Gothic: The Architecture of Deane & Woodward 1845-1861* (Princeton, 1982).

WREN, Sir Christopher (1632-1723), architect &c.

WYATT, James (1746-1813), architect of Classical and also Gothic houses, such as Fonthill Abbey, who, unfortunately, dealt ignorantly and ruthlessly with medieval buildings such as Salisbury, Durham, Hereford and Lichfield

Cathedrals, so earning him the epithet of 'The Destroyer' and the obloquy of the Victorians.

WYATT, Sir Matthew Digby (1820-1877), architect and designer, first Slade Professor of Fine Arts at Cambridge, who assisted I. K. BRUNEL on Paddington Station and who, having been appointed Surveyor to the East India Company in 1855, became architect for the interior of the India Office in collaboration with GGS for the exterior; see Nikolaus Pevsner, *Matthew Digby Wyatt* (Cambridge, 1950) and John Martin Robinson, *The Wyatts: An Architectural Dynasty* (Oxford, 1979).

WYATT, Thomas Henry (1807-1880), architect, elder brother of Matthew Digby WYATT, q.v.

YARBOROUGH, Charles Anderson Worsley, 2nd Earl of (1781-1862).

ZWIRNER, Ernst Friedrich (1802-1861), architect, appointed cathedral architect at Cologne in 1833 on the recommendation of Schinkel, carried out the completion of Cologne Cathedral after 1842.

INDEX

Main entries in this index are arranged in a single sequence of names and topics. Certain important subjects have subdivisions. Throughout, 'GGS' refers to George Gilbert Scott, senior; within the Scott family, entries and relationships ('uncle', 'third son' etc), refer to GGS.

(dem) = demolished; (fn) = footnote; (+fn) = footnote in addition to main text.

[ ] = unnamed or pseudonymous reference.

Where alternative versions of proper names are given, the first is the present day standard version, the second, GGS's.

The new appendix continues the original pagination, but Gavin Stamp's introduction is paginated alphabetically. The material in Appendix 1 and 2 is included in the index but not the 'Notes, Mainly Biographical', which is already in alphabetical order.

Saracen, 389
Saxon, 422-3
Tudor, 50, 96, 393
Vernacular, c, 226
ARCHITECTURE, *symbolism:*
140, 141, 142-4
ARLES, France, 330
ARMFIELD, Rev H. T., 305
ARMSTEAD, Henry Hugh, 265, 266, 297,
478
ARNHEM/ARNHEIM, Holland, 129
ARTHINGTON HALL/AITHINGTON
HOUSE, *see* GGS Architectural Works
ASHBEE, Mr (Clerk of Works, Gloucester
Cathedral), 337, 481
ASSISI, Italy, 330, 404
ASTON SANDFORD, Bucks., xix, 14, 15,
29
ATKINSON, Thomas Witlam, 119
AUGSBURG, Confession of, 136
AUSTEN, Mr, Mrs of Goring, 257
AUSTEN, Jane, 28 (fn)
AUSTRIA, 161
AVIGNON, France, 330
AYLESBURY, Bucks., 29, 149, 150, 241
St Mary's Church, *see* GGS
Architectural Works

B_____ (a plotter), *see* DONALDSON,
Professor T. L.
BACHARACH, Germany, 115
BACON, Lord (Francis), 423, 424
'Bacon Chapel', 423-5
BAGOT, Richard, dean of Canterbury,
later, bishop of Oxford, 94
BAIAE, Italy, 330
BAILEY, Charles, 88
BAKER, Miss
Northamptonshire Glossary, 438
BALIOL, family, 468
BAMBERG, Germany, 147
BANGOR, 467
cathedral, *see* GGS Architectural Works
see also ARCHITECTURE
BANKS, Robert Richardson, 180, 181, 447
BAPTISTS, *see* CHRISTIANITY
BARLOW, William Henry, 271
BARMOUTH, N. Wales, 467
BARNET, Herts., 84
BARRY, Sir Charles, c, 76, 85, 87, 110, 111,
179, 199, 385, [391]

BARRY, Charles, junior, h, 180,
181 (+fn), 183, 189, 382, 447, 448, 449,
456
BARRY, Edward Middleton, c, iv, 274-5,
276
eulogy on GGS, 382-6
BARTLETT, family, 442, 467
BARTLETT, Edward, 442
BARTLETT, Rev John, 442, 467
BARTLETT, Robert, 442
BARTLETT, Thomas, 54
BATH, Som., 412
Partis College, *see* GGS Architectural
Works
BATTLES,
Bosworth Field, 417
See also WARS
BAYLEY, Stephen, a
BEANLAND, Messrs, of Bradford,
builders, 311, 480
BEAUCHAMP, Frederick Lygon, 6th
Earl, 180 (fn), 304, 487
BECKETT, Sir Edmund,
see DENISON, E. B.
BEDDGELERT, Wales, 467
BEDFORD, 443
BEDFORDSHIRE SOCIETY, 150
BELGIUM, 114, 404
BELL, Alfred (of Clayton and Bell), 202,
217 (fn), 221-2, 223, 305
BELL, Doyne Courtenay, 328
BELLAMY, Thomas, 181 (fn)
BELPER, Derbys.
workhouse *see* GGS Architectural
Works
BENTHAM, Rev James, Canon of Ely,
281
BERESFORD-HOPE, Alexander James,
see HOPE
BERGUES, France, 134
BERLIN, 157
BERNASCONI, Francis, 293, 391
BEVERLEY/BEVERLY, Yorks., 70, 88
Foljambe Chapel, 96
Minster, *see* GGS Architectural Works
St Mary's Church, *see* GGS
Architectural Works
BIBLE, themes in ecclesiastical decoration,
143
Old Testament:
Isaiah, 471, 474

Moses and Aaron, 417, 418
Nehemiah, 476
Pentateuch, 380, 417, 418, 465
Psalms, 485
New Testament:
Acts, 469
St John's Gospel, 469, 470, 473
St Luke's Gospel, 469
St Mark's Gospel, 470, 475
See also ECCLESIASTICAL SUBJECTS
BIBLE SOCIETY, 14, 53, 233, 450
BICESTER, Oxon, 438
BICKERSTETH, Edward, dean of
Lichfield, 294
BIDDLE, Gordon, a
BIDDULPH, Sir Thomas, 328
BILDWAS, Salop, *see* BUILDWAS
BILLERICAY, Essex
workhouse *see* GGS Architectural
Works
BILTON, Yorks., 148
BIRMINGHAM,
St Martin's Church (dem), *see* GGS
Architectural Works
Grammar school, 74
Oratory, m
BISCOVEY, l
BLACK FOREST, Germany, 329
BLAND, archdeacon of Durham, 353, 489
BLEDLOW, Bucks., 14, 443
BLOMFIELD, Sir Arthur William, 190
BLORE, Edward, k, xvii, 51, 92, 151, 153,
166, 299, 481
BODLEY, Dr William, 243
BODLEY, George Frederick, d, k, l, 449,
450
BODLEY, Georgina (later Mrs King), l,
243, [458]
BOHEMIA, royal arms, 431
BOISERÉE, Sulpiz/Sulpice, 127
BOLBECK, family, 417
BOLOGNA, Italy, 160, 330
San Petronio, 160
San Stefano, 160
BONN, Germany, 115
BOSTON, Lincs., 2 (+fn), 66 (fn), 70, 103,
232, 240, 250, 256, 299, 460
St Botolph's Church, 66 (fn)
BOTREL D'HAZEVILLE, A., 181
BOULOGNE, France, 255
BOURNE, Capt., Margate, 35

BOYCE, Edward, 88
BOYES, Mrs, of Charterhouse Sq., 65
BRADFIELD, Berks., 97
St Andrew's Church, *see* GGS
Architectural Works
St Andrew's College, *see* GGS
Architectural Works
SS Simon & Jude Church, *see* GGS
Architectural Works
BRADFORD, Yorks., 308, 311, 480
BRANCEPETH, Co. Durham, 410
BRANDON, John Raphael, 190, 449
BRECON, Wales, 151
BREISGAU, Germany, 163
BREMEN, Germany, 129
BRIDGES and MASON, Messrs, 64
BRIDGEWATER, Som., 255
BRIDLINGTON, Yorks., 70, 148, 171
BRIDLINGTON QUAY, Yorks.,
Christ Church, *see* GGS Architectural
Works
BRIDPORT, Lord, 328
BRIDPORT, Giles, bishop of Salisbury,
297
BRIGGS, Martin S., b
BRIGHTON, Sussex, 234, 243, 244, 246,
256, 458
Brighton College, *see* GGS Architectural
Works
BRINDLEY, William, 215 (fn), 265, 266,
481, 482
BRISTOL, 251
BRITTON, John, 109
BROADWAY, Mr, chamberlain of Stowe,
40
BRODRICK/BRODERICK, Cuthbert,
181 (fn), 446
BROUGHAM, Henry, 1st Baron
Brougham & Vaux, 409
BROUGHTON, Mrs, 33, 34
BROWN, Lancelot, 2 (fn)
BROWNLEE, David B., a, b,
BRUGES, Belgium, 114
BRUNEL, Isambard Kingdom, 416
BRUNSWICK, Germany, 117, 134
BRUSSELS, Belgium, 114, 255, 330
BUCCLEUCH, Walter Francis Montagu-
Douglas Scott, 5th Duke of
Queensbury, 154

HALEY HILL, Halifax
All Souls' Church, 148, 176
HALICARNASSUS, Turkey, 267
HALIFAX, Yorks.,
church, 378, 410. *See also* GGS
Architectural Works
town hall, 148, 179
HALL, Sir Benjamin, 180
HAM, Surrey (GGS's family home), f, j,
237, 238, 254, 256, 257, 329, 330, 460,
462, 465, 485
HAM HOUSE, 465
HAMBURG, Germany, 117, 118, 120, 127,
128, 134, 161, 194, 330
Rath-Haus, 134, 148, 174
Rauman Haus, 128
St Nicholas' Church, *see* GGS
Architectural Works
HAMILTON, Rev Henry Parr, Dean of
Salisbury, 305-6
HAMILTON, Rev Walter Kerr, Bishop of
Salisbury, 303, 306
HAMMOND, Mrs, of Ham, 258
HAMPTON, Lord, *see* PAKINGTON, Sir
John
HAMPTON LUCY, Warwicks., 315
HANOVER, Germany, 117
HANWELL, Middx.,
St Mary's Church, *see* GGS
Architectural Works
HARDMAN, John, 218, 344
HARDWICK, Philip, 175
HAREWOOD, Yorks., 148
HAREWOOD, Henry Thynne Lascelles,
4th Earl of, 154
HARLECH, Wales, 467
HARROGATE/HARROWGATE,
Yorks., 148
HARROW, Middx.,
church, 86
School, 390 (fn)
HARTSHORNE, Rev E., 155
HARTWELL, Berks., 29
HARWICH, Essex, 329
HARZ/HARTZ Mountains, Germany,
330
HASTINGS, Sussex
All Saints' Church, 223
HATFIELD, Herts., Park, 325
HAUNTINGS, supernatural, 252 (fn), 254,
461-2

HAVERGAL, Rev F. T., 289, 479
HAWKSTONE, Salop.,
chapel, *see* GGS Architectural Works
HAWTREY, Rev ——, of Episcopal Jews'
Chapel, 64
HAYLING, Hants., 271
HAYLING ISLAND, Hants., 462
HAYMAN, Dr, physician, 459
HEARN, Mr, solicitor, 443
HEIDELBERG, Germany, 329
HEIDELOFF, Karl Alexander von, 119
HELPS, Sir Arthur, 327, 328
HEMLING, *see* MEMLING
HENRY I, King of England, 426
HENRY III, King of England, 393
HENRY V, King of England
tomb, Westminster Abbey, 152-3, 164
HENRY VII, King of England, 317, 320,
417, 484
Chapel, Ely Cathedral, 282, 287, 393
HENRY VIII, King of England, 371
HERALDRY, 286, 350, 431, 468
HERBERT, John Rogers, 272
HERCULANEUM, Italy, 330
HEREFORD, Cathedral, *see* GGS
Architectural Works
see also ARCHITECTURE
H. M. GOVERNMENT, 454
Office of Works, 180, 185, 193
Commissioner, 382
Postmaster-General, 382
Treasury, 456
see also GOVERNMENT BUILDINGS
HERODOTUS, 369
HESELTINE, Joanna, a
HIGGINS, William Mullinger, 72
HIGHAM FERRERS, Northants., 150, 437
HIGHNAM COURT, Gloucs., 159
HILDESHEIM, Germany, 134, 282
St Michael's Church, 282
HILL, Sir Roland, 4th Baronet, 2nd
Viscount, MP, 192
HILL, Rev ——, Archdeacon of
Chesterfield, 96
HILLESDEN/HILLESDON/
HILLESDEAN, Bucks., 20, 42-4, 57,
289, [417-19]
church, 44-6, 47
HOFLAND, *see* COE & HOFLAND

HOLBECK, Yorks.,
St John's Church (dem), *see* GGS
Architectural Works
HOLKER/HOLKAR, Lancs., 50
HOLLAND (Netherlands), 129
HOLYHEAD, Anglesey, 467
HOLY ROMAN EMPIRE, *see*
GERMANY: Empire
HOOK, Rev Walter Farquhar, Dean of
Chichester, 384
HOOK MEMORIAL CHURCH, *see*
LEEDS, Yorks.
HOPE, Alexander James Beresford, MP, i,
180, 279, 306, 382, 477
HORNE, Miss, [233], 450
HOUGH, Rev —, 453-4
HOUGHTON CONQUEST, Beds.,
church, xv
HOVE, Sussex, 235, 246
HOWARD, Henry Edward John, Dean of
Chichester, 293-4, 297, [478]
HOWDEN, Northumberland, 70
church, 171
HOWSON, Rev John Saul, Dean of
Chester, 247 (fn), 335, [484]
HUDSON/HUDON, Octavius, 291, 293,
331, 479
HULL, Yorks., 70, 71, 88, 127, 243, 250,
443
St Mary's Church, 240 (fn), 443
HULL, Mr, geologist, 425 (fn)
HUNGARY, royal arms, 431
HUNGERFORD MARKET, *see*
LONDON
HUNT, Sir Henry Arthur, 196, 198
HUNTER, Michael, a
HUNTINGTOWER, Lady Catherine
Elizabeth Camilla, [257]-259, 463
HUSSEY, Richard Charles, 330, 331, 336
HUTCHINS, Mr (Clerk of Works,
Salisbury Cathedral), 302, 480
HUTCHINSON, precentor of Lichfield
Cathedral, 294, 478

ILAM HALL, Staffs., 100
INDIA, 181, 197
Governor General, 315
India Office, *see* GOVERNMENT
BUILDINGS
Secretary of State for, 181

INSTITUTE of BRITISH ARCHITECTS
(= INSTITUTE of ARCHITECTS),
see ROYAL INSTITUTE of BRITISH
ARCHITECTS
INTERLACHEN, Switzerland, 330
IONA CROSS, 262
IRVINE, James Thomas, 351
IRVINGISM, 64
ISENHAMPSTEAD CHEYNIES, *see*
CHEYNIES
ISENHAMPSTEAD LATIMERS, *see*
LATIMERS
ISLE OF WIGHT, 252-3, 327, 461
ISLIP, Oxon, 152
ITALY, 403-4
GGS'S tours:
1851, 157-62
1877, 329-30
Gothic architecture, 122
influence of French architecture in, 162
invasion by France, 185
'Italian mania', 373
Romanesque period, 140

JACKSON, Charles, 171
JACKSON, Sir Thomas Graham, j-k
JAMES, Duke of York, later King James II
of England and VII of Scotland, 296,
478
JAMES, Rev Thomas, 154-5
JAMES, Sir Walter, 154
JAMES, Messrs, of London, 302
JENNER, Edward, 406
JERSEY, Channel Islands, 232
JERUSALEM, 431
'JEWS' CHAPEL', *see* LONDON: Bethnal
Green
JOHN de CELLA, 377
JOHNSON, ?John, architect and
draughtsman, 101
JOHNSON, Samuel, 294
JONES, Canon, of Bradford, 308
JONES, Mr, drawing master, 24-5, 42, 44
JONES, Mr, Methodist, of Finsbury
Square, 35
JONES, Dr Henry Bence, 247
JONES, Inigo, 383, 425
JONES, Rev William Basil, 312
JOURNEYS, Scott family:
to Manchester, 466-7
to North Wales, 467

to Lake District, 467
JULIUS, Dr, physician, 238, [451]

'K.H.' of Ham, Middx., *see*
HUNTINGTOWER, Lady
KASSEL/CASSEL, Germany, 117
KAYE, John, bishop of Lincoln, 74, 79
KEELE, Staffs., 97
KELHAM HALL, Notts., *see* GGS
Architectural Works
KELK, John, 267
KELSALL, family, Cheshire, 2
KELSALL, Edward, vicar of Boston,
Lincs., 2
KELSO ABBEY, 404
KEMPTHORNE/KEMTHORNE,
Sampson, 76-7, 78, 81, 444
KENT, county, 259, 468
KING, Elizabeth, (née Scott) (GGS's aunt),
29, 31, 49, 68, 232, 443, 450
KING, Richard John, 412 (fn)
KING, Rev Samuel (GGS's uncle), 29, 31,
47, 53, 68, 75, 86, 232, 320, 450, 468
KING, 'Tailor', 22-3
KING, Thomas (or George?) (GGS's
great-uncle), 29, 53, 63, 257
KING'S COLLEGE, Cambridge, *see*
CAMBRIDGE UNIVERSITY
KING'S COLLEGE, London, *see*
LONDON UNIVERSITY
KING'S LANGLEY, Herts., 68-9
KINGSLEY, Charles, 430
KIRBY, John Joshua, 56
KOBLENZ/COBLENTZ, Germany, 115,
116

LAACH, Germany, 115
LACE-MAKING, 5, 17, 18
LAKE DISTRICT, 467
LANCE, Adolphe, 174
LANE, family, Wrotham, Kent, 465
LANFRANC, archbishop of Canterbury,
435
LANGE, [?Ludwig], German architect, 119
LANGLEY, Batty, 383
LATIMERS, Bucks., 31, 48, 49-51, 54, 68-9,
250, 256, 320
LAUD, William, Archbishop of
Canterbury, xviii
LAW, Mr, farmer, of Gawcott, 16, 22, 380

LAW COURTS, *see* ROYAL COURTS
OF JUSTICE
LAWRENCE, Mrs, of Studley Park, 53
LAYARD, Sir Austen Henry, 267, 269,
270, 276
LEAMINGTON, Warwicks., 443, 450
LEAR, Mrs Sidney, 6, 304, 487
LECHMERE, Sir Edmund Anthony
Harley, MP, 367, 491
LEE, Sir George, 29
LEEDS, Yorks., 148, 151, 225
All Souls' Church (Hook Memorial), *see*
GGS Architectural Works
bank, 279
Old Bank, 272
St John's Church, 410
LEGHORN/LIVORNO, Italy, 163
LEICESTER, 468
LEICESTER, 1st Earl of, *see* COKE,
Thomas William
LEICESTER, 2nd Earl of, 289
LEIGHTON BUZZARD, Beds., 59
LEITH HILL, Surrey, j, 462
'Parkhurst', j, 462
LELAND, John, 308
Le MARCHANT, Sir Denis, 3
Le MESURIER, Rev J, 157
LENBOROUGH, Bucks., 16
LEOPOLD I, King of the Belgians, 92
LE PUY, France, 330
LE STRANGE, Henry L'Estrange
Styleman, 282, 283
LEVERTON, Notts., 232
LEWIS, Joseph, 271
LIBRARIES
British Architectural L., a
LICHFIELD, Staffs., 97, 467
cathedral, *see* GGS Architectural Works
see also ARCHITECTURE
LIÈGE, Belgium, 114
LILLE, France
cathedral, 206, 209, 374
LINCOLN, 70, 79, 460
bishop, 74, 79
cathedral/minster, 205, 281 (fn), 297
St Nicholas' Church, *see* GGS
Architectural Works
LINCOLNSHIRE, 1, 2 (fn), 83, 252
Scott family in, 468
LITTLEHAMPTON, Sussex, 311, 480

LOUIS XVIII, King of France, 29
LOUTH, Lincs., 2 (fn)
LOUVAIN, Belgium, 114, 138
LÜBECK, Germany, 117, 128
LUCCA, Italy, 330
LUCERNE, Switzerland, 330
LUCY, Rev John, 315, 483
LUCY, Rev William, Bishop of St David's, 315, 483
LUTHER, Martin, 137
LYGON, Frederick, see BEAUCHAMP, 6th Earl of
LYNCH, Dr (GGS's grandfather), 2, 32
LYNCH, Mrs (GGS's grandmother), 31-2, 38
LYNCH, Euphemia (GGS's mother), see SCOTT, Mrs Thomas
LYNCH, Dr John of Dunmow (GGS's uncle), 32, 443
LYNCH, Nathaniel (GGS's uncle), 443
LYNTON, Devon, 255
LYONS, France, 330
LYSONS, Daniel and Samuel
    Magna Britannia, 109
LYTTELTON, Lord, 344

MACAULAY, Thomas Babington, Baron, g
MacBRIDE, Dr John David, 89
MACCLESFIELD, Cheshire
    workhouse, see GGS Architectural Works
MACDONALD, Major, 89, 442, 443
MADDOX, George, 58, 68, 88
MADELEY, Salop., 36
MADSEN, Stephen Tschudi, b
MAGDEBURG, Germany, 117, 134
MAIDENHEAD, Berks., 216
MAIDS' MORTON, Bucks., 46, 57
MAINZ/MAYENCE, Germany, 115
MALVERN, Worcs., 251
MAN, Isle of, royal arms, 431
MANCHESTER
    art exhibition, 466
    cathedral, 389
MANNERS, Lord John James Robert, 7th Duke of Rutland, MP, 180, [181], 184, 186, 382
MANNERS-SUTTON, John Henry, MP, 148, 212 (fn)
MANTUA, Italy

cathedral, 160
MARBURG, Germany
    St Elizabeth's Church, 117, 264
MARGATE, Kent, 33-6, 442
MARLOW, Christopher, 390
MAROCHETTI, Baron Carlo, 267
MARSEILLES, France, 330
MARSHALL, Mr (Clerk of Works, Chichester Cathedral), 311, 380
MARTIN, père, 221
MARY I, queen of England, 284
MASFEN, Mr, church historian, 98, 445
MATLOCK, Derbys., 251, 466
MATTHEW PARIS, 308, 325 (fn)
MATTHEW of WESTMINSTER, 308
MAYENCE, Germany, see MAINZ
MEADS, 'Cracky', 21-2
MEADS, Zachary/Zachery, farmer, 16
MECHLIN/MECHELEN, Belgium, 114
MELROSE, Abbey, 396
MEMLING ('Hemling'), Hans, 417
MERIVALE, Charles, dean of Ely, 390 (fn)
MEUSE, River, France, 255
MICKLETHWAITE, John Thomas, 325
MILAN, Italy, 162
MILMAN, Henry Hart, Dean of St Paul's, 392
MILNER, Dr John, 308
MILTON, John, 389
MINDEN, Germany, 134
MINEHEAD, Somerset, 255
MINTON, Herbert, 87
    see also ARCHITECTURE: *ornamentation*
MISSIONARIES, 33, 34
MITFORD, Algernon Bertram Freeman, 382
MOBERLY, Rev George, Bishop of Salisbury, 306
MODENA, Italy, 160
MOFFATT, Mr, senior, builder, 67-8
MOFFATT, William Bonython, h, 67, 75, 79-80, 81, 82-3, 85, 90, 91, 130-3, 148, 248, 251, 316, 444, [445], 445, [446]
MOLLER, Dr Georg, 114
MONS, Belgium, 114
MONUMENTS,
    Albert Memorial, see GGS Architectural Works
    to Denton family, 479

548

to Dean Howard, 297, [478]
Eleanor Crosses, 59, 62, 89, 354
in Hereford Cathedral, 289, [486]
to Mr Lear, 487
to Bishop Lonsdale, 297, 478
Martyrs' Memorial, Oxford, see GGS
Architectural Works
in Westminster Abbey, 486
MOORE, archdeacon of Lichfield, 294, 478
MORDAUNT, Sir Charles, 10th Baronet,
MP, 148, 212
MORIARTY, Mr, barrister, k
MORRIS DANCERS, 438-9
MORRIS, William, c, 367, 434, 435, 491
MORRIS & CO., 224 (fn), [450]
MORTIMER, Mr (Clerk of Works,
Nikolaikirche, Hamburg), 129
MÜLLER, Emilius, 118, 119, 127
MUMMERS, 437-8
MUNICH, Germany, 330
painters, 223
MÜNSTER, Germany, 129
MURRAY, John, publisher, 280 (fn)
Murray's *Guide to St Albans*, 427
MUSEUMS
Victoria and Albert, a
MUSGRAVE, Thomas, archbishop of
York, [172]
MUTHESIUS, Stefan, b
MYERS, George, 88-9

NAMUR, Belgium, 255
NANTWICH, Cheshire
St Mary's Church, see GGS
Architectural Works
NAPLES, Italy, 330
NAPOLEON III, emperor of France,
[185], 398
NASH, Edwin, 58-9, 75, 444
NASH, John, 315
NAVARRE, France, royal arms, 431
NEALE, Rev John Mason, 447
NEALE, John Preston, 427, 428
NEUSS, Germany, 134
NEWARK-on-TRENT, Notts., 70, 148
Kelham Hall, see GGS Architectural
Works
St Mary Magdalene's Church, see GGS
Architectural Works
NEWFOUNDLAND, 389
NEWMAN, John Henry, Cardinal, m

NEWSTEAD ABBEY, Notts., 297
NEWTON, Sir Charles Thomas, 267
NEWTON, John, 4
NEW ZEALAND, 33-4
NICHOLSON, Dr, of St Albans, 322, 325,
326
NICHOLSON, Peter, 67
NÎMES/NISMES, France, 330
NITON, Isle of Wight, 253
NORBITON, Surrey:
St Peter's Church, see GGS
Architectural Works
NORMANDY, France, 330
NORTHAMPTON
Eleanor Cross, 59
St Peter's Church, 151
St Sepulchre's Church, 151
NORTHAMPTON, Lords of, 3
NORTHAMPTONSHIRE, 83, 154, 155,
438
Architectural Society, 155
Northamptonshire Society, 150
NORTHCOTE, Sir Stafford, Bart, MP,
184
NORTH FERRIBY, Yorks., 443
NORTON, John, 190
NORWAY, royal arms, 431
NOTTINGHAM
St Mary's Church, see GGS
Architectural Works
NUREMBERG, Germany, 147
NUTLEY, Hants., 44

OAKINGTON, Cambs., 443
OBERWESEL, Germany, 115
O'CONNELL, Daniel, 76
O'CONNOR, Dr, Roman Catholic priest,
41
OFFA, King of Mercia, 321
OLDRID, Caroline (later Mrs G. G. Scott),
66, 68-70, 71, 80, 84, 249-61
OLDRID, Fanny (later Mrs Thomas Scott),
66, 249, 250, 256
OLDRID, Helen (GGS's sister-in-law), 249,
256, 461, 485
OLDRID, J., of Boston, Lincs. (GGS's
father-in-law), 66, 103, 460, 461
OLDRID, Mrs J., née Scott (GGS's
mother-in-law), 78, 103, 232, 249, [443]

RATTEE & KETT, Messrs, 284
RAVENNA, Italy, 330
READING, Berks., 255
  gaol, see GGS Architectural Works
REDFERN, James Frank, 265, [266], 306-7,
  487
REDGRAVE, Richard, 168, [169], 382
REED, Dr Andrew, 91
REFORMATION, Protestant, 347, 371,
  388, 389, 390, 392, 410, 412, 414, 416
REICHENSPERGER, August, 147
REMAGEN, Germany, 115
RESTORATION, architectural, b, f, g, l,
  m, 385, 400-1, 402-3, 405
  for individual restorations see GGS
    Architectural Works
  Restoration movement, 398
  restoration techniques, 287
  see also ANTI-RESTORATION
  MOVEMENT
REYNOLDS, Sir Joshua, 25, 385
RHEIMS/REIMS, France, 330
  cathedral, 49, 109
RHEINDORF, Germany, 115
RHINE, River, 115, 130
RICHARD, Earl of Cornwall, 'King of the
  Romans', 431
RICHMOND, Charles Henry
  Gordon-Lennox, 6th Duke of
  Richmond and Lennox, 309
RICHMOND, George, iv, 466
RICKMAN, Thomas, 48, 343, 489
RIDSDALE JUDGMENT, 493
RIPON, Yorks.
  cathedral, see GGS Architectural Works
RIPON, George Frederick Samuel
  Robinson, 2nd Earl and 1st Marquis of,
  327, 328
ROBERTS, David, 159
ROBERTS, Henry, 73, 74, 75
ROBESPIERRE, M. F. M. I. de, 37
ROCHEAD, John Thomas, 181 (fn)
ROCHESTER, Kent
  cathedral, see GGS Architectural Works
ROGERS, family, Bucks., 442
ROME, 330, 403-404
  St Peter's, 393
ROPER, David Riddall, 72
ROSE, Rev Henry John, xv
ROSSLYN/ROSLIN, Scotland
  chapel, 109

ROTHERHAM, Yorks., 2 (fn), 468
ROTTERDAM, 129, 329
ROUEN, France
  cathedral, 162 (fn)
ROUNDHEADS (Parliamentarians), 379
ROYAL ACADEMY, k, iv, 74, 111, 151,
  175, 199, 200, 280, 373, 379, 382, 383,
  385, 491
ROYAL COURTS OF JUSTICE, b, f, l,
  273, 454
ROYAL EXCHANGE, 182 (fn)
ROYAL INSTITUTE OF BRITISH
  ARCHITECTS, a, c, l, m, 151, 180,
  183, 279, [354], 359, 367, 382, [403],
  [404], [406], [407], [408], 410, 421, 429,
  [448]
  Catalogue of Drawings, a
  GGS, papers to, 398, 402, 435
  GGS, President, 329, 373, 402
  Library, h, l
  Pugin Studentship, 404
RUDDLE & THOMPSON, Messrs,
  builders, 291, 342, 482
RUINS, architectural, treatment of, 420
RUMSEY, Mr, physician, Chesham, 51,
  [74]
RUMSEY, Henry, 74, 75, 320
RUMSEY, Robert, 63
RUSKIN, John, c, 158, 166-7, 201, 204,
  210, 278, 326, 358, 373, 396 (fn), 401,
  403-4
  Ruskinism, 210
RUSSELL, family, Cheynies, 50
RUSSELL, Mr, H.M. Inspector of Prisons,
  94-5
RUSSELL, Jesse Watts, 100
RUSSELL, Lord John, MP, 76
RYDE, Isle of Wight, 253

ST ALBANS, Herts., 320-1, [323]
  Abbey, see GGS Architectural Works
  Grammar School, 325
  St Michael's Church, see GGS
    Architectural Works
  Woolpack Inn, 321
ST ASAPH
  cathedral, see GGS Architectural Works
ST AUBYN, James Pearse, 190
ST DAVID'S
  cathedral, see GGS Architectural Works

STRASBOURG/STRASBURG, 147, 282, 330
STREET, George Edmund, d, e, k, l, 118, 160, 166, 179, 203, 215, 216, 275, 276, 429, 449
STUART, James, 48, 56
STUDLEY PARK, Yorks., l, 53
SURRIDGE, Mr, tutor to Albert Scott, 456
SUSSEX COUNTY HOSPITAL, 243
SUTTON, see MANNERS-SUTTON, J. H.
SWARTZ, Germany, 115
SWEDEN, royal arms, 431
SWIFT, Jonathan, 405
SWITZERLAND, 'the Saxon Switzerland', 146, 157, 158, 330

TANDRIDGE, Surrey, c
TAN Y BWLCH, 467
TARRANT, Dorset, 308
TATTERSHALL, Lincs., 70
    castle, 250
TAYLOR, Rev Jeremy, 460
TAYLOR, Sir Robert, j
TEFFONT, Wilts., quarry, 301
TEMPLE, Cowper, see COWPER
TENBY, Pembs., 315
TENISON, Rev Thomas, Archbishop of Canterbury, 432, 433, 434
TEULON, Samuel Sanders, 190
TEWKESBURY, Gloucs.
    Abbey, see GGS Architectural Works
THACKERAY, William Makepeace, g
THIRLWALL/ THIRLWELL, Connop, Bishop of St David's, 312, 315, 487
THOMSON, Alexander, i
THOMSON, Dr Allen/Allan, 379
THORNE, James, 423, 424
THORNE, Robert, b
THORNHILL, Sir James, 436
THORP/THORPE, Rev Thomas, Archdeacon, 104
THYNNE, Rev Lord John, Sub-Dean of Westminster, 147, 152, 153, 154, 287-8, 486
TILSON, family, of Goring, 257
TINGEWICK, Bucks.
    church, 46-7
TINNEY, Col., MP, 184
TINTERN, Monmouthshire
    abbey, 396

TISBURY, Wilts.
    quarry, 300, 301
TITE, Sir William, MP, 180, 182, 186, 189, 279, 448
TOLLEMACHE, family, 465
TOLLEMACHE, Hon. Frederick, MP, 463
TOMLINE, Rev Sir George Prettyman, Bishop of Lincoln, 5
TOPLIS, Ian, a
TORREGIANO, Italy
    ciborium, 285
TOURNAI/TOURNAY, Belgium, 114
TOWCESTER, Northants., 39
TRACTARIAN MOVEMENT, 384
TRANSPORT:
    chaise, 251, 252, 255
    coach, 241, 466, 467
        'Manchester Telegraph', 84
    Railways, f, h, 446, 466, 467
        Great Northern, 173 (fn)
        Midland, 271, 279
        Stations:
            King's Cross, a
            St Pancras, a, e, m,
TREES, in landscape, 299-300
TRENCH, Rev Richard Chenevix, Dean of Westminster, 486
TRIER/TREVES, Germany, 116
TRIESTE, Italy, 157
TRING, Herts., 233, 442
TRIQUETI, Henri Joseph François, Baron de, 224, 272-3
TRUMPINGTON, Abbot, 377
TUCKER, S. T., herald, Rouge Croix, 350
TURNHAM GREEN, Middx.
    Christ Church, see GGS Architectural Works
TUSCANY, Italy, 161
TYDD ST GILES, Cambs., 51
TYNEMOUTH, Northumbria
    priory, 404

'UNIONS', see WORKHOUSES
UNITED STATES OF AMERICA, 36, 37, 327
    New York, NY, a
UNIVERSITIES:
    Bombay, d
    Cambridge, see CAMBRIDGE UNIVERSITY

Glasgow, *see* GLASGOW
UNIVERSITY
London, *see* LONDON UNIVERSITY
Oxford, *see* OXFORD UNIVERSITY
UTRECHT, Holland, 129
UTTOXETER, Staffs., 97

van EYCK, Jan, 46, 417
VAUGHAN, Edward, Bishop of St
David's, 313
VENICE, 157, 158-9, 192, 403
Fondaco dei Turchi, 159, 403
Murano, 159
St Mark's, 159
Torcello, 159
VENTNOR, Isle of Wight, 461
VERONA, Italy, 159
fortifications, 161
St Zeno's, 160
VERULAM, 423, 426, 430
chapel, 423
See also ST ALBANS
VICENZA, Italy, 159
VICTORIA, Queen, c, f, 239, 263, 265,
267, 270, 327, 328, 382, 385
VIENNA, 159, 330
St Stephen's, 157, 159
VIOLLET-LE-DUC, Eugène-Emmanuel,
280
VITRUVIUS POLLIO, Marcus, 56
VOYSEY, Annesley, 76-7, 444

WAKEFIELD, Yorks.
St Mary's Church (bridge chapel), *see*
GGS Architectural Works
WALCOTT, Mackenzie Edward Charles,
326
WALES, 316-17, 467
WALKER, John, farmer, 16-17, 20
WALKER, 'Tom O'Gawcott', 18
WALLACE, Robert, architect, 61
WALLER, Mr, surveyor, 71
WALLER, Frederick Sandham (of Messrs
FULLJAMES & WALLER), 337, 338,
480, 481
WALPOLE, Horace, 4th earl of Orford,
390
WALSINGHAM, Alan of, *see* ALAN of
WALSINGHAM
WALTHAM ABBEY, Essex
Eleanor Cross, 59

WALTON HALL, Warwicks., *see* GGS
Architectural Works
WANSTEAD, Essex,
Infant Orphanage Asylum, *see* GGS
Architectural Works
WAPPENHAM, Northants., 38, 74, 75,
79, 80, 230, 231, 256 (fn), 461
WARD, Mr, friend of Albert Scott, 457
WARE, Abbot, 286
WARR, family, 18, 19, 23, 439-40, 441
WARR, Benjamin, farmer, 16
WARR, Molly, 18, 439, 440, 441
WARS:
Edwardian, 317
English Civil War/Great Rebellion, 379,
432
Napoleonic, 35, 36
of the Roses, 417
see also BATTLES
WARWICK, 148, 441
WARWICKSHIRE, 265, 443
WATERLOO (battlefield), Belgium, 114
WATERHOUSE, Alfred, b, e, 275, 456
WATERMORE, nr Cirencester, 148
WATSON, Mrs (née Lynch) (GGS's aunt),
443
WATTS, George Frederic, 297, 478
WATTS, Isaac, 394
WAYET, Mary, 2, 3 (fn)
WEATHERLEY, William Samuel, 305
WEBB, Rev Benjamin, 87-8
WEBSTER, Rev Thomas (GGS's father's
cousin), 443
WEETON, Yorks., 148
WELDON, Rev George Warburton, 259,
451, 464
WELLINGTON COLLEGE, Som.,
Chapel, *see* GGS Architectural Works
WENLOCK EDGE, Salop., 467
abbey, 467
WESLEY, Rev John, 3, 11, 36, 37, 38,
232-3 (fn)
WEST, John, of Gawcott, 4-5, 9, 18, 36, 53,
54, 78, 439
WESTCOTT/WESTCOTE, Rev Brooke
Fox, Canon of Peterborough, 487
WEST DERBY, Liverpool, 148
St Mary's Church, *see* GGS
Architectural Works
WEST INDIES, 2, 32, 63
WESTLAKE, Dr, physician, 378

WESTMINSTER:
Abbey, *see* GGS Architectural Works
architectural museum, 165, 203
Broad Sanctuary houses, *see* GGS
  Architectural Works
Cannon Row, 166
College Gardens, 287
Government Offices, *see*
  GOVERNMENT OFFICES
King Street, 181, 189, 197
New Palace of Westminster, *see*
  PARLIAMENT, Houses of
St Margaret's Church, *see* GGS
  Architectural Works
St Stephen's Hall, *see* PARLIAMENT,
  Houses of
School of Arts, 165-70
WESTMINSTER, Matthew of, *see*
  MATTHEW of WESTMINSTER
WESTON UNDERWOOD, Bucks., 3
WESTPHALIA, 134
WESTWARD HO!, Devon, 255
WHEWELL, Rev William, 114
WHINSTON, *see* WINSTON
WHITE, Mr, builder, Salisbury, 480
WHITE, Nanny, 19-20, 440
WHITE, William, 190
WHITEHALL, architecture, *see*
  GOVERNMENT OFFICES
WHITMORE, Lady Dorothea, 35
WHITTLEBURY, Northants., 39
WIFE-BEATING, customs concerning, 439
WILBERFORCE, Rev Dr Samuel, Bishop
  of Oxford, 149
WILBERFORCE, William, 399, 407
WILD/WYLDE, James William, 202
WILKES, John, 399
WILLEMENT, Thomas, 165
WILLIAM ('English' W.), 435
WILLIAM I, King of England, 'the
  Conqueror', 371
WILLIAM III, King, 2
WILLIAM of SENS, 435
WILLIAM de VALENCE, 325
WILLIAM of WYKEHAM, Bishop of
  Winchester, 47, 371
WILLIAMS, Rev Sir Erasmus Henry
  Griffies, 2nd Baronet, Chancellor of St
  David's, [315-16], 483, 488
WILLIS, Robert, 283, 295, 434, 435, 478
WILLIS' ROOMS, St Albans, 323, 490

WILLMORE, Mr, builder, Bucks., 54, 74
WILSON, Broadley, 53
WILSON, Joseph, 53
WILTSHIRE, 79, 255
WINCHESTER, Hants.,
  cathedral, *see* GGS Architectural Works
  bishop's palace, 62
WINCHESTER, Lord, 62
WINCHESTER HOUSE, 62
WINDSOR, Berks:
  castle, 45, 224, 272, 389
    Wolsey's Chapel, 224, 272
  parish church, 108
  workhouse, *see* GGS Architectural
  Works
WING, Bucks.
  church, 149
WINSTON/WHINSTON, Charles, 219
WISBECH, Cambs. 51
WOBURN, Beds., 31, 50
WOLFF, Dr Joseph, 64
WOLSEY, Cardinal, 224, 272
WOLVERHAMPTON, Staffs., 467
WOOD, Mr, builder, of Worcester, 312
WOOD, Sir Charles, 2nd Baronet, MP, 197
WOOD, John, the younger, 412
WOODROFFE, Rev —, 31-2, 33
WOODWARD, Benjamin, 179, 181 (fn)
WORCESTER, 312
  cathedral, *see* GGS Architectural Works
  dean, 343, 344
WORKHOUSES (= 'UNIONS') (*For those
  by GGS, see him; otherwise, see individual
  places.*)
WORSLEY, Lancs.
  St Mark's Church, *see* GGS
  Architectural Works
WORTHING, Sussex, 256
WREKIN, the, Salop, 467
WREN, Sir Christopher, c, e, 375, 383
  Pembroke College Chapel, m
  St Michael's, Cornhill, l
WROCKWARDINE, Salop, 36
WROTHAM, Kent, 259
  Wrotham Place, 259
WYATT, James, xvii, 288, 292-3, 296, 304,
  308, 478, 479
WYATT, Sir Matthew Digby, 180, 181-2,
  184, 197, 198-9, 200, 278, 449
WYATT, Thomas Henry, 59
WYCOMBE, Bucks., 31

WYLDE, *see* WILD

XANTEN, Germany, 129

YARBOROUGH, Charles Anderson
    Worsley, 2nd Earl of, 462
YATE, Mr, of Madeley, 36
YATE, Anne, 36
YATE, Rev George, 37
YORK:
    Minster, 171, 281 (fn), 320, 340, 482,
        490
      archbishops, 172, 468

YORKSHIRE, early perpendicular
    architecture in, 171
YPRES, Belgium
    Halles (Cloth Hall), 134

ZINZIG/ZINGST, Germany, 116
ZWIRNER, Ernst Friederich, 127, 128, 147

✠   ✠

The Remains of SIR GEORGE GILBERT SCOTT
will be laid in WESTMINSTER ABBEY, on *Saturday*,
the *6th of April.*

Those desiring to attend will assemble in the
CLOISTERS, at 11.30 A.M.

✠

This Card should be presented at the entrance to the Cloisters in Dean's Yard.

✠   ✠